THEORY OF STRUCTURES

AUTHOR

Dr. Arunachalam Subramanian Balu

Associate Professor, Department of Civil Engineering,
National Institute of Technology, Karnataka,
Surathkal, Mangalore, Karnataka

REVIEWER

Dr. Swati Ajay Kulkarni

Associate Professor, Department of Applied
Science and General Engineering
Army Institute of Technology, Dighi Hills,
Pune, Maharashtra

KHANNA BOOK PUBLISHING CO. (P) Ltd.
4C/4344, Ansari Road, Darya Ganj,
New Delhi, India

All India Council for Technical Education
Nelson Mandela Marg, Vasant Kunj,
New Delhi, India

Dear Readers,

To prevent the piracy, this book is secured with HIGH SECURITY HOLOGRAM on the front title cover. In case you don't find the hologram on the front cover title, please write us to at contact@khannabooks.com or whatsapp us at +91-99109 09320 and avail special gift voucher for yourself.

Specimen of Hologram on front Cover title:

Moreover, there is a SPECIAL DISCOUNT COUPON for you with EVERY HOLOGRAM.

How to avail this SPECIAL DISCOUNT:

Step 1: Scratch the hologram

Step 2: Under the scratch area, your "coupon code" is available

Step 3: Logon to www.khannabooks.com

Step 4: Use your "coupon code" in the shopping cart and get your copy at a special discount

Step 5: Enjoy your reading!

ISBN: 978-93-5538-733-2

Book Code: DIP462EN

Theory Of Structures

by Dr. Arunachalam Subramanian Balu

First Edition: 2026

Originally Published by:

All India Council for Technical Education, Ministry of Education, GOI

Exclusively Published & Distributed by:

Khanna Book Publishing Co. (P) Ltd.
4C/4344, Ansari Road, Daryaganj,
New Delhi (INDIA)

Visit us at: **www.khannabooks.com**
Write us at: **contact@khannabooks.com**

To view complete list of books,
Please scan the QR Code:

KPH

Printed in Bharat.

प्रो. टी. जी. सीताराम
अध्यक्ष
Prof. T. G. Sitharam
Chairman

सत्यमेव जयते

आज़ादी का अमृत महोत्सव

अखिल भारतीय तकनीकी शिक्षा परिषद्
(भारत सरकार का एक सांविधिक निकाय)
(शिक्षा मंत्रालय, भारत सरकार)
नेल्सन मंडेला मार्ग, वसंत कुंज, नई दिल्ली-110070
दूरभाष : 011-26131498
ई-मेल : chairman@aicte-india.org

ALL INDIA COUNCIL FOR TECHNICAL EDUCATION
(A STATUTORY BODY OF THE GOVT. OF INDIA)
(Ministry of Education, Govt. of India)
Nelson Mandela Marg, Vasant Kunj, New Delhi-110070
Phone : 011-26131498
E-mail : chairman@aicte-india.org

FOREWORD

Engineers are the backbone of any modern society. They are the ones responsible for the marvels as well as the improved quality of life across the world. Engineers have driven humanity towards greater heights in a more evolved and unprecedented manner.

The All India Council for Technical Education (AICTE), have spared no efforts towards the strengthening of the technical education in the country. AICTE is always committed towards promoting quality Technical Education to make India a modern developed nation emphasizing on the overall welfare of mankind.

An array of initiatives has been taken by AICTE in last decade which have been accelerated now by the National Education Policy (NEP) 2020. The implementation of NEP under the visionary leadership of Hon'ble Prime Minister of India envisages the provision for education in regional languages to all, thereby ensuring that every graduate becomes competent enough and is in a position to contribute towards the national growth and development through innovation & entrepreneurship.

One of the spheres where AICTE had been relentlessly working since past couple of years is providing high quality original technical contents at Under Graduate & Diploma level prepared and translated by eminent educators in various Indian languages to its aspirants. For students pursuing 2nd year of their Engineering education, AICTE has identified 87 books, which shall be translated into 12 Indian languages - Hindi, Tamil, Gujarati, Odia, Bengali, Kannada, Urdu, Punjabi, Telugu, Marathi, Assamese & Malayalam. In addition to the English medium, books in different Indian Languages are going to support the students to understand the concepts in their respective mother tongue.

On behalf of AICTE, I express sincere gratitude to all distinguished authors, reviewers and translators from the renowned institutions of high repute for their admirable contribution in a record span of time.

AICTE is confident that these outcomes based original contents shall help aspirants to master the subject with comprehension and greater ease.

T.G. Sitharam

(Prof. T. G. Sitharam)

ACKNOWLEDGEMENT

I am grateful to the authorities of AICTE, particularly Prof. T. G. Sitharam, Chairman; Prof. M P Poonia, Vice-Chairman; Prof. Rajive Kumar, Member-Secretary and Dr. Amit Kumar Srivastava, Director, Faculty Development Cell for their planning to publish the book on Theory of Structures. I sincerely acknowledge Dr. Kulkarni Swati Ajay, Associate Professor, Army Institute of Technology, Pune for her valuable contributions during the review of the book. I am grateful to National Institute of Technology Karnataka for providing the facilities to write this book.

I am eternally grateful to my parents Mrs. A S Gandhi and Mr. A Subramanian, my uncle Mr. A Natarajan and my brother Mr. A S Raja. I express my indebtedness to my teachers Prof. K Chinnaraju, Prof. B N Rao and Prof. Devdas Menon. I am also grateful to my family members, friends and colleagues for their support. I appreciate the contributions by my doctoral students Mr. Akshay Kumar and Ms. Sushma.

My greatest appreciation is for my wife, Dr. G Deepa, who is a constant source of support and energy. A lifelong partner makes both the journey and destination worthwhile.

Dr. Arunachalam Subramanian Balu

AICTE'S LIST OF PRESCRIBED TEXTBOOKS

As Per Model Curriculum & Outcome Based Education
aligned with
NATIONAL EDUCATION POLICY 2020

UNDERGRADUATE COURSE BOOKS

S.No.	ISBN	Book Name	Author
1	9789355382160	Advanced Electrical Machines: Theory and Practicals	Bharat Singh Rajpurohit
2	9789355382139	Analog Electronic Circuits: Theory and Practical	Venu Sonti, Sachin Jain
3	9789355383808	Analog Electronic Devices: Theory and Practicals	N. B Balamurugan
4	9789391505158	Basic Electrical Engineering (with Lab Manual)	S.K. Sahdev
5	9789355388087	Basic of Electronics	Brijesh Iyer
6	9789355387127	Basics of Electrical Machines: Theory and Practicals	D. K. Palwalia, U. K. Kalla, R. K. Kumawat
7	9789355389381	Basics of Mechanics	Shubhankar Bhowmick, N. Venkata Swamy Naidu
8	9789355386250	Basics of Thermodynamics	Parmod Kumar, Atul Dhar
9	9789355386984	Biology for Engineers	Annamma Odaneth
10	9789391505141	Chemistry-I	Manisha Agarwal
11	9789355384843	Civil Engineering Societal and Global Impact	Shakuntala Acharya
12	9789355382184	Computer Aided Civil Engineering Drawing	D. Chandra Mouli, B. Swathi
13	9789355382580	Computer Aided Design & Analysis	Hari Kumar Voruganti
14	9789355387592	Computer Architecture	D. Vaithiyanathan
15	9789355385093	Computer Networks	Hari Prabhat Gupta
16	9789355385307	Construction Engineering & Management	Sparsh Johari
17	9789355388728	Control Systems	S.N. Deepa
18	9789355385420	Data Structure and Algorithms	Ranbir Singh Sanasam
19	9789355386700	Design and Analysis of Algorithms	Hari P. Gupta, Rahul Mishra
20	9789355388872	Digital Electronics and System	Abhishek Bhatt
21	9789355386571	Digital Signal Processing	Sanjeev Sharma
22	9789355383396	Disaster management	Pradeep K. Goyal, Anil K. Gupta
23	9789355385222	Discrete Mathematical Structures	Narendra S. Chaudhari, Sharmila S. P.
24	9789355387868	Effective Technical Communication	Pritee Sharma, Sanchita Verma
25	9789355383389	Electrical Circuit Analysis and Network Theory	Shouri Chatterjee
26	9789355388957	Electromagnetic Waves	Uttam M. Pal, Srijith K.
27	9789355384652	Electronic Communication	Vimal Bhatia
28	9789355388711	Embedded Systems	Santanu Chattopadhyay
29	9789355385147	Energy Science and Engineering	M. Rizwan, Majid Jamil
30	9789355387929	Engineering Economics, Estimation & Costing	Yogesh C. Joshi
31	9789355384669	Engineering Geology	R. N. Khare, Ketan Chourasia
32	9789391505066	Engineering Graphics & Design	Pradeep Jain
33	9789391505097	English (with Lab Manual)	Kulbhushan Kumar
34	9789355385963	Environmental Engineering	Chandra Sekhar Matli
35	9789355388117	Fluid Mechanics	Shreenivas N. Londhe, Pradnya R. Dixit
36	9789355388377	Fluid Mechanics & Fluid Machines	R.P. Saini
37	9789355387103	Geotechnical Engineering	Paramita Bhattacharya

UNDERGRADUATE COURSE BOOKS

S.No.	ISBN	Book Name	Author
38	9789355385130	Hydraulic Engineering	Sayantan Ganguly
39	9789355385550	Hydrology & Water Resources Engineering	Mitthan Lal Kansal, P.K. Agarwal
40	9789355389688	Information Technology Workshop in MATLAB	Hari Prabhat Gupta
41	9789355383235	Instrumentation for Civil Engineering Applications	Ashim Kanti Dey, Manita Das
42	9789355387042	Introduction to Civil Engineering	Manabendra Saharia, Nagendra R. Velaga
43	9789355384805	Introduction to Database Systems	Vikram Singh
44	9789355387509	Machine Element & System Design	Sabah Khan
45	9789355385383	Machine Learning	Himanshu Mittal
46	9789355388414	Manufacturing Automation	Chitragupt Swaroop Chitransh
47	9789355387233	Manufacturing Processes	Dheerendra Kumar Dwivedi
48	9789355389886	Materials Engineering	Dheerendra Kumar Dwivedi
49	9789391505172	Mathematics - I Calculus and Linear Algebra [For Non-Computer Science Engineering Branches]	Reena Garg
50	9789391505271	Mathematics - I Calculus and Linear Algebra [For Computer Science Engineering Branches]	Reena Garg
51	9789355384607	Measurements & Metrology	V.P. Chandramohan
52	9789355383730	Mechanics of Materials	Arvind Vyavahare
53	9789355383358	Mechatronics, Robotics & Control	J. Srinivas
54	9789355385116	Microprocessor and Microcontroller	Saurabh Chaudhury, Risha Mal
55	9789355386083	Microprocessors	Yogendra Kumar Gupta
56	9789355389169	Mobile Communication and Networks	Vimal Bhatia
57	9789355385475	Operating Systems	Sukomal Pal
58	9789355385604	Operating Systems	Sanjaya Kumar Panda
59	9789391505134	Physics (Oscillations, Waves and Optics) With lab manual	A.B. Bhattacharya, Atanu Nag
60	9789391505257	Physics (Quantum Mechanics for Engineers) With lab manual	A.B. Bhattacharya, Atanu Nag
61	9789391505165	Physics (Introduction to Electromagnetic Theory) (with Lab Manual)	A.B. Bhattacharya, Atanu Nag
62	9789391505059	Physics (Introduction to Mechanics) (with Lab Manual)	A.B. Bhattacharya, Atanu Nag
63	9789355385956	Power Electronics: Theory and Practicals	Lalit Chandra Saikia
64	9789355384942	Power Systems-I	Suresh Mikkili
65	9789355386236	Power Systems-II	Arun Rahul S, Manas K. Jena
66	9789355383754	Product Innovation & Entrepreneurship	Vigneswaran C
67	9789355384584	Production & Operation Management	Navin Kumar Dev
68	9789391505219	Programming for Problem Solving (with Lab Manual)	R.S. Salaria
69	9789355385451	Signals and Systems	Sanjay L. Nalbalwar
70	9789355386021	Strength of Materials	Uday Shanker Dixit, Nelson Muthu, S. M. Kamal
71	9789355383792	Structural Engineering	T.D. Gunneswara Rao, D. Ravi Prasad
72	9789355387004	Surveying and Geomatics	P. K. Garg
73	9789355384317	Testing & Evaluation of Civil Engineering Materials	Sandeep Chaudhary, Kashyap A Patel
74	9789355382306	Theory of Computation	Debi Prasanna Acharjya
75	9789355384928	Transportation Engineering	A.K. Raji
76	9789355385208	VLSI Design	Mahendra Sakare, Shonal Chouksey
77	9789391505332	Workshop / Manufacturing Practices (with Lab Manual)	Veeranna D.K.

DIPLOMA COURSE BOOKS

S.No.	ISBN	Book Name	Author
1	9789355382481	Aanandam An Act of Community Service	Shuchi Sharma
2	9789355385567	Advanced Manufacturing Processes	Ranjeet Kumar Sahu, Devendra Laxman Kamble
3	9789355385109	Advanced Surveying: Theory & Practice	Ramakant Agrawal, Parshottam Sarathe
4	9789355384546	Algorithms	Piyoosh P, Arnab Sarkar
5	9789391505448	Applied Chemistry (with Lab Manual)	Anju Rawlley, Devdatta Vinayakrao Saraf
6	9789391505431	Applied Physics-I (with Lab Manual)	Vinod Kumar Yadav, Mina Talati
7	9789391505578	Applied Physics-II (with Lab Manual)	Hussain Jeevakhan
8	9789355387530	Basic Mechanical Engineering	Dharmendra Singh, Chandra Shekhar Rajoria
9	9789355387394	Building Construction	Rinku Kumar, Sandeep Panchal
10	9789355383280	Building Electrification	Arnab Ghosh
11	9789355384379	Building Planning and Drawing	Aparna Dwivedi
12	9789391505493	Communication Skills in English	Anjana Tiwari
13	9789355383570	Computer Aided Machine Drawing Practice	Kanak Kalita
14	9789355388964	Computer Networking and Data Communication	Sanjaya Shankar Tripathy
15	9789355382986	Computer Networks: Theory & Practicals	Brijendra Pratap Singh, Manoj Madhava Gore
16	9789355382672	Computer Programming: Theory and Practicals	Satyendra Singh Chouhan
17	9789355387714	Computer System Organization	Sonal Yadav
18	9789355382658	Concrete Technology: Theory and Practice	Sasankasekhar Mandal, Vishwajit Anand, Sushil K. Agarwala
19	9789355383334	Construction Materials and Testing	Vanita Aggarwal
20	9789355383501	Consumer Electronics	Amit M. Joshi, Maulin M. Joshi, Urvashi Prakash Shukla
21	9789355387684	Data Structures: Theory & Practicals	NB Venkateswarlu
22	9789355388513	Design of Machine Elements	A. Kumaravel, M. Kathirselvam
23	9789355388360	Design of Steel and RCC Structure	Sparsh Johari
24	9789355383303	Digital Communication	Muralidhar Kulkarni, K. S. Shivaprakasha
25	9789355387295	Digital Electronics	Menka Yadav
26	9789355389435	Electric Circuits and Networks	Jamuna K., Nilanjan Tewari
27	9789355388452	Electric Motors and Transformers (Theory and Practicals)	Sanjay B. Bodkhe
28	9789355385901	Electric Power Transmission and Distribution	Sudhir Sharma
29	9789355389466	Electrical & Electronics Measurements and Instrumentation	Sudarsan Sahoo, Vipin Chandra Pal, Sudipta Chakraborty
30	9789355382696	Electronic Communication	M. D. Selvaraj, P. Nagaradjane
31	9789355387202	Electronic Devices and Circuits	Ankesh Jain
32	9789355386373	Electronic Equipment Maintenance	Chanchal Sharma
33	9789355384690	Embedded Systems	Deepa M, G. Santhanamari, Susithra. N
34	9789355384867	Energy Conservation and Audit	M. Rizwan, Majid Jamil
35	9789391505509	Engineering Graphics	Sharad K. Pradhan, K.K. Jain
36	9789391505608	Engineering Mechanics (with Lab Manual)	Bhankhar Bharat, Gokaldas Vandana Somkuwar

DIPLOMA COURSE BOOKS

S.No.	ISBN	Book Name	Author
37	9789391505516	Engineering Workshop Practice	A. K. Sarathe
38	9789391505653	Environmental Science	Subrat Roy
39	9789355384966	Estimating, Costing and valuation	Sandeep Panchal
40	9789355389510	Fluid Mechanics & Hydraulic Machinery	Suman Chakraborty, Sourav Mitra, Aditya Bandopadhyay
41	9789391505592	Fundamentals of Electrical and Electronics Engineering (with Lab Manual)	Susan S. Mathew, Saji T. Chacko
42	9789355387240	Fundamentals of Power Electronics	Soumitra Kumar Mandal
43	9789355389602	Geotechnical Engineering (Theory & Practicals)	Neelima Satyam
44	9789355386137	Induction, Synchronous, and Special Electrical Machines	K. Selvajyothi, S. Tamilselvi, Sarat Kumar Sahoo
45	9789355382290	Industrial Engineering & Management	A. Manimaran
46	9789355384959	Internet of Things	Sujata Pal
47	9789355388650	Introduction to DBMS: Theory & Practicals	Myneni Madhu Bala
48	9789355384294	Introduction to e-Governance	Kamal Kant Verma
49	9789355386564	Introduction to Electric Generation Systems	Lalit Chandra Saikia, Nalin Behari, Deb Choudhury
50	9789391505585	Introduction to IT Systems (with Lab Manual)	Prashant Joshi
51	9789355382900	Linear Integrated Circuit	B. T. Krishna
52	9789355388148	Manufacturing Engineering	Santosh Kumar
53	9789355383877	Material Science & Engineering	Vinod Kumar, Nisheeth k. Prasad
54	9789391505424	Mathematics-I	Deepak Singh
55	9789391505523	Mathematics-II	Garima Singh
56	9789355385994	Measurements and Metrology	A. Gnanavelbabu, M. Santhana kumar, R. Saranraj
57	9789355388131	Mechanics of Materials and their Testing	R. Velmurugan, Pragathi
58	9789355385048	Microcontroller Applications	Ritula Thakur
59	9789355385062	Microcontrollers and Applications	Santanu Chattopadhyay
60	9789355388100	Mobile and Wireless Communication	Maulin Joshi, Urvashi P. Shukla
61	9789355387790	Production & Operations Management	Mayank Kumar Agrawal
62	9789355388704	Public Health Engineering	Rinku Kumar
63	9789355387455	Python Programming	Rupesh Nasre
64	9789355387189	Renewable Energy Technologies	Sanjay Agrawal, Rajeev K. Mishra
65	9789355387479	Software Engineering	Salman Abdul Moiz
66	9789355389749	Theory of Machines & Mechanisms	G. C. Mohan Kumar
67	9789355387332	Theory of Structures	Arunachalam Subramanian Balu
68	9789355389015	Thermal Engineering - I	V. Raghavan
69	9789355389831	Thermal Engineering - II	Parvesh Antil
70	9789355386779	Transportation Engineering (Theory & Practice)	A.K. Raji, K.K. Babu
71	9789355384287	Water Resource Engineering (Theory & Practice)	Prakash C. Swain, Dillip K. Ghose
72	9789355383051	Web Technologies: Theory & Practical	Raman Dugyala

PREFACE

A structure can be defined as a fully functional object formed by connecting the elements together. Natural structures vary from the very smallest part of an atom to the entire cosmology of the universe. Trees, animals and human beings could also be treated as structures. Man-made structures include buildings, bridges, dams, ships, aeroplanes, rockets, trains, cars, artefacts, and sculptures etc.

The primary objective of civil engineering structures is to function as an integral unit in transmitting loads to the supporting medium safely. This physical structures become reality after going through many phases like Conceptual plan, Structural analysis and design, and Construction. *Structural analysis* mainly focusses on predicting the response of structures subjected to specified arbitrary external loads. *Structural design* aims at determining the most suitable proportions, dimensions and details of the elements and connections for satisfying the requirements set by the responses resulted in the analysis.

All too often in today's world, advanced computer programs are being used for the analysis and design. A proper understanding of the basic principles concerning how structures really work is essential for using the computer-based tools effectively and sensibly. *Theory of structures* underscores the fundamental concepts behind the analysis and design. Therefore, the primary goal of this book is to impart a basic understanding of structural behaviour to students (at diploma level in particular) interested in analysis and design of structures subjected to different types of loads. The contents of this book are limited to analysis of structures wherein the force and displacement responses of structural elements are obtained.

The book is presented in five units to cater the requirements of model curriculum prescribed by *All India Council for Technical Education*. The first unit presents the analysis procedure to determine the stresses in vertical members such as columns and chimneys, and analysis of dams. The second unit presents the analytical methods for obtaining the displacement responses of statically determinate structures. It is presumed that the students have thorough background knowledge for analysing statically determinate beams for the force responses, which are the basic requirements for getting the displacement responses. The third unit presents the techniques to solve statically indeterminate structures such as fixed beams and two-span continuous beams using the conventional force method. The fourth unit presents an iterative numerical procedure to solve statically indeterminate structures for the force responses. The last unit presents different techniques to analyse the pin-jointed statically determinate truss structures.

The emphasis throughout is on clarity in basic understanding of concepts and their applications to a wide variety of problems. Wherever possible, a visual language of structural behaviour is considered for a qualitative understanding of the response of structure. Students must bear in mind that the numbers resulting from the analysis should not be viewed as mere numbers, because they may bear significant values intrinsically.

எண் ணனண் ப ஏனன எழ ூதண் ணதனண் ப இவ் வரிரண் டுமம்
கண் ணனன் ப வாழும் உயிரக்கு.
Numbers and letters are the two discerning eyes for all mankind to make the best of life. (Thirukkural No. 392).

Dr. Arunachalam Subramanian Balu

OUTCOME BASED EDUCATION

For the implementation of an outcome based education the first requirement is to develop an outcome based curriculum and incorporate an outcome based assessment in the education system. By going through outcome based assessments, evaluators will be able to evaluate whether the students have achieved the outlined standard, specific and measurable outcomes. With the proper incorporation of outcome based education there will be a definite commitment to achieve a minimum standard for all learners without giving up at any level. At the end of the programme running with the aid of outcome based education, a student will be able to arrive at the following outcomes:

Programme Outcomes (POs) are statements that describe what students are expected to know and be able to do upon graduating from the program. These relate to the skills, knowledge, analytical ability attitude and behaviour that students acquire through the program. The POs essentially indicate what the students can do from subject-wise knowledge acquired by them during the program. As such, POs define the professional profile of an engineering diploma graduate.

National Board of Accreditation (NBA) has defined the following seven POs for an Engineering diploma graduate:

PO1. Basic and Discipline specific knowledge: Apply knowledge of basic mathematics, science and engineering fundamentals and engineering specialization to solve the engineering problems.

PO2. Problem analysis: Identify and analyses well-defined engineering problems using codified standard methods.

PO3. Design/ development of solutions: Design solutions for well-defined technical problems and assist with the design of systems components or processes to meet specified needs.

PO4. Engineering Tools, Experimentation and Testing: Apply modern engineering tools and appropriate technique to conduct standard tests and measurements.

PO5. Engineering practices for society, sustainability and environment: Apply appropriate technology in context of society, sustainability, environment and ethical practices.

PO6. Project Management: Use engineering management principles individually, as a team member or a leader to manage projects and effectively communicate about well-defined engineering activities.

PO7. Life-long learning: Ability to analyse individual needs and engage in updating in the context of technological changes.

COURSE OUTCOMES

By the end of the course, students are expected to be familiar with the following.

CO-1: Fundamentals of stresses and safety conditions in columns, chimneys and dams

CO-2Different methods for evaluating displacement responses of structures

CO-3: Analysis of statically indeterminate structures for force responses

CO-4: Determination of salient parameters required for design of structural elements

CO-5: Analysis of simple truss structures

Mapping of Course Outcomes with Programme Outcomes

Course Outcomes	Expected Mapping with Programme Outcomes (1- Weak Correlation; 2- Medium correlation; 3- Strong Correlation)						
	PO-1	PO-2	PO-3	PO-4	PO-5	PO-6	PO-7
CO-1	3	3	3	2	1	1	3
CO-2	3	3	2	2	1	1	3
CO-3	3	3	2	1	1	1	3
CO-4	3	3	3	1	1	1	3
CO-5	3	3	2	1	1	1	3

GUIDELINES FOR TEACHERS

To implement Outcome Based Education (OBE) knowledge level and skill set of the students should be enhanced. Teachers should take a major responsibility for the proper implementation of OBE. Some of the responsibilities (not limited to) for the teachers in OBE system may be as follows:

- Within reasonable constraint, they should manipulate time to the best advantage of all students.
- They should assess the students only upon certain defined criterion without considering any other potential ineligibility to discriminate them.
- They should try to grow the learning abilities of the students to a certain level before they leave the institute.
- They should try to ensure that all the students are equipped with the quality knowledge as well as competence after they finish their education.
- They should always encourage the students to develop their ultimate performance capabilities.
- They should facilitate and encourage group work and team work to consolidate newer approach.
- They should follow Blooms taxonomy in every part of the assessment.

Bloom's Taxonomy

Level	Teacher should Check	Student should be able to	Possible Mode of Assessment
Create	Students ability to create	Design or Create	Mini project
Evaluate	Students ability to justify	Argue or Defend	Assignment
Analyse	Students ability to distinguish	Differentiate or Distinguish	Project/Lab Methodology
Apply	Students ability to use information	Operate or Demonstrate	Technical Presentation/ Demonstration
Understand	Students ability to explain the ideas	Explain or Classify	Presentation/Seminar
Remember	Students ability to recall (or remember)	Define or Recall	Quiz

GUIDELINES FOR STUDENTS

Students should take equal responsibility for implementing the OBE. Some of the responsibilities (not limited to) for the students in OBE system are as follows:

- Students should be well aware of each Unit Outcome (UO) before the start of a unit in each and every course.
- Students should be well aware of each Course Outcome (CO) before the start of the course.
- Students should be well aware of each Programme Outcome (PO) before the start of the programme.
- Students should think critically and reasonably with proper reflection and action.
- Learning of the students should be connected and integrated with practical and real life consequences.
- Students should be well aware of their competency at every level of OBE.

ABBREVIATIONS AND SYMBOLS

BC	Boundary Condition
BMD	Bending Moment Diagram
COF	Carry Over Factor
COM	Carry Over Moment
DKI	Degree of Kinematic Indeterminacy
DSI	Degree of Static Indeterminacy
FEM	Fixed End Moment
FS	Factor of Safety
SFD	Shear Force Diagram

A	Area
b	Breadth
C	Compression
d	Depth, Internal diameter
D	External diameter
e	Eccentricity
E	Modulus of elasticity
F	Force
h	Height
H	Horizontal reaction, height
I	Moment of inertia
j	Joint
K	Stiffness factor
k	Wind resistance
L	Length
M	Moment
P	Load, Thrust
p	Pressure
r	Radius of gyration, Reaction
R	Radius of curvature, Resultant
S	Shear
T	Tension
V	Shear, Vertical reaction, Volume
w	Distributed load
W	Load, Weight
ψ	Chord rotation
κ	Curvature

Δ	Deflection
δ	Deformation
ρ	Density
γ	Distribution factor
θ	Slope
ε	Strain
o	Stress
δL	Change in length
μ	Coefficient of friction

LIST OF FIGURES

Unit 1

Unit 2

Unit 3

Unit 4

Unit 5

LIST OF TABLES

CONTENTS

1 Direct and Bending Stresses

UNIT SPECIFICS

This unit discusses the following aspects.

- Principles of structural analysis
- Concepts of direct and bending stresses
- Analysis of vertical members such as columns, chimneys and dams

RATIONALE

Basic concepts of structural analysis are highlighted to understand the importance of this course. Structural design process requires the information of stress resultants as necessary input. Therefore, most of the structural analysis procedures aim at estimating the stresses developed in the elements due to application of loads. This chapter explains the detailed procedure for analysing vertical structural elements for the resultant stresses.

UNIT OUTCOMES

List of outcomes of this unit is as follows.

U1-O1: Describe the need for structural analysis
U1-O2: Describe the concepts of stresses
U1-O3: Describe the procedure for obtaining resultant stresses
U1-O4: Analyse solid and hollow chimneys
U1-O5: Analyse and check the conditions of stability for rectangular and trapezoidal dams

Mapping of Unit-1 Outcomes with Course Outcomes *

	CO-1	CO-2	CO-3	CO-4	CO-5
U1-O1	3	3	3	3	3
U1-O2	3	1	2	2	2
U1-O3	3	1	1	1	1
U1-O4	3	1	1	1	1
U1-O5	3	1	1	1	1

* (1- Weak correlation; 2- Medium correlation; 3- Strong correlation)

1.1 Introduction

Everything has *structure*. The function of a structure is to provide the form and shape on which other functions can operate. In a *building* context, structure is a device for channelling loads (i.e., dead or live loads that act on structures) to the ground. Though a structure functions as a whole, students must realise that a typical building is composed of a seemingly endless array of individual elements like beams and columns. These elements are invariably so positioned and interrelated as to enable the overall structure to function as a whole in carrying either vertically or horizontally acting loads to the ground. No matter how some individual elements are located and attached to one another, if the resultant configuration and interrelation of all elements does not function as a whole unit in channelling all anticipated types of loads to the ground, the configuration cannot be said to be a *structure*.

1.2 Structural Analysis

Theory of structure is a broader area of structural engineering in which *analysis* is the determination of responses of a structure to the loads that act upon it, whereas *design* is the creation and subsequent modification of the physical configuration of a structure to achieve a desired response. This book is limited to serve the purpose of the former as indicated in Figure 1.1. The loads may be directly (e.g., concentrated, uniformly distributed, varying loads/forces, etc.), or indirectly (e.g., differential support settlement, environmental effects, etc.) applied to the structure. Similarly, responses are broadly classified into force (e.g., shear force, bending moment, torsional moment, etc.), and displacement (elongation/contraction, slope, deflection, curvature, etc.) responses. The force responses are required for proportioning the elements whereas the displacement responses are required for checking the serviceability conditions during the design process.

Students should bear in mind that the physical structures and loads are converted into idealized mathematical models for performing the analysis for the desired response quantities. Therefore, each *number* is very important, because it may bear different *values*. This essentially means that understanding the *physics of mathematics* is important.

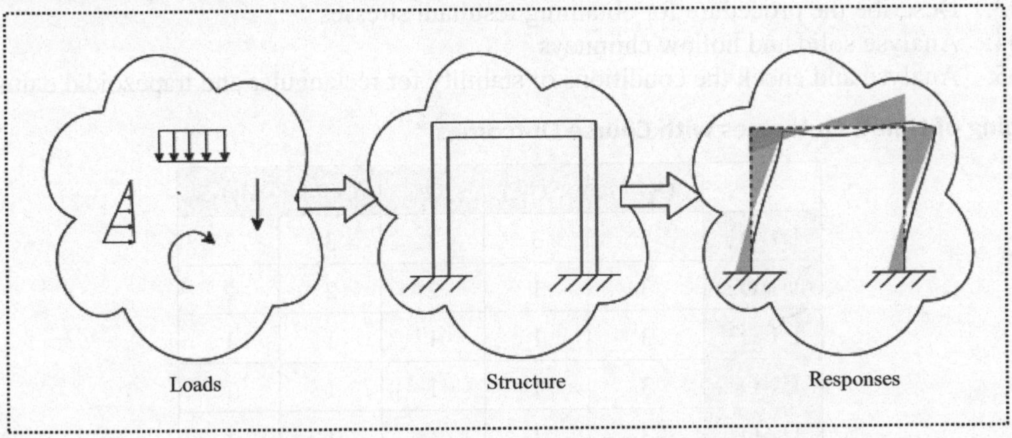

Figure 1.1 Process in structural analysis

1.3 Basic Equations

Material continuity without discontinuities or cracks is a logical assumption in solid mechanics. This assumption leads to a mathematical description of geometric relations of a continuous medium known as *continuum* expressed as compatibility conditions.

In order to establish a solution in any solid mechanics problem in which structural engineering is one of its applications, the following three basic sets of relations have to be fulfilled.

i) *Equilibrium conditions*, which guarantee that the body is always in equilibrium
ii) *Compatibility conditions*, which guarantee that the body remains continuous
iii) *Constitutive relations*, which connect stresses and strains of a material behaviour

In short, the mechanics analysis of a given structural problem or a proposed structural design must involve the mathematical formulation of the above three sets of equations and solutions. It does not mean that the solution procedure necessitates the application of all the above equations. Depending on the nature of the problem, some of the conditions are explicitly satisfied to arrive at a solution while other conditions are implicitly satisfied. The interrelationship of these three sets of basic equations for static analysis is shown in Figure 1.2.

1.4 Indeterminacy

Simple structures like cantilever and simply supported beams can be solved by the application of the three equations of statical equilibrium (i.e., all horizontal forces must balance, all vertical forces must balance, and all moments must balance). Consequently, for a solution to be found, there can be three unknowns. This means, if the solution of a structure is statically determinable, the structure is termed as *statically determinate*. However, virtually all real structures have more than three unknowns, which cannot be solved by the three equations of equilibrium alone. Hence, if the solution of a structure is not statically determinable, the structure is termed as *statically indeterminate*. Therefore, the *degree of static indeterminacy* (DSI) is the number of redundant forces (i.e., extra forces) present in the structure more than required for mere equilibrium. It represents the difference between the number of static unknowns (reactions and internal forces) and the number of static equations (equilibrium equations). For a given structure the degree of static indeterminacy is unique, but redundant forces can be different.

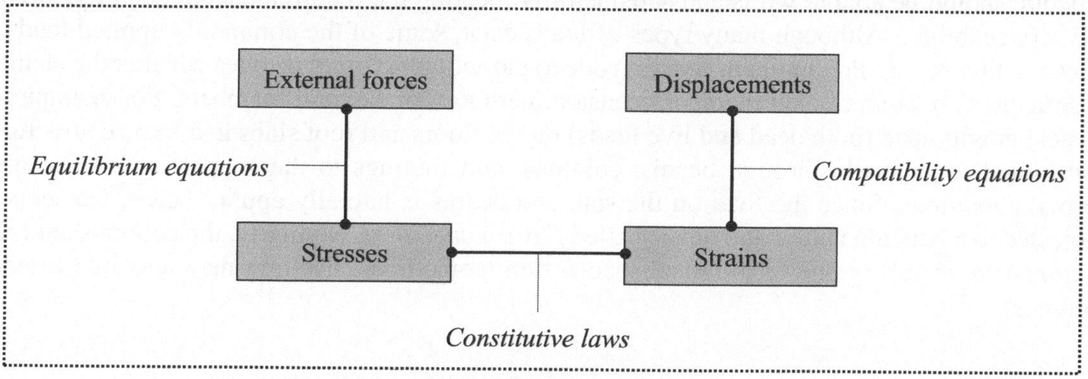

Figure 1.2 Interrelation of basic equations

There is another allied concept called *kinematic indeterminacy*, which is usually associated with *degrees of freedom* (i.e., independent co-ordinates required to define the displaced configuration of structure). Theoretically, a structure has infinite degrees of freedom, because it is a continuum. However, in a skeletal structure, the actual degrees of freedom are limited to the ones at the joints where different joint elements converge. Therefore, the *degree of kinematic indeterminacy* (DKI) is defined as the total number of *degrees of freedom* at the various joints in a skeletal structure.

Methods of structural analysis are broadly grouped in to two categories, namely *flexibility methods* and *stiffness methods*. The flexibility methods use the degree of static indeterminacy while the stiffness methods use the degree of kinematic indeterminacy. Since the degree of indeterminacy decides the complexity of computations involved during the solution process, it is wise to adopt an appropriate method of analysis by appraising both the indeterminacies. Table 1.1 presents the details of degrees of static and kinematic indeterminacies for different beam structures.

Table 1.1 Beams with indeterminacies

Type of beam		DSI	DKI
Cantilever beam (Fixed at A & free at B)		0	$2\ (\theta_B \,\&\, \Delta_B)$
Simply supported beam (Hinge at A & Roller at B)		0	$2\ (\theta_A \,\&\, \theta_B)$
Propped cantilever beam (Fixed at A & Roller at B)	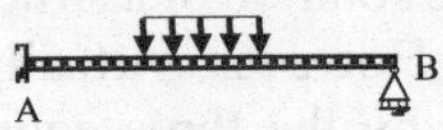	1	$1\ (\theta_B)$
Fixed beam (Fixed at A & B)	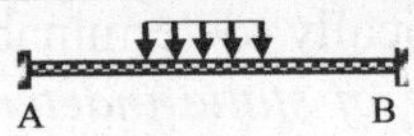	3	0

1.5 Loads

Loads act on a structure, causing it to undergo internal stresses and displacements, which the structure should be able to withstand satisfactorily meeting the requirements of stability, strength and serviceability. Although many types of loads exist, some of the commonly applied loads are shown in Figure 1.3. Predominant function due to the action of forces decides whether the elements of structures are compression members, tension members, or flexural members. For example, the vertical gravity load (both dead and live loads) on the floors and roof slabs in a framed structure is transmitted sequentially through beams, columns, and footings to the supporting ground under normal conditions. Since the load on the slab and beams is laterally applied, these elements are subjected to a bending nature and hence called *flexural members*. Similarly, the columns are called *compression members* due to the axial load action (sometimes, bending may also be present in columns).

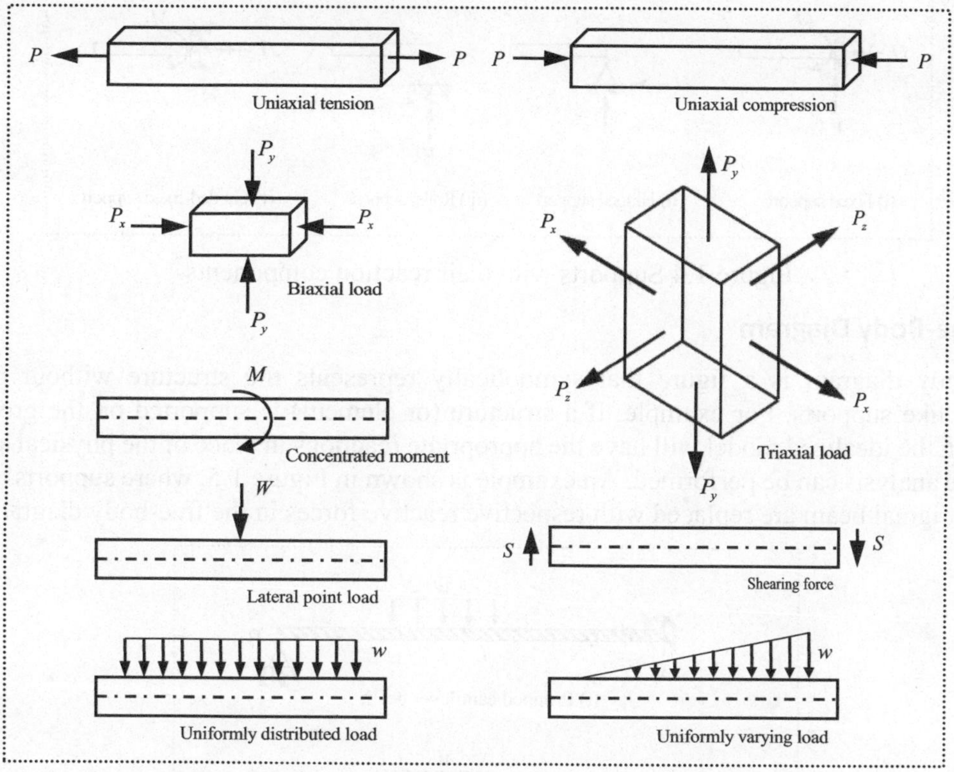

Figure 1.3 Types of loads applied on structural elements

1.6 Supports

Structural elements are assembled to make a whole structure which is supported on ground in such a way that the load is transmitted through the supports. In turn, the supports develop reactions depending on the nature of support conditions. For example, if the support restrains linear movements in a particular direction, then a reaction is developed in the opposite direction. Similarly, the support offers moment reaction when the rotational movement is restrained. Figure 1.4 presents a few types of supports and their respective reaction components. In case of a fixed support, as the support restrains all the movements, it offers resistance in horizontal, vertical and rotational directions by developing *H*, *V* and *M* respectively. Hinged support permits the member to rotate freely, hence no resistance is observed in the rotational direction. However, it offers resistance to both horizontal and vertical directions by developing *H* and *V* respectively. Roller support permits the member to rotate freely in rotational direction, and to move freely horizontal direction, hence no resistance is observed in those directions. Therefore, it offers resistance only to vertical direction by developing *V*. Another type of support called guided-fixed support offers resistance to horizontal and rotational directions, but not in vertical direction, hence *H* and *M* are developed.

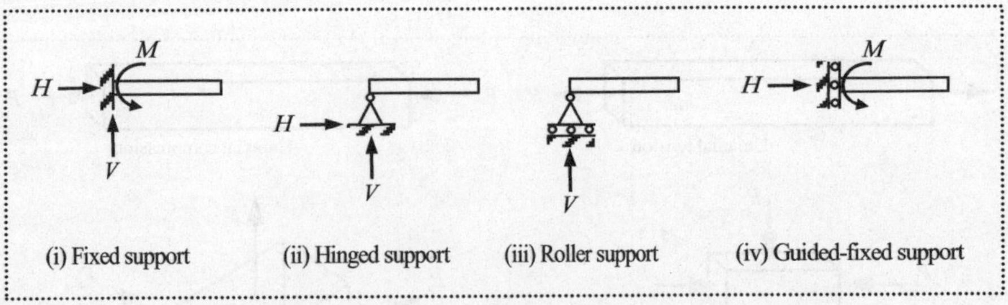

Figure 1.4 Supports with their reaction components

1.7 Free-Body Diagram

A free-body diagram is a figure that symbolically represents the structure without physical attributes like supports. For example, if a structure (or element) is supported on the ground (or wall), then the idealized model will have the appropriate reactions in place of the physical supports so that the analysis can be performed. An example is shown in Figure 1.5, where supports at A and B in the original beam are replaced with respective reactive forces in the free-body diagram.

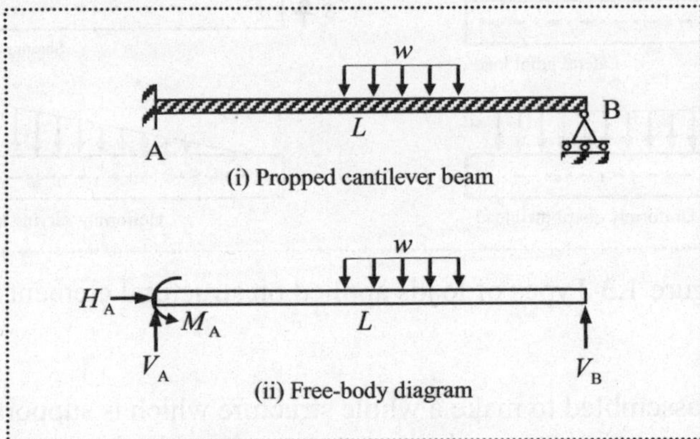

Figure 1.5 Free-body diagram

1.8 Concept of Stress

At the rudimentary level of understanding, *stress* and *strain* are defined in the context of an axial tensile test of a longitudinal specimen. If F_x is the axial tensile force applied through the centroid of a specimen with cross-sectional area A_x, the corresponding *axial stress* σ_x is defined as

$$\sigma_x = \frac{F_x}{A_x} \tag{1.1}$$

in which, the subscript "x" indicates that both force and cross-section face in the direction of the longitudinal axis of the member.

Because the member elongates when acted on by the tensile force, the concept of axial strain is as a measure of the change in length. The *axial strain* ε_x is defined as

$$\varepsilon_x = \frac{\delta L}{L_0} \tag{1.2}$$

in which δL is the experimentally measured extension that occurs in the pre-established reference length L_0, termed the *gauge length*.

The axial stress and axial strain (Eq. 1.1 and Eq. 1.2) are average values. The stress is averaged over the cross-sectional area, and the strain is averaged over the gauge length. In this sense, the stress is considered to be "uniformly distributed over the cross section", and the strain is considered to be "constant over the gauge length".

Consider a member made-up of fibres (represented by dotted lines) arranged along the longitudinal direction as shown in Figure 1.6.

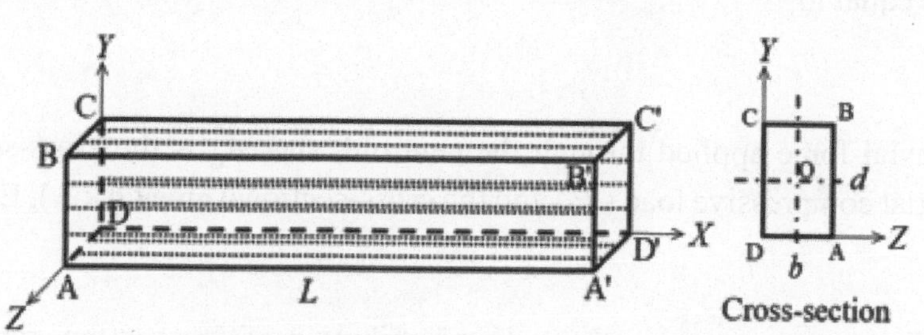

Figure 1.6 Member with represented fibres

If a load P is applied at the centroid (i.e., at O) in the direction of the longitudinal axis (i.e., X), then each fibre is considered to be subjected to the same magnitude. At the same time, the applied load is internally resisted at each point in the fibre, and this force is called stress, which is equal at all points. This is called *direct stress,* σ_0. Incidentally, all fibres will shorten or elongate equally depending on the nature of concentrated load applied (i.e., compression or tension respectively).

If a load P is applied at a point other than the centroid (i.e., eccentric), then the fibres will not have an equal displacement. Moreover, some fibres may experience shortening while some may have expansion, which leads to the bending of fibres in a lateral direction. The corresponding stress is called *bending stress,* σ_b.

This kind of phenomenon can also be evidenced when the load is laterally applied on the length (i.e., in the Y or Z direction). But, another kind of stress across the section, called *shear stress*, is also developed in this case. It is noted that direct and bending stresses will act perpendicular to the section whereas shear stress will act along the section. Therefore, the resultant stress is obtained by combining the direct and bending stresses as

$$\sigma = \sigma_0 \pm \sigma_b \tag{1.3}$$

where σ_0 is the direct stress, and σ_b is the bending stress. Here, σ_b takes positive or negative depending on the fibre whether it is under compression or tension due to the bending.

1.9 Analysis of Vertical Members

In structures, the loads acting on beams are transmitted to the supporting medium through vertical members like columns. Columns are predominantly subjected to axial compression, and they can be circular, square, rectangular, standard or built-up section in their cross sections.

1.9.1 Analysis of Axially Loaded Members

If the axis of load coincides with the longitudinal axis of the member, then the load applied is called axial or direct load, and the member is called *axially loaded member*. Consider a vertical member (e.g., column) of rectangular section supported at the base and loaded at the top as shown in Figure 1.7. Since the load is applied at the centroid of the section, the stress developed at the fibres is uniform, which is equal to

$$\sigma_x = \frac{F_x}{A_x} \tag{1.4}$$

where F_x is the axial force applied through the centroid, and A_x is the cross-sectional area. By substituting the axial compressive load (P) and the cross-sectional area ($b \times d$), Eq. (1.4) becomes:

$$\sigma_0 = \frac{P}{b \cdot d} \tag{1.5}$$

where σ_0 is the direct stress (compression). The distribution of stress at the edges across breadth and width directions are also shown in Figure 1.7.

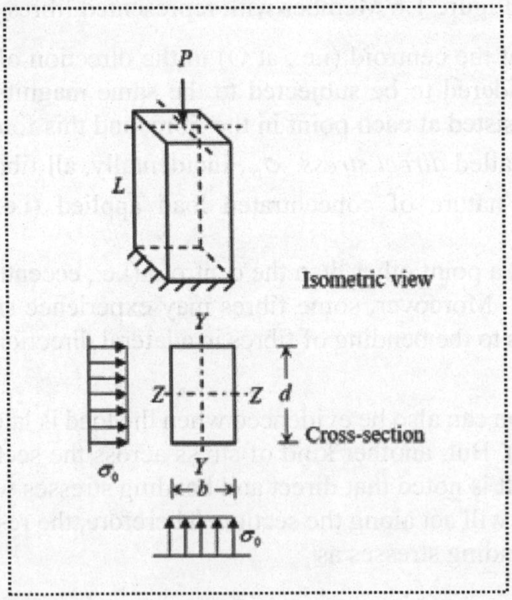

Figure 1.7 Stress distribution of axially loaded member

1.9.2 Analysis of Eccentrically Loaded Members

If the axis of load does not coincide with the longitudinal axis of the member (i.e., the load is applied at a distance " e " from the centroid), the member is called an *eccentrically loaded member*. Consider a column of rectangular section supported at the base and loaded at the top as shown in Figure 1.8. Since the load is eccentrically applied, it will bend the member, which will result in non-uniform stress distribution across the section. The bent configuration of the member in one direction is also shown in Figure 1.8 so as to visualise the effects of bending due to which the extreme faces are subjected to compression and tension.

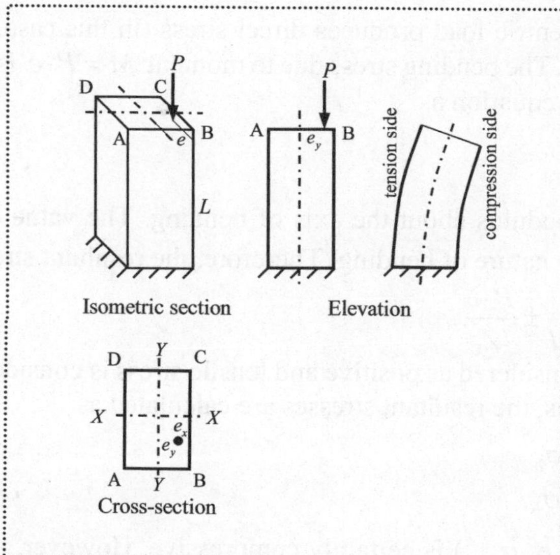

Figure 1.8 Eccentrically loaded member

To understand the effects of eccentric loads, let a load P act eccentric to one axis as shown in Figure 1.9(i).

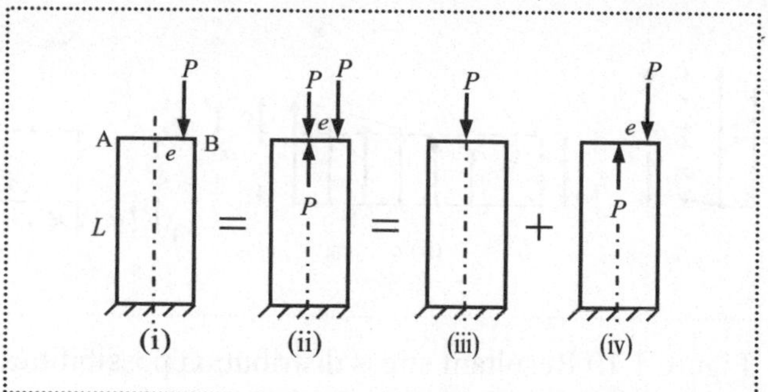

Figure 1.9 Load acting eccentric to one axis

The evolution of the resultant stresses due to the eccentric load can be realized as follows.

i) Assume two equal and opposite loads (equal to P) are introduced in the axis of the member (Figure 1.9(ii)). As these loads cancel out each other, their introduction does not make any difference to the actual loading of the member.

ii) The above scenario is effectively the same as the combination of Figure 1.9(iii) and Figure 1.9(iv).

iii) Figure 1.9(iii) results in the direct stress (i.e., uniform compressive stress across the section), and Figure 1.9(iv) results in the bending stress due to the clockwise couple of magnitude $P \times e$.

iv) Therefore, an eccentric load produces direct stress (in this case, compression) as well as the bending stress. The bending stress due to moment $M = P \cdot e$ is obtained from the simple theory of bending equation as

$$\sigma_b = \frac{M}{Z} \tag{1.6}$$

where Z is the section modulus about the axis of bending. The value of σ_b can be positive or negative depending on the nature of bending. Therefore, the resultant stress is obtained as

$$\sigma = \sigma_0 \pm \sigma_b = \frac{P}{b \cdot d} \pm \frac{P \cdot e}{Z} \tag{1.7}$$

If compressive stress is considered as positive and tensile stress is considered negative, for the load acting eccentric to one axis, the resultant stresses are calculated as

Stress at B, $\sigma = \sigma_0 + \sigma_b$

Stress at A, $\sigma = \sigma_0 - \sigma_b$

In this case, stress at B (i.e., σ_{max}) is certainly compressive. However, stress at A (i.e., σ_{min}) will offer three possibilities as shown in Figure 1.10. If $\sigma_b = \sigma_0$, then $\sigma_{min} = 0$. If $\sigma_b < \sigma_0$, then σ_{min} will also be positive, hence compression. If $\sigma_b > \sigma_0$, then σ_{min} will be negative, hence the tension.

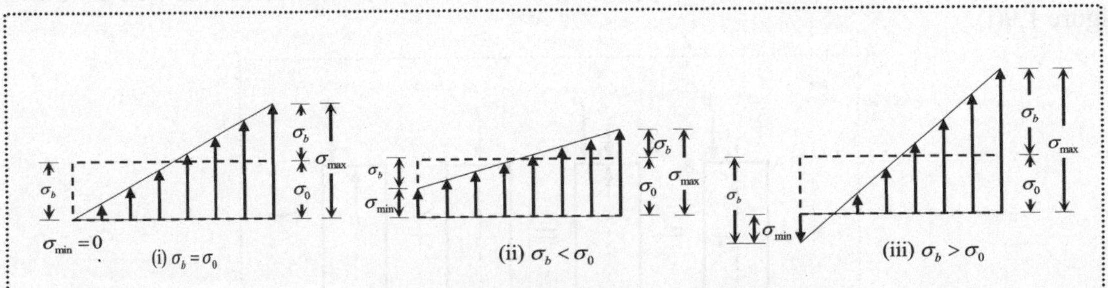

Figure 1.10 Resultant stress distribution possibilities

Similarly, assume that the load is acting eccentric to both axes (i.e., X and Y) as shown in Figure 1.11. Since the load is assumed to be acting in the first quadrant, both eccentricities (e_x and e_y) are considered positive.

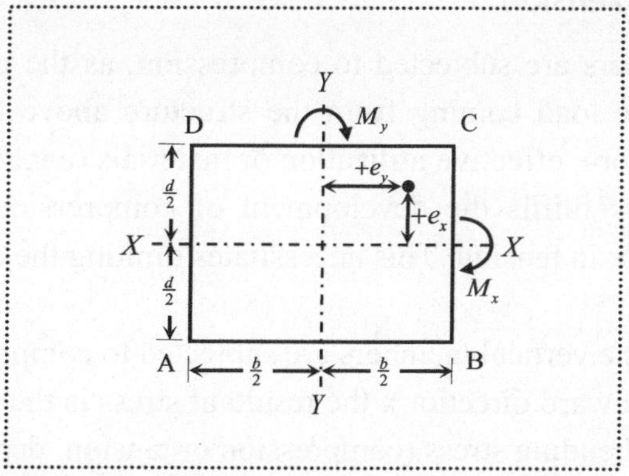

Figure 1.11 Load acting eccentric to both axes

The system can be assumed to consist of the following.

i) An axial load P acting at the centroid. This results in the direct stress, $\sigma_0 = \dfrac{P}{b \cdot d}$

ii) A couple $P \cdot e_x$ about X-axis. This results in the bending stress, $\sigma_{b_x} = \dfrac{P \cdot e_x}{Z_{xx}}$

iii) A couple $P \cdot e_y$ about Y-axis. This results in the bending stress, $\sigma_{b_y} = \dfrac{P \cdot e_y}{Z_{yy}}$

Therefore, stress at any point is given by

$$\sigma = \frac{P}{b \cdot d} \pm \frac{P \cdot e_x}{Z_{xx}} \pm \frac{P \cdot e_y}{Z_{yy}} \tag{1.8}$$

where

e_x is the eccentricity measured from XX-axis in Y-direction

e_y is the eccentricity measured from YY-axis in X-direction

Z_{xx} is the section modulus about XX axis, $Z_{xx} = \dfrac{bd^2}{6}$

Z_{yy} is the section modulus about YY axis, $Z_{yy} = \dfrac{db^2}{6}$

1.9.3 Neutral Axis

In the resultant stress distribution diagram, when both compressive and tensile stresses are present, and in between these stresses, there is a layer of fibres which has neither compression nor tension. This layer is called the neutral layer or neutral surface. The intersection of this neutral surface with the axial plane of symmetry is called the neutral axis. At the neutral axis, the stress is zero.

1.9.4 Condition for No Tension

Most of the vertical members are subjected to compression, as the predominant action of these members is to transmit the load coming from the structure above to the ground which is the direction of gravity. Therefore, effective utilization of materials (e.g., stone, timber, brick etc.) for constructing such members fulfils the development of compression with no tension as these materials are relatively weak in tension. This necessitates limiting the eccentricity " e " to a certain value for different sections.

From Eq. (1.7), when the vertical members are subjected to compressive loads (i.e., the load is applied at the top in a downward direction), the resultant stress is the combination of direct stress (always compression) and bending stress (compression or tension, depending on the eccentricity). Therefore, bending stress is the deciding factor for transiting compression into tension.

If σ_b exceeds σ_0, the resultant stress (σ) in Eq. (1.7) results in a tensile stress in one layer. Hence, $\sigma_b \le \sigma_0$ should be the required condition to ensure no tension across the section.

$$\sigma_b \le \sigma_0 \Rightarrow \frac{P \cdot e}{Z} \le \frac{P}{A} \tag{1.9}$$

$$\boxed{e \le \frac{Z}{A}} \tag{1.10}$$

Eq. (1.10) means, $e_x \le \frac{Z_{xx}}{A}$ and $e_y \le \frac{Z_{yy}}{A}$.

The above expression can also be written in terms of radius of gyration as

$$\frac{P \cdot e}{Z} \le \frac{P}{A} \Rightarrow \frac{P \cdot e}{I/y} \le \frac{P}{A}$$

$$\frac{P \cdot e}{(A \cdot r^2)/y} \le \frac{P}{A} \tag{1.11}$$

$$\boxed{e \le \frac{r^2}{y}} \tag{1.12}$$

where " r " is the radius of gyration with regard to neutral axis and " y " is the distance of extreme fibre from the neutral axis.

For a rectangular section the limiting value of eccentricity to ensure no tension conditions can be obtained as

$$e_x \le \frac{Z_{xx}}{A} \Rightarrow e_x \le \frac{\left(bd^2/6\right)}{bd} \tag{1.13}$$

$$\boxed{e_x \le \frac{d}{6}} \tag{1.14}$$

Similarly, $e_y \leq \frac{Z_{yy}}{A} \Rightarrow e_y \leq \frac{\left(db^2/6\right)}{bd}$

$$\boxed{e_y \leq \frac{b}{6}} \tag{1.15}$$

Thus, the value of eccentricity can be on either side of the geometrical axis, which means, if the load line is within the middle third of the section $\left(\text{i.e., } d/6+d/6=d/3 \text{ and } b/6+b/6=b/3\right)$, the resultant stress will ensure no tension condition. This is called the *middle third rule*.

Similarly for solid circular sections, the limiting values of eccentricity to ensure no-tension, is $D/8$, where D is the diameter of section. If the load acts within the middle quarter $\left(\text{i.e., } D/8+D/8=D/4\right)$, the resultant stress will ensure no tension condition. Hence, this is called the *middle quarter rule*.

In a similar way, for hollow circular sections, the limiting values of eccentricity to ensure no tension is $\left(-\frac{D^2+d^2}{8D} \leq e \leq \frac{D^2+d^2}{8D}\right)$ (where D is external diameter and d is internal diameter).

1.9.5 *Core of a Section*

For a given cross-section, it is of interest to define a region around the centroid within which the load P will induce compression over the entire section. This region is called the *core* or *Kernel* of the section. For the rectangular section, the core is as shown in Figure 1.12. Therefore, the core of the rectangular section is the area of the shaded portion.

$$\text{Core of rectangle} = 4\times\left(\frac{1}{2}\times\frac{b}{6}\times\frac{d}{6}\right)$$

$$= \frac{bd}{18}$$

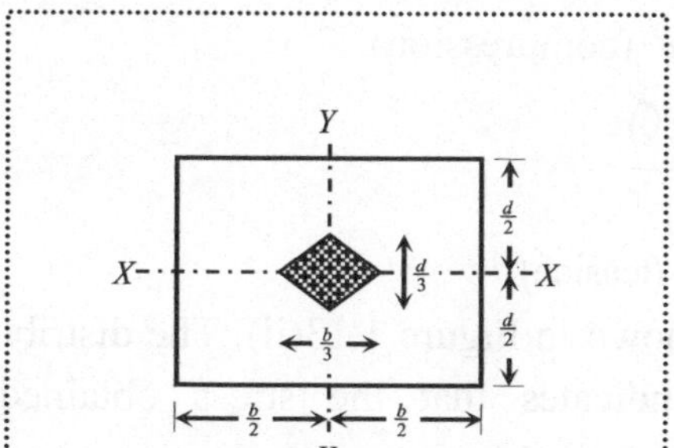

Figure 1.12 Core of rectangular section

1.9.6 Numerical Examples

Example 1.1: A rectangular column of breadth 300 mm and width 200 mm carries a load of 120 kN at an eccentricity of 80 mm in a plane bisecting the width. Find the maximum and minimum stresses in the section.

Solution:

The eccentricity is with respect to *Y*-axis as shown in Figure 1.13(i). Therefore, the moment causing the bending stress is $M_y = P \cdot e_y$.

Since the load is applied with an eccentricity in one direction, the fibre BC develops compressive stresses due to both direct and bending actions, and the fibre AD develops compressive stress due to direct action and tensile stress due to bending action. The resultant stress is obtained using the following formulas.

$$\sigma_{\text{BC}} = \frac{P}{A} + \frac{P \cdot e_y}{Z_{yy}}$$

$$\sigma_{\text{AD}} = \frac{P}{A} - \frac{P \cdot e_y}{Z_{yy}}$$

where

$$P = 120 \text{ kN} = 120 \times 10^3 \text{ N}$$

$$A = b \times d$$

$$= 300 \times 200 = 60 \times 10^3 \text{ mm}^2$$

$$e_y = 80 \text{ mm}$$

$$Z_{yy} = \frac{db^2}{6}$$

$$= \frac{200(300)^2}{6} = 3 \times 10^6 \text{ mm}^3$$

$$\sigma_{\text{BC}} = \frac{120 \times 10^3}{60 \times 10^3} + \frac{(120 \times 10^3)(80)}{3 \times 10^6}$$

$$= 2.0 + 3.2 = 5.2 \text{ N/mm}^2 \text{ (compression)}$$

$$\sigma_{\text{AD}} = \frac{120 \times 10^3}{60 \times 10^3} - \frac{(120 \times 10^3)(80)}{3 \times 10^6}$$

$$= 2.0 - 3.2 = -1.2 \text{ N/mm}^2 \text{ (tension)}$$

The stress distribution is shown in Figure 1.13(ii). The distribution is same for the fibre DC. The subscript BC in σ_{BC} indicates that the stress obtained is uniform from B to C (i.e., 5.2 N/mm^2), and similarly, the subscript AD in σ_{AD} indicates that the stress obtained is uniform from A to D (i.e., -1.2 N/mm^2). Therefore, the maximum stress is 5.2 N/mm^2 (compression), and the minimum stress is -1.2 N/mm^2 (tension).

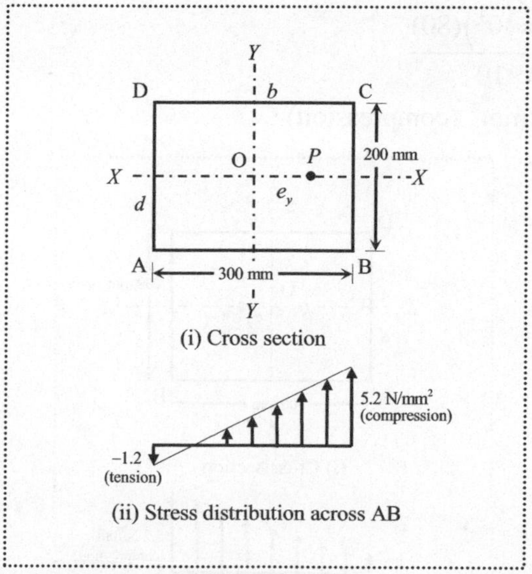

Figure 1.13 Section and stress distribution (Example 1.1)

Example 1.2: A rectangular column of breadth 300 mm and width 200 mm carries a load of 120 kN at an eccentricity of 30 mm in a plane bisecting the width. Find the maximum and minimum stresses in the section.

Solution:

The eccentricity is with respect to *Y*-axis as shown in Figure 1.14(i). Therefore, the moment causing the bending stress is $M_y = P \cdot e_y$.

Similar to Example 1.1, the fibre BC develops compressive stresses due to both direct and bending actions, and the fibre AD develops compressive stress due to direct action and tensile stress due to bending action. The resultant stress is obtained using the following formulas.

$$\sigma_{\text{BC}} = \frac{P}{A} + \frac{P \cdot e_y}{Z_{yy}} \text{ and } \sigma_{\text{AD}} = \frac{P}{A} - \frac{P \cdot e_y}{Z_{yy}}$$

where

$$P = 120 \text{ kN} = 120 \times 10^3 \text{ N}$$
$$A = b \times d = 300 \times 200 = 60 \times 10^3 \text{ mm}^2$$
$$e_y = 30 \text{ mm}$$
$$Z_{yy} = db^2/6 = 3 \times 10^6 \text{mm}^3$$

$$\sigma_{\text{BC}} = \frac{120 \times 10^3}{60 \times 10^3} + \frac{(120 \times 10^3)(30)}{3 \times 10^6}$$
$$= 2.0 + 1.2 = 3.2 \text{ N/mm}^2 \text{ (compression)}$$

$$\sigma_{AD} = \frac{120\times10^3}{60\times10^3} - \frac{(120\times10^3)(80)}{3\times10^6}$$
$$= 2.0 - 1.2 = 0.8 \text{ N/mm}^2 \text{ (compression)}$$

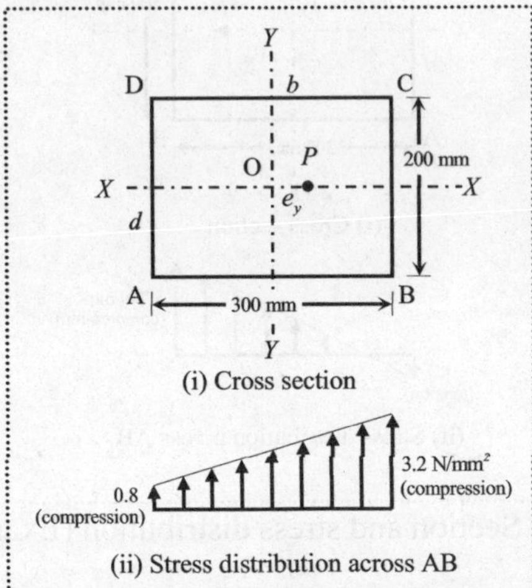

Figure 1.14 Section and stress distribution (Example 1.2)

The stress distribution is shown in Figure 1.14(ii). The distribution is same for the fibre DC. The subscript BC in σ_{BC} indicates that the stress obtained is uniform from B to C (i.e., 3.2 N/mm^2), and similarly, the subscript AD in σ_{AD} indicates that the stress obtained is uniform from A to D (i.e., 0.8 N/mm^2). Therefore, the maximum stress is 3.2 N/mm^2 (compression), and the minimum stress is 0.8 N/mm^2 (compression). Unlike in Example 1.1, the resultant stress at all fibres is compressive.

Example 1.3: A rectangular column of breadth 300 mm and width 200 mm carries a load of 120 kN at an eccentricity of 50 mm in a plane bisecting the width. Find the maximum and minimum stresses in the section.

Solution:

Here the eccentricity is with respect to *Y*-axis as shown in Figure 1.15(i). Therefore, moment causing the bending stress is $M_y = P \cdot e_y$.

Similar to Example 1.1, the fibre BC develops compressive stresses due to both direct and bending actions, and the fibre AD develops compressive stress due to direct action and tensile stress due to bending action. The resultant stress is obtained using the following formulas.

$$\sigma_{BC} = \frac{P}{A} + \frac{P\cdot e_y}{Z_{yy}}$$

$$\sigma_{AD} = \frac{P}{A} - \frac{P \cdot e_y}{Z_{yy}}$$

where

$$P = 120 \text{ kN} = 120 \times 10^3 \text{ N}$$

$$A = b \times d = 300 \times 200 = 60 \times 10^3 \text{ mm}^2$$

$$e_y = 50 \text{ mm}$$

$$Z_{yy} = \frac{db^2}{6} = \frac{200(300)^2}{6} = 3 \times 10^6 \text{ mm}^3$$

$$\sigma_{BC} = \frac{120 \times 10^3}{60 \times 10^3} + \frac{(120 \times 10^3)(50)}{3 \times 10^6}$$

$$= 2.0 + 2.0 = 4.0 \text{ N/mm}^2 \text{ (compression)}$$

$$\sigma_{AD} = \frac{120 \times 10^3}{60 \times 10^3} - \frac{(120 \times 10^3)(50)}{3 \times 10^6}$$

$$= 2.0 - 2.0 = 0 \text{ N/mm}^2$$

The stress distribution is shown in Figure 1.15(ii), and the distribution is same for the fibre DC. The subscript BC in σ_{BC} indicates that the stress obtained is uniform from B to C (i.e., 4.0 N/mm^2), and similarly, the subscript AD in σ_{AD} indicates that the stress obtained is uniform from A to D (i.e., 0 N/mm^2). Therefore, the maximum stress is 4.0 N/mm^2 (compression), and the minimum stress is 0 N/mm^2. Unlike in Example 1.1, the resultant stress, no tensile stress is resulted and stress is zero at one fibre.

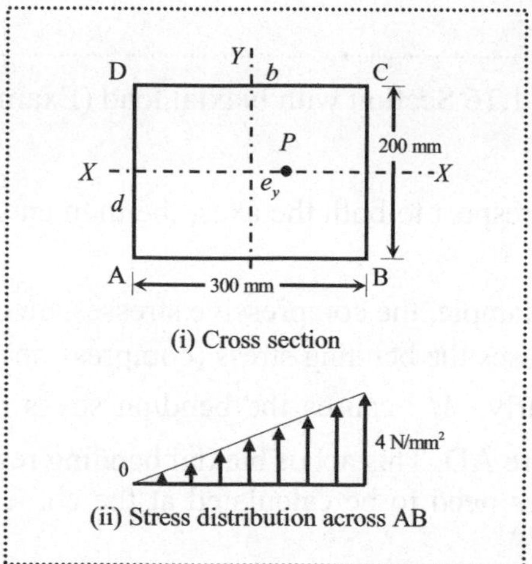

Figure 1.15 Section and stress distribution (Example 1.3)

Note:

i) In Examples 1.1–1.3, all the data except the value of eccentricity are same. The different values of bending stresses due to different eccentricities offered three possibilities of resultant stresses as explained in Figure 1.10.

ii) If the load was applied eccentrically in a plane bisecting the breadth, then the bending stress would be $M_{xx} = P \cdot e_x$, and the corresponding bending stress would be Pe_x / Z_{xx}, where $Z_{xx} = bd^2/6$. These stresses need to be computed in the fibres AB and DC. Hence the stress variation would be across BC, which is same as AD.

Example 1.4: A rectangular column of breadth 300 mm and depth 200 mm carries a load of 120 kN at an eccentricity of 90 mm and 75 mm with respect to *YY* and *XX* axes respectively as shown in Figure 1.16. Find the resultant stresses at extreme corners, and draw the distribution along all four edges.

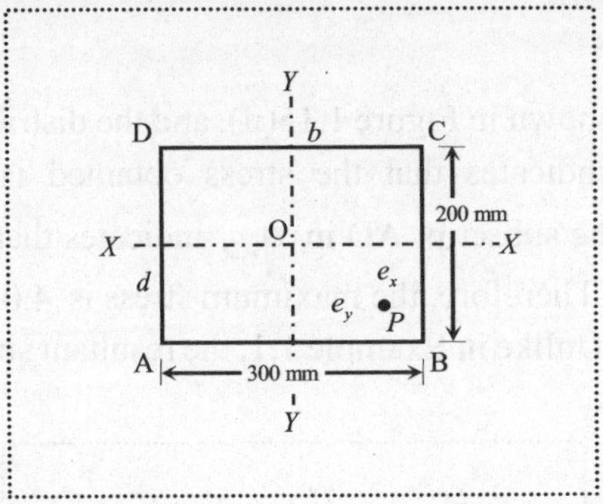

Figure 1.16 Section with biaxial load (Example 1.4)

Solution:

Since the eccentricity is with respect to both the axes, the moments causing the bending stress are $M_x = P \cdot e_x$ and $M_y = P \cdot e_y$.

As seen in the previous example, the compressive stresses are developed on all edges as direct stress. Independently, M_x causes the bending stress (compression) in fibre AB and bending stress (tension) in fibre CD. Similarly, M_y causes the bending stress (compression) in fibre CB and bending stress (tension) in fibre AD. This act of biaxial bending results in non-uniform stresses on all four edges. Hence, stresses need to be calculated at the corners to obtain the distribution of stresses along the edges.

$$\text{Resultant stresses at the corners} = \frac{P}{A} \pm \frac{P \cdot e_x}{Z_{xx}} \pm \frac{P \cdot e_y}{Z_{yy}}$$

where

$$P = 120 \text{ kN} = 120 \times 10^3 \text{ N}$$

$$A = b \times d = 300 \times 200 = 60000 \text{ mm}^2$$

$$e_x = 75 \text{ mm}; \; e_y = 90 \text{ mm}$$

$$M_x = P \cdot e_x = 120 \times 10^3 \times 75 = 9.0 \times 10^6 \text{ Nmm}$$

$$M_y = P \cdot e_y = 120 \times 10^3 \times 90 = 10.8 \times 10^6 \text{ Nmm}$$

$$Z_{xx} = \frac{bd^2}{6} = \frac{300(200)^2}{6} = 2 \times 10^6 \text{ mm}^3$$

$$Z_{yy} = \frac{db^2}{6} = \frac{200(300)^2}{6} = 3 \times 10^6 \text{ mm}^3$$

$$\frac{P}{A} = \frac{120 \times 10^3}{60 \times 10^3} = 2.0 \text{ N/mm}^2$$

$$\frac{M_x}{Z_{xx}} = \frac{9 \times 10^6}{2 \times 10^6} = 4.5 \text{ N/mm}^2$$

$$\frac{M_y}{Z_{yy}} = \frac{10.8 \times 10^6}{3 \times 10^6} = 3.6 \text{ N/mm}^2$$

$$\text{Stress at A, } \sigma_A = \frac{P}{A} + \frac{M_x}{Z_{xx}} - \frac{M_y}{Z_{yy}}$$

$$= 2.0 + 4.5 - 3.6 = 2.9 \text{ N/mm}^2 \text{ (compression)}$$

$$\text{Stress at B, } \sigma_B = \frac{P}{A} + \frac{M_x}{Z_{xx}} + \frac{M_y}{Z_{yy}}$$

$$= 2.0 + 4.5 + 3.6 = 10.1 \text{ N/mm}^2 \text{ (compression)}$$

$$\text{Stress at C, } \sigma_C = \frac{P}{A} - \frac{M_x}{Z_{xx}} + \frac{M_y}{Z_{yy}}$$

$$= 2.0 - 4.5 + 3.6 = 1.1 \text{ N/mm}^2 \text{ (compression)}$$

$$\text{Stress at D, } \sigma_D = \frac{P}{A} - \frac{M_x}{Z_{xx}} - \frac{M_y}{Z_{yy}}$$

$$= 2.0 - 4.5 - 3.6 = -6.1 \text{ N/mm}^2 \text{ (tension)}$$

The stress along the edge AB varies from 2.9 to 10.1 N/mm^2, and across the edge DC it varies from -6.1 to 1.1 N/mm^2. Similarly, in the other direction, the stress varies from 10.1 to 1.1 N/mm^2 across the edge BC, and -6.1 to 10.1 N/mm^2 across the edge AD. These stress distributions are shown in Figure 1.17. All positive stress values are considered compressive and negative stress values are considered tensile.

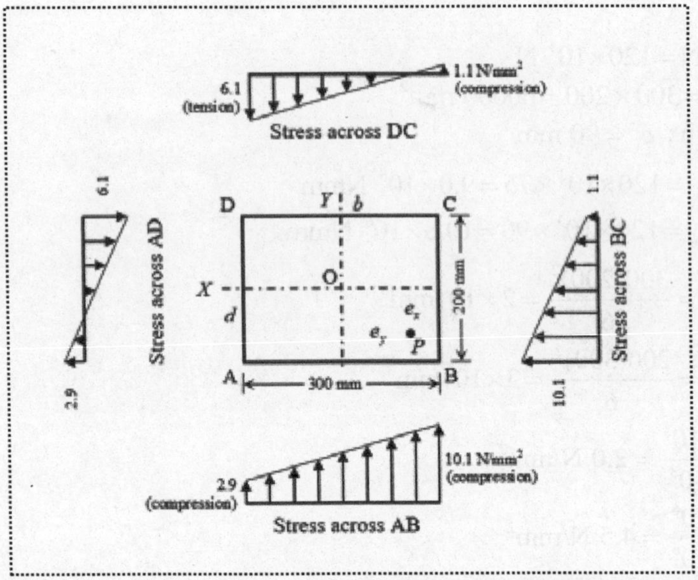

Figure 1.17 Stress distribution across the edges (Example 1.4)

Example 1.5: A hollow rectangular column with external dimensions of 1500×2500 mm and internal dimensions of 900×1600 mm carries a compressive load of 1500 kN at an eccentricity of 700 mm in a plane bisecting the breadth. Find the maximum and minimum stresses in the section.

Solution:

The eccentricity is with respect to *X*-axis as shown in Figure 1.18(i). Therefore, the moment causing the bending stress is $M_x = P \cdot e_x$.

Since the load is applied with an eccentricity in one direction, the fibre CD develops compressive stresses due to both direct and bending actions, and the fibre AB develops compressive stress due to direct action and tensile stress due to bending action. The resultant stresses along the extreme fibres are obtained using the following formulas.

The maximum stress, $\sigma_{CD} = \dfrac{P}{A} + \dfrac{P \cdot e_x}{Z_{xx}}$

The minimum stress, $\sigma_{AB} = \dfrac{P}{A} - \dfrac{P \cdot e_x}{Z_{xx}}$

where

$$P = 1500 \text{ kN} = 1500 \times 10^3 \text{ N}$$

$$A = (B \times D - b \times d) = 1500 \times 2500 - 900 \times 1600 = 2.31 \times 10^6 \text{ mm}^2$$

$$e_x = 700 \text{ mm}$$

$$Z_{xx} = \frac{1}{6}\left(\frac{BD^3 - bd^3}{D}\right) = \frac{1}{6}\left(\frac{1500 \times 2500^3 - 900 \times 1600^3}{2500}\right) = 1.31674 \times 10^9 \text{ mm}^3$$

$$\text{Stress at fibre CD, } \sigma_{CD} = \frac{1500\times10^3}{2.31\times10^6} + \frac{(1500\times10^3)(700)}{1.31674\times10^9}$$

$$= 0.649 + 0.797 = 1.446 \text{ N/mm}^2 \text{ (compression)}$$

$$\text{Stress at fibre AB, } \sigma_{AB} = \frac{1500\times10^3}{2.31\times10^6} - \frac{(1500\times10^3)(700)}{1.31674\times10^9}$$

$$= 0.649 - 0.797 = -0.148 \text{ N/mm}^2 \text{ (tension)}$$

The stress distribution is shown in Figure 1.18(ii). The maximum stress is 1.446 N/mm^2 (compression), and the minimum stress is 0.148 N/mm^2 (tension).

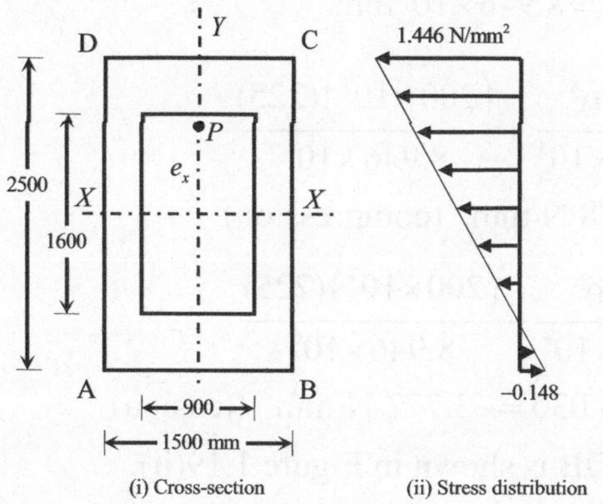

Figure 1.18 Section and stress distribution (Example 1.5)

Note:

The load applied in the hollow portion does not necessarily mean that the load is not transmitted through the column. Similarly, the stress will exist at the base under the hollow portion as shown in Figure 1.18(ii). However, the stress distribution needs to be represented only for the solid portion when the distribution is drawn at a section other than the base (e.g., at mid-height).

Example 1.6: If a solid circular column of diameter 450 mm is subjected to a load of 200 kN at the outer edge, determine the maximum and minimum stresses in the section.

Solution:

Since the load is applied at the outer edge of circle, the eccentricity is the same at all the edges from the centroid of the circular section. Therefore, the maximum stress (i.e., compression) occurs at the location of load, and the minimum stress (i.e., tension) occurs at the opposite edge of the circular section. Let the eccentricity be considered with respect to *Y*-axis as shown in Figure 1.19(i).

$$\sigma_{max} = \sigma_D = \frac{P}{A} + \frac{P \cdot e_y}{Z_{yy}}$$

$$\sigma_{min} = \sigma_B = \frac{P}{A} - \frac{P \cdot e_y}{Z_{yy}}$$

where

$$P = 200 \text{ kN} = 200 \times 10^3 \text{ N}$$

$$A = \frac{\pi D^2}{4} = \frac{\pi (450)^2}{4} = 159.043 \times 10^3 \text{ mm}^2$$

$$e_y = 225 \text{ mm}$$

$$Z_{yy} = \frac{\pi D^3}{32} = \frac{\pi (450)^3}{32} = 8.946 \times 10^6 \text{ mm}^3$$

$$\text{Stress at D, } \sigma_D = \frac{200 \times 10^3}{159.043 \times 10^3} + \frac{(200 \times 10^3)(225)}{8.946 \times 10^6}$$

$$= 1.258 + 5.030 = 6.288 \text{ N/mm}^2 \text{ (compression)}$$

$$\text{Stress at B, } \sigma_B = \frac{200 \times 10^3}{159.043 \times 10^3} - \frac{(200 \times 10^3)(225)}{8.946 \times 10^6}$$

$$= 1.258 - 5.030 = -3.772 \text{ N/mm}^2 \text{ (tension)}$$

The stress distribution across DB is shown in Figure 1.19(ii).

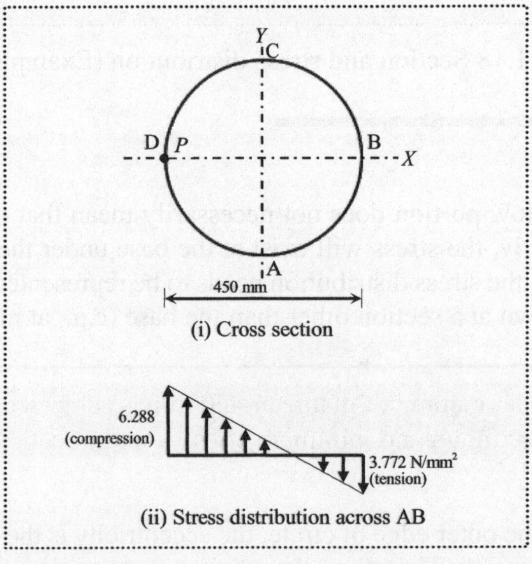

Figure 1.19 Section and stress distribution (Example 1.6)

Example 1.7: A hollow circular column of outer diameter 450 with 75 mm thickness is subjected to a load of 200 kN applied at an eccentricity of 100 mm with respect to *X*-axis. Find the maximum and minimum stresses in the section.

Solution:

The eccentricity is with respect to *X*-axis as shown in Figure 1.20(i). The maximum stress at A and minimum stress at C are calculated using the following formulas.

$$\sigma_{\max} = \sigma_{\text{A}} = \frac{P}{A} + \frac{P \cdot e_x}{Z_{xx}} \text{ and } \sigma_{\min} = \sigma_{\text{C}} = \frac{P}{A} - \frac{P \cdot e_x}{Z_{xx}}$$

where

$$P = 200 \text{ kN} = 200 \times 10^3 \text{ N}$$

$$e_x = 100 \text{ mm}$$

$$A = \frac{\pi\left(D^2 - d^2\right)}{4} = \frac{\pi\left(450^2 - 300^2\right)}{4} = 88.357 \times 10^3 \text{ mm}^2$$

$$Z_{xx} = \frac{\pi\left(D^4 - d^4\right)}{32D} = \frac{\pi\left(450^4 - 300^4\right)}{32(450)} = 7.179 \times 10^6 \text{ mm}^3$$

$$\text{Stress at A, } \sigma_{\text{A}} = \frac{200 \times 10^3}{88.357 \times 10^3} + \frac{\left(200 \times 10^3\right)(100)}{7.179 \times 10^6}$$

$$= 2.264 + 2.786 = 5.050 \text{ N/mm}^2 \text{ (compression)}$$

$$\text{Stress at C, } \sigma_{\text{C}} = \frac{200 \times 10^3}{88.357 \times 10^3} - \frac{\left(200 \times 10^3\right)(100)}{7.179 \times 10^6}$$

$$= 2.264 - 2.786 = -0.522 \text{ N/mm}^2 \text{ (tension)}$$

The stress distribution across AC at the base is shown in Figure 1.20(ii).

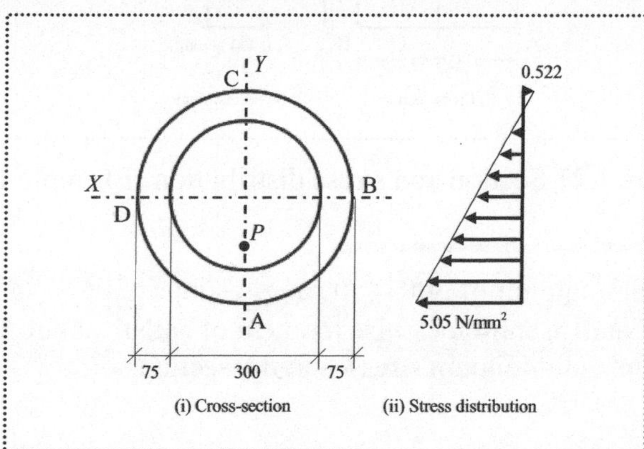

Figure 1.20 Section and stress distribution (Example 1.7)

Example 1.8: A rectangular column of 300×450 mm is subjected to an anti-clockwise moment of 5 kNm about *X*-axis. Find the maximum and minimum stresses in the section.

Solution:

The column is not subjected to any axial or eccentric loads as shown in Figure 1.21(i). Therefore, no direct stress is developed at the base. However, the moment applied causes bending stresses. The maximum and minimum stresses at the opposite sides are obtained as follows.

$$\sigma = \frac{P}{A} \pm \frac{M_x}{Z_{xx}}$$

$$\text{Stress at fibre AB, } \sigma_{AB} = 0 + \frac{5\times10^6}{\left(300\times450^2\right)/6}$$

$$= 0.494 \text{ N/mm}^2 \text{ (compression)}$$

$$\text{Stress at fibre CD, } \sigma_{CD} = 0 - \frac{5\times10^6}{\left(300\times450^2\right)/6}$$

$$= -0.494 \text{ N/mm}^2 \text{ (tension)}$$

Since the magnitude of the stress is same at the two opposite edges, the maximum compressive and tensile stresses are equal to 0.494 N/mm^2. The stress distribution at the base is shown in Figure 1.21(ii)

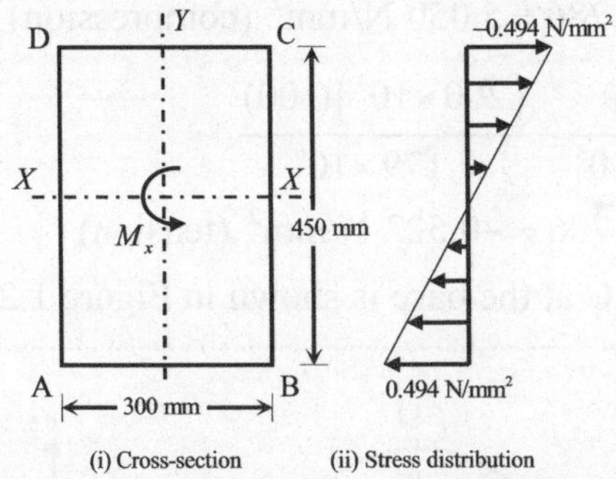

Figure 1.21 Section and stress distribution (Example 1.8)

Example 1.9: A rectangular column of 300×450 mm is subjected to a load of 10 kN at the mid-point of extreme fibre DC and an anti-clockwise moment of 5 kNm about *X* axis as shown in Figure 1.22(i). Find the maximum and minimum stresses in the section.

Solution:

The point load (i.e., 10 kN) causes the direct stress (compression) across the entire section. It also develops a clockwise moment of 2.25 kNm (i.e., 10×0.225) which causes the bending stress (compression) in fibre DC and the bending stress (tension) in fibre AB. In addition, the moment applied (i.e., 5 kNm) causes bending stress (compression) in fibre AB and bending stress (tension) in fibre DC.

Therefore, the resultant stresses are calculated using the following formula.

$$\sigma = \frac{P}{A} \pm \frac{P \cdot e_x}{Z_{xx}} \pm \frac{M_x}{Z_{xx}}$$

Stress at fibre AB, $\sigma_{AB} = \frac{10\times10^3}{(300\times450)} - \frac{(10\times10^3)(225)}{(300\times450^2)/6} + \frac{5\times10^6}{(300\times450^2)/6}$

$$= 0.074 - 0.222 + 0.494 = 0.346 \text{ N/mm}^2 \text{ (compression)}$$

Stress at fibre DC, $\sigma_{DC} = \frac{10\times10^3}{(300\times450)} + \frac{(10\times10^3)(225)}{(300\times450^2)/6} - \frac{5\times10^6}{(300\times450^2)/6}$

$$= 0.074 + 0.222 - 0.494 = -0.198 \text{ N/mm}^2 \text{ (tension)}$$

The maximum stress is 0.346 N/mm² (compression) at the extreme fibre AB and the minimum stress is 0.198 N/mm² (tension) at the extreme fibre DC as shown in Figure 1.22(ii).

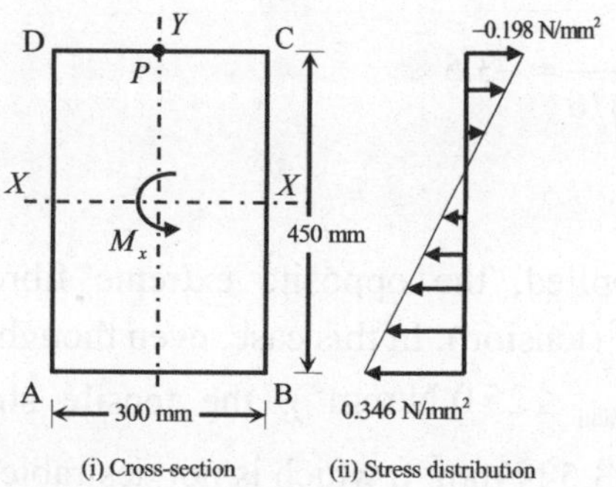

Figure 1.22 Section and stress distribution (Example 1.9)

Note:

In the numerical examples, the nature of bending stress is diagnosed by realising the moment whether it causes the compression or the tension. The results can also be obtained by properly substituting the coordinates of eccentricity (i.e., + or –) in the resultant stress equation as $\sigma = \frac{P}{A} + \frac{P \cdot e_x}{Z_{xx}} + \frac{P \cdot e_y}{Z_{yy}}$.

Example 1.10: A column of 300×300 mm is made up of concrete with maximum allowable compressive stress of 25 N/mm² and maximum allowable tensile stress of 3.5 N/mm². Find the greatest load that can be applied with an eccentricity limited to 75 mm on the column.

Solution:

Since the maximum and minimum stresses are limited to 25 N/mm² (compression) and 3.5 N/mm² (tension) respectively, the appropriate formulas can be used as follows.

$$\sigma_{max} = \frac{P}{A} + \frac{P \cdot e}{Z} = 25.0$$

$$\sigma_{min} = \frac{P}{A} - \frac{P \cdot e}{Z} = -3.5$$

From the maximum stress equation,

$$\frac{P}{(300 \times 300)} + \frac{P(75)}{(300 \times 300^2)/6} = 25.0$$

$$\boxed{P = 900 \times 10^3 \text{ N}}$$

Similarly, from the minimum stress equation,

$$\frac{P}{(300 \times 300)} - \frac{P(75)}{(300 \times 300^2)/6} = -3.5$$

$$\boxed{P = 630 \times 10^3 \text{ N}}$$

When $P = 900 \times 10^3$ N is applied, the opposite extreme fibres will result in 25.0 N/mm² (compression) and 5.0 N/mm² (tension). In this case, even though the compressive stress is within the allowable value ($\sigma_{compression} \leq 25.0$ N/mm²), the tensile stress (5.0 N/mm²) exceeds the allowable value (i.e., $\sigma_{tension} \nleq 3.5$ N/mm²), which is not desirable.

On the other hand, when $P = 630 \times 10^3$ N is applied, the opposite extreme fibres will result in 17.5 N/mm² (compression) and 3.5 N/mm² (tension), which satisfies the conditions. Therefore, the greatest load that can be applied safely is $P = 630 \times 10^3$ N.

Example 1.11: A steel column shown in Figure 1.23 carries a vertical compressive load of 2100 kN. Find the maximum allowable eccentricity of the load from *X*-axis (e_x) if the maximum tensile stress is not to exceed 200 N/mm².

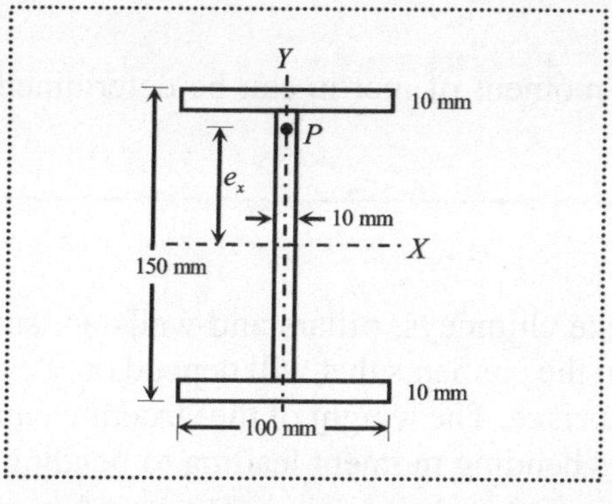

Figure 1.23 Steel column with I-section (Example 1.11)

Solution:

Since the tensile stress is limited to 200 N/mm^2, the eccentricity can be obtained from the following formula.

$$\frac{P}{A}-\frac{P\cdot e_x}{Z_{xx}}=-200$$

where

$$P=2100\text{ kN}=2100\times10^3\text{ N}$$

$$A=(100\times10+10\times130+100\times10)=3300\text{ mm}^2$$

As the section is symmetrical about both the axes, the moment of inertial can be obtained by considering the section as hollow rectangular section with 100×150 mm as outer dimensions and 90×130 mm as inner dimensions.

$$I_{xx}=\frac{\left(100\times150^3\right)-\left(90\times130^3\right)}{12}=11.6475\times10^6\text{ mm}^4$$

$$Z_{xx}=\frac{I_{xx}}{(150/2)}=155.3\times10^3\text{ mm}^3$$

$$\frac{2100\times10^3}{3300}-\frac{\left(2100\times10^3\right)\cdot e_x}{155.3\times10^3}=-200$$

$$636.364-13.522e_x=-200$$

$$\boxed{e_x=61.852\text{ mm}}$$

The limiting value of eccentricity from the *X*-axis is 61.852 mm to satisfy the allowable tensile stress criterion. If the same example were to be solved by limiting the maximum compressive stress of 200 N/mm^2, then the eccentricity would be 32.271 mm.

Note:

For the built-up sections, the moment of inertia can be determined by applying the parallel axis theorem.

1.10 Analysis of Chimney

Vertical structural elements like chimneys, pillars and walls are subjected to wind pressure. This wind pressure induces loads on the elements that will depend on the angle at which the wind strikes, and the shape of the exposed surface. The weight of the structure causes direct stress (compression) while the wind load introduces bending moment leading to bending stresses at the base.

Wind force (P) is equal to the product of the intensity of wind pressure (p) and the surface area (A_e) exposed to wind as shown in Figure 1.24.

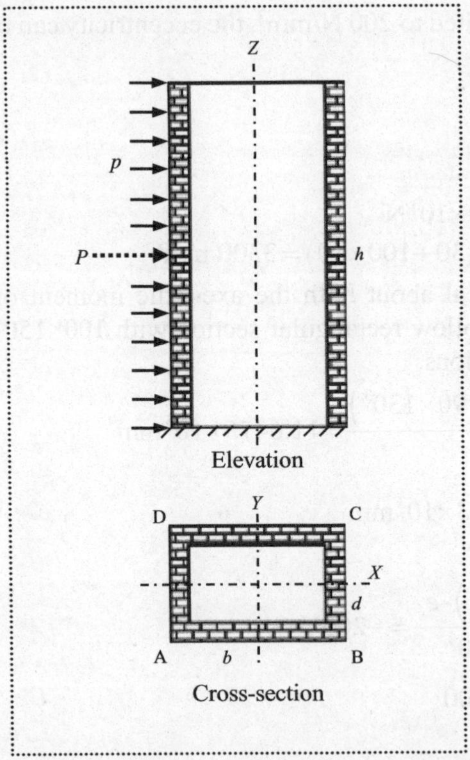

Figure 1.24 Wind pressure on chimney

However, this wind force is obtained by introducing the coefficient of wind resistance (k) when the pressure acts on circular or inclined surfaces. If the wind pressure is assumed to be uniform on the entire surface, the wind force can be considered to be concentrated at the centroid of the exposed area.

$$P = k \cdot p \cdot A_e \tag{1.16}$$

where P is concentrated wind force, p is wind pressure, and A_e is exposed area. The coefficient of wind resistance is obtained as

$$k = \sin^2 \theta \tag{1.17}$$

where θ is the angle of wind direction with the surface. If the wind pressure is acting perpendicular to a flat surface, then $k = 1$. For inclined surfaces (e.g., $\theta = 45°$), $k = 0.5$, and for circular surfaces, $k = 2/3$.

Mostly, chimneys are massive in nature. Hence, the weight of the chimney acts as a compressive vertical load which causes direct stress, and the wind force acts as horizontal (lateral) load causing the bending stress at the base. The resultant stress is obtained using the following formula.

$$\sigma = \frac{W}{A} \pm \frac{M}{Z} \tag{1.18}$$

where $W = V \cdot \rho$ is the weight of the structure

V is the volume of the structure,

ρ is the density of the structure,

A is the area of cross-section,

M is the moment due to wind force,

Z is the section modulus about the axis of bending.

1.10.1 Numerical Examples

Example 1.12: A square chimney of 12.5 m high has an opening of 1.2×1.2 m inside. The wall thickness is 450 mm. If the horizontal wind pressure is 1.1 kN/m^2 and the weight density of chimney is 18 kN/m^3, determine the maximum and minimum stresses at the base.

Solution:

The dimensions of the chimney are shown in Figure 1.25. Let the wind pressure act on the side AD.

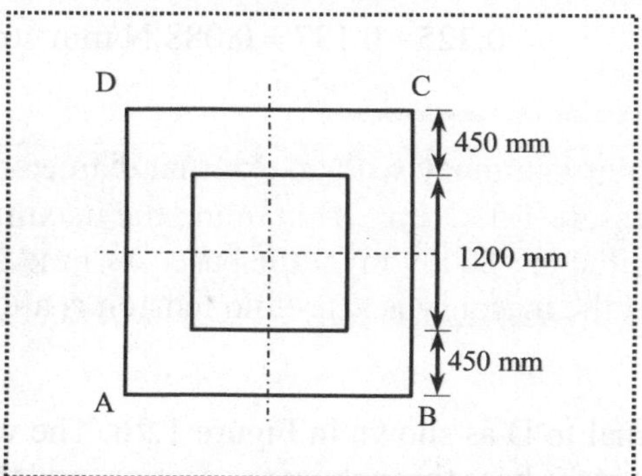

Figure 1.25 Section of hollow square chimney (Example 1.12)

The weight of chimney causes the direct stress (compression) at base throughout the section, and the wind force causes bending stresses at the base, precisely compression at fibre BC and tension at fibre AD. Therefore, the maximum stress will occur at BC and minimum stress will occur at AD.

$$\text{The maximum stress, } \sigma_{\max} = \sigma_{BC} = \frac{W}{A} + \frac{M}{Z_{yy}}$$

$$\text{The minimum stress, } \sigma_{\min} = \sigma_{AD} = \frac{W}{A} - \frac{M}{Z_{yy}}$$

where

$$\text{Cross-sectional area, } A = (2.1\times2.1) - (1.2\times1.2) = 2.97\ \text{m}^2 = 2.97\times10^6\ \text{mm}^2$$

$$\text{Weight, } W = V\cdot\rho = (A\cdot h)\rho = (2.97\times12.5)(18.0) = 668.25\ \text{kN}$$

$$\text{Moment, } M = P\cdot\frac{h}{2} = (k\cdot p\cdot A_e)\frac{h}{2}$$

$$= (1.0\times1.15\times(2.1\times12.5))\left(\frac{12.5}{2}\right) = 188.672\ \text{kNm}$$

$$\text{Moment of inertia, } I_{yy} = \frac{(2.1\times2.1^3) - (1.2\times1.2^3)}{12} = 1.447875\ \text{m}^4$$

$$\text{Section modulus, } Z_{yy} = \frac{I_{yy}}{(2.1/2)} = 1.37893\ \text{m}^3 = 1.37893\times10^9\ \text{mm}^3$$

$$\text{The maximum stress, } \sigma_{\max} = \sigma_{BC} = \frac{668.25\times10^3}{2.97\times10^6} + \frac{188.672\times10^6}{1.37893\times10^9}$$

$$= 0.225 + 0.137 = 0.362\ \text{N/mm}^2\ \text{(compression)}$$

$$\text{The minimum stress, } \sigma_{\min} = \sigma_{AD} = \frac{668.25\times10^3}{2.97\times10^6} - \frac{188.672\times10^6}{1.37893\times10^9}$$

$$= 0.225 - 0.137 = 0.088\ \text{N/mm}^2\ \text{(compression)}$$

Example 1.13: A circular masonry chimney with an external diameter 1.2 m and internal diameter 0.6 m is subjected to wind pressure 1.5 kN/m^2. Determine the maximum height of the chimney if the stress (compression) is limited to 120 kN/m^2 at the base. Assume the unit weight of masonry is 18 kN/m^3. Also check whether the masonry is safe if no tension is allowed.

Solution:

Let the wind pressure act normal to D as shown in Figure 1.26. The weight of the chimney causes the direct stress (compression) at the base throughout the section, and the wind force causes bending stresses at B (compression) and at D (tension).

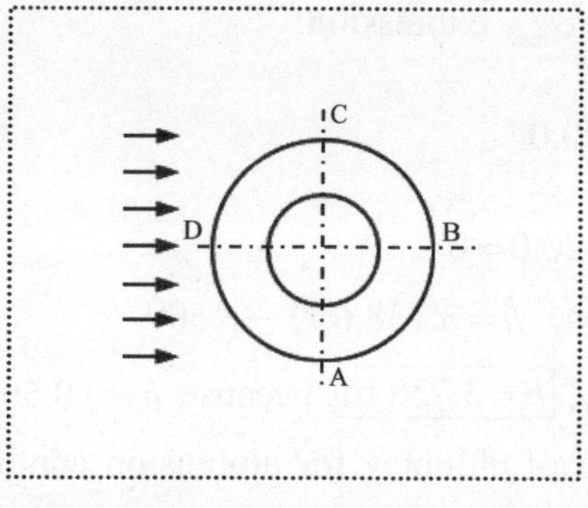

Figure 1.26 Wind pressure on chimney (Example 1.13)

The maximum stress will occur at B and minimum stress will occur at D.

$$\sigma_{max} = \sigma_B = \frac{W}{A} + \frac{M}{Z_{yy}}$$

$$\sigma_{min} = \sigma_D = \frac{W}{A} - \frac{M}{Z_{yy}}$$

Here, the height of chimney needs to be determined so that the maximum stress is 120 kN/m^2.

Therefore, $\frac{W}{A} + \frac{M}{Z_{yy}} = 120$.

Let the height of chimney be "h" in metres.

$$\text{Cross sectional area, } A = \frac{\pi\left(1.2^2 - 0.6^2\right)}{4} = 0.848230 \text{ m}^2$$

$$\text{Area exposed to wind, } A_e = 1.2 \times h = 1.2\, h \text{ m}^2$$

$$\text{Volume, } V = A \cdot h = 0.84823\, h \text{ m}^3$$

$$\text{Weight, } W = V \cdot \rho = (0.84823\, h)(18.0) = 15.26814\, h \text{ kN}$$

$$\text{Wind force, } P = k \cdot p \cdot A_e = \frac{2}{3} \times 1.5 \times (1.2\, h) = 1.2\, h \text{ kN}$$

$$\text{Moment due to wind force, } M = P \cdot \frac{h}{2} = (1.2\, h)\frac{h}{2} = 0.6\, h^2 \text{ kNm}$$

$$\text{Section modulus about Y-axis, } Z_{yy} = \frac{I_{yy}}{(D/2)} = \frac{\frac{\pi}{64}\left(D^4 - d^4\right)}{(D/2)} = \frac{\pi}{32D}\left(D^4 - d^4\right)$$

$$= \frac{\pi}{32(1.2)}\left(1.2^4 - 0.6^4\right) = 0.159043 \text{ m}^3$$

Substituting the above values in σ_{max} expression:

$$\frac{15.26814\,h}{0.84823}+\frac{0.6\,h^2}{0.159043}=120.0$$

$$3.772565\,h^2+18.0\,h-120.0=0$$

By solving the quadratic equation, $h=3.738$ (or) -8.509

Therefore, the height of chimney, $\boxed{h=3.738\text{ m}}$, because $h=-8.509$ is inadmissible.

In order to determine the height of chimney for no-tension condition, the minimum stress at D should be zero.

$$\frac{W}{A}-\frac{M}{Z_{yy}}=0$$

$$\frac{15.26814\,h}{0.84823}-\frac{0.6\,h^2}{0.159043}=0$$

$$18.0\,h=3.772565\,h^2$$

$$\boxed{h=4.771\text{ m}}$$

Since the height already obtained (i.e, 3.738 m) is less than height required to develop tension (i.e, 4.771 m), the masonry with $h=3.738$ m is safe.

Note:

The maximum and minimum stresses for different values of height are presented in Table 1.2.

Table 1.2 Maximum and minimum stresses

h (m)	W/A (kN/m^2)	M/Z (kN/m^2)	σ_{max} (kN/m^2)	σ_{min} (kN/m^2)
8.0	144.0	241.4	+385.4	–97.4
7.0	126.0	184.9	+310.9	–58.9
6.0	108.0	135.8	+243.8	–27.8
5.0	90.0	94.3	+184.3	–4.3
4.771	85.9	85.9	+171.8	0
4.0	72.0	60.4	+132.4	+11.6
3.738	67.3	52.7	+120.0	+14.6
3.0	54.0	34.0	+88.0	+20.0

From the above table, when the height is 3.738 m, the stress (compressive) at B reaches the limiting value (i.e., 120 kN/m^2), while stress at D is also compressive (+14.6 kN/m^2). However, when the height is 4.771 m, even though the stress at D satisfies the no-tension condition (i.e., 0 kN/m^2), the stress (compressive) at B (i.e., 171.8 kN/m^2) exceeds the limiting value of the material (i.e., 120 kN/m^2), which is not desirable.

Example 1.14: Design a hollow rectangular chimney that develops no-tension at the base with the following details.

Outer breadth of chimney $= B$

Outer depth of chimney, $D = \frac{2}{3}B$

Inner breadth of chimney, $b = B/2$

Inner depth of chimney, $d = D/2$

Height of chimney, $h = 10B$

Unit weight of chimney, $\rho = 24\ \text{kN/m}^3$

Wind pressure acting on the shorter side, $p = 1.5\ \text{m}^2$

Solution:

The design of chimney necessarily means obtaining the dimensions of the chimney by satisfying the given condition (i.e., no-tension at the base). Since only one condition is available to be satisfied, we can solve for only one unknown. In this case, all the geometric dimensions of the chimney can be represented in terms of outer breadth (B).

$$\frac{W}{A} - \frac{M}{Z_{yy}} = 0 \tag{1.19}$$

Cross-sectional area, $A = (BD - bd)$

$$= \left(B \times \frac{2}{3}B - \frac{B}{2} \cdot \frac{\left(\frac{2}{3}B\right)}{2}\right) = \frac{B^2}{2}$$

Exposed area to wind, $A_e = D \times h$

$$= \left(\frac{2}{3}B\right)(10B) = \frac{20}{3}B^2$$

Volume of chimney, $V = A \cdot h$

$$= \left(\frac{B^2}{2} \times 10B\right) = 5B^3$$

Weight of chimney, $W = V \cdot \rho$

$$= (5B^3)(24.0) = 120B^3$$

Wind force, $P = k \cdot p \cdot A_e$

$$= 1.0 \times 1.5 \times \left(\frac{20}{3}B^2\right) = 10B^2$$

$$\text{Moment due to wind force, } M = P\cdot\left(\frac{h}{2}\right)$$

$$= \left(10B^2\right)\left(\frac{10B}{2}\right) = 50B^3$$

$$\text{Section modulus, } Z_{yy} = \frac{I_{yy}}{(B/2)}$$

$$= \frac{\left(DB^3 - db^3\right)/12}{(B/2)} = \frac{\left(\frac{2}{3}B\cdot B^3 - \frac{1}{3}B\cdot\left(\frac{1}{2}B\right)^3\right)/12}{(B/2)} = \frac{5B^3}{48}$$

Substituting the above in Eq. (1.19)

$$\frac{120B^3}{\left(B^2/2\right)} - \frac{50B^3}{\left(5B^3/48\right)} = 0$$

$$\boxed{B = 2.0\text{ m}}$$

Since, the value of B is known, all the remaining dimensions can be obtained.

$$D = \frac{2}{3}B = \frac{2}{3}(2.0) = 1.333\text{ m}$$

$$b = \frac{B}{2} = \frac{2.0}{2} = 1.0\text{ m}$$

$$d = \frac{D}{2} = \frac{1.333}{2} = 0.667\text{ m}$$

1.11 Analysis of Dams

A gravity dam is a solid structure, generally made of masonry or concrete, constructed across a river to create a reservoir on its upstream. The forces acting on gravity dams such as self-weight, water pressure etc. are resisted by their own weight. Rectangular and trapezoidal are the commonly preferred shapes for solid gravity dams, and a typical section is shown in Figure 1.27.

Analysis of dams involves the determination of stresses at the base, and checking the conditions of stability against tension, sliding and overturning by considering a unit length of the structure. The impounding water exerts pressure on the vertical wall in upstream side, and this pressure varies linearly from zero at the surface of water to γh at the bottom, where γ is the unit weight of water, and h is the height of water. Since the pressure distribution is a triangle, the horizontal thrust is the area of the distribution which acts at $h/3$ from the base.

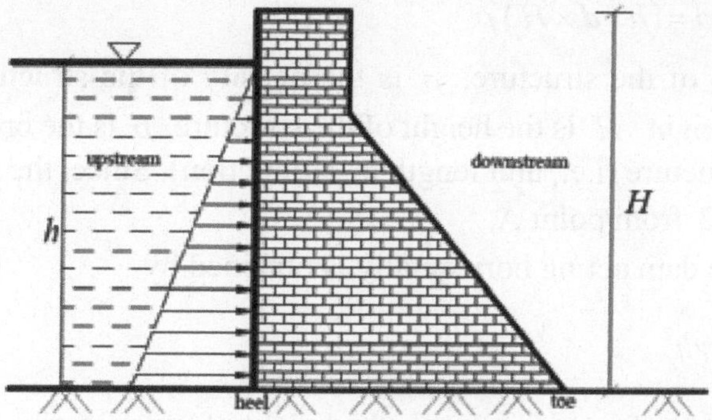

Figure 1.27 A typical section of gravity dam

1.11.1 *Analysis of Rectangular Dam*

Consider a rectangular dam that retains water on one of its vertical sides as shown in Figure 1.28.

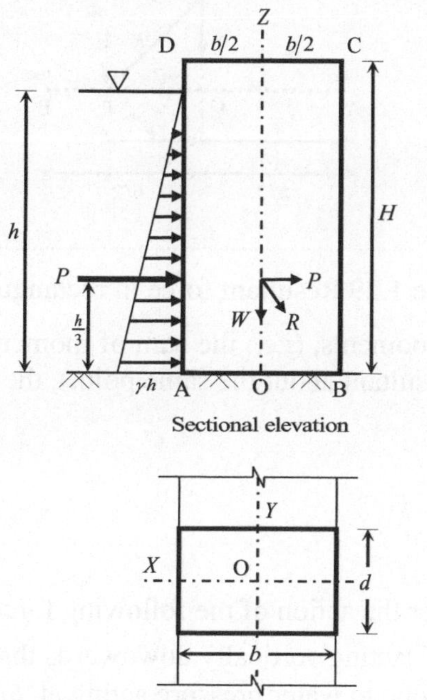

Figure 1.28 Rectangular dam

The weight of the dam acting vertically is obtained by

$$W = V \cdot \rho = (A \cdot H)\rho = (b \times d \times H)\rho \tag{1.20}$$

where V is the volume of the structure, ρ is the density of the structure, A is the area of the structure resisting the weight, H is the height of the structure, b is the breadth of the structure and d is the width of the structure (i.e., unit length in Y-direction). Since, the section is a rectangle, the centre of gravity $\bar{x} = b/2$ from point A.

Lateral thrust on the dam acting horizontally is obtained by

$$P = \frac{1}{2}\gamma h \cdot h = \frac{1}{2}\gamma h^2 \tag{1.21}$$

where γ is the unit weight of water, and h is the height of water retained.

The dam is subjected to two forces, W and P. Let the resultant R meet the base at E at a distance "e" from O as shown in Figure 1.29.

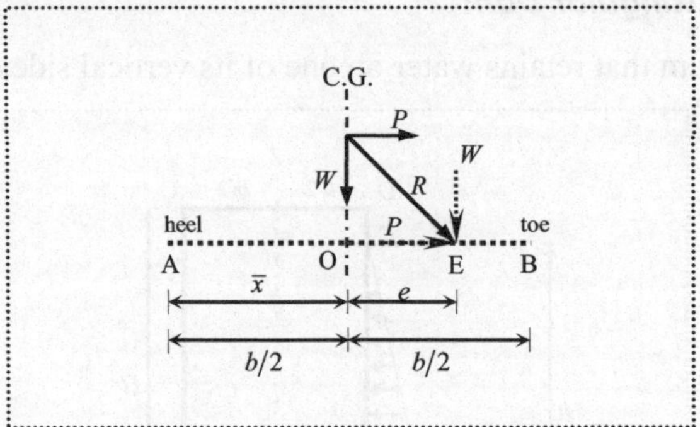

Figure 1.29 Resultant force in rectangular dam

Using Varignon's theorem of moments, (i.e., the sum of moments of all forces about any point is equal to the moment of their resultant about the same point), the eccentricity (e) is calculated as

$$P \times \frac{h}{3} - W \times e = R \times 0$$

$$\boxed{e = \frac{P}{W} \cdot \frac{h}{3}} \tag{1.22}$$

The dam is in equilibrium under the action of the following forces:

i) Weight of the dam (W) acting vertically downwards through the centre of gravity
ii) Horizontal thrust (P) due to water pressure acting at $h/3$ from the base
iii) Reaction offered at the base for the resultant (R) in opposite direction.

The horizontal component of R at E is resisted by frictional resistance against sliding at the base, and the vertical component of R is resisted by normal reaction at the base. Since this vertical component acts at an eccentricity e from O, the section at the base will be subjected to both direct and bending stresses.

Therefore, $\sigma = \frac{W}{A} \pm \frac{M}{Z}$

where

Weight of dam, $W = V \times \rho = (A \cdot H) \cdot \rho$

Area of section resisting the weight, $A = (b \times d) = (b \times 1) = b$

Moment causing the bending stress, $M = W \cdot e$

Section modulus, $Z = \frac{db^2}{6} = \frac{(1)b^2}{6} = \frac{b^2}{6}$

Eccentricity, $e = \frac{P}{W} \cdot \frac{h}{3}$

Substituting the above expressions in the resultant stresses equation,

$$\sigma = \frac{W}{b} \pm \frac{W \cdot e}{(b^2/6)} = \frac{W}{b}\left(1 \pm \frac{6e}{b}\right) \tag{1.23}$$

The maximum stress occurs at B (always compression), and minimum stress occurs at A (compression or tension depending on the value of eccentricity).

$$\boxed{\sigma_{\max} = \sigma_{\text{B}} = \frac{W}{b}\left(1 + \frac{6e}{b}\right)} \tag{1.24}$$

$$\boxed{\sigma_{\min} = \sigma_{\text{A}} = \frac{W}{b}\left(1 - \frac{6e}{b}\right)} \tag{1.25}$$

1.11.2 *Analysis of Trapezoidal Dam*

Consider a trapezoidal dam that retains water on its vertical side as shown in Figure 1.30. Similar to the rectangular dam, the lateral (horizontal) thrust acting at $h/3$ from the base is

$$P = \frac{1}{2}\gamma h^2 \tag{1.26}$$

The weight of the dam is calculated by considering the average breadth of the section

$$W = V \times \rho = \left(\frac{a+b}{2}\right) d \cdot H \cdot \rho \tag{1.27}$$

Unlike the rectangular section (in which the centre of gravity $\bar{x} = b/2$), for trapezoidal section, the centre of gravity (C.G.) is calculated using a formula. If $\bar{x}$ is the centre of gravity (at which W acts vertically) measured from the face of the vertical wall, then

$$\bar{x} = \frac{1}{3}\left(\frac{a^2 + ab + b^2}{a+b}\right) \tag{1.28}$$

where " a " is the top side and " b " is the bottom side, and the value of $\bar{x}$ always lies between $b/3$ and $b/2$ for all the general conditions where $a \leq b$.

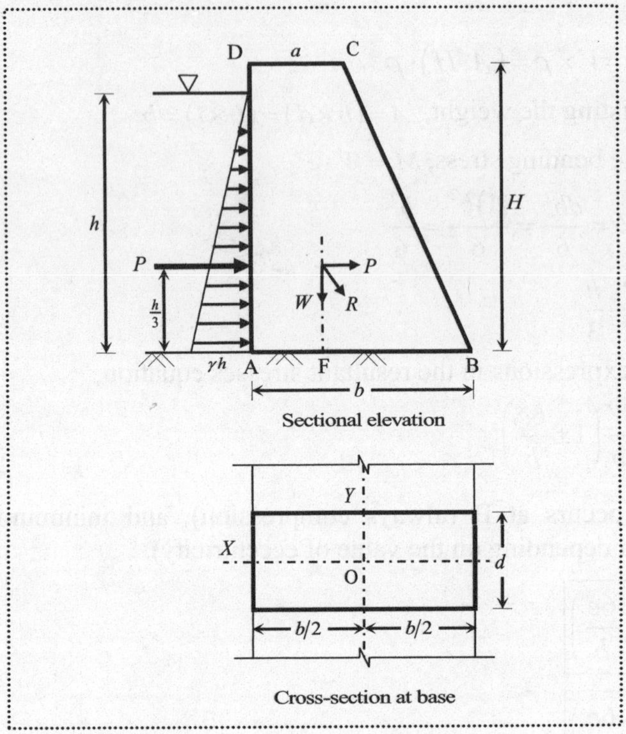

Figure 1.30 Trapezoidal dam

Let point F be the distance of C.G. from A (i.e., AF= $\bar{x}$), and point O be the mid-point at the base (i.e., AO= $b/2$). The resultant (R) of weight (i.e., W , acting vertically at point F) and lateral thrust (i.e., P, acting horizontally at $h/3$) meets the base at E at a distance of e from O as shown in Figure 1.31.

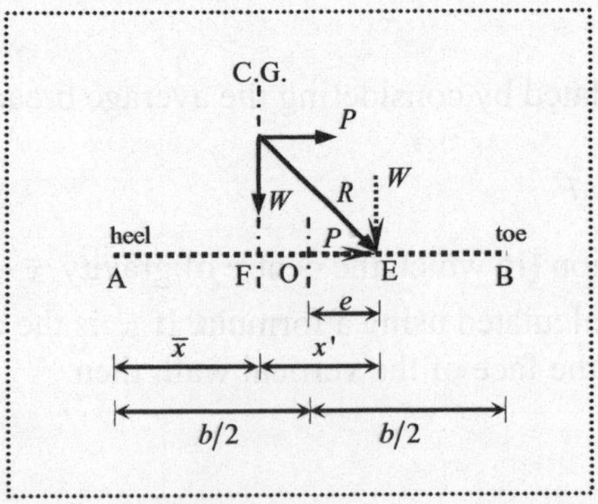

Figure 1.31 Resultant force in trapezoidal dam

Similar to the rectangular section, apply Varignon's theorem by equating the sum of moments of P and W about point E, with the moment of R about point E.

$$\left(P\times\frac{h}{3}\right)-(W\times x')=(R\times 0)$$

$$x'=\frac{P}{W}\cdot\frac{h}{3} \tag{1.29}$$

Let x_{E} be the distance between A and E.

$$x_{\mathrm{E}}=\bar{x}+x' \tag{1.30}$$

Since the vertical component of R acting at E is eccentric to the centroid of base, it causes both direct and bending stresses. The eccentricity that causes bending stresses is

$$\boxed{e=x_{\mathrm{E}}-\frac{b}{2}} \tag{1.31}$$

The maximum and minimum stresses are determined using the same equation used for rectangular section.

1.11.3 *Condition to Avoid Tension*

Since the section at the base is rectangle, the value of eccentricity is limited to $b/6$ for ensuring compressive stress at the base without development of any tension (i.e., $e\leq b/6$).

1.11.4 *Condition to Prevent Sliding*

The horizontal component of R (i.e., P) is resisted by the frictional force between the bottom of the dam and the ground beneath, and it should be less than the limiting frictional resistance (F) for ensuring safety against sliding. Therefore, the frictional resistance is obtained as

$$F=\mu\times W \tag{1.32}$$

where μ is the coefficient of friction between the dam and the soil on which it rests.

The factor of safety is the ratio between the resistance offered by the frictional force and the horizontal force which causes sliding, and the value should not be less than 1.0.

$$FS_{\text{sliding}}=\frac{F}{P}=\frac{\mu\cdot W}{P} \tag{1.33}$$

It is usual to design the dam such that the factor of safety against sliding is at least 1.50.

1.11.5 *Condition to Avoid Overturning*

For ensuring safety against overturning, it is necessary that the resultant must strike the base within its breadth (i.e., point E should lie within the base AB). That means the overturning of the dam occurs if the clockwise moment due to water thrust (P) about B exceeds the restoring moment due to W about B.

The overturning moment is the product of horizontal thrust and the distance of the force from the base.

$$M_O = \frac{Ph}{3} \tag{1.34}$$

The restoring moment is the product of the weight and its CG distance from the toe.

$$M_R = W(b - \bar{x}) \tag{1.35}$$

The factor of safety is the ratio between the restoring moment and the overturning moment, and the value should not be less than 1.0.

$$FS_{\text{overturning}} = \frac{M_R}{M_O} \tag{1.36}$$

It is usual to design the dam such that the factor of safety against overturning is at least 1.50.

1.11.6 Numerical Examples

Example 1.15: A trapezoidal masonry dam is as shown in Figure 1.32. Determine the maximum and minimum stresses at the base if the unit weight of masonry is 18 kN/m^3 and weight of water is 10 kN/m^3.

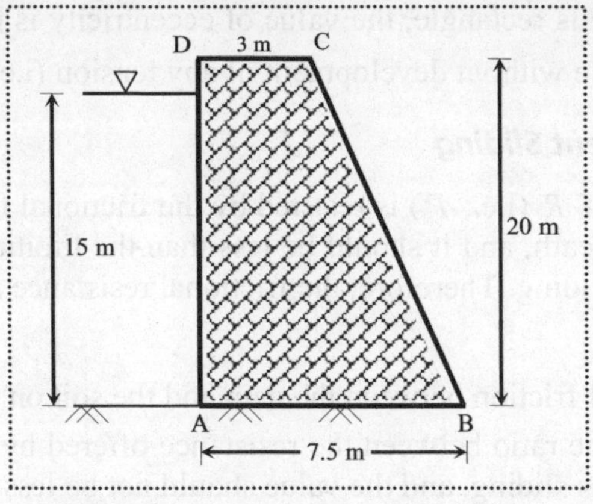

Figure 1.32 Dimensions of trapezoidal dam (Example 1.15)

Solution:

Given data for the analysis are as follows.

Top breadth of dam, $a = 3.0$ m
Bottom breadth of dam, $b = 7.5$ m
Width of dam, $d = 1.0$ m (i.e., unit length)
Height of dam, $H = 20.0$ m
Height of water, $h = 15.0$ m
Density of water, $\gamma = 10.0$ kN/m^3
Density of masonry, $\rho = 18.0$ kN/m^3

As the dam is trapezoidal, the weight, $W = \left(\dfrac{a+b}{2}\right) \times H \times \rho$

$$= \left(\frac{3.0+7.5}{2}\right) \times 20 \times 18.0 = 1890.0 \text{ kN}$$

Lateral thrust due to water pressure, $P = \dfrac{1}{2} \times \gamma \times h^2$

$$= \frac{1}{2} \times 10.0 \times (15.0)^2 = 1125.0 \text{ kN}$$

Distance of centre of gravity from A, $\bar{x} = \dfrac{1}{3}\left(\dfrac{a^2+ab+b^2}{a+b}\right)$

$$= \frac{1}{3}\left(\frac{3.0^2+(3.0)(7.5)+7.5^2}{3.0+7.5}\right) = 2.786 \text{ m}$$

Location of R from A, $x_E = \bar{x} + x' = \bar{x} + \dfrac{P}{W} \cdot \dfrac{h}{3}$

$$= 2.786 + \frac{1125.0}{1890.0}\left(\frac{15}{3}\right) = 5.762 \text{ m}$$

Therefore, eccentricity, $e = x_E - \dfrac{b}{2}$

$$= 5.762 - \frac{7.5}{2} = 2.012 \text{ m}$$

The maximum and minimum stresses are calculated as

$$\sigma_{max} = \sigma_B = \frac{W}{b}\left(1+\frac{6e}{b}\right)$$

$$= \frac{1890.0}{7.5}\left(1+\frac{6\times 2.012}{7.5}\right) = 657.62 \text{ kN/m}^2 \text{ (compression)}$$

$$\sigma_{min} = \sigma_A = \frac{W}{b}\left(1-\frac{6e}{b}\right)$$

$$= \frac{1890.0}{7.5}\left(1-\frac{6\times 2.012}{7.5}\right) = -153.62 \text{ kN/m}^2 \text{ (tension)}$$

Example 1.16: A rectangular masonry dam of 18 m high is used to reserve water up to 15 m. Find the minimum base width required if the unit weight of masonry is 22 kN/m^3 and weight of water is 10 kN/m^3. Take the coefficient of friction between masonry and ground is 0.6.

Solution:

Let the width of base be "b".

Weight of masonry, $W=(b\times d\times H)\rho$

$$=(b\times 1.0\times 18.0)22=396.0\,b\text{ kN}$$

Lateral thrust on the dam, $P=\frac{1}{2}\gamma h^2$

$$=\frac{1}{2}\times 10\times(15.0)^2=1125.0\text{ kN}$$

Eccentricity, $e=\frac{P}{W}\cdot\frac{h}{3}$

$$=\frac{(1125.0\times 15.0)}{(396.0b\times 3)}=\frac{625.0}{44.0\,b}\text{ m}$$

Minimum width required to avoid tension at base is obtained by satisfying the condition $\sigma_{\min}=0$.

$$\sigma_{\min}=\frac{W}{b}\left(1-\frac{6e}{b}\right)=0 \text{ (this is same as } e\le b/6\text{)}$$

$$\frac{625.0}{44.0b}=\frac{b}{6}$$

$$\boxed{b=9.232\text{ m}}$$

Minimum width required to avoid sliding is obtained by equating the horizontal thrust with the frictional resistance.

$$P=\mu\times W$$

$$1125.0=0.6\times 396.0b$$

$$\boxed{b=4.735\text{ m}}$$

Since the minimum width required at the base to avoid sliding is less than the width required to avoid tension, it is safe to provide $b=9.232$ m.

Example 1.17: A trapezoidal masonry dam of 18 m high is used to reserve water up to 15 m. Find the minimum base width required if the unit weight of masonry is 22 kN/m^3, weight of water is 10 kN/m^3, and the maximum normal pressure at the base varies from zero at one side to 550 kN/m^2 at the other side.

Solution:

Let the top width be a, and bottom width be b.

Weight of masonry, $W=\left(\frac{a+b}{2}\times d\times H\right)\rho$

$$=\left(\frac{a+b}{2}\times 1.0\times 18.0\right)\times 22.0=198.0(a+b)\text{ kN}$$

Lateral thrust on the dam, $P=\frac{1}{2}\gamma h^2$

$$=\frac{1}{2}\times 10\times(15.0)^2=1125.0\text{ kN}$$

Since the stress varies from zero to 550 kN/m² at the base, no-tension condition is satisfied.

$\sigma_{\text{min}}=\frac{W}{b}\left(1-\frac{6e}{b}\right)=0$, this leads to $e=b/6$.

Substituting $e=b/6$ in the maximum stress condition,

$$\sigma_{\text{max}}=\frac{W}{b}\left(1+\frac{6e}{b}\right)=550$$

$$\frac{W}{b}\left(1+\frac{6(b/6)}{b}\right)=550$$

$$\boxed{\frac{W}{b}=275.0}$$

Substituting the value of W in the above equation,

$$\frac{198.0(a+b)}{b}=275.0\Rightarrow 198.0a+198.0b=275.0b$$

$$198.0a=77.0b\Rightarrow \boxed{a=0.389b}$$

Distance of centre of gravity $\bar{x}=\frac{1}{3}\left(\frac{a^2+ab+b^2}{a+b}\right)$

$$=\frac{1}{3}\left(\frac{(0.389b)^2+0.389b\cdot b+b^2}{0.389b+b}\right)=0.370b$$

Distance of point at which R strikes, $x_{\text{E}}=\bar{x}+x'$

$$=\bar{x}+\frac{P}{W}\cdot\frac{h}{3}$$

$$= 0.370b + \frac{1125.0}{198.0(0.389b + b)}\left(\frac{15}{3}\right)$$

$$= 0.370b + \frac{20.453}{b}$$

Therefore, eccentricity, $e = x_E - \frac{b}{2}$

$$= 0.370b + \frac{20.453}{b} - \frac{b}{2}$$

$$= \frac{20.453}{b} - 0.130b$$

For no-tension condition to be satisfied, $e = b/6$.

$$\frac{20.453}{b} - 0.130b = \frac{b}{6}$$

$$20.453 = 0.297b^2$$

$$\boxed{b = 8.303 \text{ m}}$$

Therefore top width, $a = 3.230$ m, and bottom width $b = 8.303$ m are provided.

UNIT SUMMARY

- ✓ Basic equations to be satisfied while solving any structural analysis problem are Equilibrium conditions, Compatibility conditions and Constitutive relations.
- ✓ Two types of indeterminacies to classify the structures are Static and Kinematic indeterminacies
- ✓ Free-body diagram is a diagram that represents the structure graphically by replacing the supports with respective reaction components
- ✓ In axially loaded vertical members, the stress developed is the direct stress, $\sigma_0 = \frac{P}{b \cdot d}$
- ✓ In eccentrically loaded vertical members, the stresses developed are the direct and bending stresses: $\sigma_0 = \frac{P}{A}$ and $\sigma_b = \frac{M}{Z}$
- ✓ The resultant stress is obtained by using $\sigma = \frac{P}{b \cdot d} \pm \frac{P \cdot e_x}{Z_{xx}} \pm \frac{P \cdot e_y}{Z_{yy}}$
- ✓ Neutral axis is the layer within the section under bending where the stress is zero.
- ✓ In a rectangular section, the limiting value of eccentricity to avoid tension is $b/6$ or $d/6$.
- ✓ The wind force acting on chimneys is calculated as $P = k \cdot p \cdot A_e$
- ✓ The conditions to be satisfied for the dams are safety against tension, sliding and overturning
- ✓ Horizontal thrust on the dam due to water is calculated as $P = \frac{1}{2}\gamma h^2$

EXERCISES

1.1. Distinguish between axial and eccentric loads.

1.2. Define bending stress.

1.3. Explain the different possibilities of resultant stresses.

1.4. What is meant by core or Kernel? Write the importance of it.

1.5. Write the stability conditions of masonry dam.

1.6. A circular column of 300 mm diameter carries an eccentric compressive load of 50 kN at an eccentricity of 50 mm. Find the maximum and minimum stresses at the base.

1.7. A rectangular hollow column with outer dimensions of 300×450 mm and wall thickness of 50 mm is subjected to compressive load of 100 kN acting at one of the exterior corners. Find the maximum and minimum stresses at the base, and draw the stress distribution across all four edges.

1.8. A hollow circular column with outer diameter of 200 mm and inner diameter of 150 mm is subjected to an eccentric compressive load of 75 kN. Find the limiting value of eccentricity to avoid tension at the base.

1.9. A cylindrical chimney with external diameter of 5 m and internal diameter of 2 m is subjected to a wind pressure of 1.2 kN/m^2. If the height of the chimney is 25 m, weight density of the chimney is 22 kN/m^3 and coefficient of wind pressure is 0.6, find the maximum and minimum stresses at the base.

1.10. A masonry dam 9 m high, 1.25 m wide at the top and 5.75 m wide at the base retains water to a depth of 8.4 m, the water face of the dam being vertical. Find the maximum and minimum stress intensities at the base. Water and masonry weigh 10 kN/m^3 and 22 kN/m^3 respectively.

1.11. A masonry dam of rectangular section 4 m high retains water. Find the width of the dam section so that tensile stresses are just avoided. For this condition, find the maximum stress in masonry for the base section. Water and masonry weigh 10 kN/m^3 and 22 kN/m^3 respectively.

1.12. A trapezoidal masonry dam 9 m high retains water up to the top. The water face of the dam is vertical. If the top width of the dam is 1.5 m, find the minimum bottom width required to avoid tension in masonry. Take weight densities of water and masonry as 10 kN/m^3 and 22 kN/m^3 respectively.

1.13. A masonry dam of trapezoidal section has a vertical water face and a height of 9 m. The depth of water impounded is 8.4 m. If the top width of the section is 1.5 m, find the minimum base width required for the condition of no-tension in masonry and also the condition of no-slip for $\mu = 0.6$. Take weight densities of water and masonry as 10 kN/m^3 and 22 kN/m^3 respectively.

QR Code for *Direct and Bending Stresses*

NPTEL Lecture: https://www.youtube.com/watch?v=iNG4bLMyeFA

This page is intentionally left blank

2 Slope and Deflection

UNIT SPECIFICS

This unit discusses the following aspects.

- Concept of slope and deflection
- Relationship among forces and displacements
- Double integration and Macaulay's methods for displacement responses

RATIONALE

Force responses obtained from the analysis are primarily utilized to decide the dimensioning of section during the design process. Displacement responses are employed to validate the design in the form of serviceability requirement. In statically indeterminate structures, the displacement responses serve as additional equations to analyse the structures for even force responses. This chapter presents basic analytical approach of solving statically determinate structures for displacement responses such as slope and deflection.

UNIT OUTCOMES

List of outcomes of this unit is as follows.

U2-O1: Describe the concept of displacement responses
U2-O2: Describe the concepts of stiffness and its importance
U2-O3: Describe the relationship among forces and displacements
U2-O4: Application of double integration method to determine slope and deflection
U2-O5: Application of Macaulay's method to determine slope and deflection

Mapping of Unit-2 Outcomes with Course Outcomes *

	CO-1	CO-2	CO-3	CO-4	CO-5
U2-O1	1	3	2	2	1
U2-O2	1	3	2	2	1
U2-O3	1	3	2	2	1
U2-O4	1	3	1	1	1
U2-O5	1	3	1	1	1

* (1- Weak correlation; 2- Medium correlation; 3- Strong correlation)

2.1 Introduction

As already discussed, the force responses (e.g., maximum shear force and maximum bending moment) are the primary input to the structural design process for dimensioning the sections. However, displacement responses (e.g., maximum deflection) sometimes decide the proportioning of sections for ensuring the serviceability requirements. In case of statically indeterminate structures, when the available equilibrium equations are inadequate to solve for the unknown reactions present in the free-body diagram, the solution process demands the displacement responses for invoking the compatibility conditions in order to get the solution. Therefore, it is essential to develop the ability to estimate displacements in statically determinate (just-rigid) structures.

2.2 Stiffness

Stiffness is defined as the force required to cause displacement, which is inherent with the material, and the inverse of stiffness is called flexibility. For example, in a bar element, if an axial load (P) results in a deformation (δ) then the stiffness of the bar is P/δ, which is further written as AE/L after substituting PL/AE for δ, where AE is termed as *axial rigidity*. Similarly, when the bending causes the deformation in elements or structures, the bending stiffness can be defined.

2.3 Flexural Deformation

When loads applied on a structure induce bending, the structure assumes a configuration that satisfies external equilibrium under the combined action of the loads and reactions. Simultaneously, internal forces are developed in the form of shear and moments throughout the structure. At any point within the structure, there is a curvature consistent with the moment. These curvatures accumulate as angle changes along the lengths, causing the member to deform into a bent configuration. The elements of the deformed structure fit together in a compatible mode by satisfying all the displacement boundary conditions.

2.4 Sign Conventions

Consider a beam subjected to arbitrary lateral loads as shown in Figure 2.1(i). An element length dx of the beam at a distance x from the left support is acted upon by an external lateral load, and internal shearing forces and bending moments. The bending moments on the elemental length dx tend to convert the straight beam *concave* on its upper surface and *convex* on its lower surface (i.e., compression in the upper fibers and tension in the lower fibers). This phenomenon is called sagging, and the corresponding moments are called *sagging* bending moments. The shearing forces on the elemental length tend to rotate the element in a *clockwise* sense.

The *clockwise* shearing forces (Figure 2.1(ii)) and *sagging* bending moments (Figure 2.1(iii)) are considered positive. When the variations of shearing force and bending moment are represented graphically along the beam (i.e., shear force and bending moment diagrams respectively), the quantities are plotted above the centre line of the beam when positive, and below when negative.

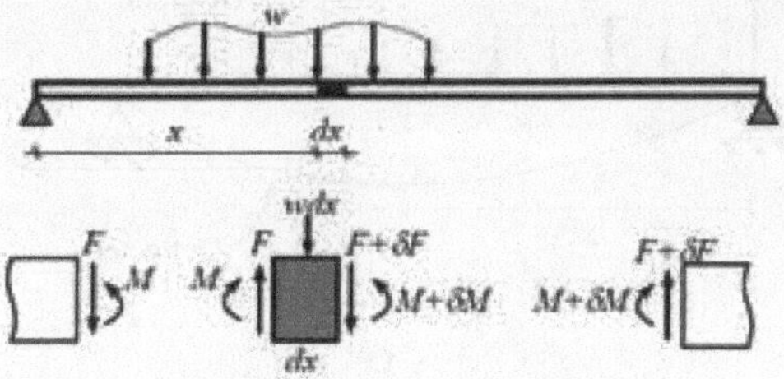

(i) Forces in an element

(ii) Clockwise shearing forces

(iii) Sagging bending moment

Figure 2.1 Forces and their sign conventions

2.5 Flexural Force-Displacement Relationship

The straight beam takes curved profile due to the bending nature of loading which is termed as flexural behaviour. The measurement of any point on the bent configuration from the original position is called displacement. The measurement of displacement in linear direction is called *deflection* while in rotational direction is *slope*. Typically, for a flexural member, the force-displacement relationships must relate the end moments to the corresponding end rotations of the member. Actually, shears and transverse deflections at the end need to be considered, but they are neglected in the current formulation.

Consider a flexural member as shown in Figure 2.2. Let AB be an isolated element subjected to sagging moment M as shown in Figure 2.2. As the element bends, the bottom fibres are elongated while the top fibres are contracted. In between, there is a longitudinal fibre, called *neural fibre*, whose length remains unchanged. The plane cross sections are assumed to remain plane even after bending when the beam deflects.

The extensions of lines through cross sections at A and B intersect at O, called *centre of curvature*, by forming an angle $d\theta$. If the tangents to the deflected neutral fibre are constructed at points A and B, it is evident that $d\theta$ also measures the angular deformation over the length of the beam element. The line BD constructed parallel to the deflected cross section at A creating triangle BCD. Then, for small angles, comparing triangles BCD and OAB,

$$d\theta \simeq \frac{dx}{R} \simeq \frac{dl}{y} \tag{2.1}$$

where R is the radius of curvature of the element, y is the distance from the neutral fibre to the topmost fibre, and dl is the shortening of the top fibre.

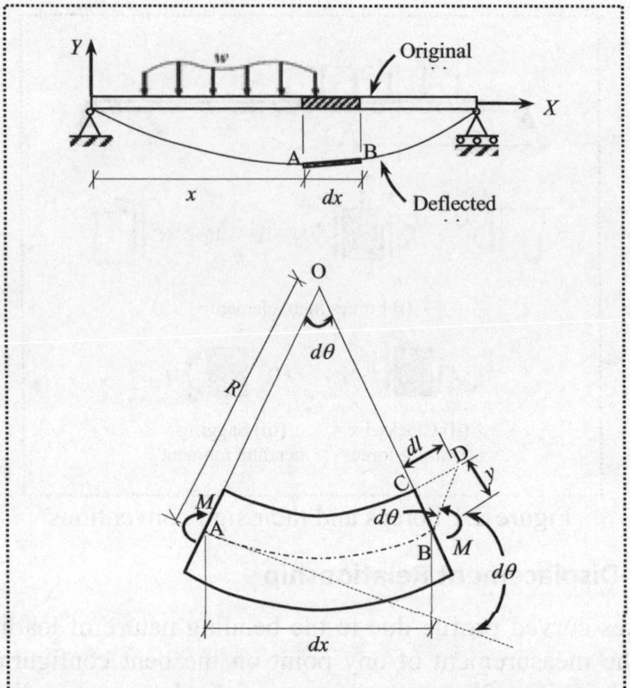

Figure 2.2 Flexural deformation of beam element

Eq. (2.1) can be written as

$$\frac{dl}{dx} = \frac{y}{R} \tag{2.2}$$

As the topmost fibre is essentially an axially loaded element, the application of respective expressions for axial strain and subsequently axial stress in Eq. (2.1),

$$\sigma = E\frac{y}{R} \tag{2.3}$$

where σ is the stress in the top fibre and E is the modulus of elasticity. This fibre stress could also be expressed by the familiar expression from basic mechanics that

$$\sigma = \frac{M \cdot y}{I} \tag{2.4}$$

where M is the moment acting on the element, and I is the moment of inertia. From Eq. (2.3) and Eq. (2.4),

$$\frac{1}{R} = \frac{M}{EI} \tag{2.5}$$

The transverse displacement Δ of the deflected structure can be related to the radius of the curvature according to the elementary calculus relationship as

$$\kappa = \frac{1}{R} = \frac{\dfrac{d^2\Delta}{dx^2}}{\pm\left[1+\left(\dfrac{d\Delta}{dx}\right)^2\right]^{3/2}} \tag{2.6}$$

where κ (pronounced as Kappa) is defined as curvature. Here, $\Delta(x)$ is the deflection at a distance x from the origin, and the gradient $\dfrac{d\Delta}{dx}$ is the slope. Since the value of $d\Delta/dx$ is small compared to unity, Eq. (2.6) reduces to

$$\kappa = \frac{1}{R} = \pm\frac{d^2\Delta}{dx^2} \tag{2.7}$$

Therefore, from Eq. (2.5) and Eq. (2.7)

$$\frac{d^2\Delta}{dx^2} = \pm\frac{M}{EI} \tag{2.8}$$

Eq. (2.8) is a force- deformation relationship. If the slope is represented as $\theta = d\Delta/dx$ then

$$\frac{d}{dx}\left(\frac{d\Delta}{dx}\right) = \frac{d\theta}{dx} = \pm\frac{M}{EI} \tag{2.9}$$

Solution of Eq. (2.9) results in the quantities of slope and deflection as

$$\frac{d\Delta}{dx} = \theta = \int\frac{M}{EI}\,dx + C_1 \tag{2.10}$$

$$\Delta = \int\theta\,dx + C_2 \tag{2.11}$$

where EI is called *flexural rigidity*, C_1 and C_2 are the constants of integration.

Table 2.1 presents the relationship among the responses. From the curvature (which is generally obtained as the bending moment divided by the flexural rigidity), first integration yields respective slope quantities, and further integration of the slopes yields the deflections. This can also be visualized in differential form starting from the deflection.

Table 2.1 Relationship among the responses

Differentiation (↓)	Response	Integration (↑)
	Deflection, Δ	
	Slope, $\theta = \dfrac{d\Delta}{dx}$	
	Moment, $M = EI\dfrac{d^2\Delta}{dx^2}$	
	Shear, $V = \dfrac{dM}{dx} = EI\dfrac{d^3\Delta}{dx^3}$	
	Load, $w = \dfrac{dV}{dx} = EI\dfrac{d^4\Delta}{dx^4}$	

Different methods to estimate the slope and deflection quantities are as follows.

(i) Direct integration methods
(ii) Graphical methods
(iii) Energy methods

Direct integration methods (Double integration method and Macaulay's method) use the force-deformation relationship as a differential equation. Solution of this differential equation by applying appropriate boundary conditions yields the explicit expressions for slope ($d\Delta/dx$), and deflection (Δ). The primary advantage of the integration methods is the ability to get the displacement quantities at any point along the length using the obtained explicit expressions. The integration method is of greatest value when the loading is such as to produce a moment diagram that is a continuous function over the entire length of the beam (e.g., cantilever beam subjected to a point load at the free end; cantilever beam or a simply supported beam subjected to a uniformly distributed load over the entire span). However, when the moment diagram has discontinuities (i.e., due to concentrated loads or internal reaction points occurring along the span), additional constants of integration should be evaluated by applying continuity conditions. In those situations, graphical methods (Moment-area method and Conjugate beam method) are considered to be superior for general loading cases.

2.6 Double Integration Method

The governing differential equation of the elastic curve presented in Eq. (2.8) is written as

$$EI\frac{d^2\Delta}{dx^2} = \pm M_x \tag{2.12}$$

Eq. (2.12) can be directly integrated to obtain the solutions as

$$EI\frac{d\Delta}{dx} = \pm\int M_x dx + C_1 \tag{2.13}$$

$$EI\Delta = \pm\int\left[\int M_x dx + C_1\right]dx + C_2 = \int\left[\int M_x dx\right]dx + C_1 x + C_2 \tag{2.14}$$

where C_1 and C_2 are the constants of integration. These constants can be determined using boundary conditions, which are specific values of slope and deflection known at particular locations along the span. Table 2.2 presents the boundary conditions for common types of supports.

Table 2.2 Boundary conditions

Support	Slope	Deflection
Fixed support	$\theta = 0$	$\Delta = 0$
Hinged support	$\theta \neq 0$	$\Delta = 0$
Roller support	$\theta \neq 0$	$\Delta = 0$
Intermediate	$\theta \neq 0$	$\Delta = 0$
Free end	$\theta \neq 0$	$\Delta \neq 0$

For example, at the location of the fixed support in a beam, both $\theta = 0$ and $\Delta = 0$ can be considered as two boundary conditions to solve for two constants of integration. In case of hinged or roller supports, the non-zero boundary condition cannot be applied, hence $\Delta = 0$ can only be applied. However, while solving simply-supported beam examples, $\Delta = 0$ at two support locations offer two boundary conditions required for solving two constants of integration. After replacing the values of the constants, Eq. (2.13) and Eq. (2.14) render the explicit expressions for determining the values of slope and deflection respectively at any location along the span.

It is important to decide the sign (positive or negative) on the right side of Eq. (2.12). Consider a beam subjected to sagging moments as shown in Figure 2.3. The value of rotation $(d\Delta/dx)$ diminishes along the length as x increases. This means, a sagging moment results in negative curvature. Therefore, the governing differential equation is written as

$$\boxed{EI\frac{d^2\Delta}{dx^2} = -M} \tag{2.15}$$

where M is the *sagging* bending moment.

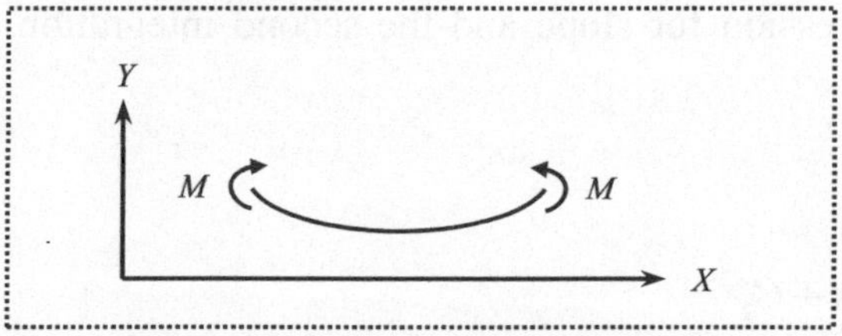

Figure 2.3 Sagging bending moment

2.6.1 Numerical Examples

Example 2.1: A cantilever beam of span L is subjected to a concentrated load W at the free-end. Using the double integration method, determine the slope and the deflection at the free-end. Also find the slope and deflection at the mid-span.

Solution:

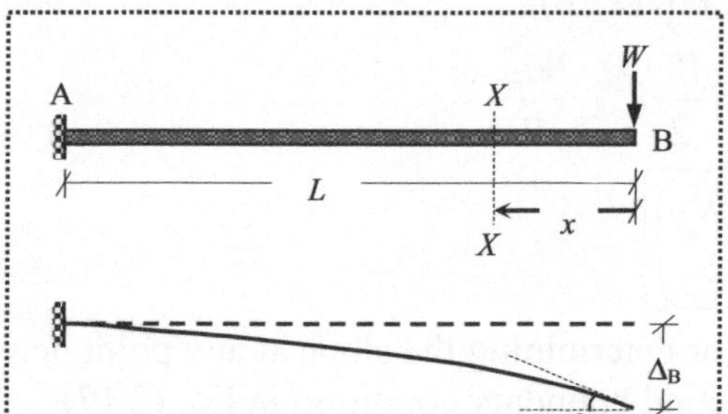

Figure 2.4 Cantilever beam with a concentrated load at free-end (Example 2.1)

The cantilever beam with loading and the deflected shape are shown in Figure 2.4. Slope at B (i.e., θ_B) is the angular deviation of point B with respect to the horizontal axis, and deflection at B (i.e., Δ_B) is the displacement of point in lateral direction as shown in Figure 2.4. The governing differential equation of the elastic curve as given in Eq. (2.15) is

$$EI\frac{d^2\Delta}{dx^2} = -M$$

Take moment of all forces to the right of section *XX* by keeping the free end B as origin,

$$M = -W \times x$$

Since the bending of the beam due to the load is hogging in nature, it is considered negative, and this moment variation is a single continuous function for the entire span (i.e., for $0 \le x \le L$). Substituting the moment expression in the governing equation,

$$EI\frac{d^2\Delta}{dx^2} = -(-Wx) = Wx$$

As already discussed, the above equation is a second-order differential equation, and the first integration yields the expression for slope and the second integration yields the expression for deflection as

$$EI\frac{d\Delta}{dx} = W \times \frac{x^2}{2} + C_1 \tag{2.16}$$

$$EI\ \Delta = W \times \frac{x^3}{6} + C_1 \times x + C_2 \tag{2.17}$$

where C_1 and C_2 are the constants of integration, which need to be evaluated using the boundary conditions (BC) as follows.

BC (i): At the fixed end, the value of slope is zero, $x = L \rightarrow \frac{d\Delta}{dx} = 0$

BC (ii): At the fixed end, the value of deflection is zero, $x = L \rightarrow \Delta = 0$

Substituting the first boundary condition in Eq. (2.16),

$$EI(0) = W \times \frac{(L)^2}{2} + C_1 \Rightarrow C_1 = \frac{-WL^2}{2}$$

Substitute the value of C_1 in Eq. (2.16),

$$EI\frac{d\Delta}{dx} = W \times \frac{x^2}{2} - \frac{WL^2}{2} = \frac{W}{2}x^2 - \frac{WL^2}{2}$$

$$\boxed{\frac{d\Delta}{dx} = \frac{1}{EI}\left(\frac{W}{2}x^2 - \frac{WL^2}{2}\right)} \tag{2.18}$$

Eq. (2.18) is the expression for determining the slope at any point between $x = 0$ and $x = L$. Similarly, substituting the second boundary condition in Eq. (2.17),

$$EI(0) = W \times \frac{L^3}{6} + C_1 \times L + C_2$$

The value of C_1 is already obtained. Therefore, by substituting C_1,

$$0=\frac{WL^3}{6}-\frac{WL^2}{2}\times L+C_2 \Rightarrow C_2=\frac{WL^3}{3}$$

Now, substitute the values of C_1 and C_2 in Eq. (2.17),

$$EI\,\Delta=\frac{W}{6}x^3-\frac{WL^2}{2}x+\frac{WL^3}{3}$$

$$\boxed{\Delta=\frac{1}{EI}\left(\frac{W}{6}x^3-\frac{WL^2}{2}x+\frac{WL^3}{3}\right)} \qquad (2.19)$$

Eq. (2.19) is the expression for determining the deflection at any point between $x=0$ and $x=L$.

(i) For determining the value of slope at the free-end (i.e., at B), substitute $x=0$ in Eq. (2.18).

$$\frac{d\Delta}{dx}=\frac{1}{EI}\left(\frac{W}{2}\times(0)^2-\frac{WL^2}{2}\right)=\frac{-WL^2}{2EI}$$

$$\boxed{\theta_B=\frac{-WL^2}{2EI}}$$

(ii) For determining the value of deflection at the free-end (i.e., at B), substitute $x=0$ in Eq. (2.19).

$$\Delta=\frac{1}{EI}\left(\frac{W}{6}\times(0)^3-\frac{WL^2}{2}\times(0)+\frac{WL^3}{3}\right)=\frac{WL^3}{3EI}$$

$$\boxed{\Delta_B=\frac{WL^3}{3EI}}$$

(iii) Similarly, for determining the value of slope at the mid-span (i.e., at C), substitute $x=L/2$ in Eq. (2.18).

$$\frac{d\Delta}{dx}=\frac{1}{EI}\left(\frac{W}{2}\times(L/2)^2-\frac{WL^2}{2}\right)=\frac{-3}{8}\frac{WL^2}{EI}$$

$$\boxed{\theta_C=\frac{-3}{8}\frac{WL^2}{EI}}$$

(iv) Similarly, for determining the value of deflection at the mid-span (i.e., at C), substitute $x=L/2$ in Eq. (2.19).

$$\Delta=\frac{1}{EI}\left(\frac{W}{6}\times(L/2)^3-\frac{WL^2}{2}\times(L/2)+\frac{WL^3}{3}\right)=\frac{5}{48}\frac{WL^3}{EI}$$

$$\boxed{\Delta_C=\frac{5}{48}\frac{WL^3}{EI}}$$

The values of slope and deflection are indicated in Figure 2.5.

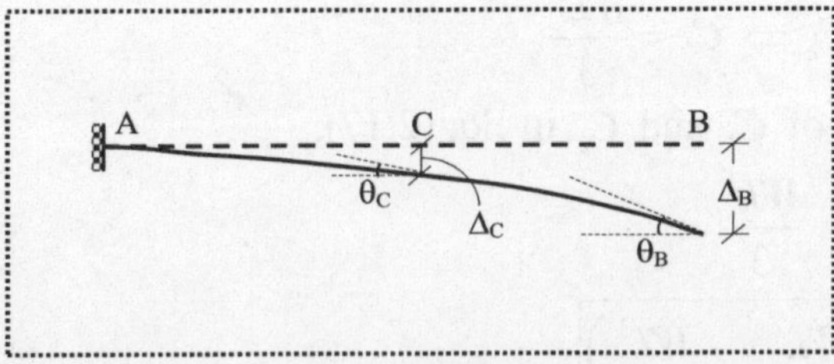

Figure 2.5 Representation of slopes and deflections (Example 2.1)

In general, in cantilever beams under normal loading conditions, both the maximum slope and deflection occur at the free end only. Therefore,

$$\boxed{\theta_{max} = \theta_B = \frac{WL^2}{2EI}}$$

$$\boxed{\Delta_{max} = \Delta_B = \frac{WL^3}{3EI}}$$

Example 2.2: A cantilever beam of span L is subjected to a uniformly distributed load over the entire length. Using the double integration method, determine the slope and deflection at the free-end. Also determine the slope and deflection at the mid-span.

Solution:

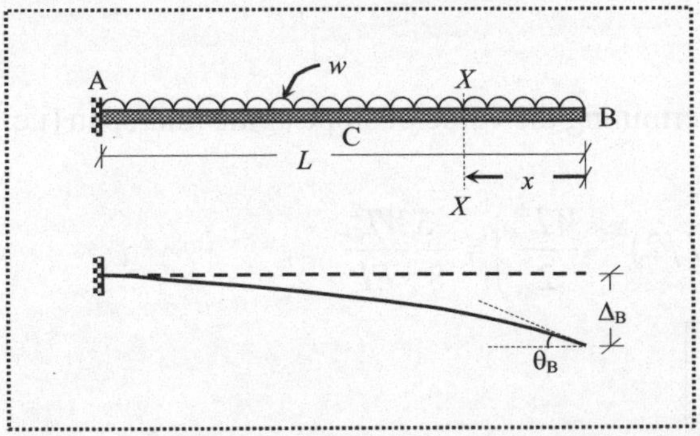

Figure 2.6 Cantilever beam with uniformly distributed load (Example 2.2)

The loading and the deflected shape are shown in Figure 2.6. The governing differential equation of the elastic curve as given in Eq. (2.15) is

$$EI\frac{d^2\Delta}{dx^2} = -M$$

Take moment of all forces to the right of section XX by keeping the free end B as origin,

$$M = -w \times x \times \frac{x}{2} = -\frac{w}{2}x^2$$

The bending moment is considered negative due to hogging nature, and the variation of moment is a single continuous function for the entire span (i.e., for $0 \le x \le L$). Substituting the moment expression in the governing equation,

$$EI\frac{d^2\Delta}{dx^2} = -\left(-\frac{w}{2}x^2\right) = \frac{w}{2}x^2$$

The first and second integrations yield the expressions for slope and deflection respectively as

$$EI\frac{d\Delta}{dx} = \frac{w}{2}\times\frac{x^3}{3} + C_1 \tag{2.20}$$

$$EI\ \Delta = \frac{w}{2}\times\frac{x^4}{12} + C_1 \times x + C_2 \tag{2.21}$$

where C_1 and C_2 are the constants of integration, which need to be evaluated using the boundary conditions as follows.

BC (i): At the fixed end, the value of slope is zero, $x = L \rightarrow \dfrac{d\Delta}{dx} = 0$

BC (ii): At the fixed end, the value of deflection is zero, $x = L \rightarrow \Delta = 0$

Substituting the first boundary condition in Eq. (2.20)

$$EI(0) = \frac{w}{6}\times(L)^3 + C_1 \Rightarrow C_1 = \frac{-wL^3}{6}$$

Substitute the value of C_1 in Eq. (2.20)

$$EI\frac{d\Delta}{dx} = \frac{w}{6}x^3 - \frac{wL^3}{6}$$

$$\boxed{\frac{d\Delta}{dx} = \frac{1}{EI}\left(\frac{w}{6}x^3 - \frac{wL^3}{6}\right)} \tag{2.22}$$

Eq. (2.22) is the complete expression for determining the slope at any point between $x = 0$ and $x = L$.

Similarly, substituting the second boundary condition in Eq. (2.21),

$$EI(0) = \frac{w}{24}\times(L)^4 + C_1\times(L) + C_2$$

The value of C_1 is already obtained. Therefore, substituting C_1,

$$0 = \frac{wL^4}{24} - \frac{wL^3}{6}\times L + C_2 \Rightarrow C_2 = \frac{wL^4}{8}$$

Now, substitute the values of C_1 and C_2 in Eq. (2.21)

$$EI\ \Delta = \frac{w}{24}x^4 - \frac{wL^3}{6}x + \frac{wL^4}{8}$$

$$\boxed{\Delta = \frac{1}{EI}\left(\frac{w}{24}x^4 - \frac{wL^3}{6}x + \frac{wL^4}{8}\right)} \tag{2.23}$$

Eq. (2.23) is the expression for determining the deflection at any point between $x = 0$ and $x = L$.

(i) For determining the value of slope at the free-end (i.e., at B), substitute $x = 0$ in Eq. (2.22).

$$\frac{d\Delta}{dx} = \frac{1}{EI}\left[\frac{w}{6} \times (0)^3 - \frac{wL^3}{6}\right] = \frac{-wL^3}{6EI}$$

$$\boxed{\theta_B = \frac{-wL^3}{6EI}}$$

(ii) For determining the value of deflection at the free-end (i.e., at B), substitute $x = 0$ in Eq. (2.23).

$$\Delta = \frac{1}{EI}\left[\frac{w}{24} \times (0)^4 - \frac{wL^3}{6} \times (0) + \frac{wL^4}{8}\right] = \frac{wL^4}{8EI}$$

$$\boxed{\Delta_B = \frac{wL^4}{8EI}}$$

(iii) Similarly, for determining the value of slope at the mid-span (i.e., at C), substitute $x = L/2$ in Eq. (2.22).

$$\frac{d\Delta}{dx} = \frac{1}{EI}\left[\frac{w}{6} \times (L/2)^3 - \frac{wL^3}{6}\right] = \frac{-7}{48}\frac{wL^3}{EI}$$

$$\boxed{\theta_C = \frac{-7}{48}\frac{wL^3}{EI}}$$

(iv) Similarly, for determining the value of deflection at the mid-span (i.e., at C), substitute $x = L/2$ in Eq. (2.23).

$$\Delta = \frac{1}{EI}\left[\frac{w}{24} \times (L/2)^4 - \frac{wL^3}{6} \times (L/2) + \frac{wL^4}{8}\right] = \frac{17}{384}\frac{wL^4}{EI}$$

$$\boxed{\Delta_C = \frac{17}{384}\frac{wL^4}{EI}}$$

For this loading case also, both the maximum slope and deflection occur at the free end only. Therefore,

$$\boxed{\theta_{max} = \theta_B = \frac{wL^3}{6EI}}$$

and $$\boxed{\Delta_{max} = \Delta_B = \frac{wL^4}{8EI}}$$

Example 2.3: A cantilever beam of span L is subjected to a uniformly varying load of w at the fixed end and zero at the free end. Using the double integration method, determine the slope and deflection at the free-end.

Solution:

The uniformly varying load considered is a triangle load with the intensity varying from w (per unit length) at the fixed end A and zero at the free end B as shown in Figure 2.7.

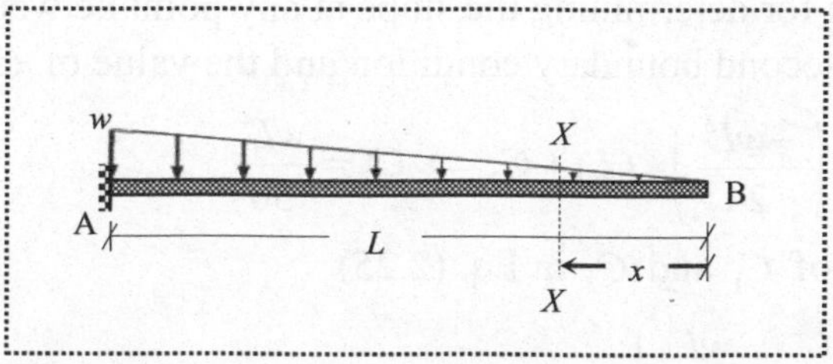

Figure 2.7 Cantilever beam with uniformly varying load (Example 2.3)

The governing differential equation of the elastic curve as given in Eq. (2.15) is

$$EI\frac{d^2\Delta}{dx^2} = -M$$

Take moment of all forces to the right of section *XX* by keeping the free end B as origin,

$$M = -\left(\frac{1}{2}\times x\times\frac{wx}{L}\right)\left(\frac{1}{3}\times x\right) = -\frac{w}{6L}x^3$$

The bending moment is considered negative due to hogging nature, and the variation of moment is a single continuous function for the entire span (i.e., for $0\le x\le L$). Substituting the moment expression in the governing equation,

$$EI\frac{d^2\Delta}{dx^2} = -\left(-\frac{w}{6L}x^3\right) = \frac{w}{6L}x^3$$

The first and second integrations yield the expressions for slope and deflection respectively as

$$EI\frac{d\Delta}{dx} = \frac{w}{6L}\times\frac{x^4}{4} + C_1 \tag{2.24}$$

$$EI\,\Delta = \frac{w}{6L}\times\frac{x^5}{20} + C_1\times x + C_2 \tag{2.25}$$

where C_1 and C_2 are the constants of integration, which need to be evaluated using the boundary conditions as follows.

BC (i): At the fixed end, the value of slope is zero, $x = L \rightarrow \frac{d\Delta}{dx} = 0$

BC (ii): At the fixed end, the value of deflection is zero, $x = L \rightarrow \Delta = 0$

Substituting the first boundary condition in Eq. (2.24)

$$EI(0) = \frac{w}{24L}\times(L)^4 + C_1 \Rightarrow C_1 = \frac{-wL^3}{24}$$

Substitute the value of C_1 in Eq. (2.24)

$$EI\frac{d\Delta}{dx}=\left(\frac{w}{24L}x^4-\frac{wL^3}{24}\right)$$

$$\boxed{\frac{d\Delta}{dx}=\frac{1}{EI}\left(\frac{w}{24L}x^4-\frac{wL^3}{24}\right)} \qquad (2.26)$$

Eq. (2.26) is the expression for determining the slope at any point between $x=0$ and $x=L$. Similarly, substituting the second boundary condition and the value of C_1 in Eq. (2.25),

$$EI(0)=\frac{w}{120L}\times(L)^5+\left(\frac{-wL^3}{24}\right)\times(L)+C_2 \Rightarrow C_2=\frac{wL^4}{30}$$

Now, substitute the values of C_1 and C_2 in Eq. (2.25)

$$EI\,\Delta=\left(\frac{w}{120L}x^5-\frac{wL^3}{24}x+\frac{wL^4}{30}\right)$$

$$\boxed{\Delta=\frac{1}{EI}\left(\frac{w}{120L}x^5-\frac{wL^3}{24}x+\frac{wL^4}{30}\right)} \qquad (2.27)$$

Eq. (2.27) is the expression for determining the deflection at any point between $x=0$ and $x=L$.

(i) The value of slope at the free-end (i.e., at B) can be obtained by substituting $x=0$ in Eq. (2.26).

$$\frac{d\Delta}{dx}=\frac{1}{EI}\left[\frac{w}{24L}\times(0)^4-\frac{wL^3}{24}\right]=\frac{-wL^3}{24EI}$$

$$\boxed{\theta_B=\frac{-wL^3}{24EI}}$$

(ii) The value of deflection at the free-end (i.e., at B) can be obtained by substituting $x=0$ in Eq. (2.27).

$$\Delta=\frac{1}{EI}\left[\frac{w}{120L}\times(0)^5-\frac{wL^3}{24}\times(0)+\frac{wL^4}{30}\right]=\frac{wL^4}{30EI}$$

$$\boxed{\Delta_B=\frac{wL^4}{30EI}}$$

For this loading case also, both the maximum slope and deflection occur at the free end only. Therefore,

$$\boxed{\theta_{max}=\theta_B=\frac{wL^3}{24EI}} \text{ and } \boxed{\Delta_{max}=\Delta_B=\frac{wL^4}{30EI}}$$

Example 2.4: A cantilever beam of span L is subjected to a clockwise moment M_1 at the free end. Using the double integration method, determine the slope and deflection at the free-end.

Solution:

The applied load is the concentrated moment at the free end as shown in Figure 2.8. The governing differential equation of the elastic curve as given in Eq. (2.15) is

$$EI\frac{d^2\Delta}{dx^2}=-M$$

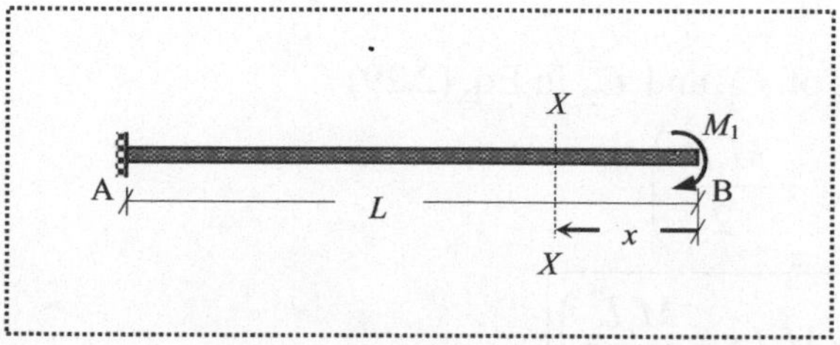

Figure 2.8 Cantilever beam with a moment at the free end (Example 2.4)

Take moment of all forces to the right of section *XX* by keeping the free end B as origin,

$$M=-M_1$$

The bending moment is considered negative due to hogging nature, and the variation of moment is a single continuous function for the entire span (i.e., for $0\le x\le L$). Substituting the moment expression in the governing equation,

$$EI\frac{d^2\Delta}{dx^2}=-(-M_1)=M_1$$

The first and second integrations yield the expressions for slope and deflection respectively as

$$EI\frac{d\Delta}{dx}=M_1\times x+C_1 \tag{2.28}$$

$$EI\ \Delta=M_1\times\frac{x^2}{2}+C_1\times x+C_2 \tag{2.29}$$

where C_1 and C_2 are the constants of integration, which need to be evaluated using the boundary conditions as follows.

BC (i): At the fixed end, the value of slope is zero, $x=L\ \rightarrow\ \frac{d\Delta}{dx}=0$

BC (ii): At the fixed end, the value of deflection is zero, $x=L\ \rightarrow\ \Delta=0$

Substituting the first boundary condition in Eq. (2.28)

$$EI(0)=M_1\times(L)+C_1\Rightarrow C_1=-M_1L$$

Substitute the value of C_1 in Eq. (2.28)

$$EI\frac{d\Delta}{dx}=(M_1\times x-M_1L)$$

$$\frac{d\Delta}{dx} = \frac{1}{EI}(M_1 x - M_1 L) \tag{2.30}$$

Eq. (2.30) is the expression for determining the slope at any point between $x = 0$ and $x = L$. Similarly, substituting the second boundary condition and the value of C_1 in Eq. (2.29),

$$EI(0) = M_1 \times \frac{(L)^2}{2} - M_1 L \times (L) + C_2$$

$$\Rightarrow C_2 = \frac{M_1 L^2}{2}$$

Now, substitute the values of C_1 and C_2 in Eq. (2.29)

$$EI\ \Delta = \left(\frac{M_1}{2} x^2 - M_1 L x + \frac{M_1 L^2}{2} \right)$$

$$\Delta = \frac{1}{EI}\left(\frac{M_1}{2} x^2 - M_1 L x + \frac{M_1 L^2}{2} \right) \tag{2.31}$$

Eq. (2.31) is the expression for determining the deflection at any point between $x = 0$ and $x = L$.

(i) The value of slope at the free-end (i.e., at B) can be obtained by substituting $x = 0$ in Eq. (2.30).

$$\frac{d\Delta}{dx} = \frac{1}{EI}[M_1 \times (0) - M_1 L] = \frac{-M_1 L}{EI}$$

$$\theta_B = \frac{-M_1 L}{EI}$$

(ii) The value of deflection at the free-end (i.e., at B) can be obtained by substituting $x = 0$ in Eq. (2.27).

$$\Delta = \frac{1}{EI}\left[\frac{M_1}{2} \times (0)^2 - M_1 L \times (0) + \frac{M_1 L^2}{2} \right] = \frac{M_1 L^2}{2EI}$$

$$\Delta_B = \frac{M_1 L^2}{2EI}$$

For this loading case also, both the maximum slope and deflection occur at the free end only. Therefore,

$$\theta_{max} = \theta_B = \frac{M_1 L}{EI}$$

and $\Delta_{max} = \Delta_B = \dfrac{M_1 L^2}{2EI}$

Example 2.5: A cantilever steel beam of span 6 m is subjected a uniformly distributed load of 20 kN/m over the entire length, a point load of 50 kN at the free end, and an anti-clockwise moment of 75 kNm at the free end. The cross-section of the beam is 200×300 mm, and the modulus of elasticity is 210×10^6 kN/m^2. Determine the slope and deflection at the free-end.

Solution:

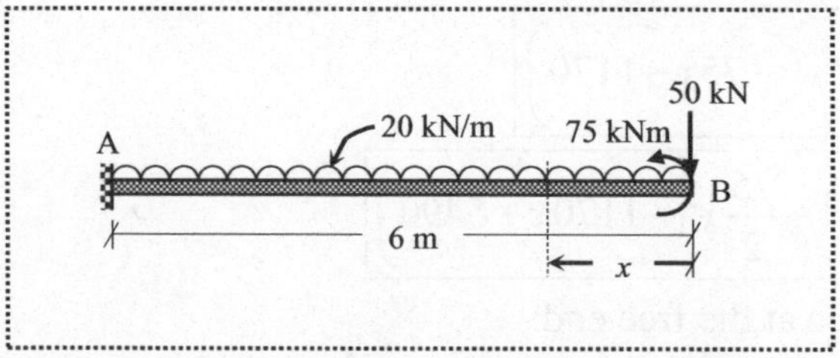

Figure 2.9 Cantilever beam with multiple loads (Example 2.5)

The loading on the beam is as shown in Figure 2.9. The governing differential equation of the elastic curve as given in Eq. (2.15) is

$$EI\frac{d^2\Delta}{dx^2}=-M$$

Take moment of all forces to the right of section *XX* by keeping the free end B as origin,

$$M=-50\times x-20\times x\times\frac{x}{2}+75=\left(-50x-10x^2+75\right)$$

in which $(-50x)$ is the hogging moment due to the point load, $(-10x^2)$ is the hogging moment due to the uniformly distributed load over a span of "x", and (75) is the sagging moment. The variation of moment is a single continuous function for the entire span (i.e., for $0\le x\le 6$). Substituting the moment expression in the governing equation,

$$EI\frac{d^2\Delta}{dx^2}=-\left(-50x-10x^2+75\right)=\left(50x+10x^2-75\right)$$

The first and second integrations yield the expressions for slope and deflection respectively as

$$EI\frac{d\Delta}{dx}=50\times\frac{x^2}{2}+10\times\frac{x^3}{3}-75\times x+C_1 \qquad (2.32)$$

$$EI\ \Delta=+50\times\frac{x^3}{6}+10\times\frac{x^4}{12}-75\times\frac{x^2}{2}+C_1\times x+C_2 \qquad (2.33)$$

where C_1 and C_2 are the constants of integration, which need to be evaluated using the boundary conditions as follows.

BC (i): At the fixed end, the value of slope is zero, $x=6\ \rightarrow\ d\Delta/dx=0$

BC (ii): At the fixed end, the value of deflection is zero, $x=6\ \rightarrow\ \Delta=0$

Substituting the first boundary condition in Eq. (2.32),

$$EI\left(0\right)=+50\times\frac{(6)^2}{2}+10\times\frac{(6)^3}{3}-75\times(6)+C_1\Rightarrow C_1=-1170$$

Similarly, substituting the second boundary condition and the value of C_1 in Eq. (2.33),

$$EI(0) = +50\times\frac{(6)^3}{6} + 10\times\frac{(6)^4}{12} - 75\times\frac{(6)^2}{2} - 1170\times(6) + C_2 \Rightarrow C_2 = 5490$$

Therefore, the expressions respectively for finding the slope and deflections at any point between $x = 0$ and 6 are,

$$\boxed{\frac{d\Delta}{dx} = \frac{1}{EI}\left(\frac{10}{3}x^3 + 25x^2 - 75x - 1170\right)} \tag{2.34}$$

$$\boxed{\Delta = \frac{1}{EI}\left(\frac{5}{6}x^4 + \frac{25}{3}x^3 - \frac{75}{2}x^2 - 1170x + 5490\right)} \tag{2.35}$$

Using Eq. (2.34), the slope at the free end:

$$\theta_B = \left.\frac{d\Delta}{dx}\right|_{x=0} = \frac{1}{EI}\left(\frac{10}{3}\times(0)^3 + 25\times(0)^2 - 75\times(0) - 1170\right) = \frac{-1170}{EI}$$

Substituting the values of $E = 210\times10^6$ kN/m^2 and $I = \dfrac{bd^3}{12} = \dfrac{(0.2)(0.3)^3}{12} = 450\times10^{-6}$ m^4,

$$\theta_B = \frac{-1170}{\left(210\times10^6\right)\left(450\times10^{-6}\right)} = -0.01238 \text{ radians}$$

Similarly, using Eq. (2.35), the deflection at the free end is,

$$\Delta_B = \Delta|_{x=0} = \frac{1}{EI}\left(\frac{5}{6}\times(0)^4 + \frac{25}{3}\times(0)^3 - \frac{75}{2}\times(0)^2 - 1170\times(0) + 5490\right) = \frac{5490}{EI}$$

Substituting the values of E and I,

$$\Delta_B = \frac{5490}{\left(210\times10^6\right)\left(450\times10^{-6}\right)} = 0.05810 \text{ m}$$

The above answers can be directly obtained using the standard formulas that are already derived in Examples 2.1, 2.2 and 2.4. The directions of the point load and uniformly distributed loads in this example are same as in Examples 2.1 and 2.2. However, the direction of the applied moment is opposite to the one in Example 2.4. Therefore, the signs for the respective slope and deflection formulas should be changed accordingly.

$$\theta_B = -\frac{WL^2}{2EI} - \frac{wL^3}{6EI} + \frac{M_1L}{EI}$$

$$\theta_B = -\frac{(50)(6)^2}{2EI} - \frac{(20)(6)^3}{6EI} + \frac{(75)(6)}{EI} = \frac{-1170}{EI} \text{ radians}$$

$$\Delta_B = -\frac{WL^3}{3EI} - \frac{wL^4}{8EI} + \frac{M_1L^2}{2EI}$$

$$\Delta_B = \frac{(50)(6)^3}{3EI} + \frac{(20)(6)^4}{8EI} - \frac{(75)(6)^2}{2EI} = \frac{5490}{EI} \text{ m}$$

Note:

(i) The maximum slope and the maximum defection normally occur at the free end of cantilever for the general loading cases. Therefore, no separate calculation is required for obtaining the maximum quantities.

(ii) Instead of the free end of cantilever, the fixed end can also be taken as origin for taking the moment of all forces to the left of section *XX* by properly including the effects of support reactions (i.e, vertical reaction and moment reaction).

Example 2.6: A simply supported beam of span L and flexural rigidity EI is subjected to a uniformly distributed load over the entire length. Using the double integration method, determine the slope at the support locations and deflection at the mid-span location.

Solution:

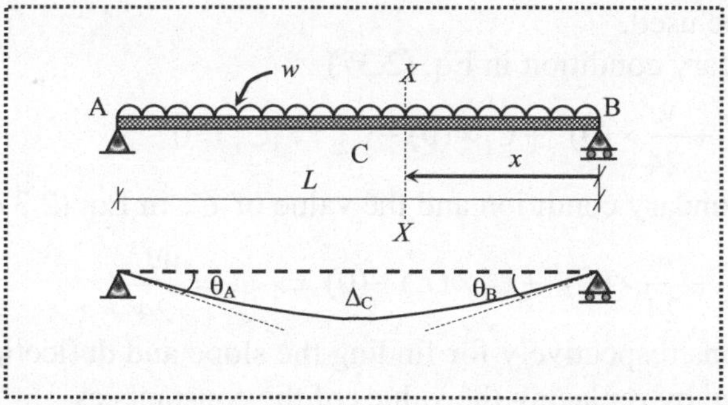

Figure 2.10 Simply supported beam with uniformly distributed load (Example 2.6)

The loading on the beam and the deflected shape are shown in Figure 2.10. The governing differential equation of the elastic curve as given in Eq. (2.15):

$$EI\frac{d^2\Delta}{dx^2} = -M$$

Since the loading on the simply supported beam is symmetrical, both the vertical reactions at A and B will be equal to $\dfrac{wL}{2}$.

$$V_A = V_B = \frac{wL}{2}$$

Take moment of all forces to the right of section *XX* by keeping the support B as origin,

$$M = V_B \times x - w \times x \times \frac{x}{2} = \frac{wL}{2}x - \frac{w}{2}x^2$$

The bending moment is considered positive due to sagging nature, and the variation of moment is a single continuous function for the entire span (i.e., for $0 \le x \le L$). Substituting the moment expression in the governing equation,

$$EI\frac{d^2\Delta}{dx^2}=-\left(\frac{wL}{2}x-w\frac{x^2}{2}\right)=-\frac{wL}{2}x+\frac{w}{2}x^2$$

The first and second integrations yield the expressions for slope and deflection respectively as

$$EI\frac{d\Delta}{dx}=-\frac{wL}{2}\times\frac{x^2}{2}+\frac{w}{2}\times\frac{x^3}{3}+C_1 \tag{2.36}$$

$$EI\,\Delta=-\frac{wL}{2}\times\frac{x^3}{6}+\frac{w}{2}\times\frac{x^4}{12}+C_1\times x+C_2 \tag{2.37}$$

where C_1 and C_2 are the constants of integration, which need to be evaluated using the boundary conditions as follows.

BC (i): At support B, the value of deflection is zero, $x=0 \rightarrow \Delta=0$

BC (ii): At support A, the value of deflection is zero, $x=L \rightarrow \Delta=0$

Unlike in cantilever beams, both the boundary conditions are related to deflection values, hence Eq. (2.37) only should be used.

Applying the first boundary condition in Eq. (2.37)

$$EI(0)=-\frac{wL}{12}\times(0)^3+\frac{w}{24}\times(0)^4+C_1\times(0)+C_2\Rightarrow C_2=0$$

Applying the second boundary condition and the value of C_2 in Eq. (2.37)

$$EI(0)=-\frac{wL}{12}\times(L)^3+\frac{w}{24}\times(L)^4+C_1\times(L)+(0)\Rightarrow C_1=\frac{wL^3}{24}$$

Therefore, the expressions respectively for finding the slope and deflections at any point between $x=0$ and L are obtained by replacing the values of the constants as,

$$\boxed{\frac{d\Delta}{dx}=\frac{1}{EI}\left(\frac{w}{6}x^3-\frac{wL}{4}x^2+\frac{wL^3}{24}\right)} \tag{2.38}$$

$$\boxed{\Delta=\frac{1}{EI}\left(\frac{w}{24}x^4-\frac{wL}{12}x^3+\frac{wL^3}{24}x\right)} \tag{2.39}$$

(i) For obtaining the value of slope at B, substitute $x=0$ in Eq. (2.38).

$$\frac{d\Delta}{dx}=\frac{1}{EI}\left(\frac{w}{6}\times(0)^3-\frac{wL}{4}\times(0)^2+\frac{wL^3}{24}\right)=\frac{wL^3}{24EI}$$

$$\boxed{\theta_B=\frac{wL^3}{24EI}}$$

(ii) For obtaining the value of slope at A, substitute $x=L$ in Eq. (2.38).

$$\frac{d\Delta}{dx}=\frac{1}{EI}\left(\frac{w}{6}\times(L)^3-\frac{wL}{4}\times(L)^2+\frac{wL^3}{24}\right)=\frac{-wL^3}{24EI}$$

$$\boxed{\theta_A=\frac{-wL^3}{24EI}}$$

(iii) For obtaining the value of deflection at C (i.e., mid-span), substitute $x = L/2$ in Eq. (2.39).

$$\Delta = \frac{1}{EI}\left(\frac{w}{24}\times(L/2)^4 - \frac{wL}{12}\times(L/2)^3 + \frac{wL^3}{24}\times(L/2)\right) = \frac{5}{384}\frac{wL^4}{EI}$$

$$\boxed{\Delta_C = \frac{5}{384}\frac{wL^4}{EI}}$$

The maximum slope, $\boxed{\theta_{max} = -\theta_A = \theta_B = \frac{wL^3}{24EI}}$

The maximum deflection, $\boxed{\Delta_{max} = \Delta_C = \frac{5}{384}\frac{wL^4}{EI}}$

Note:

In general, in simply supported beams subjected to symmetrical loads, the maximum slope occurs at the supports (both supports will have same magnitude, but opposite sign), and the maximum deflection occurs at the mid-span. For unsymmetrically loaded beams, the maximum slope occurs at one of the supports and the maximum deflection occurs in between the supports where the direction of the slope changes (i.e., slope is zero).

Example 2.7 A simply supported beam of span L and flexural rigidity EI is subjected to a uniformly varying load over the entire length. Using the double integration method, determine the slope at the support locations and deflection at the mid-span location.

Solution:

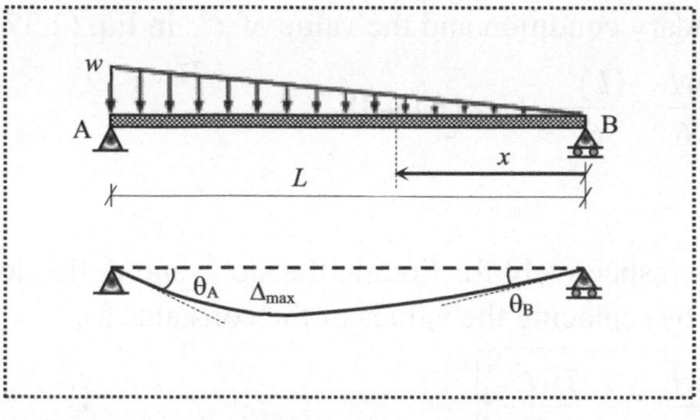

Figure 2.11 Simply supported beam with uniformly varying load (Example 2.7)

The loading on the beam and the deflected shape are shown in Figure 2.11. The governing differential equation of the elastic curve as given in Eq. (2.15) is

$$EI\frac{d^2\Delta}{dx^2} = -M$$

Since the loading on the simply supported beam is unsymmetrical, by applying vertical force equilibrium and moment equilibrium conditions, the vertical reactions at A and B are obtained.

$$V_A = \frac{wL}{3} \text{ and } V_B = \frac{wL}{6}$$

Take moment of all forces to the right of section *XX* by keeping the support B as origin,

$$M = V_B \times x - \left(\frac{1}{2} \times x \times \frac{wx}{L}\right)\left(\frac{1}{3} \times x\right) = \frac{wL}{6}x - \frac{w}{6L}x^3$$

The variation of moment is a single continuous function for the entire span (i.e., for $0 \le x \le L$). Substituting the moment expression in the governing equation,

$$EI\frac{d^2\Delta}{dx^2} = -\left(\frac{wL}{6}x - \frac{w}{6L}x^3\right) = \frac{w}{6L}x^3 - \frac{wL}{6}x$$

The first and second integrations yield the expressions for slope and deflection respectively as

$$EI\frac{d\Delta}{dx} = \frac{w}{6L} \times \frac{x^4}{4} - \frac{wL}{6} \times \frac{x^2}{2} + C_1 \tag{2.40}$$

$$EI\,\Delta = \frac{w}{6L} \times \frac{x^5}{20} - \frac{wL}{6} \times \frac{x^3}{6} + C_1 \times x + C_2 \tag{2.41}$$

where C_1 and C_2 are the constants of integration, which need to be evaluated using the boundary conditions as follows.

BC (i): At support B, the value of deflection is zero, $x = 0 \rightarrow \Delta = 0$

BC (ii): At support A, the value of deflection is zero, $x = L \rightarrow \Delta = 0$

Applying the first boundary condition in Eq. (2.37)

$$EI(0) = \frac{w}{6L} \times \frac{(0)^5}{20} - \frac{wL}{6} \times \frac{(0)^3}{6} + C_1 \times (0) + C_2$$

$$\Rightarrow C_2 = 0$$

Applying the second boundary condition and the value of C_2 in Eq. (2.37)

$$EI(0) = \frac{w}{6L} \times \frac{(L)^5}{20} - \frac{wL}{6} \times \frac{(L)^3}{6} + C_1 \times (L) + (0)$$

$$\Rightarrow C_1 = \frac{7wL^3}{360}$$

Therefore, the expressions respectively for finding the slope and deflections at any point between $x = 0$ and L are obtained by replacing the values of the constants as,

$$\boxed{\frac{d\Delta}{dx} = \frac{1}{EI}\left(\frac{w}{24L}x^4 - \frac{wL}{12}x^2 + \frac{7wL^3}{360}\right)} \tag{2.42}$$

$$\boxed{\Delta = \frac{1}{EI}\left(\frac{w}{120L}x^5 - \frac{wL}{36}x^3 + \frac{7wL^3}{360}x\right)} \tag{2.43}$$

(i) For obtaining the value of slope at B, substitute $x = 0$ in Eq. (2.42).

$$\frac{d\Delta}{dx} = \frac{1}{EI}\left(\frac{w}{24L} \times (0)^4 - \frac{wL}{12} \times (0)^2 + \frac{7wL^3}{360}\right) = \frac{7}{360}\frac{wL^3}{EI}$$

$$\boxed{\theta_B = \frac{7}{360}\frac{wL^3}{EI}}$$

(ii) For obtaining the value of slope at A, substitute $x = L$ in Eq. (2.42).

$$\frac{d\Delta}{dx} = \frac{1}{EI}\left(\frac{w}{24L} \times (L)^4 - \frac{wL}{12} \times (L)^2 + \frac{7wL^3}{360}\right) = \frac{-wL^3}{45EI}$$

$$\boxed{\theta_A = \frac{-wL^3}{45EI}}$$

(iii) For obtaining the value of deflection at the mid-span, substitute $x = L/2$ in Eq. (2.43).

$$\Delta_{\text{mid-span}} = \frac{1}{EI}\left(\frac{w}{120L} \times (L/2)^5 - \frac{wL}{36} \times (L/2)^3 + \frac{7wL^3}{360} \times (L/2)\right) = \frac{5}{768}\frac{wL^4}{EI}$$

$$\boxed{\Delta_{\text{mid-span}} = \frac{5}{768}\frac{wL^4}{EI}} = 0.00651\frac{wL^4}{EI}$$

Since the loading on the beam is not symmetrical, the maximum deflection does not occur at the mid-span. The location of the maximum deflection can be obtained by equating the slope equation to zero.

$$\frac{d\Delta}{dx} = \frac{1}{EI}\left(\frac{w}{24L}x^4 - \frac{wL}{12}x^2 + \frac{7wL^3}{360}\right) = 0$$

$$15x^4 - 30L^2x^2 + 7L^4 = 0$$

The solution of the above polynomial equation results in the following roots.

$$x = (+1.315L, +0.519L, -0.519L, -1.315L)$$

in which $+0.519L$ is only the admissible root. Therefore, the maximum deflection occurs at $x = 0.519L$ from the support B.

The maximum deflection is

$$\Delta_{\max} = \Delta|_{x=0.519L} = \frac{1}{EI}\left(\frac{w}{120L}\cdot(0.519L)^5 - \frac{wL}{36}\cdot(0.519L)^3 + \frac{7wL^3}{360}\cdot(0.519L)\right)$$

$$= 0.006522\frac{wL^4}{EI}$$

Example 2.8: A simply supported beam of span L and flexural rigidity EI is subjected to an anti-clockwise moment M_1 at support B. Using the double integration method, determine the slope at the support locations and deflection at the mid-span location.

Solution:

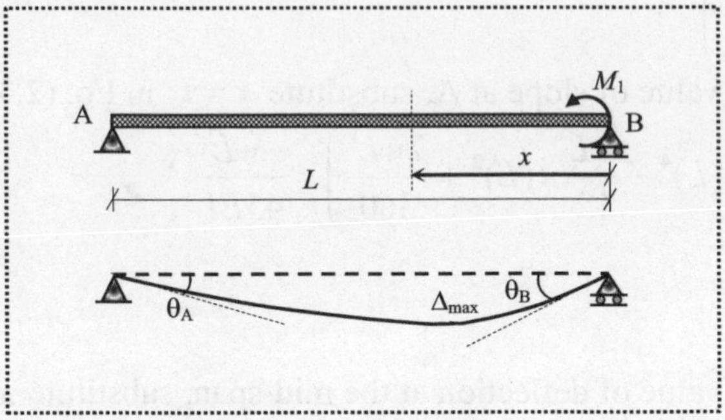

Figure 2.12 Simply supported beam with a moment at one support (Example 2.8)

The loading on the beam and the deflected shape are shown in Figure 2.12. The governing differential equation of the elastic curve as given in Eq. (2.15) is

$$EI\frac{d^2\Delta}{dx^2} = -M$$

The beam is not subjected to any lateral loading. However, the concentrated moment (anti-clockwise) applied at B causes bending of the beam which is sagging in nature. The equilibrium equations are applied to determine the reactions at A and B (i.e., V_A and V_B are assumed to be acting in upward direction).

$$\sum F_y = 0 \Rightarrow V_A + V_B = 0 \text{ (i.e., sum of all forces in vertical direction is equal to zero)}$$

$$\sum M = 0 \Rightarrow V_A \times L - M_1 = 0 \text{ (i.e., sum of all moments about B is equal to zero)}$$

$$V_A = \frac{+M_1}{L} \text{ (+ indicates that the assumed upward direction is correct)}$$

$$V_B = \frac{-M_1}{L} \text{ (– indicates that the assumed upward direction is not correct; hence it is downwards)}$$

Take moment of all forces to the right of section XX by keeping the support B as origin,

$$M = -V_B \times x + M_1 = \frac{-M_1}{L}x + M_1$$

in which, $(-M_1x/L)$ is hogging due to the reaction, and (M_1) is sagging due to the applied moment. The variation of moment is a single continuous function for the entire span (i.e., for $0 \le x \le L$). Substituting the moment expression in the governing equation,

$$EI\frac{d^2\Delta}{dx^2} = -\left(\frac{-M_1}{L}x + M_1\right) = \frac{M_1}{L}x - M_1$$

The first and second integrations yield the expressions for slope and deflection respectively as

$$EI\frac{d\Delta}{dx}=\frac{M_1}{L}\times\frac{x^2}{2}-M_1\times x+C_1 \tag{2.44}$$

$$EI\,\Delta=\frac{M_1}{L}\times\frac{x^3}{6}-M_1\times\frac{x^2}{2}+C_1\times x+C_2 \tag{2.45}$$

where C_1 and C_2 are the constants of integration, which need to be evaluated using the boundary conditions as follows.

BC (i): At support B, the value of deflection is zero, $x=0 \rightarrow \Delta=0$

BC (ii): At support A, the value of deflection is zero, $x=L \rightarrow \Delta=0$

Applying the first boundary condition in Eq. (2.45)

$$EI(0)=\frac{M_1}{6L}\times(0)^3-\frac{M_1}{2}\times(0)^2+C_1\times(0)+C_2$$

$$\Rightarrow C_2=0$$

Applying the second boundary condition and the value of C_2 in Eq. (2.45)

$$EI(0)=\frac{M_1}{6L}\times(L)^3-\frac{M_1}{2}\times(L)^2+C_1\times(L)+(0)$$

$$\Rightarrow C_1=\frac{M_1L}{3}$$

Therefore, the expressions respectively for finding the slope and deflections at any point between $x=0$ and L are obtained by replacing the values of the constants as,

$$\boxed{\frac{d\Delta}{dx}=\frac{1}{EI}\left(\frac{M_1}{2L}x^2-M_1x+\frac{M_1L}{3}\right)} \tag{2.46}$$

$$\boxed{\Delta=\frac{1}{EI}\left(\frac{M_1}{6L}x^3-\frac{M_1}{2}x^2+\frac{M_1L}{3}x\right)} \tag{2.47}$$

(i) For obtaining the value of slope at B, substitute $x=0$ in Eq. (2.44).

$$\frac{d\Delta}{dx}=\frac{1}{EI}\left(\frac{M_1}{2L}\times(0)^2-M_1\times(0)+\frac{M_1L}{3}\right)=\frac{M_1L}{3EI}$$

$$\boxed{\theta_B=\frac{M_1L}{3EI}}$$

(ii) For obtaining the value of slope at A, substitute $x=L$ in Eq. (2.44).

$$\frac{d\Delta}{dx}=\frac{1}{EI}\left(\frac{M_1}{2L}\times(L)^2-M_1\times(L)+\frac{M_1L}{3}\right)=\frac{-M_1L}{6EI}$$

$$\boxed{\theta_B=\frac{-M_1L}{6EI}}$$

(iii) For obtaining the value of deflection at the mid-span, substitute $x=L/2$ in Eq. (2.45).

$$\Delta_{\text{mid-span}}=\frac{1}{EI}\left(\frac{M_1}{6L}\times(L/2)^3-\frac{M_1}{2}\times(L/2)^2+\frac{M_1L}{3}\times(L/2)\right)=\frac{M_1L^2}{16EI}$$

$$\boxed{\Delta_{\text{mid-span}} = \frac{M_1 L^2}{16EI}} = 0.0625\frac{M_1 L^2}{EI}$$

Since the loading on the beam is not symmetrical, the maximum deflection does not occur at the mid-span. The location of the maximum deflection can be obtained by equating the slope equation to zero.

$$\frac{d\Delta}{dx} = \frac{1}{EI}\left(\frac{M_1}{2L}x^2 - M_1 x + \frac{M_1 L}{3}\right) = 0$$

$$3x^2 - 6Lx + 2L^2 = 0$$

The solution of the above polynomial equation results in the following roots.

$$x = (+1.577L, +0.423L)$$

in which $+0.423L$ is the admissible root. Therefore, the maximum deflection occurs at $x = 0.423L$ from the support B.

The maximum deflection is

$$\Delta_{\max} = \Delta\big|_{x=0.423L} = \frac{1}{EI}\left(\frac{M_1}{6L}\times(0.423L)^3 - \frac{M_1}{2}\times(0.423L)^2 + \frac{M_1 L}{3}\times(0.423L)\right)$$

$$= 0.06415\frac{M_1 L^2}{EI}$$

The double integration method was successfully adopted to solve the problems (Examples 2.1-2.8) due to the fact that, in each example, the moment variation throughout the length was represented by a single continuous function. However, when discontinuities exist, multiple functions are required to represent the moment variation, and consequently each function will result in two constants of integration during the integration process for slope and deflection.

Consider a simply-supported beam of uniform flexural rigidity (EI) and length (L), which carries a concentrated lateral load (W) at a distance "a" from B as shown in Figure 2.13. The reactions at A and B are $V_A = \frac{Wa}{L}$ and $V_B = \frac{W(L-a)}{L}$.

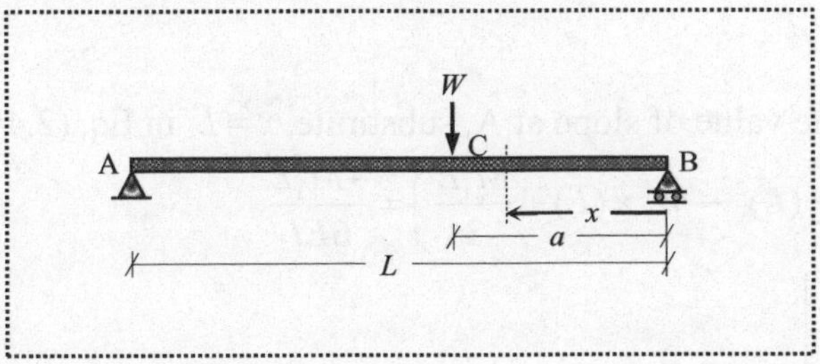

Figure 2.13 Simply supported beam with a point load

Consider a section at a distance "x" from B; the bending moment at the section is

if $x < a$ then $M = V_B \times x = \dfrac{W(L-a)}{L}x$; and

if $x > a$ then $M = V_B \times x - W \times (x-a) = \dfrac{W(L-a)}{L}x - W(x-a)$

$$EI\frac{d^2\Delta}{dx^2} = \begin{cases} -\dfrac{W(L-a)}{L}x & \text{if } x < a \\ -\dfrac{W(L-a)}{L}x + W(x-a) & \text{if } x > a \end{cases} \tag{2.48}$$

The first and second integrations yield the expressions for slope and deflection respectively as

$$\text{if } x < a;\ EI\frac{d\Delta}{dx} = -\frac{W(L-a)}{L} \times \frac{x^2}{2} + C_1 \tag{2.49}$$

$$\text{if } x > a;\ EI\frac{d\Delta}{dx} = -\frac{W(L-a)}{L} \times \frac{x^2}{2} + W\left(\frac{x^2}{2} - a \times x\right) + D_1 \tag{2.50}$$

$$\text{if } x < a;\ EI\Delta = -\frac{W(L-a)}{L} \times \frac{x^3}{6} + C_1 \times x + C_2 \tag{2.51}$$

$$\text{if } x > a;\ EI\Delta = -\frac{W(L-a)}{L} \times \frac{x^3}{6} + W\left(\frac{x^3}{6} - a \times \frac{x^2}{2}\right) + D_1 \times x + D_2 \tag{2.52}$$

in which C_1, C_2, D_1 and D_2 are the arbitrary constants. The boundary conditions ($\Delta = 0$ when $x = 0$; and $\Delta = 0$ when $x = L$) are insufficient to evaluate the constants. Therefore, continuity conditions need to be used further.

For $x = a$, the values of the slopes given by Eq. (2.49) and Eq. (2.50) are equal, and the deflections given by Eq. (2.51) and Eq. (2.52) are equal as there is continuity of the deflected form of the beam through the point C. By applying all the conditions, the constants are evaluated.

$$C_1 = \frac{Wa}{6L}(L-a)(2L-a)$$

$$C_2 = 0$$

$$D_1 = \frac{Wa}{6L}\left(2L^2 + a^2\right)$$

$$D_2 = \frac{-Wa^3}{6}$$

Therefore, the final slope and deflection equations become

$$\text{if } x < a;\ EI\frac{d\Delta}{dx} = -\frac{W(L-a)}{2L}x^2 + \frac{Wa}{6L}\left(2L^2 - 3La + a^2\right) \tag{2.53}$$

$$\text{if } x > a;\ EI\frac{d\Delta}{dx} = -\frac{W(L-a)}{2L}x^2 + \frac{W}{2}\left(x^2 - 2ax\right) + \frac{Wa}{6L}\left(2L^2 + a^2\right) \tag{2.54}$$

Eq. (2.54) can be written as

$$\text{if } x>a;\ EI\frac{d\Delta}{dx}=-\frac{W(L-a)}{2L}x^2+\frac{Wa}{6L}\left(2L^2-3La+a^2\right)+\frac{W}{2}(x-a)^2 \tag{2.55}$$

Eq. (2.53) and Eq. (2.54) differ only by the last term of Eq. (2.55); if the last term of Eq. (2.55) is discarded when $x\le a$, then Eq. (2.55) may be used to determine the slope in all parts of the beam.

Similarly, for deflection,

$$\text{if } x<a;\ EI\Delta=-\frac{W(L-a)}{6L}x^3+\frac{Wa}{6L}\left(2L^2-3aL+a^2\right)x \tag{2.56}$$

$$\text{if } x>a;\ EI\Delta=-\frac{W(L-a)}{6L}x^3+\frac{W}{6}\left(x^3-3ax^2\right)+\frac{Wa}{6L}\left(2L^2+a^2\right)x+\frac{-Wa^3}{6} \tag{2.57}$$

Eq. (2.57) can be written as

$$\text{if } x>a;\ EI\Delta=-\frac{W(L-a)}{6L}x^3+\frac{Wa}{6L}\left(2L^2-3aL+a^2\right)x+\frac{W}{6}(x-a)^3 \tag{2.58}$$

Eq. (2.56) and Eq. (2.57) differ only by the last term of Eq. (2.58); if the last term of Eq. (2.58) is discarded when $x<a$, then Eq. (2.58) may be used to define the deflected form in all parts of the beam. This kind of situations can be easily handled by adopting Macaulay's method as explained in Section 2.7.

2.7 Macaulay's Method

The double integration method gives the equation of the elastic curve for a beam when the moment variation can be expressed by a continuous function throughout the entire length. When discontinuities occur (e.g., cantilever beam subjected to multiple loads, simply supported beam with point loads or distributed loads for a portion of the span), the double integration method is adopted using *Macaulay* terms.

Consider a cantilever beam with general loading as shown in Figure 2.14.

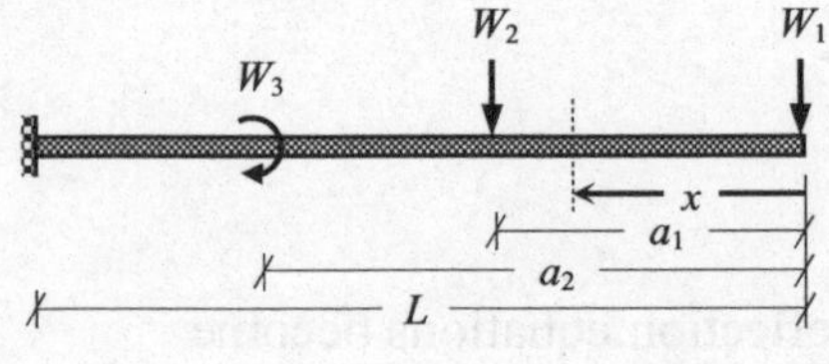

Figure 2.14 Cantilever beam with multiple loads

The governing differential equation of the elastic curve is written as

$$EI\frac{d^2\Delta}{dx^2}=-M$$

By taking the free end as origin, the variation of moment can be expressed in the form

$$M=-W_1\times x-W_2\times[x-a_1]^1-W_3\times[x-a_2]^0 \tag{2.59}$$

where quantities $W_i[x-a_i]$ represent the bending moments due to concentrated loads, and the square brackets $[\cdots]$ are called *Macaulay* brackets which are defined as

$$[x-a_i]=\begin{cases}0 & \text{if } x\le a_i\\ x-a_1 & \text{if } x>a_i\end{cases} \tag{2.60}$$

Typically, when $W_i(x-a_i)$ is integrated, we get

$$\int W_i(x-a_i)=W_i\times\left(\frac{x^2}{2}-a_i\times x\right)+C \tag{2.61}$$

However, when $W_i[x-a_i]$ is integrated, we get

$$\int W_i[x-a_i]=W_i\times\frac{[x-a_i]^2}{2}+C_{\mathrm{M}} \tag{2.62}$$

with the difference between the two expressions being contained in the constant C_{M}. This integration rules make use of the *double integration method* suitable for determining displacements of beams with discontinuous functions. Therefore, the term $W_i[x-a_i]$ should be integrated with respect to $[x-a_i]$ and not x. Also, the term $W_i[x-a_i]$ is applicable only for $x>a_i$ or $[x-a_i]$ is positive. That means, *Macaulay* terms should be integrated with respect to themselves and must be neglected when they are negative.

2.7.1 Numerical Examples

Example 2.9: A simply supported beam of span L is subjected to a mid-span point load W. Using the Macaulay's method, determine the slope at the supports and deflection at the mid-span.

Solution:

The simply supported beam with mid-span point load and the displacement responses are shown in Figure 2.15. By applying the equilibrium conditions, the reactions are obtained.

$$V_{\mathrm{A}}=\frac{W}{2} \text{ and } V_{\mathrm{B}}=\frac{W}{2}.$$

The governing differential equation of the elastic curve is

$$EI\frac{d^2\Delta}{dx^2}=-M$$

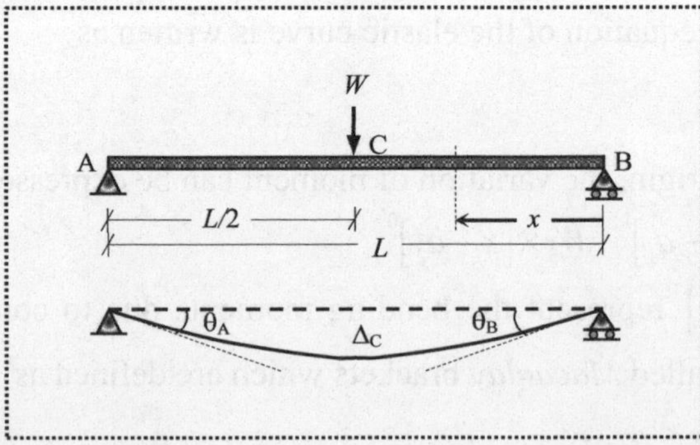

Figure 2.15 Simply supported beam with mid-span point load (Example 2.9)

In this example, the moment variation cannot be expressed by a single equation for the entire length. By taking B as origin, the moment at the section *XX* is expressed as

$$M=\begin{cases}\dfrac{W}{2}\times x & \text{if } 0\le x\le\dfrac{L}{2}\\ \dfrac{W}{2}\times x-W\times\left(x-\dfrac{L}{2}\right) & \text{if } \dfrac{L}{2}\le x\le L\end{cases} \tag{2.63}$$

The first line of Eq. (2.63) is valid, if the value of x lies between 0 and $L/2$ from B, and the second line is valid, if the value of x lies between $L/2$ and L from B. However, the term $\frac{W}{2}x$ is common in both the expressions. Therefore, Eq. (2.63) is written as

$$M=\frac{W}{2}x\ \vdots\ -W\left[x-\frac{L}{2}\right] \tag{2.64}$$

The expression is partitioned by dotted lines. The first segment in Eq. (2.64) is considered when the moment is evaluated between B and C, and both first and second segments together are considered when the moment is evaluated between C and A, by keeping the origin as B.

Substituting M in the governing equation, and use of Macaulay's terms as

$$EI\frac{d^2\Delta}{dx^2}=-\frac{W}{2}x\ \vdots\ +W\left[x-\frac{L}{2}\right] \tag{2.65}$$

The first and second integrations yield the expressions for slope and deflection respectively as

$$EI\frac{d\Delta}{dx}=-\frac{W}{2}\times\frac{x^2}{2}+C_1\ \vdots\ +W\times\frac{\left[x-\frac{L}{2}\right]^2}{2} \tag{2.66}$$

$$EI\ \Delta=-\frac{W}{2}\times\frac{x^3}{6}+C_1\times x+C_2\ \vdots\ +W\times\frac{\left[x-\frac{L}{2}\right]^3}{6} \tag{2.67}$$

From Eq. (2.66) and Eq. (2.67), two important observations can be made.

Firstly, the constants of integration C_1 and C_2 are placed within the first segment only as they are common for the entire expression. If these constants are written at the end, there might be chance of omitting the constants while evaluating the first segment alone whenever needed.

Secondly, bracket terms are integrated with respect to themselves. That means, the term $[x-L/2]$ is integrated as $\dfrac{[x-L/2]^2}{2}$, but not as $\left[\dfrac{x^2}{2}-\dfrac{L}{2}\times x\right]$.

Two boundary conditions are identified as follows.

BC (i): At the roller support B, the value of deflection is zero, $x=0 \rightarrow \Delta=0$

BC (ii): At the hinged support A, the value of deflection is zero, $x=L \rightarrow \Delta=0$

Since both the boundary conditions are corresponding to the deflection at two locations, Eq. (2.67) only can be used. Substituting the first boundary condition (consider the first segment only as $x=0$ lies in $0 \le x \le L/2$),

$$EI\ (0) = -\frac{W}{12}\times(0)^3 + C_1\times(0) + C_2 \Rightarrow C_2 = 0$$

Similarly, substituting the second boundary condition (consider both the first and second segments together), and the value of C_2,

$$EI\ (0) = -\frac{W}{12}\times(L)^3 + C_1\times(L) + 0 \vdots + \frac{W}{6}\times\left[L-\frac{L}{2}\right]^3 \Rightarrow C_1 = \frac{WL^2}{16}$$

Therefore, substituting the values of constants in Eq. (2.66) and Eq. (2.67) respectively gives the complete expressions for slope and deflection.

$$\boxed{\frac{d\Delta}{dx} = \frac{1}{EI}\left(-\frac{W}{4}x^2 + \frac{WL^2}{16} \vdots + \frac{W}{2}\left[x-\frac{L}{2}\right]^2\right)} \quad (2.68)$$

$$\boxed{\Delta = \frac{1}{EI}\left(-\frac{W}{12}x^3 + \frac{WL^2}{16}x \vdots + \frac{W}{6}\left[x-\frac{L}{2}\right]^3\right)} \quad (2.69)$$

(i) For determining the value of slope at B, substitute $x=0$ in Eq. (2.68) (by considering the first segment only).

$$\frac{d\Delta}{dx} = \frac{1}{EI}\left(-\frac{W}{4}\times(0)^2 + \frac{WL^2}{16}\right)$$

$$\boxed{\theta_B = +\frac{WL^2}{16EI}}$$

(ii) For determining the value of slope at A, substitute $x=L$ in Eq. (2.68) (by considering the first and second segments together).

$$\frac{d\Delta}{dx} = \frac{1}{EI}\left(-\frac{W}{4}\times(L)^2 + \frac{WL^2}{16} + \frac{W}{2}\times\left[(L)-\frac{L}{2}\right]^2\right)$$

$$\theta_A = -\frac{WL^2}{16EI}$$

(iii) For determining the value of deflection at C (i.e., mid-span), substitute $x = L/2$ in Eq. (2.69) (by considering the first segment only).

$$\Delta = \frac{1}{EI}\left[-\frac{W}{12}\times\left(\frac{L}{2}\right)^3 + \frac{WL^2}{16}\times\left(\frac{L}{2}\right)\right]$$

$$\Delta_C = \frac{WL^3}{48EI}$$

Since the beam is symmetrically loaded, the maximum slope occurs at the supports, and the maximum deflection occurs at the mid-span location.

$$\theta_{max} = \frac{WL^2}{16EI}$$

and $\Delta_{max} = \Delta_C = \dfrac{WL^3}{48EI}$

Example 2.10: A simply supported beam of span L is subjected to a point load W at a distance of "a" from the right support. Using the Macaulay's method, determine the slope at the support locations and deflection under the load. Also find the maximum deflection.

Solution:

The simply supported beam with a point load is shown in Figure 2.16. By applying the equilibrium conditions, the reactions are obtained.

$$V_A = \frac{Wa}{L}$$

$$V_B = \frac{W(L-a)}{L}$$

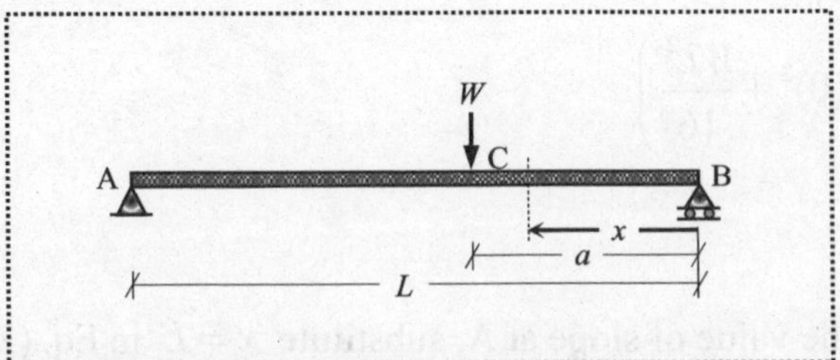

Figure 2.16 Simply supported beam with a point load (Example 2.10)

The governing differential equation of the elastic curve is

$$EI\frac{d^2\Delta}{dx^2} = -M$$

In this example, the moment variation cannot be expressed by a single equation for the entire length. By taking B as origin, the moment at the section is expressed as

$$M = \begin{cases} \dfrac{W(L-a)}{L}\times x & \text{if } 0 \le x \le a \\ \dfrac{W(L-a)}{L}\times x - W\times(x-a) & \text{if } a \le x \le L \end{cases} \tag{2.70}$$

The first line of Eq. (2.70) is valid, if the value of x lies between 0 and a from B, and the second line is valid, if the value of x lies between a and L from B. However, the term $\frac{W(L-a)}{L}x$ is common in both the expressions. Therefore, Eq. (2.70) is written as

$$M = \frac{W(L-a)}{L}x \,\vdots -W[x-a] \tag{2.71}$$

The expression is partitioned by dotted lines. The first segment in Eq. (2.71) is considered when the moment is evaluated between B and C, and both the first and second segments together are considered when the moment is evaluated between C and A, by keeping the origin as B.

Substituting M in the governing equation, and use of Macaulay's terms as

$$EI\frac{d^2\Delta}{dx^2} = -\frac{W(L-a)}{L}x \,\vdots + W[x-a] \tag{2.72}$$

The first and second integrations yield the expressions for slope and deflection respectively as

$$EI\frac{d\Delta}{dx} = -\frac{W(L-a)}{L}\times\frac{x^2}{2} + C_1 \,\vdots + W\times\frac{[x-a]^2}{2}$$

$$EI\,\Delta = -\frac{W(L-a)}{L}\times\frac{x^3}{6} + C_1\times x + C_2 \,\vdots + W\times\frac{[x-a]^3}{6}$$

Two boundary conditions are identified as follows.

BC (i): At the roller support B, the value of deflection is zero, $x=0 \rightarrow \Delta=0$

BC (ii): At the hinged support A, the value of deflection is zero, $x=L \rightarrow \Delta=0$

Substituting the first boundary condition (as $x=0$ lies in the first segment, consider the first segment only),

$$EI(0) = -\frac{W(L-a)}{L}\times\frac{(0)^3}{6} + C_1\times(0) + C_2 \Rightarrow C_2 = 0$$

Similarly, substituting the second boundary condition (as $x=L$ lies in the second segment, consider both the first and second segments together),

$$EI(0)=-\frac{W(L-a)}{L}\times\frac{(L)^3}{6}+C_1\times(L)+(0)+W\times\frac{[L-a]^3}{6}\Rightarrow C_1=\frac{W}{6L}\left(2L^2a-3La^2+a^3\right)$$

Therefore, the expressions for slope and deflection are

$$\boxed{\frac{d\Delta}{dx}=\frac{1}{EI}\left(-\frac{W(L-a)}{2L}x^2+\frac{W}{6L}\left(2L^2a-3La^2+a^3\right)\vdots+\frac{W}{2}[x-a]^2\right)} \tag{2.73}$$

$$\boxed{\Delta=\frac{1}{EI}\left(-\frac{W(L-a)}{6L}x^3+\frac{W}{6L}\left(2L^2a-3La^2+a^3\right)x\vdots+\frac{W}{6}[x-a]^3\right)} \tag{2.74}$$

(i) For determining the value of slope at B, substitute $x=0$ in Eq. (2.73) (by considering the first segment only).

$$\frac{d\Delta}{dx}=\frac{1}{EI}\left(-\frac{W(L-a)}{2L}\times(0)^2+\frac{W}{6L}\left(2L^2a-3La^2+a^3\right)\right)=\frac{Wa}{6EIL}\left(2L^2-3La+a^2\right)$$

$$\boxed{\theta_B=\frac{Wa}{6EIL}\left(2L^2-3La+a^2\right)}$$

(ii) For determining the value of slope at A, substitute $x=L$ in Eq. (2.73) (by considering the first and second segments together).

$$\frac{d\Delta}{dx}=\frac{1}{EI}\left(-\frac{W(L-a)}{2L}\times(L)^2+\frac{W}{6L}\left(2L^2a-3La^2+a^3\right)+\frac{W}{2}[(L)-a]^2\right)=\frac{-Wa}{6EIL}\left(L^2-a^2\right)$$

$$\boxed{\theta_A=\frac{-Wa}{6EIL}\left(L^2-a^2\right)}$$

(iii) For determining the value of deflection the mid-span, substitute $x=L/2$ in Eq. (2.74);

$$\Delta_{\text{mid-span}}=\frac{1}{EI}\left(-\frac{W(L-a)}{6L}\times\left(\frac{L}{2}\right)^3+\frac{W}{6L}\left(2L^2a-3La^2+a^3\right)\times\left(\frac{L}{2}\right)+\frac{W}{6}\left[\left(\frac{L}{2}\right)-a\right]^3\right)$$

$$=\frac{W}{48EI}\left(3L^2a-4a^3\right)$$

$$\boxed{\Delta_{\text{mid-span}}=\frac{W}{48EI}\left(3L^2a-4a^3\right)}$$

The location of the maximum deflection can be obtained by equating the slope equation to zero. If $a<L/2$,

$$\frac{1}{EI}\left(-\frac{W(L-a)}{2L}x^2+\frac{W}{6L}\left(2L^2a-3La^2+a^3\right)+\frac{W}{2}[x-a]^2\right)=0$$

By solving the above equation, the admissible root obtained as; $x = L - \frac{1}{3}\sqrt{3\left(L^2 - a^2\right)}$. Therefore, the maximum deflection is

$$\boxed{\Delta_{max} = \frac{W}{EI}\frac{a\left(L^2 - a^2\right)^{3/2}}{9\sqrt{3}L}}$$

When the load acts at the mid-span, the above formulas can be verified with Example 2.8 by substituting $a = L/2$.

Example 2.11: A cantilever beam of span 6 m is subjected to three concentrated loads of 30 kN, 25 kN and 20 kN respectively at 3 m, 5 m and 6 m from the fixed end. Using the Macaulay's method, determine the slope and deflection at the salient locations.

Solution:

The cantilever beam with loads is shown in Figure 2.17. The governing differential equation of the elastic curve is

$$EI\frac{d^2\Delta}{dx^2} = -M$$

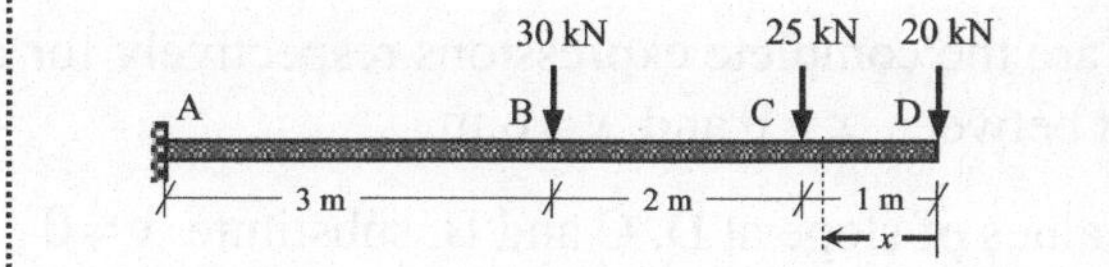

Figure 2.17 Cantilever beam with multiple loads (Example 2.11)

Take moment of all forces to the right of section by keeping the free end D as origin,

$$M = -20\times x \,\vdots - 25\times[x-1] \,\vdots - 30\times[x-3]$$

Substituting the moment expression in the governing equation,

$$EI\frac{d^2\Delta}{dx^2} = +20x \,\vdots + 25[x-1] \,\vdots + 30[x-3]$$

The first and second integrations yield the expressions for slope and deflection respectively as

$$EI\frac{d\Delta}{dx} = 20\times\left(\frac{x^2}{2}\right) + C_1 \,\vdots + 25\times\frac{[x-1]^2}{2} \,\vdots + 30\times\frac{[x-3]^2}{2}$$

$$EI\Delta = 20\times\left(\frac{x^3}{6}\right) + C_1\times x + C_2 \,\vdots + 25\times\frac{[x-1]^3}{6} \,\vdots + 30\times\frac{[x-3]^3}{6}$$

where C_1 and C_2 are the constants of integration, which need to be evaluated using the boundary conditions as follows.

BC (i): At the fixed end, the value of slope is zero, $x=6 \rightarrow d\Delta/dx=0$

BC (ii): At the fixed end, the value of deflection is zero, $x=6 \rightarrow \Delta=0$

Substituting the first boundary condition in the slope equation

$$EI(0)=20\times\frac{(6)^2}{2}+C_1\vdots+25\times\frac{[6-1]^2}{2}\vdots+30\times\frac{[6-3]^2}{2} \Rightarrow C_1=-807.5$$

Similarly, substituting the second boundary condition and the value of C_1 in the deflection equation

$$EI(0)=20\times\left(\frac{6^3}{6}\right)-807.5\times(6)+C_2\vdots+25\times\frac{[6-1]^3}{6}\vdots+30\times\frac{[6-3]^3}{6}$$

$$\Rightarrow C_2=3469.167$$

Therefore, after substituting the value of C_1 and C_2, the slope and deflection equations

$$\frac{d\Delta}{dx}=\frac{1}{EI}\left(10x^2-807.5\vdots+\frac{25}{2}[x-1]^2\vdots+15[x-3]^2\right) \quad (2.75)$$

$$\Delta=\frac{1}{EI}\left(\frac{10}{3}x^3-807.5x+3469.167\vdots+\frac{25}{6}[x-1]^3\vdots+5[x-3]^3\right) \quad (2.76)$$

Eq. (2.75) and Eq. (2.76) are the complete expressions respectively for determining the slope and the deflection at any point between $x=0$ and $x=6$ m.

(i) For determining the values of slope at D, C and B, substitute $x=0$, 1 and 3 in Eq. (2.75). The first segment only is considered for θ_D. Both the first and second segments are considered for θ_C, and the first, second and third segments are considered for θ_B.

$$\theta_D=\left.\frac{d\Delta}{dx}\right|_{x=0}=\frac{1}{EI}\left(10\times(0)^2-807.5\right)=\frac{-807.5}{EI} \text{ radians}$$

$$\theta_C=\left.\frac{d\Delta}{dx}\right|_{x=1}=\frac{1}{EI}\left(10\times(1)^2-807.5+\frac{25}{2}\times[(1)-1]^2\right)=\frac{-797.5}{EI} \text{ radians}$$

$$\theta_B=\left.\frac{d\Delta}{dx}\right|_{x=3}=\frac{1}{EI}\left(10\times(3)^2-807.5+\frac{25}{2}\times[(3)-1]^2+15\times[(3)-3]^2\right)=\frac{-667.5}{EI} \text{ radians}$$

(ii) For determining the values of deflection at D, C and B, substitute $x=0$, 1 and 3 in Eq. (2.76). The first segment only is considered for Δ_D. Both first and second segments are considered for Δ_C, and the first, second and third segments are considered for Δ_B.

$$\Delta_D=\Delta|_{x=0}=\frac{1}{EI}\left(\frac{10}{3}\times(0)^3-807.5\times(0)+3469.167\right)=\frac{3469.167}{EI} \text{ m}$$

$$\Delta_C = \Delta\big|_{x=1} = \frac{1}{EI}\left(\frac{10}{3}\times(1)^3 - 807.5\times(1) + 3469.167 + \frac{25}{6}\times[(1)-1]^3\right) = \frac{2665.0}{EI}\ \text{m}$$

$$\Delta_B = \Delta\big|_{x=3} = \frac{1}{EI}\left(\frac{10}{3}\times(3)^3 - 807.5\times(3) + 3469.167 + \frac{25}{6}\times[(3)-1]^3 + 5\times[(3)-3]^3\right)$$

$$= \frac{1170.0}{EI}\ \text{m}$$

Example 2.12: A cantilever beam of span 6 m is subjected to three loads: (i) 25 kN at the free end; (ii) 20 kN at 1 m from the free end; and (iii) 10 kN/m over the span of 3 m from the fixed end. Using the Macaulay's method, determine the slope and deflection at the salient locations.

Solution:

The cantilever beam with loads is shown in Figure 2.18. The governing differential equation of the elastic curve is

$$EI\frac{d^2\Delta}{dx^2} = -M$$

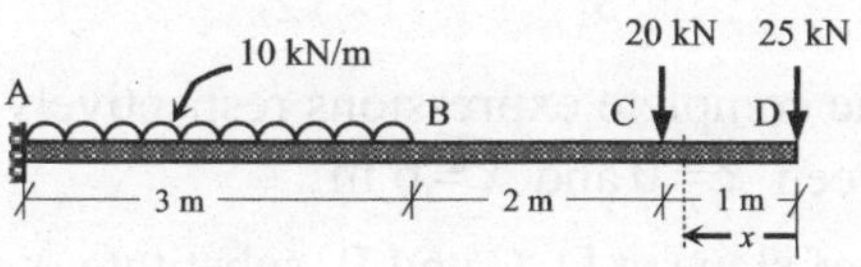

Figure 2.18 Cantilever beam with multiple loads (Example 2.12)

Take moment of all forces to the right of section by keeping the free end D as origin,

$$M = -25\times x \;\vdots\; -20\times[x-1] \;\vdots\; -10\times[x-3]\times\frac{[x-3]}{2}$$

Substituting the moment expression in the governing equation,

$$EI\frac{d^2\Delta}{dx^2} = 25x \;\vdots\; +20[x-1] \;\vdots\; +5[x-3]^2$$

The first and second integrations yield the expressions for slope and deflection respectively as

$$EI\frac{d\Delta}{dx} = 25\times\left(\frac{x^2}{2}\right) + C_1 \;\vdots\; +20\times\frac{[x-1]^2}{2} \;\vdots\; +5\times\frac{[x-3]^3}{3}$$

$$EI\Delta = 25\times\left(\frac{x^3}{6}\right) + C_1\times x + C_2 \;\vdots\; +20\times\frac{[x-1]^3}{6} \;\vdots\; +5\times\frac{[x-3]^4}{12}$$

where C_1 and C_2 are the constants of integration, which need to be evaluated using the boundary conditions as follows.

BC (i): At the fixed end, the value of slope is zero, $x=6 \rightarrow d\Delta/dx=0$

BC (ii): At the fixed end, the value of deflection is zero, $x=6 \rightarrow \Delta=0$

Substituting the first boundary condition in the slope equation

$$EI(0)=25\times\left(\frac{6^2}{2}\right)+C_1\vdots+20\times\frac{[6-1]^2}{2}\vdots+5\times\frac{[6-3]^3}{3} \Rightarrow C_1=-745.0$$

Similarly, substituting the second boundary condition and the value of C_1 in the deflection equation

$$EI(0)=25\times\left(\frac{6^3}{6}\right)+745.0\times6+C_2\vdots+20\times\frac{[6-1]^3}{6}\vdots+5\times\frac{[6-3]^4}{12}$$

$$\Rightarrow C_2=3119.583$$

Therefore, after substituting the value of C_1 and C_2, the slope and deflection equations

$$\frac{d\Delta}{dx}=\frac{1}{EI}\left(\frac{25}{2}x^2-745\vdots+10[x-1]^2\vdots+\frac{5}{3}[x-3]^3\right) \tag{2.77}$$

$$\Delta=\frac{1}{EI}\left(\frac{25}{6}x^3-745x+3119.583\vdots+\frac{10}{3}[x-1]^3\vdots+\frac{5}{12}[x-3]^4\right) \tag{2.78}$$

Eq. (2.77) and Eq. (2.78) are the complete expressions respectively for determining the slope and the deflection at any point between $x=0$ and $x=6$ m.

For determining the values of slope at D, C and B, substitute $x=0$, 1 and 3 in Eq. (2.77). The first segment only is considered for θ_D. Both the first and second segments are considered for θ_C and the first, second and third segments are considered for θ_B.

$$\theta_D=\left.\frac{d\Delta}{dx}\right|_{x=0}=\frac{1}{EI}\left(\frac{25}{2}\times(0)^2-745\right)=\frac{-745}{EI}\text{ radians}$$

$$\theta_C=\left.\frac{d\Delta}{dx}\right|_{x=1}=\frac{1}{EI}\left(\frac{25}{2}\times(1)^2-745\vdots+10\times[(1)-1]^2\right)=\frac{-732.5}{EI}\text{ radians}$$

$$\theta_B=\left.\frac{d\Delta}{dx}\right|_{x=3}=\frac{1}{EI}\left(\frac{25}{2}\times(3)^2-745\vdots+10\times[(3)-1]^2\vdots+\frac{5}{3}\times[(3)-3]^3\right)=\frac{-592.5}{EI}\text{ radians}$$

For determining the values of deflection at D, C and B, substitute $x=0$, 1 and 3 in Eq. (2.78). The first segment only is considered for Δ_D. Both the first and second segments are considered for Δ_C, and the first, second and third segments are considered for Δ_B.

$$\Delta_D=\Delta|_{x=0}=\frac{1}{EI}\left(\frac{25}{6}\times(0)^3-745\times(0)+3119.583\right)=\frac{3119.583}{EI}\text{ m}$$

$$\Delta_C = \Delta|_{x=1} = \frac{1}{EI}\left(\frac{25}{6}\times(1)^3 - 745\times(1) + 3119.583 + \frac{10}{3}\times[(1)-1]^3\right) = \frac{2378.75}{EI}\text{ m}$$

$$\Delta_B = \Delta|_{x=3} = \frac{1}{EI}\left(\frac{25}{6}\times(3)^3 - 745\times(3) + 3119.583 + \frac{10}{3}\times[(3)-1]^3 + \frac{5}{12}\times[(3)-3]^4\right)$$

$$= \frac{1023.75}{EI}\text{ m}$$

Example 2.13: A cantilever beam of span 7 m is subjected to a concentrated load of 25 kN at 1 m from the fixed end, and a uniformly distributed load of 10 kN/m over a span of 4 m from the free end. Using the Macaulay's method, determine the slope and deflection at the salient locations.

Solution:

The cantilever beam with loads is shown in Figure 2.19(i). The governing differential equation of the elastic curve is

$$EI\frac{d^2\Delta}{dx^2} = -M$$

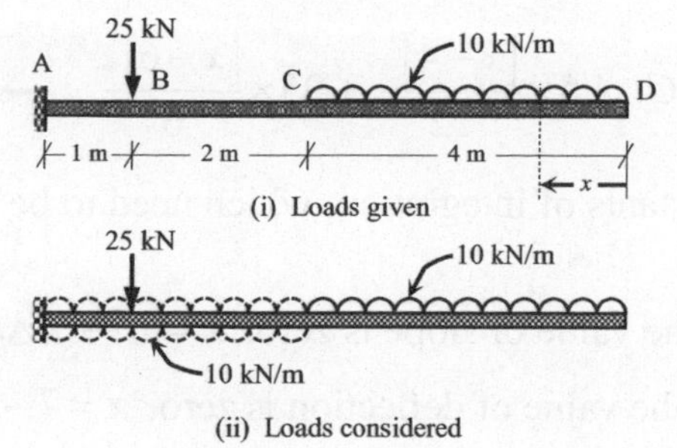

Figure 2.19 Cantilever beam with multiple loads (Example 2.13)

Take moment of all forces to the right of section in Figure 2.19(i) by keeping the free end D as origin,

$$M = \begin{cases} -10\times x\times x/2 & \text{if } 0\le x\le 4 \\ -10\times 4\times(x-2) & \text{if } 4\le x\le 6 \\ -10\times 4\times(x-2) - 25\times(x-6) & \text{if } 6\le x\le 7 \end{cases}$$

In order to use the Macaulay's method, the moment expression obtained for the first segment should appear in the moment expression of the second segment. Similarly, the moment expression obtained for the second segment should appear in the moment expression of the third segment. Since the uniformly distributed load is terminated at C, the moment of this force in the first, second and third segments will not remain the same; and this is possible only if the distributed load is continued till the end of the last segment. Therefore, the uniformly distributed load (with same magnitude) is assumed to continue till the end (i.e., A) from C, and a uniformly distributed load (with same magnitude) in the opposite direction is included between C and A to neutralize the effect of the assumed load as shown in Figure 2.19(ii).

Therefore, the moment expression becomes

$$M=-10\times x\times\frac{x}{2}\;\vdots\;+10\times[x-4]\times\frac{[x-4]}{2}\;\vdots\;-25\times[x-6]$$

Substituting the moment expression in the governing equation,

$$EI\frac{d^2\Delta}{dx^2}=5x^2\;\vdots\;-5[x-4]^2\;\vdots\;+25[x-6]$$

The first and second integrations yield the expressions for slope and deflection respectively as

$$EI\frac{d\Delta}{dx}=5\times\left(\frac{x^3}{3}\right)+C_1\;\vdots\;-5\times\frac{[x-4]^3}{3}\;\vdots\;+25\times\frac{[x-6]^2}{2}$$

$$EI\Delta=5\times\left(\frac{x^4}{12}\right)+C_1\times x+C_2\;\vdots\;-5\times\frac{[x-4]^4}{12}\;\vdots\;+25\times\frac{[x-6]^3}{6}$$

where C_1 and C_2 are the constants of integration, which need to be evaluated using the boundary conditions as follows.

BC (i): At the fixed end, the value of slope is zero, $x=7\rightarrow d\Delta/dx=0$

BC (ii): At the fixed end, the value of deflection is zero, $x=7\rightarrow\Delta=0$

Substituting the first boundary condition in the slope equation

$$EI(0)=5\times\left(\frac{7^3}{3}\right)+C_1\;\vdots\;-5\times\frac{[7-4]^3}{3}\;\vdots\;+25\times\frac{[7-6]^2}{2}$$

$$\Rightarrow C_1=-539.167$$

Similarly, substituting the second boundary condition and the value of C_1 in the deflection equation

$$EI(0)=5\times\left(\frac{7^4}{12}\right)-539.167\times(7)+C_2\;\vdots\;-5\times\frac{[7-4]^4}{12}\;\vdots\;+25\times\frac{[7-6]^3}{6}$$

$$\Rightarrow C_2=2803.336$$

Therefore, after substituting the value of C_1 and C_2, the slope and deflection equations

$$\frac{d\Delta}{dx}=\frac{1}{EI}\left(\frac{5}{3}x^3-539.167\vdots-\frac{5}{3}[x-4]^3\vdots+\frac{25}{2}[x-6]^2\right) \quad (2.79)$$

$$\Delta=\frac{1}{EI}\left(\frac{5}{12}x^4-539.167x+2803.336\vdots-\frac{5}{12}[x-4]^4\vdots+\frac{25}{6}[x-6]^3\right) \quad (2.80)$$

Eq. (2.79) and Eq. (2.80) are the complete expressions respectively for determining the slope and the deflection at any point between $x=0$ and $x=7$ m.

For determining the values of slope at D, C and B, substitute $x=0$, 4 and 6 in Eq. (2.79). The first segment only is considered for θ_D. Both the first and second segments are considered for θ_C and the first, second and third segments are considered for θ_B.

$$\theta_D=\left.\frac{d\Delta}{dx}\right|_{x=0}=\frac{1}{EI}\left(\frac{5}{3}\times(0)^3-539.167\right)=\frac{-539.167}{EI}\text{ radians}$$

$$\theta_C=\left.\frac{d\Delta}{dx}\right|_{x=4}=\frac{1}{EI}\left(\frac{5}{3}\times(4)^3-539.167\vdots-\frac{5}{3}\times[4-4]^3\right)=\frac{-432.5}{EI}\text{ radians}$$

$$\theta_B=\left.\frac{d\Delta}{dx}\right|_{x=6}=\frac{1}{EI}\left(\frac{5}{3}\times(6)^3-539.167\vdots-\frac{5}{3}\times[6-4]^3\vdots+\frac{25}{2}\times[6-6]^2\right)=\frac{-192.5}{EI}\text{ radians}$$

For determining the values of deflection at D, C and B, substitute $x=0$, 4 and 6 in Eq. (2.80). The first segment only is considered for Δ_D. Both the first and second segments are considered for Δ_C, and the first, second and third segments are considered for Δ_B.

$$\Delta_D=\Delta|_{x=0}=\frac{1}{EI}\left(\frac{5}{12}\times(0)^4-539.167\times(0)+2803.336\right)=\frac{2803.336}{EI}\text{ m}$$

$$\Delta_C=\Delta|_{x=4}=\frac{1}{EI}\left(\frac{5}{12}\times(4)^4-539.167\times(4)+2803.336\vdots-\frac{5}{12}\times[4-4]^4\right)$$

$$=\frac{753.335}{EI}\text{ m}$$

$$\Delta_B=\Delta|_{x=6}=\frac{1}{EI}\left(\frac{5}{12}\times(6)^4-539.167\times(6)+2803.336\vdots-\frac{5}{12}\times[6-4]^4\vdots+\frac{25}{6}\times[6-6]^3\right)$$

$$=\frac{101.667}{EI}\text{ m}$$

Example 2.14: A cantilever beam of span 9 m is subjected to a concentrated load of 30 kN at the free end, and a uniformly distributed load of 20 kN/m over a span of 4 m starting at 2 m from the fixed end. Using the Macaulay's method, determine the slope and deflection at the salient locations.

Solution:

The cantilever beam with loads is shown in Figure 2.20(i).

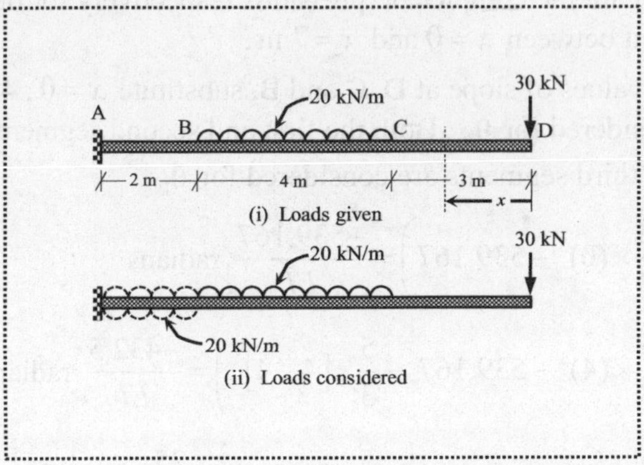

Figure 2.20 Cantilever beam with multiple loads (Example 2.14)

The governing differential equation of the elastic curve is

$$EI\frac{d^2\Delta}{dx^2} = -M$$

Similar to Example 2.13, the uniformly distributed load of 20 kN/m is added in the segment AB both in downward and upward directions as shown in Figure 2.20(ii). Take moment of all forces to the right of section in Figure 2.19(ii) by keeping the free end D as origin,

$$M = -30\times x \,\vdots -20\times[x-3]\times\frac{[x-3]}{2} \,\vdots +20\times[x-7]\times\frac{[x-7]}{2}$$

Substituting the moment expression in the governing equation,

$$EI\frac{d^2\Delta}{dx^2} = 30x \,\vdots +10[x-3]^2 \,\vdots -10[x-7]^2$$

The first and second integrations yield the expressions for slope and deflection respectively as

$$EI\frac{d\Delta}{dx} = 30\times\left(\frac{x^2}{2}\right) + C_1 \,\vdots +10\times\frac{[x-3]^3}{3} \,\vdots -10\times\frac{[x-7]^3}{3}$$

$$EI\Delta = 30\times\left(\frac{x^3}{6}\right) + C_1\times x + C_2 \,\vdots +10\times\frac{[x-3]^4}{12} \,\vdots -10\times\frac{[x-7]^4}{12}$$

where C_1 and C_2 are the constants of integration, which need to be evaluated using the boundary conditions as follows.

BC (i): At the fixed end, the value of slope is zero, $x=9 \rightarrow d\Delta/dx=0$

BC (ii): At the fixed end, the value of deflection is zero, $x=9 \rightarrow \Delta=0$

Substituting the first boundary condition in the slope equation

$$EI(0)=30\times\left(\frac{9^2}{2}\right)+C_1\vdots+10\times\frac{[9-3]^3}{3}\vdots-10\times\frac{[9-7]^3}{3} \Rightarrow C_1=-1908.333$$

Similarly, substituting the second boundary condition and the value of C_1 in the deflection equation

$$EI(0)=30\times\left(\frac{9^3}{6}\right)-1908.333\times(9)+C_2\vdots+10\times\frac{[9-3]^4}{12}\vdots-10\times\frac{[9-7]^4}{12} \Rightarrow C_2=12463.330$$

Therefore, after substituting the value of C_1 and C_2, the slope and deflection equations

$$\frac{d\Delta}{dx}=\frac{1}{EI}\left(15x^2-1908.333\vdots+\frac{10}{3}[x-3]^3\vdots-\frac{10}{3}[x-7]^3\right) \tag{2.81}$$

$$\Delta=\frac{1}{EI}\left(5x^3-1908.333x+12463.330\vdots+\frac{5}{6}[x-3]^4\vdots-\frac{5}{6}[x-7]^4\right) \tag{2.82}$$

Eq. (2.81) and Eq. (2.82) are the complete expressions respectively for determining the slope and the deflection at any point between $x=0$ and $x=9$ m.

For determining the values of slope at D, C and B, substitute $x=0$, 3 and 7 in Eq. (2.77). The first segment only is considered for θ_D. Both the first and second segments are considered for θ_C and the first, second and third segments are considered for θ_B.

$$\theta_D=\left.\frac{d\Delta}{dx}\right|_{x=0}=\frac{1}{EI}\left(15\times(0)^3-1908.333\right)=\frac{-1908.333}{EI} \text{ radians}$$

$$\theta_C=\left.\frac{d\Delta}{dx}\right|_{x=3}=\frac{1}{EI}\left(15\times(3)^2-1908.333\vdots+\frac{10}{3}\times[3-3]^3\right)=\frac{-1773.333}{EI} \text{ radians}$$

$$\theta_B=\left.\frac{d\Delta}{dx}\right|_{x=7}=\frac{1}{EI}\left(15\times(7)^2-1908.333\vdots+\frac{10}{3}\times[7-3]^3\vdots-\frac{10}{3}\times[7-7]^3\right)=\frac{-960.0}{EI} \text{ radians}$$

For determining the values of deflection at D, C and B, substitute $x=0$, 3 and 7 in Eq. (2.82). The first segment only is considered for Δ_D. Both the first and second segments are considered for Δ_C, and the first, second and third segments are considered for Δ_B.

$$\Delta_D=\Delta|_{x=0}=\frac{1}{EI}\left(5\times(0)^3-1908.333\times(0)+12463.330\right)=\frac{14463.330}{EI} \text{ m}$$

$$\Delta_C=\Delta|_{x=3}=\frac{1}{EI}\left(5\times(3)^3-1908.333\times(3)+12463.330\vdots+\frac{5}{6}\times[3-3]^4\right)=\frac{6873.331}{EI} \text{ m}$$

$$\Delta_B = \Delta|_{x=7} = \frac{1}{EI}\left(5\times(7)^3 - 1908.333\times(7) + 12463.330 \vdots + \frac{5}{6}\times[7-3]^4 \vdots - \frac{5}{6}\times[7-7]^4\right)$$

$$= \frac{1033.332}{EI}\ \text{m}$$

Example 2.15: A cantilever beam of span 10 m is subjected to the lateral loads as shown in Figure 2.21. Using the Macaulay's method, determine the slope and deflection at the salient locations.

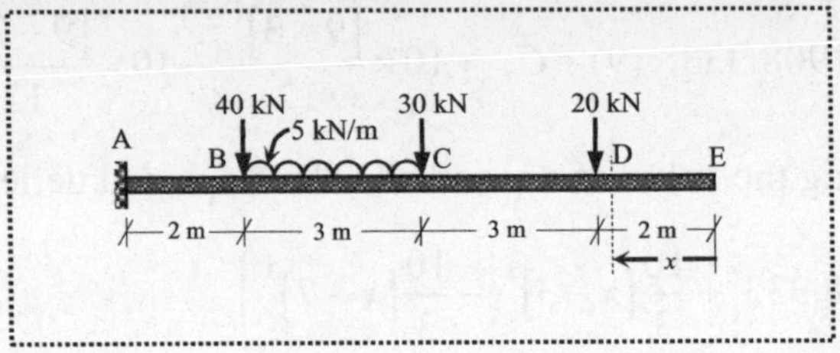

Figure 2.21 Cantilever beam with multiple loads (Example 2.15)

Solution:

The governing differential equation of the elastic curve is

$$EI\frac{d^2\Delta}{dx^2} = -M$$

Similar to Example 2.13, the uniformly distributed load of 5 kN/m is added in the segment BA both in downward and upward directions. Take moment of all forces to the right of section by keeping the free end E as origin,

$$M = -0\times x \vdots - 20\times[x-2] \vdots - 30\times[x-5] - 5\times[x-5]\times\frac{[x-5]}{2} \vdots - 40\times[x-8] + 5\times[x-8]\times\frac{[x-8]}{2}$$

Since no lateral load is applied in the segment ED, there is no bending moment in the segment. However, due to the bending of other segments, both slope and deflection will exist in the segment ED. Moreover, the constants of integration should appear in the first segment only. Therefore, zero moment is kept in the first segment.

Substituting the moment expression in the governing equation,

$$EI\frac{d^2\Delta}{dx^2} = 0 \vdots + 20[x-2] \vdots + 30[x-5] + \frac{5}{2}[x-5]^2 \vdots + 40[x-8] - \frac{5}{2}[x-8]^2$$

The first and second integrations yield the expressions for slope and deflection respectively as

$$EI\frac{d\Delta}{dx} = 0 + C_1 \vdots + 20\times\frac{[x-2]^2}{2} \vdots + 30\times\frac{[x-5]^2}{2} + \frac{5}{2}\times\frac{[x-5]^3}{3} \vdots + 40\times\frac{[x-8]^2}{2} - \frac{5}{2}\times\frac{[x-8]^3}{3}$$

$$EI\Delta = 0 + C_1 \times x + C_2 \vdots + 20\times\frac{[x-2]^3}{6} \vdots + 30\times\frac{[x-5]^3}{6} + \frac{5}{2}\times\frac{[x-5]^4}{12} \vdots + 40\times\frac{[x-8]^3}{6} - \frac{5}{2}\times\frac{[x-8]^4}{12}$$

where C_1 and C_2 are the constants of integration, which need to be evaluated using the boundary conditions as follows.

BC (i): At the fixed end, the value of slope is zero, $x=10 \rightarrow d\Delta/dx = 0$

BC (ii): At the fixed end, the value of deflection is zero, $x=10 \rightarrow \Delta = 0$

Substituting the first boundary condition in the slope equation,

$$EI(0) = 0 + C_1 \vdots + 20\times\frac{[10-2]^2}{2} \vdots + 30\times\frac{[10-5]^2}{2} + \frac{5}{2}\times\frac{[10-5]^3}{3} \vdots + 40\times\frac{[10-8]^2}{2} - \frac{5}{2}\times\frac{[10-8]^3}{3}$$

$$\Rightarrow C_1 = -1192.5$$

Similarly, substituting the second boundary condition and the value of C_1 in the deflection equation

$$EI(0) = 0 - 1192.5\times(10) + C_2 \vdots + 20\times\frac{[10-2]^3}{6} \vdots + 30\times\frac{[10-5]^3}{6}$$
$$+\frac{5}{2}\times\frac{[10-5]^4}{12} \vdots + 40\times\frac{[10-8]^3}{6} - \frac{5}{2}\times\frac{[10-8]^4}{12}$$

$$\Rightarrow C_2 = 9413.125$$

Therefore, after substituting the value of C_1 and C_2, the slope and deflection equations:

$$\frac{d\Delta}{dx} = \frac{1}{EI}\left(-1192.5 \vdots + 10[x-2]^2 \vdots + 15[x-5]^2 + \frac{5}{6}[x-5]^3 \vdots + 20[x-8]^2 - \frac{5}{6}[x-8]^3\right) \quad (2.83)$$

$$\Delta = \frac{1}{EI}\left(\begin{array}{l} -1192.5x + 9413.125 \vdots + \frac{10}{3}[x-2]^3 \vdots + 5[x-5]^3 + \frac{5}{24}[x-5]^4 \vdots \\ +\frac{20}{3}[x-8]^3 - \frac{5}{24}[x-8]^4 \end{array}\right) \quad (2.84)$$

Eq. (2.83) and Eq. (2.84) are the complete expressions respectively for determining the slope and the deflection at any point between $x=0$ and $x=10$ m.

For determining the values of slope at E, D, C and B, substitute $x=0$, 2, 5 and 8 in Eq. (2.83). The first segment only is considered for θ_E. Both the first and second segments are considered for θ_D. The first, second and third segments are considered for θ_C, and all four segments are considered for θ_B.

$$\theta_E = \left.\frac{d\Delta}{dx}\right|_{x=0} = \frac{1}{EI}(-1192.5) = \frac{-1192.5}{EI} \text{ radians}$$

$$\theta_D = \left.\frac{d\Delta}{dx}\right|_{x=2} = \frac{1}{EI}\left(-1192.5 \vdots +10\times[2-2]^2 \vdots\right) = \frac{-1192.5}{EI} \text{ radians}$$

$$\theta_C = \left.\frac{d\Delta}{dx}\right|_{x=5} = \frac{1}{EI}\left(-1192.5 \vdots +10\times[5-2]^2 \vdots +15\times[5-5]^2 + \frac{5}{6}\times[5-5]^3\right)$$

$$= \frac{-1102.5}{EI} \text{ radians}$$

$$\theta_B = \left.\frac{d\Delta}{dx}\right|_{x=8} = \frac{1}{EI}\left(\begin{matrix}-1192.5 \vdots +10\times[8-2]^2 \vdots +15\times[8-5]^2 + \frac{5}{6}\times[8-5]^3 \vdots \\ +20\times[8-8]^2 - \frac{5}{6}\times[8-8]^3\end{matrix}\right)$$

$$= \frac{-675.0}{EI} \text{ radians}$$

For determining the values of deflection at E, D, C and B, substitute $x = 0$, 2, 5 and 8 in Eq. (2.84). The first segment only is considered for Δ_E. Both the first and second segments are considered for Δ_D. The first, second and third segments are considered for Δ_C, and all the four segments are considered for Δ_B.

$$\Delta_E = \Delta|_{x=0} = \frac{1}{EI}(-1192.5\times 0 + 9413.125) = \frac{9413.125}{EI} \text{ m}$$

$$\Delta_D = \Delta|_{x=2} = \frac{1}{EI}\left(-1192.5\times(2) + 9413.125 \vdots + \frac{10}{3}\times[2-2]^3\right) = \frac{7028.125}{EI} \text{ m}$$

$$\Delta_C = \Delta|_{x=5} = \frac{1}{EI}\left(\begin{matrix}-1192.5\times(5) + 9413.125 \vdots + \frac{10}{3}\times[5-2]^3 \vdots \\ +5\times[5-5]^3 + \frac{5}{24}\times[5-5]^4\end{matrix}\right) = \frac{3540.625}{EI} \text{ m}$$

$$\Delta_B = \Delta|_{x=8} = \frac{1}{EI}\left(\begin{matrix}-1192.5\times(8) + 9413.125 \vdots + \frac{10}{3}\times[8-2]^3 \vdots +5\times[8-5]^3 + \frac{5}{24}\times[8-5]^4 \vdots \\ + \frac{20}{3}\times[8-8]^3 - \frac{5}{24}\times[8-8]^4\end{matrix}\right)$$

$$= \frac{745.0}{EI} \text{ m}$$

Example 2.16: A simply supported beam of span 9 m is subjected to two concentrated loads of 40 kN and 30 kN at 2 m and 5 m respectively from the left support. Using the Macaulay's method, determine (i) the slope at the supports, (ii) the slope at the loading points, (iii) the deflection at the loading points, and (iv) the maximum deflection.

Solution:

The simply supported beam with two point loads is shown in Figure 2.22.

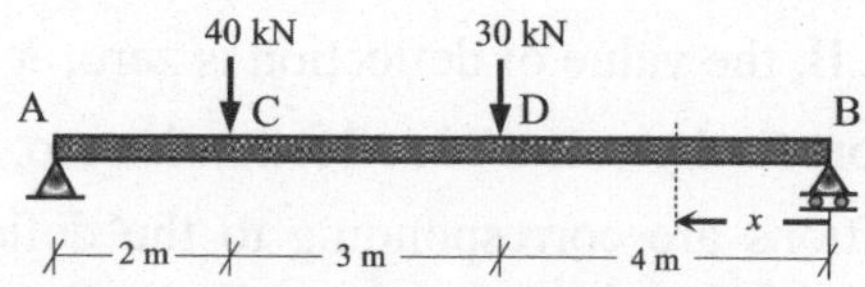

Figure 2.22 Simply supported beam with two point loads (Example 2.16)

The reactions at the supports are obtained by applying the equilibrium conditions as

$$\sum F_y = 0 \Rightarrow V_A + V_B - 40 - 30 = 0$$

$$\Rightarrow V_A + V_B = 70$$

$$\sum M_B = 0 \Rightarrow V_A \times 9 - 40 \times 7 - 30 \times 4 = 0$$

$$V_A = 44.444 \text{ kN}$$

$$V_B = 25.556 \text{ kN}$$

By taking B as origin, the moment of all the forces on the right of the section is

$$M = V_B \times x \,\vdots\, - 30 \times [x-4] \,\vdots\, - 40 \times [x-7] = 25.556x \,\vdots\, - 30[x-4] \,\vdots\, - 40[x-7]$$

The expression is partitioned by dotted lines. The first segment is considered when the moment is evaluated between B and D; both the first and second segments together are considered when the moment is evaluated between D and C; and the first, second and third segments together are considered when the moment is evaluated between C and A by keeping the origin as B.

The governing differential equation of the elastic curve is

$$EI\frac{d^2\Delta}{dx^2} = -M$$

Substituting M in the governing equation,

$$EI\frac{d^2\Delta}{dx^2} = -25.556x \,\vdots\, + 30[x-4] \,\vdots\, + 40[x-7]$$

The first and second integrations yield the expressions for slope and deflection respectively as

$$EI\frac{d\Delta}{dx} = -25.556\times\frac{x^2}{2} + C_1 \vdots + 30\times\frac{[x-4]^2}{2} \vdots + 40\times\frac{[x-7]^2}{2}$$

$$EI\ \Delta = -25.556\times\frac{x^3}{6} + C_1\times x + C_2 \vdots + 30\times\frac{[x-4]^3}{6} \vdots + 40\times\frac{[x-7]^3}{6}$$

where C_1 and C_2 are the constants of integration, which need to be evaluated using the boundary conditions as follows.

BC (i): At the roller support B, the value of deflection is zero, $x=0 \rightarrow \Delta=0$

BC (ii): At the hinged support A, the value of deflection is zero, $x=9 \rightarrow \Delta=0$

Since both the boundary conditions are corresponding to the deflection at two locations, only deflection equation should be used for evaluating the constants C_1 and C_2.

By applying the first boundary condition;

$$EI\ (0) = -25.556\times\frac{(0)^3}{6} + C_1\times(0) + C_2$$

$$\Rightarrow C_2 = 0$$

By applying the second boundary condition and the substituting the value of C_2;

$$EI\ (0) = -25.556\times\frac{(9)^3}{6} + C_1\times(9) + 0 \vdots + 30\times\frac{[9-4]^3}{6} \vdots + 40\times\frac{[9-7]^3}{6}$$

$$\Rightarrow C_1 = 269.636$$

Therefore, the complete expressions for slope and deflection:

$$\frac{d\Delta}{dx} = \frac{1}{EI}\left(-12.778x^2 + 269.636 \vdots + 15[x-4]^2 \vdots + 20[x-7]^2\right) \tag{2.85}$$

$$\Delta = \frac{1}{EI}\left(-4.259x^3 + 269.636x \vdots + 5[x-4]^3 \vdots + 6.667[x-7]^3\right) \tag{2.86}$$

(i) The values of slope at the supports:

$$\theta_B = \left.\frac{d\Delta}{dx}\right|_{x=0} = \frac{1}{EI}\left(-12.778\times(0)^2 + 269.636\right) = \frac{269.636}{EI} \text{ radians}$$

$$\theta_A = \left.\frac{d\Delta}{dx}\right|_{x=9} = \frac{1}{EI}\left(-12.778\times(9)^2 + 269.636 \vdots + 15\times[9-4]^2 \vdots + 20\times[9-7]^2\right)$$

$$= \frac{-310.382}{EI} \text{ radians}$$

(ii) The values of slope at the loading points:

$$\theta_D = \left.\frac{d\Delta}{dx}\right|_{x=4} = \frac{1}{EI}\left(-12.778\times(4)^2+269.636 \vdots +15\times[4-4]^2\right) = \frac{65.188}{EI}\text{ m}$$

$$\theta_C = \left.\frac{d\Delta}{dx}\right|_{x=7} = \frac{1}{EI}\left(-12.778\times(7)^2+269.636 \vdots +15\times[7-4]^2 \vdots +20\times[7-7]^2\right) = \frac{-221.43}{EI}\text{ m}$$

(iii) The values of deflection at the loading points:

$$\Delta_D = \left.\Delta\right|_{x=4} = \frac{1}{EI}\left(-4.259\times(4)^3+269.636\times(4) \vdots +5\times[4-4]^3\right) = \frac{805.968}{EI}\text{ m}$$

$$\Delta_C = \left.\Delta\right|_{x=7} = \frac{1}{EI}\left(-4.259\times(7)^3+269.636\times(7) \vdots +5\times[7-4]^3 \vdots +6.667[7-7]^3\right)$$

$$= \frac{561.615}{EI}\text{ m}$$

(iv) Maximum deflection:

The maximum deflection in simply supported beams occurs where the direction of slope changes (i.e., $d\Delta/dx = 0$). Assume the direction of slope changes in the first segment (i.e., BD). Therefore, only the first segment should be considered.

$$\frac{d\Delta}{dx} = \frac{1}{EI}\left(-12.778x^2+269.636\right) = 0$$

$$-12.778x^2+269.636 = 0 \Rightarrow x_1 = -4.594 \text{ and } x_2 = +4.594$$

Both the values of x are inadmissible because they do not lie in the segment BD. Therefore, the assumption is not correct.

Now, assume the direction of slope changes in the second segment (i.e., DC). Therefore, the first and second segments together should be considered.

$$\frac{d\Delta}{dx} = \frac{1}{EI}\left(-12.778x^2+269.636 \vdots +15[x-4]^2\right) = 0$$

$$2.222x^2+120x+509.636 = 0 \Rightarrow x_1 = 49.359 \text{ and } x_2 = +4.647$$

Therefore, $x = 4.647$ m is the admissible root.

$$\Delta_{max} = \left.\Delta\right|_{x=4.647} = \frac{1}{EI}\left(-4.259\times(4.647)^3+269.636\times(4.647) \vdots +5\times[4.647-4]^3\right)$$

$$= \frac{826.961}{EI}\text{ m}$$

Example 2.17: A simply supported beam of span 6 m is subjected to three concentrated loads of 60 kN, 100 kN and 40 kN at 1 m, 3 m and 4 m respectively from the left support. Using the Macaulay's method, determine the maximum slope and deflection.

Solution:

The simply supported beam with three point loads is shown in Figure 2.23.

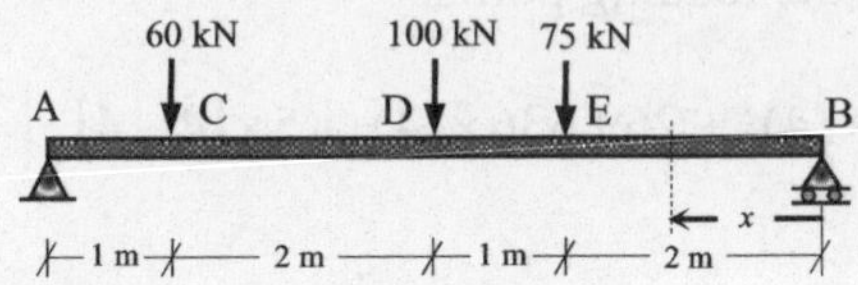

Figure 2.23 Simply supported beam with three point loads (Example 2.17)

The reactions at the supports are obtained by applying the equilibrium conditions as

$$\sum F_y = 0 \Rightarrow V_A + V_B - 60 - 100 - 75 = 0$$

$$\Rightarrow V_A + V_B = 235$$

$$\sum M_B = 0 \Rightarrow V_A \times 5 - 60 \times 5 - 100 \times 3 - 75 \times 2 = 0$$

Therefore, $V_A = 125.0$ kN and $V_B = 110.0$ kN.

By taking B as origin, the moment of all the forces on the right of the section is

$$M = V_B \times x \,\vdots - 75 \times [x-2] \,\vdots - 100 \times [x-3] \,\vdots - 60 \times [x-5]$$

$$= 110x \,\vdots - 75[x-2] \,\vdots - 100[x-3] \,\vdots - 60[x-5]$$

The expression is partitioned by dotted lines for different segments. The governing differential equation of the elastic curve after substituting M is

$$EI\frac{d^2\Delta}{dx^2} = -110x \,\vdots + 75[x-2] \,\vdots + 100[x-3] \,\vdots + 60[x-5]$$

The first and second integrations yield the expressions for slope and deflection respectively as

$$EI\frac{d\Delta}{dx} = -110 \times \frac{x^2}{2} + C_1 \,\vdots + 75 \times \frac{[x-2]^2}{2} \,\vdots + 100 \times \frac{[x-3]^2}{2} \,\vdots + 60 \times \frac{[x-5]^2}{2}$$

$$EI\,\Delta = -110 \times \frac{x^3}{6} + C_1 \times x + C_2 \,\vdots + 75 \times \frac{[x-2]^3}{6} \,\vdots + 100 \times \frac{[x-3]^3}{6} \,\vdots + 60 \times \frac{[x-5]^3}{6}$$

where C_1 and C_2 are the constants of integration, which need to be evaluated using the boundary conditions as follows.

BC (i): At the roller support B, the value of deflection is zero, $x=0 \rightarrow \Delta=0$
BC (ii): At the hinged support A, the value of deflection is zero, $x=6 \rightarrow \Delta=0$

Since both the boundary conditions are corresponding to the deflection at two locations, only deflection equation should be used for evaluating the constants C_1 and C_2.
By applying the first boundary condition;

$$EI\ (0)=-110\times\frac{(0)^3}{6}+C_1\times(0)+C_2$$

$$\Rightarrow C_2=0$$

By applying the second boundary condition and the substituting the value of C_2;

$$EI\ (0)=-110\times\frac{(6)^3}{6}+C_1\times(6)+0\vdots+75\times\frac{[6-2]^3}{6}\vdots+100\times\frac{[6-3]^3}{6}\vdots+60\times\frac{[6-5]^3}{6}$$

$$\Rightarrow C_1=450.0$$

Therefore, the complete expressions for slope and deflection;

$$\frac{d\Delta}{dx}=\frac{1}{EI}\left(-55x^2+450\vdots+37.5[x-2]^2\vdots+50[x-3]^2\vdots+30[x-5]^2\right) \qquad (2.87)$$

$$\Delta=\frac{1}{EI}\left(-18.333x^3+450x\vdots+12.5[x-2]^3\vdots+16.667[x-3]^3\vdots+10[x-5]^3\right) \qquad (2.88)$$

(i) Maximum slope:
The maximum slope in simply supported beam occurs at one of the support locations.

$$\theta_B=\left.\frac{d\Delta}{dx}\right|_{x=0}=\frac{1}{EI}\left(-55\times(0)^2+450\right)=\frac{450}{EI}\text{ radians}$$

$$\theta_A=\left.\frac{d\Delta}{dx}\right|_{x=6}=\frac{1}{EI}\left(-55\times(6)^2+450\vdots+37.5\times[6-2]^2\vdots+50\times[6-3]^2\vdots+30\times[6-5]^2\right)$$

$$=\frac{-450}{EI}\text{ radians}$$

Therefore, the maximum slope is $\theta_{max}=\frac{450}{EI}$ radians

(ii) Maximum deflection:
The maximum deflection in simply supported beams occurs where the direction of slope changes (i.e., $d\Delta/dx=0$). Since the values of slope at the supports (i.e., ends) are same but opposite in sign, the change of sign mostly occurs around the mid-point. Assume the direction of slope changes in the second segment (i.e., ED). Therefore, the first and second segments together are considered.

$$\frac{d\Delta}{dx}=\frac{1}{EI}\left(-55x^2+450\vdots+37.5[x-2]^2\right)=0$$

$$-17.5x^2 - 150x + 600 = 0$$

$$\Rightarrow x_1 = 2.971 \text{ and } x_2 = -11.542$$

Therefore, $x = 2.971$ m is the admissible solution.

$$\Delta_{\max} = \Delta\Big|_{x=2.971} = \frac{1}{EI}\left(-18.333\times(2.971)^3 + 450\times(2.971) + 12.5[2.971-2]^3\right) = \frac{867.619}{EI}\text{ m}$$

Note: The deflection at the mid-span is, $\Delta_{\text{mid-spam}} = \Delta\Big|_{x=3} = \dfrac{867.509}{EI}$ m

Example 2.18: A simply supported beam of span 10 m is subjected to a uniformly distributed load of 10 kN/m over a span of 6 m from the left support, and a point load of 20 kN at 3 m from the right support. Using the Macaulay's method, determine the maximum slope and deflection.

Solution:

The simply supported beam with multiple loads is shown in Figure 2.24.

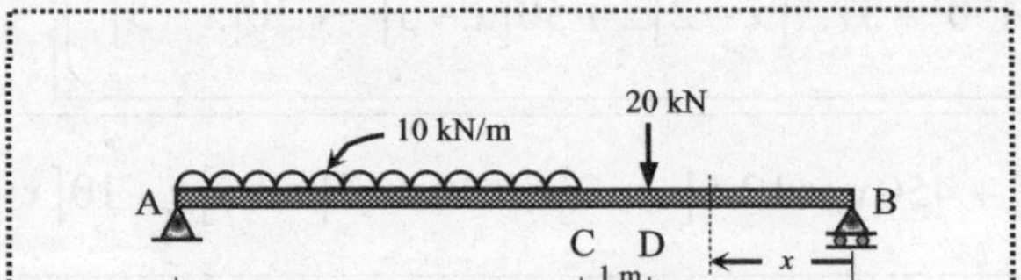

Figure 2.24 Simply supported beam with multiple loads (Example 2.18)

The reactions at the supports are obtained by applying the equilibrium conditions as

$$\sum F_y = 0 \Rightarrow V_A + V_B - 10\times 6 - 20 = 0$$

$$\Rightarrow V_A + V_B = 80$$

$$\sum M_B = 0 \Rightarrow V_A \times 10 - 10\times 6\times\left(\frac{6}{2}+4\right) - 20\times 3 = 0$$

$$V_A = 48.0 \text{ kN}$$

$$V_B = 32.0 \text{ kN}$$

By taking B as origin, the moment of all the forces on the right of the section is

$$M = V_B \times x - 20\times[x-3] - 10\times[x-4]\times\frac{[x-4]}{2} = 32x - 20[x-3] - 5[x-4]^2$$

The expression is partitioned by dotted lines for different segments. The governing differential equation of the elastic curve is

$$EI\frac{d^2\Delta}{dx^2} = -32x \vdots + 20[x-3] \vdots + 5[x-4]^2$$

The first and second integrations yield the expressions for slope and deflection respectively as

$$EI\frac{d\Delta}{dx} = -32\times\frac{x^2}{2} + C_1 \vdots + 20\times\frac{[x-3]^2}{2} \vdots + 5\times\frac{[x-4]^3}{3}$$

$$EI\,\Delta = -32\times\frac{x^3}{6} + C_1\times x + C_2 \vdots + 20\times\frac{[x-3]^3}{6} \vdots + 5\times\frac{[x-4]^4}{12}$$

where C_1 and C_2 are the constants of integration, which need to be evaluated using the boundary conditions as follows.

BC (i): At the roller support B, the value of deflection is zero, $x=0 \rightarrow \Delta=0$

BC (ii): At the hinged support A, the value of deflection is zero, $x=10 \rightarrow \Delta=0$

Since both the boundary conditions are corresponding to the deflection at two locations, only deflection equation should be used for evaluating the constants C_1 and C_2.
By applying the first boundary condition;

$$EI\ (0) = -32\times\frac{(0)^3}{6} + C_1\times(0) + C_2$$

$$\Rightarrow C_2 = 0$$

By applying the second boundary condition and the substituting the value of C_2;

$$EI\ (0) = -32\times\frac{10^3}{6} + C_1\times(10) + (0) \vdots + 20\times\frac{[10-3]^3}{6} \vdots + 5\times\frac{[10-4]^4}{12}$$

$$\Rightarrow C_1 = 365.0$$

Therefore, the complete expressions for slope and deflection:

$$\boxed{\frac{d\Delta}{dx} = \frac{1}{EI}\left(-16x^2 + 365 \vdots + 10[x-3]^2 \vdots + 1.667[x-4]^3\right)} \quad (2.89)$$

$$\boxed{\Delta = \frac{1}{EI}\left(-5.333x^3 + 365x \vdots + 3.333[x-3]^3 \vdots + 0.417[x-4]^4\right)} \quad (2.90)$$

(iii) Maximum slope:

The maximum slope in simply supported beam occurs at one of the support locations.

$$\theta_B = \left.\frac{d\Delta}{dx}\right|_{x=0} = \frac{1}{EI}\left(-16\times(0)^2 + 365\right) = \frac{365}{EI}\ \text{radians}$$

$$\theta_A = \left.\frac{d\Delta}{dx}\right|_{x=10} = \frac{1}{EI}\left(-16\times(10)^2 + 365 \vdots + 10\times[10-3]^2 \vdots + 1.667\times[10-4]^3\right)$$

$$= \frac{-384.928}{EI} \text{ radians}$$

Therefore, the maximum slope is $\theta_{max} = \dfrac{384.928}{EI}$ radians

(iv) Maximum deflection:

The maximum deflection in simply supported beam occurs where the direction of slope changes (i.e., $d\Delta/dx = 0$). Since the values of the slopes at end ends are nearly same but opposite in sign, the change of sign mostly occurs around the mid-point. Assume the direction of slope changes in the third segment (i.e., CA). Therefore, all the three segments together are considered.

$$\frac{d\Delta}{dx} = \frac{1}{EI}\left(-16x^2 + 365 \vdots +10[x-3]^2 \vdots +1.667[x-4]^3\right) = 0$$

$$1.667x^3 - 26x^2 + 20x + 348.312 = 0$$

$$x_1 = 13.580,\ x_2 = 5.058 \text{ and } x_3 = -3.042$$

Therefore, $x = 5.058$ m is the admissible solution.

$$\Delta_{max} = \Delta|_{x=5.058} = \frac{1}{EI}\left(\begin{array}{l} -5.333\times(5.058)^3 + 365\times(5.058) \vdots +3.333\times[5.058-3]^3 \vdots \\ +0.417\times[5.058-4]^4 \end{array}\right)$$

$$= \frac{1185.650}{EI} \text{ m}$$

Example 2.19: A simply supported beam of span 10 m is subjected to a point load of 50 kN at 6 m from the right support, and a uniformly distributed load of 10 kN/m spanning over 6 m from the left hand support. Determine the maximum slope and deflection.

Solution:

The simply supported beam with multiple loads is shown in Figure 2.25.

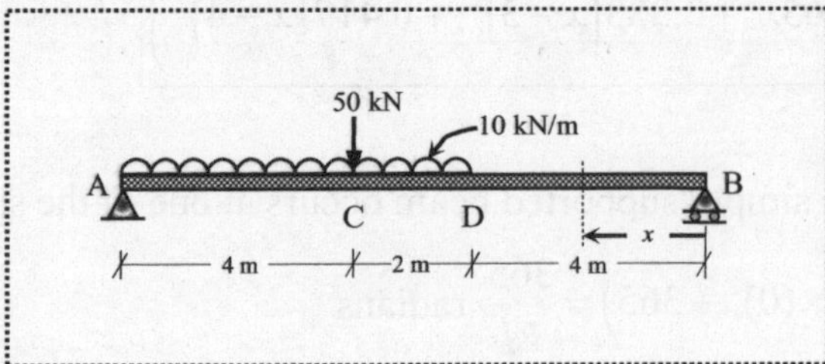

Figure 2.25 Simply supported beam with multiple loads (Example 2.19)

The reactions at the supports are obtained by applying the equilibrium conditions as

$$\sum F_y = 0 \Rightarrow V_A + V_B - 10\times 6 - 50 = 0$$

$$\Rightarrow V_A + V_B = 110$$

$$\sum M_B = 0 \Rightarrow V_A \times 10 - 10\times 6\times\left(\frac{6}{2}+4\right) - 50\times 6 = 0$$

Therefore, $V_A = 72.0$ kN and $V_B = 38.0$ kN.

By taking B as origin, the moment of all the forces on the right of the section is

$$M = V_B \times x \,\vdots - 10\times[x-4]\times\frac{[x-4]}{2} \,\vdots - 50\times[x-6] = 38x \,\vdots - 5[x-4]^2 \,\vdots - 50[x-6]$$

The expression is partitioned by dotted lines for different segments. The governing differential equation of the elastic curve is

$$EI\frac{d^2\Delta}{dx^2} = -38x \,\vdots + 5[x-4]^2 \,\vdots + 50[x-6]$$

The first and second integrations yield the expressions for slope and deflection respectively as

$$EI\frac{d\Delta}{dx} = -38\times\frac{x^2}{2} + C_1 \,\vdots + 5\times\frac{[x-4]^3}{3} \,\vdots + 50\times\frac{[x-6]^2}{2}$$

$$EI\,\Delta = -38\times\frac{x^3}{6} + C_1\times x + C_2 \,\vdots + 5\times\frac{[x-4]^4}{12} \,\vdots + 50\times\frac{[x-6]^3}{6}$$

where C_1 and C_2 are the constants of integration, which need to be evaluated using the boundary conditions as follows.

BC (i): At the roller support B, the value of deflection is zero, $x = 0 \rightarrow \Delta = 0$

BC (ii): At the hinged support A, the value of deflection is zero, $x = 10 \rightarrow \Delta = 0$

Since both the boundary conditions are corresponding to the deflection at two locations, only deflection equation should be used for evaluating the constants C_1 and C_2.

By applying the first boundary condition;

$$EI\,(0) = -38\times\frac{(0)^3}{6} + C_1\cdot(0) + C_2$$

$$\Rightarrow C_2 = 0$$

By applying the second boundary condition and the substituting the value of C_2;

$$EI\,(0) = -38\times\frac{(10)^3}{6} + C_1\times(10) + 0 \,\vdots + 5\times\frac{[10-4]^4}{12} \,\vdots + 50\times\frac{[10-6]^3}{6}$$

$$\Rightarrow C_1 = 526.0$$

Therefore, the complete expressions for slope and deflection:

$$\frac{d\Delta}{dx}=\frac{1}{EI}\left(-19x^2+526\vdots+1.667[x-4]^3\vdots+25[x-6]^2\right) \tag{2.91}$$

$$\Delta=\frac{1}{EI}\left(-6.333x^3+526x\vdots+0.417[x-4]^4\vdots+8.333[x-6]^3\right) \tag{2.92}$$

(i) Maximum slope:

The maximum slope in simply supported beam occurs at one of the support locations.

$$\theta_B=\left.\frac{d\Delta}{dx}\right|_{x=0}=\frac{1}{EI}\left(-19\times(0)^2+526\right)=\frac{526}{EI}$$

$$\theta_A=\left.\frac{d\Delta}{dx}\right|_{x=10}=\frac{1}{EI}\left(-19\times(10)^2+526\vdots+1.667\times[10-4]^3\vdots+25\times[10-6]^2\right)=\frac{-613.928}{EI}\text{ radians}$$

Therefore, the maximum slope is $\theta_{max}=\frac{613.928}{EI}$ radians

(ii) Maximum deflection:

The maximum deflection in simply supported beam occurs where the direction of slope changes (i.e., $d\Delta/dx=0$). Assume the direction of slope changes in the second segment (i.e., DC).

$$\frac{d\Delta}{dx}=\frac{1}{EI}\left(-19x^2+526\vdots+1.667[x-4]^3\right)=0$$

$$1.667x^3-39x^2+80x+419.312=0$$

$$\Rightarrow x_1=20.447,\ x_2=5.279 \text{ and } x_3=-2.330$$

Therefore, $x=5.279$ m is the admissible root.

$$\Delta_{max}=\Delta|_{x=5.279}=\frac{1}{EI}\left(-6.333\times(5.279)^3+526\times(5.279)\vdots+0.417\times[5.279-4]^4\right)$$

$$=\frac{1846.195}{EI}\text{ m}$$

Note: In Examples 2.16–2.19, the moment expression can be written by keeping the left support (i.e., A) as origin. However, in Examples 2.18 and 2.19, when the moment expression is written by taking A as origin, as the uniformly distributed load is discontinued, additional load should be assumed both in downward and in upward directions for the remaining portion till the end (i.e., B). Therefore, if the distributed load is given in the left end, then taking origin from the right end, and vise-versa would simplify the moment equation.

Example 2.20: A simply supported beam of span 10 m is subjected to two concentrated loads of 30 kN and 40 kN at 2 m and 8 m from the left support, and a uniformly distributed load of 10 kN/m spanning over 5 m starting at 3 m from the left support. Determine the maximum slope and deflection.

Solution:

The simply supported beam with multiple loads is shown in Figure 2.26(i).

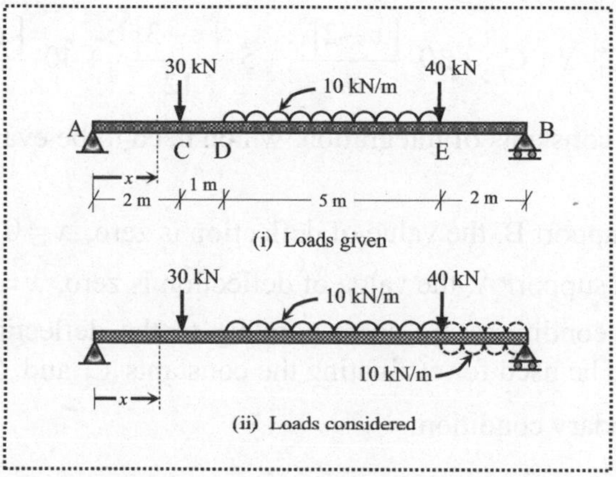

Figure 2.26 Simply supported beam with multiple loads (Example 2.20)

The reactions at the supports are obtained by applying the equilibrium conditions as

$$\sum F_y = 0 \Rightarrow V_A + V_B - 30 - 10\times 5 - 40 = 0$$

$$\Rightarrow V_A + V_B = 120$$

$$\sum M_B = 0 \Rightarrow V_A \times 10 - 30\times 8 - 10\times 5\times\left(\frac{5}{2}+2\right) - 40\times 2 = 0$$

$$V_A = 54.5 \text{ kN}$$

$$V_B = 65.5 \text{ kN}$$

For getting a continuous function (due to the distributed load) in all segments while taking A as origin, the uniformly distributed load of 10 kN/m is added in the segment EB both in downward and upward directions as shown in Figure 2.26(ii). By taking A as origin, the moment of all the forces on the left of the section is

$$M = V_A \times x \,\vdots - 30\times[x-2]\,\vdots - 10\times[x-3]\times\frac{[x-3]}{2}\,\vdots - 40\times[x-8] + 10\times[x-8]\times\frac{[x-8]}{2}$$

$$= 54.5x \,\vdots - 30[x-2]\,\vdots - 5[x-3]^2\,\vdots - 40[x-8] + 5[x-8]^2$$

The expression is partitioned by dotted lines for different segments. The governing differential equation of the elastic curve is

$$EI\frac{d^2\Delta}{dx^2} = -54.5x \vdots +30[x-2] \vdots +5[x-3]^2 \vdots +40[x-8]-5[x-8]^2$$

The first and second integrations yield the expressions for slope and deflection respectively as

$$EI\frac{d\Delta}{dx} = -54.5\times\frac{x^2}{2}+C_1 \vdots +30\cdot\frac{[x-2]^2}{2} \vdots +5\cdot\frac{[x-3]^3}{3} \vdots +40\cdot\frac{[x-8]^2}{2}-5\cdot\frac{[x-8]^3}{3}$$

$$EI\,\Delta = -54.5\times\frac{x^3}{6}+C_1\cdot x+C_2 \vdots +30\cdot\frac{[x-2]^3}{6} \vdots +5\cdot\frac{[x-3]^4}{12} \vdots +40\cdot\frac{[x-8]^3}{6}-5\cdot\frac{[x-8]^4}{12}$$

where C_1 and C_2 are the constants of integration, which need to be evaluated using the boundary conditions as follows.

BC (i): At the roller support B, the value of deflection is zero, $x=0 \rightarrow \Delta=0$

BC (ii): At the hinged support A, the value of deflection is zero, $x=10 \rightarrow \Delta=0$

Since both the boundary conditions are corresponding to the deflection at two locations, only deflection equation should be used for evaluating the constants C_1 and C_2.

By applying the first boundary condition;

$$EI\,(0) = -54.5\times\frac{(0)^3}{6}+C_1\times(0)+C_2$$

$$\Rightarrow C_2 = 0$$

By applying the second boundary condition and the substituting the value of C_2;

$$EI\,(0) = \left(\begin{array}{l} -54.5\times\frac{10^3}{6}+C_1\times(10)+0 \vdots +30\times\frac{[10-2]^3}{6} \vdots +5\times\frac{[10-3]^4}{12} \vdots \\ +40\times\frac{[10-8]^3}{6}-5\times\frac{[10-8]^4}{12} \end{array}\right)$$

$$\Rightarrow C_1 = 547.625$$

Therefore, the complete expressions for slope and deflection:

$$\frac{d\Delta}{dx} = \frac{1}{EI}\left(\begin{array}{l} -27.25x^2+547.625 \vdots +15[x-2]^2 \vdots +1.667[x-3]^3 \vdots \\ +20[x-8]^2-1.667[x-8]^3 \end{array}\right) \qquad (2.93)$$

$$\Delta = \frac{1}{EI}\left(\begin{array}{l} -9.083x^3+547.625x \vdots +5[x-2]^3 \vdots +0.417[x-3]^4 \vdots \\ +6.667[x-8]^3-0.417[x-8]^4 \end{array}\right) \qquad (2.94)$$

(iii) Maximum slope:

The maximum slope in simply supported beam occurs at one of the support locations.

$$\theta_A = \left.\frac{d\Delta}{dx}\right|_{x=0} = \frac{1}{EI}\left(-27.25\times(0)^2 + 547.625\right) = \frac{547.625}{EI} \text{ radians}$$

$$\theta_B = \left.\frac{d\Delta}{dx}\right|_{x=10} = \frac{1}{EI}\left(\begin{array}{l} -27.25\times 10^2 + 547.625 \vdots + 15\times[10-2]^2 \vdots + 1.667\times[10-3]^3 \vdots \\ +20\times[10-8]^2 - 1.667\times[10-8]^3 \end{array}\right)$$

$$= \frac{-578.930}{EI} \text{ radians}$$

Therefore, the maximum slope is $\theta_{max} = \dfrac{578.930}{EI}$ radians

(iv) Maximum deflection:

The maximum deflection in simply supported beam occurs where the direction of slope changes (i.e., $d\Delta/dx = 0$). Assume the direction of slope changes in the third segment (i.e., DE).

$$\frac{d\Delta}{dx} = \frac{1}{EI}\left(-27.25x^2 + 547.625 \vdots + 15[x-2]^2 \vdots + 1.667[x-3]^3\right) = 0$$

$$1.667x^3 - 27.25x^2 - 15x + 562.625 = 0$$

$$\Rightarrow x_1 = 15.526,\ x_2 = 5.091 \text{ and } x_3 = -4.270$$

Therefore, $x = 5.091$ m is the admissible root.

$$\Delta_{max} = \Delta|_{x=5.091} = \frac{1}{EI}\left(\begin{array}{l} -9.083\times(5.091)^3 + 547.625\times(5.091) \vdots + 5\times[5.091-2]^3 \vdots \\ +0.417\times[5.091-3]^4 \end{array}\right)$$

$$= \frac{1745.090}{EI} \text{ m}$$

Example 2.21: An overhanging beam of span 10 m is subjected to multiple lateral loads as shown in Figure 2.27(i). Determine the maximum slope and the maximum deflection.

Solution:

For getting a continuous function (due to the distributed load) in all segments while taking A as origin, the uniformly distributed load of 10 kN/m is added between C and E both in downward and upward directions as shown in Figure 2.27(ii).

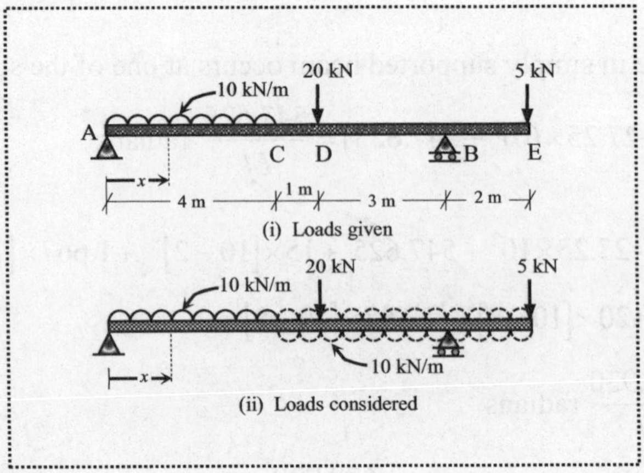

Figure 2.27 Overhanging beam with multiple loads (Example 2.21)

The reactions at the supports are obtained by applying the equilibrium conditions as

$$\sum F_y = 0 \Rightarrow V_A + V_B - 10\times 4 - 20 - 5 = 0$$

$$\Rightarrow V_A + V_B = 65$$

$$\sum M_A = 0 \Rightarrow -5\times 10 + V_B\times 8 - 20\times 5 - 10\times 4\times (4/2) = 0$$

Therefore, $V_A = 36.25$ kN and $V_B = 28.75$ kN.

By taking A as origin, the moment of all the forces on the left of the section is

$$M = V_A\times x - 10\times x\times \frac{x}{2} \vdots + 10\times[x-4]\times\frac{[x-4]}{2} \vdots - 20\times[x-5] \vdots + V_B\times[x-8]$$

$$= 36.25x - 5x^2 \vdots + 5[x-4]^2 \vdots - 20[x-5] \vdots + 28.75[x-8]$$

The expression is partitioned by dotted lines for different segments. The governing differential equation of the elastic curve is

$$EI\frac{d^2\Delta}{dx^2} = -36.25x + 5x^2 \vdots - 5[x-4]^2 \vdots + 20[x-5] \vdots - 28.75[x-8]$$

The first and second integrations yield the expressions for slope and deflection respectively as

$$EI\frac{d\Delta}{dx} = -36.25\times\frac{x^2}{2} + 5\times\frac{x^3}{3} + C_1 \vdots - 5\times\frac{[x-4]^3}{3} \vdots + 20\times\frac{[x-5]^2}{2} \vdots - 28.75\times\frac{[x-8]^2}{2}$$

$$EI\,\Delta = -36.25\times\frac{x^3}{6} + 5\times\frac{x^4}{12} + C_1\times x + C_2 \vdots - 5\times\frac{[x-4]^4}{12} \vdots + 20\times\frac{[x-5]^3}{6} \vdots - 28.75\times\frac{[x-8]^3}{6}$$

where C_1 and C_2 are the constants of integration, which need to be evaluated using the boundary conditions as follows.

BC (i): At the hinged support A, the value of deflection is zero, $x=0 \rightarrow \Delta=0$

BC (ii): At the roller support B, the value of deflection is zero, $x=8 \rightarrow \Delta=0$

Since both the boundary conditions are corresponding to the deflection at two locations, only deflection equation should be used for evaluating the constants C_1 and C_2.

By applying the first boundary condition;

$$EI\ (0)=-36.25\times\frac{(0)^3}{6}+5\times\frac{(0)^4}{12}+C_1\times(0)+C_2$$

$$\Rightarrow C_2=0$$

By applying the second boundary condition and the substituting the value of C_2;

$$EI(0)=-36.25\times\frac{(8)^3}{6}+5\times\frac{(8)^4}{12}+C_1\times(8)+0\vdots-5\times\frac{[8-4]^4}{12}\vdots+20\times\frac{[8-5]^3}{6}\vdots-28.75\times\frac{[8-8]^3}{6}$$

$$\Rightarrow C_1=175.417$$

Therefore, the complete expressions for slope and deflection:

$$\frac{d\Delta}{dx}=\frac{1}{EI}\left(\begin{array}{l}-18.125x^2+1.667x^3+175.417\vdots-1.667[x-4]^3\vdots+10[x-5]^2\vdots\\-14.375[x-8]^2\end{array}\right) \quad (2.95)$$

$$\Delta=\frac{1}{EI}\left(\begin{array}{l}-6.042x^3+0.417x^4+175.417x\vdots-0.417[x-4]^4\vdots+3.333[x-5]^3\vdots\\-4.792[x-8]^3\end{array}\right) \quad (2.96)$$

(i) Maximum slope:

The maximum slope in overhanging beam occurs at either one of the support locations or at the free end of the overhang.

$$\theta_A=\left.\frac{d\Delta}{dx}\right|_{x=0}=\frac{1}{EI}\left(-18.125\times(0)^2+1.667\times(0)^3+175.417\right)=\frac{175.417}{EI}\text{ radians}$$

$$\theta_B=\left.\frac{d\Delta}{dx}\right|_{x=8}=\frac{1}{EI}\left(-18.125\times8^2+1.667\times8^3+175.417\vdots-1.667\times[8-4]^3\vdots+10\times[8-5]^2\right)$$

$$=\frac{-147.767}{EI}\text{ radians}$$

$$\theta_B=\left.\frac{d\Delta}{dx}\right|_{x=10}=\frac{1}{EI}\left(\begin{array}{l}-18.125\times10^2+1.667\times10^3+175.417\vdots-1.667\times[10-4]^3\vdots\\+10\times[10-5]^2\vdots-14.375\times[10-8]^2\end{array}\right)$$

$$= \frac{-137.655}{EI} \text{ radians}$$

Therefore, the maximum slope is $\theta_{max} = \dfrac{175.417}{EI}$ radians

(ii) Maximum deflection:

The maximum deflection in overhanging beam occurs where the direction of slope changes (i.e., $d\Delta/dx = 0$) between the supports or at the free end.

Assume the direction of slope changes in the first segment (i.e., AC).

$$\frac{d\Delta}{dx} = \frac{1}{EI}\left(-18.125x^2 + 1.667x^3 + 175.417\right) = 0$$

$$1.667x^3 - 18.125x^2 + 175.417 = 0 \Rightarrow x_1 = -2.777,\ x_2 = 9.771 \text{ and } x_3 = 3.879$$

Therefore, $x = 3.879$ m is the admissible solution.

$$\Delta\big|_{x=3.879} = \frac{1}{EI}\left(-6.042\times(3.879)^3 + 0.417\times(3.879)^4 + 175.417\times(3.879)\right) = \frac{422.205}{EI} \text{ m}$$

$$\Delta_E = \Delta\big|_{x=10} = \frac{1}{EI}\begin{pmatrix} -6.042\times(10)^3 + 0.417\times(10)^4 + 175.417\times(10) \\ -0.417\times[10-4]^4 + 3.333\times[10-5]^3 - 4.792\times[10-8]^3 \end{pmatrix} = \frac{-279.973}{EI} \text{ m}$$

Therefore, $\Delta_{max} = \dfrac{422.205}{EI}$ m

The negative sign of Δ_E indicates that the deflection is in the opposite direction (i.e., upwards).

The standard formulas can also be used to determine the slope and deflection. This mainly helps in determining the maximum slope and the maximum deflection for cantilever beams subjected to multiple loads. Consider a cantilever beam with two point loads W_1 and W_2 as shown in Figure 2.28(i). As already seen, the maximum slope and the maximum deflection occur at the free end (i.e., at B). Therefore, the values of slope and deflection at B can be obtained by superimposing the individual effects due to the point loads W_1 and W_2 at B.

The deflected shape due to W_1 is a nonlinear curve between A and B' as shown in Figure 2.28(ii). However, the deflected shape due to W_2 is a nonlinear curve between A and C', and a linear curve (i.e., inclined line) between C' and B' as shown in Figure 2.28(iii). Therefore, the slope and the deflection at B due to W_1 can be determined directly using the respective formulas. However, the slope and the deflection at B due to W_2 cannot be directly obtained as the formulas are not available.

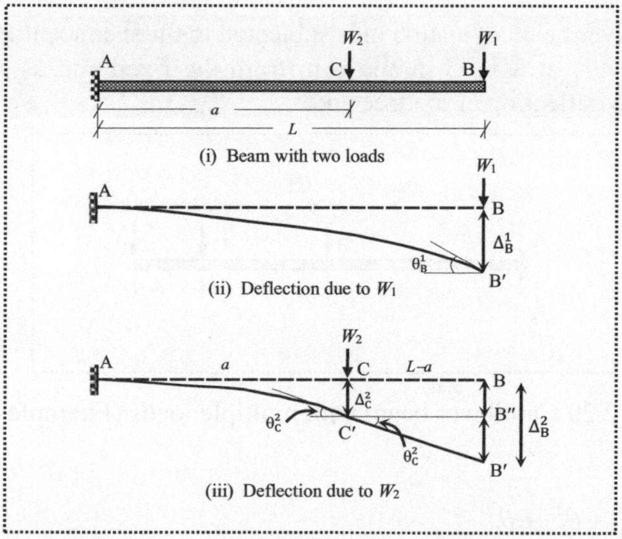

Figure 2.28 Cantilever beam with multiple loads

(i) Slope at B (θ_B):

The slope at B, $\theta_B = \theta_B^1 + \theta_B^2$

where, θ_B^1 is the slope at B due to W_1; $\theta_B^1 = \dfrac{W_1 L^2}{2EI}$

θ_B^2 is the slope at B due to W_2 which is equal to θ_B^2 as the curve C'B' is linear;

$$\theta_B^2 = \theta_C^2 = \frac{W_2 a^2}{2EI}$$

(ii) Deflection at B (Δ_B):

The deflection at B, $\Delta_B = \Delta_B^1 + \Delta_B^2$

where, Δ_B^1 is the deflection at B due to W_1; $\Delta_B^1 = \dfrac{W_1 L^3}{3EI}$

Δ_B^2 is the deflection at B due to W_2; $\Delta_B^2 = \text{BB}'' + \text{B}''\text{B}' = \Delta_C^2 + \theta_C^2 \times (L-a)$

$$= \frac{W_2 a^3}{3EI} + \frac{W_2 a^2}{2EI} \times (L-a)$$

The sign of the slope formulas (i.e., negative) for cantilever beams is ignored in the above calculations to avoid confusion while obtaining the deflections.

Example 2.22: A cantilever beam of span 6 m is subjected to three concentrated loads of 30 kN, 25 kN and 20 kN respectively at 3 m, 5 m and 6 m from the fixed end as shown in Figure 2.29. Determine the slope and deflection at the free end.

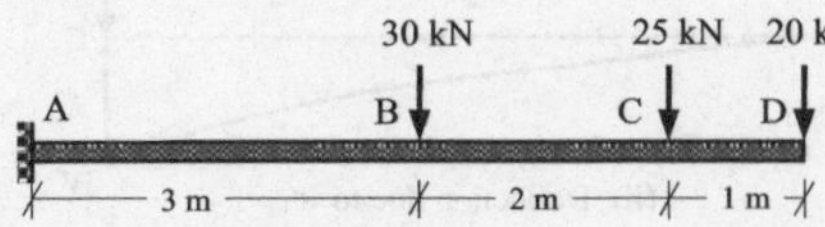

Figure 2.29 Cantilever beam with multiple loads (Example 2.22)

Solution:

The slope at D, $\theta_D = \theta_D^{20} + \theta_D^{25} + \theta_D^{30}$

Slope at D due to 20 kN; $\theta_D^{20} = \dfrac{20\times 6^2}{2EI} = \dfrac{360}{EI}$

Slope at D due to 25 kN (equal to slope at C); $\theta_D^{25} = \dfrac{25\times 5^2}{2EI} = \dfrac{312.5}{EI}$

Slope at D due to 30 kN (equal to slope at B); $\theta_D^{30} = \dfrac{30\times 3^2}{2EI} = \dfrac{135}{EI}$

Therefore, the slope at D, $\theta_D = \dfrac{360}{EI} + \dfrac{312.5}{EI} + \dfrac{135}{EI} = \dfrac{807.5}{EI}$ radians

The deflection at D, $\Delta_D = \Delta_D^{20} + \Delta_D^{25} + \Delta_D^{30}$

Deflection at D due to 20 kN; $\Delta_D^{20} = \dfrac{20\times 6^3}{3EI} = \dfrac{1440}{EI}$ m

Deflection at D due to 25 kN; $\Delta_D^{25} = \dfrac{25\times 5^3}{3EI} + \dfrac{25\times 5^2}{2EI}\times(6-5) = \dfrac{1354.167}{EI}$ m

Deflection at D due to 30 kN; $\Delta_D^{30} = \dfrac{30\times 3^3}{3EI} + \dfrac{30\times 3^2}{2EI}\times(6-3) = \dfrac{675}{EI}$ m

Therefore, the deflection at D, $\Delta_D = \dfrac{1440}{EI} + \dfrac{1354.167}{EI} + \dfrac{675}{EI} = \dfrac{3469.167}{EI}$ m

The above answers are same as the ones obtained using Macaulay's method in Example 2.11.

Example 2.23: A cantilever beam of span 6 m is subjected to three loads as shown in Figure 2.30. Determine the slope and deflection at the free end.

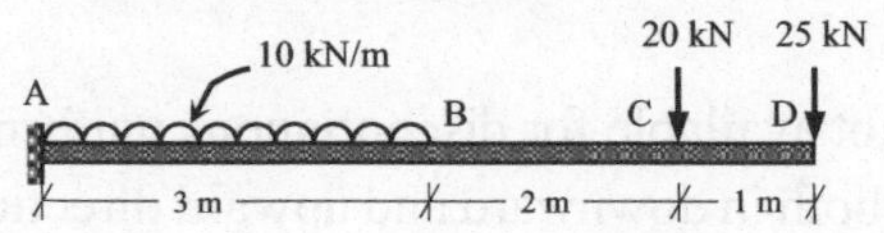

Figure 2.30 Cantilever beam with multiple loads (Example 2.23)

Solution:

The slope at D, $\theta_D = \theta_D^{25} + \theta_D^{20} + \theta_D^{10}$

Slope at D due to 25 kN; $\theta_D^{25} = \dfrac{25\times 6^2}{2EI} = \dfrac{450}{EI}$

Slope at D due to 20 kN (equal to slope at C); $\theta_D^{20} = \dfrac{20\times 5^2}{2EI} = \dfrac{250}{EI}$

Slope at D due to 10 kN/m (equal to slope at B); $\theta_D^{10} = \dfrac{10\times 3^3}{6EI} = \dfrac{45}{EI}$ (formula for UDL is used)

Therefore, the slope at D, $\theta_D = \dfrac{450}{EI} + \dfrac{250}{EI} + \dfrac{45}{EI} = \dfrac{745}{EI}$ radians

The deflection at D, $\Delta_D = \Delta_D^{25} + \Delta_D^{20} + \Delta_D^{10}$

Deflection at D due to 25 kN; $\Delta_D^{25} = \dfrac{25\times 6^3}{3EI} = \dfrac{1800}{EI}$ m

Deflection at D due to 20 kN; $\Delta_D^{20} = \dfrac{20\times 5^3}{3EI} + \dfrac{20\times 5^2}{2EI}\times(6-5) = \dfrac{1083.333}{EI}$ m

Deflection at D due to 10 kN; $\Delta_D^{10} = \dfrac{10\times 3^4}{8EI} + \dfrac{10\times 3^3}{6EI}\times(6-3) = \dfrac{236.25}{EI}$ m (formula for UDL)

Therefore, the deflection at D, $\Delta_D = \dfrac{1800}{EI} + \dfrac{1083.333}{EI} + \dfrac{236.25}{EI} = \dfrac{3119.583}{EI}$ m

The above answers are same as the ones obtained using Macaulay's method in Example 2.12.

Example 2.24: A cantilever beam of span 9 m is subjected to a point load of 30 kN at the free end, and a uniformly distributed load of 20 kN/m over a span of 4 m starting at 2 m from the fixed end as shown in Figure 2.31(i). Determine the slope and deflection at the free end.

Solution:

As the standard formulas are not available for discontinuous uniformly distributed load, the load is assumed over the segment AB both in downward and upward directions as shown in Figure 2.31(ii).

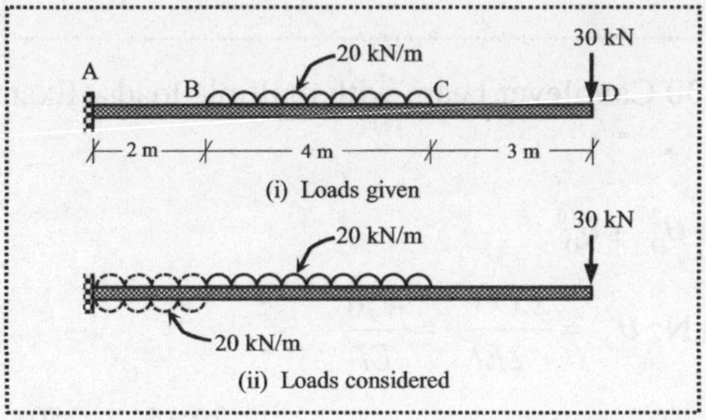

Figure 2.31 Cantilever beam with multiple loads (Example 2.24)

The slope at D, $\theta_D = \theta_D^{30} + \theta_D^{20} - \theta_D^{20upward}$

Slope at D due to 30 kN; $\theta_D^{30} = \dfrac{30 \times 9^2}{2EI} = \dfrac{1215}{EI}$

Slope at D due to 20 kN/m (equal to slope at C); $\theta_D^{20} = \dfrac{20 \times 6^3}{6EI} = \dfrac{720}{EI}$

Slope at D due to 20 kN/m (upward) (equal to slope at B); $\theta_D^{20upward} = \dfrac{20 \times 2^3}{6EI} = \dfrac{26.667}{EI}$

Therefore, the slope at D, $\theta_D = \dfrac{1215}{EI} + \dfrac{720}{EI} - \dfrac{26.667}{EI} = \dfrac{1908.333}{EI}$ radians

The deflection at D, $\Delta_D = \Delta_D^{30} + \Delta_D^{20} - \Delta_D^{20upward}$

Deflection at D due to 30 kN; $\Delta_D^{25} = \dfrac{30 \times 9^3}{3EI} = \dfrac{7290}{EI}$ m

Deflection at D due to 20 kN/m; $\Delta_D^{20} = \dfrac{20 \times 6^4}{8EI} + \dfrac{20 \times 6^3}{6EI} \times (9-6) = \dfrac{5400}{EI}$ m

Deflection at D due to 20 kN/m (upward); $\Delta_D^{20upward} = \dfrac{20 \times 2^4}{8EI} + \dfrac{20 \times 2^3}{6EI} \times (9-2) = \dfrac{226.667}{EI}$ m

Therefore, the deflection at D, $\Delta_D = \dfrac{7290}{EI} + \dfrac{5400}{EI} - \dfrac{226.667}{EI} = \dfrac{12463.333}{EI}$ m

The above answers are same as the ones obtained using Macaulay's method in Example 2.14.

The formulas for slope and deflection in cantilever and simply supported beams for standard loads are presented in Table 2.3.

Table 2.3 Formulas for slope and deflection

Beam	Slope	Deflection
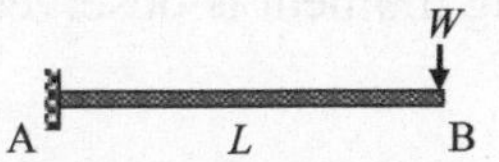	$\theta_A = 0$ $\theta_B = \dfrac{-WL^2}{2EI}$	$\Delta_A = 0$ $\Delta_B = \dfrac{WL^3}{3EI}$
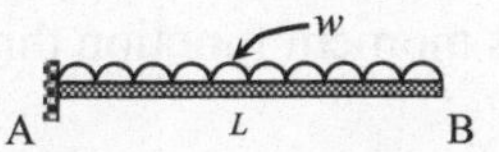	$\theta_A = 0$ $\theta_B = \dfrac{-wL^3}{6EI}$	$\Delta_A = 0$ $\Delta_B = \dfrac{wL^4}{8EI}$
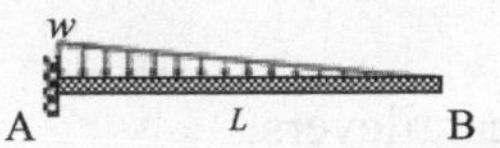	$\theta_A = 0$ $\theta_B = \dfrac{-wL^3}{24EI}$	$\Delta_A = 0$ $\Delta_B = \dfrac{wL^4}{30EI}$
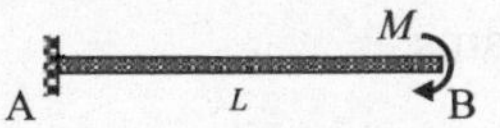	$\theta_A = 0$ $\theta_B = \dfrac{-ML}{EI}$	$\Delta_A = 0$ $\Delta_B = \dfrac{ML^2}{2EI}$
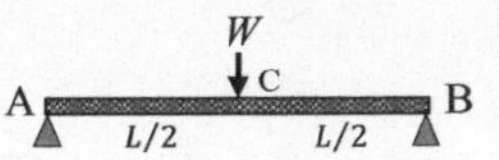	$\theta_A = \dfrac{-WL^2}{16EI}$ $\theta_B = \dfrac{WL^2}{16EI}$	$\Delta_A = \Delta_B = 0$ $\Delta_C = \dfrac{WL^3}{48EI}$
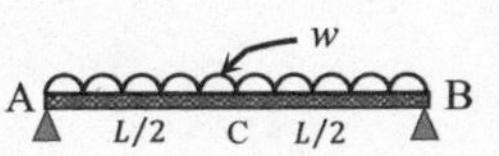	$\theta_A = \dfrac{-wL^3}{24EI}$ $\theta_B = \dfrac{wL^3}{24EI}$	$\Delta_A = \Delta_B = 0$ $\Delta_C = \dfrac{5}{384}\dfrac{wL^4}{EI}$
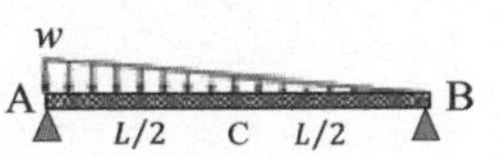	$\theta_A = \dfrac{-wL^3}{45EI}$ $\theta_B = \dfrac{7}{360}\dfrac{wL^3}{EI}$	$\Delta_A = \Delta_B = 0$ $\Delta_C = \dfrac{5}{768}\dfrac{wL^4}{EI}$ $\Delta_{max} = 0.006522\dfrac{wL^4}{EI}$ (at $0.481L$ from A)
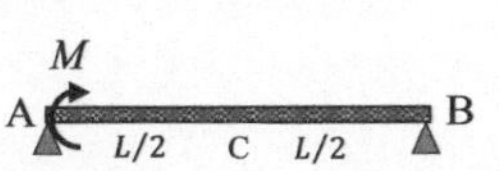	$\theta_A = \dfrac{-ML}{3EI}$ $\theta_B = \dfrac{ML}{6EI}$	$\Delta_A = \Delta_B = 0$ $\Delta_C = \dfrac{ML^2}{16EI}$ $\Delta_{max} = 0.06415\dfrac{ML^2}{EI}$ (at $0.423L$ from A)

UNIT SUMMARY

- ✓ When a structural member is subjected to lateral loads, slope is defined as the displacement in the rotational direction and the deflection is defined as the displacement in the linear direction.
- ✓ Stiffness is defined as the force required to cause the displacement.
- ✓ Governing differential equation of elastic curve when sagging moment is observed:

$$EI\frac{d^2\Delta}{dx^2} = -M$$

- ✓ The double integration method is effective when a continuous moment function throughout the length is possible.
- ✓ The known conditions of slope and deflection (usually zero values) at the ends are called boundary conditions.
- ✓ The maximum slope and deflection occur at the free end of cantilevers.
- ✓ The maximum slope occurs at the supports, and the maximum deflection occurs at a point where the direction of slope changes in simply supported beams.

EXERCISES

2.1. A cantilever beam of span 6 m is subjected to a point load of 20 kN at the tip, and a uniformly distributed load of 10 kN/m over a span of 4 m from the fixed end. Find the values of slope and deflection at the mid-span and free-end locations. Take the flexural rigidity as 6000 kNm^2.

2.2. A cantilever beam of span L is subjected to a uniformly varying load with w at the free end and zero at the fixed end. Derive the expressions for slope and deflection, and find the values of maximum slope and deflection.

2.3. A cantilever beam of span 9 m is subjected to 30 kN loads at every 3 m span. Find the maximum deflection if the cross-section is 200×300 mm, and the modulus of elasticity is 210×10^3 MPa.

2.4. A cantilever beam of span 6 m is subjected to a uniformly distributed load of 20 kN/m (downwards) over the half-span from the fixed support. Determine the point load (upwards) required at the free end to nullify the deflection (at the free end) caused due to the load applied (i.e., 20 kN/m).

2.5. Derive expressions for the slope and deflection of a cantilever beam subjected a triangular load (with zero intensity at the support and a peak value w at the free-end). Assume the beam to have a span L and a uniform flexural rigidity EI.

2.6. A simply supported beam is subjected to point loads of W each at every one-third of the span. Determine the values of maximum slope and deflection.

2.7. A simply supported beam if span 6 m is subjected to a uniformly distributed load of 25 kN/m over the half-span from the left support. Derive the expression for the slope and deflection, and determine the maximum slope and deflection.

2.8. Derive expressions for the slope and deflection of a simply supported beam subjected to a distributed gravity load of total magnitude W, having a triangular distribution (with zero intensity at the two supports and a peak value at the mid-span location). Assume the beam to have a span L and a uniform flexural rigidity EI.

2.9. A simply supported beam of span 10 m is subjected to a clockwise moment of 50 kNm at the mid-span. Determine the values of maximum slope and deflection.

2.10. A simply supported beam of span 8 m is subjected to a uniformly distributed load of 20 kN/m over the entire span, and point loads of 5 kN each at every 2 m. Find the values of maximum slope and deflection.

QR Code for *Slope and Deflection*

NPTEL Lecture: https://www.youtube.com/watch?v=q7G0RMtrKr8

3 Fixed and Continuous Beams

UNIT SPECIFICS

This unit discusses the following aspects.

- Concept of fixity and its advantages
- Force responses of fixed beams
- Force responses of continuous beams

RATIONALE

In general, many civil engineering structures are statically indeterminate. Analysis of statically indeterminate structures require understanding of both the force and displacement responses of statically determinate structures which are already covered in the earlier chapters. This chapter presents the procedure for analyzing statically indeterminate structures such as fixed and continuous beams for force responses.

UNIT OUTCOMES

List of outcomes of this unit is as follows.

U3-O1: Describe the concept of fixity
U3-O2: Describe the advantages of fixity
U3-O3: Describe the principles of superposition
U3-O4: Analysis of fixed beams
U3-O5: Analysis of continuous beams

Mapping of Unit-3 Outcomes with Course Outcomes *

	CO-1	CO-2	CO-3	CO-4	CO-5
U3-O1	1	1	3	2	1
U3-O2	1	2	3	2	1
U3-O3	1	1	3	2	1
U3-O4	1	3	3	2	1
U3-O5	1	3	3	2	1

* (1- Weak correlation; 2- Medium correlation; 3- Strong correlation)

3.1 Introduction

Statically determinate structures (e.g., cantilever and simply supported beams) can be solved by applying statics equilibrium equations. However, the solution of statically indeterminate structures is not straightforward due to their redundant nature. Most civil engineering structures are statically indeterminate, and the force responses of such structures are the primary requirement for the design. Therefore, it is essential to understand both the force and displacement responses of statically determinate structures for analyzing statically indeterminate structures such as fixed and continuous beams. The concepts covered in Chapter 2 for determining the slope and deflection of statically determinate structures are readily applied in this chapter.

3.2 Concept of Fixity

Fixity is a condition of support in which all displacements are restrained. Consequently, reactions are developed in horizontal, vertical and rotational directions in a two-dimensional system. When the ends of a beam are fixed, more reactions are developed, and the beam becomes statically indeterminate.

3.3 Fixed Beam

If the two ends of a beam are supported by fixed supports, the beam is termed as fixed beam (also called built-in or encastered beam). It can be understood in two ways:

(i) A cantilever beam has two degrees of freedom at the free end (axial deformation is ignored as it is not significant) namely rotation (i.e., slope) and the deflection. Therefore, a fixed beam can be visualized as a cantilever beam with the degrees of freedom at the free-end arrested. This means that the fixed beam typically has a degree of static indeterminacy equal to two (the vertical reaction and the moment reaction can be considered as redundant forces). Hence, two additional equations are required to solve the problem apart from the static equilibrium equations.

(ii) A simply supported beam has two degrees of freedom (i.e., one rotation at each support). Therefore, a fixed beam can be visualized as a simply supported beam with the degrees of freedom at the supports arrested. Again, the degree of static indeterminacy is two (one moment reaction at each support can be considered as redundant forces).

3.3.1 Advantages of Fixed Beam

The advantages of fixed beam are

(i) As the ends of beam are fixed, the stiffness of structure increases. Therefore, it deflects less compared to simply supported beams.

(ii) As the moments are redistributed, the maximum moment decreases. Therefore, long-span structures can be constructed.

(iii) As the moment variation along the length has both sagging and hogging nature, efficient utilization of reinforcement in concrete structures is possible wherever required.

(iv) It is more stable and stronger.

3.3.2 Principle of Superposition

When a linearly elastic structure is subjected to a number of loads, the resultant effect (i.e., force or displacement responses) is the algebraic sum of the effects produced by individual loads at a particular point. This principle is useful in solving complex structural analysis problems by superimposing the solutions of the decomposed simple problems. In a simpler sense, the statically indeterminate structures can be decomposed into a series of statically determinate structures for the purpose of performing the analysis.

3.3.3 Analysis of Fixed Beam

A fixed beam with arbitrary loading is shown in Figure 3.1. The free-body diagram of the beam shows that there are four reactions (V_A, V_B, M_{AB}^F and M_{BA}^F), in which V_A and V_B are the vertical reactions; M_{AB}^F and M_{BA}^F are the moment reactions (called *fixed-end moments*). As the degree of static indeterminacy is two, any two reactions can be considered as redundant forces so as to treat the beam as statically determinate. If V_B and M_{BA}^F are considered as redundant, then the beam is a cantilever beam with two redundant forces at B. If M_{AB}^F and M_{BA}^F are considered as redundant, then the beam is a simply supported beam with one redundant force for each support.

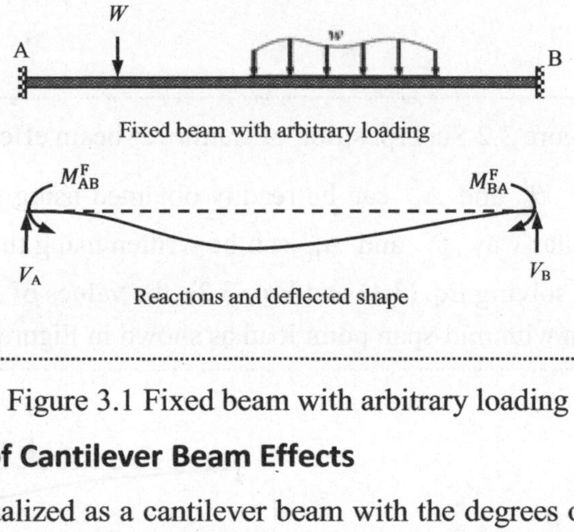

Figure 3.1 Fixed beam with arbitrary loading

3.3.4 Superposition of Cantilever Beam Effects

A fixed beam can be visualized as a cantilever beam with the degrees of freedom at the free-end arrested. Therefore, the fixed beam with arbitrary loading can be decomposed into a cantilever beam with the given loading, and a cantilever beam with redundant forces ($R_1 = V_B$ and $R_2 = M_{BA}^F$) as loading at the free end (i.e., at B) as shown in Figure 3.2.

In the original fixed structure, the slope and deflection are zero at B. Therefore, the algebraic sum of slope (at B) of (i) the cantilever beam subjected to given loading, and (ii) the cantilever beam subjected to the redundant forces as loading, is equal to zero. Similarly, the algebraic sum of deflection (at B) of (i) the cantilever beam subjected to given loading, and (ii) the cantilever beam subjected to the redundant forces as loading, is equal to zero.

$$\theta_B^L + \theta_B^R = 0 \quad (3.1)$$

$$\Delta_B^L + \Delta_B^R = 0 \quad (3.2)$$

where

θ_B^L is the slope at B due to given load (i.e., in clockwise direction)

Δ_B^L is the deflection at B due to given load (i.e., in downward direction)

θ_B^R is the slope at B due to R_1 and R_2 (i.e., in anti-clockwise direction)

Δ_B^R is the deflection at B due to R_1 and R_2 (i.e., in upward direction)

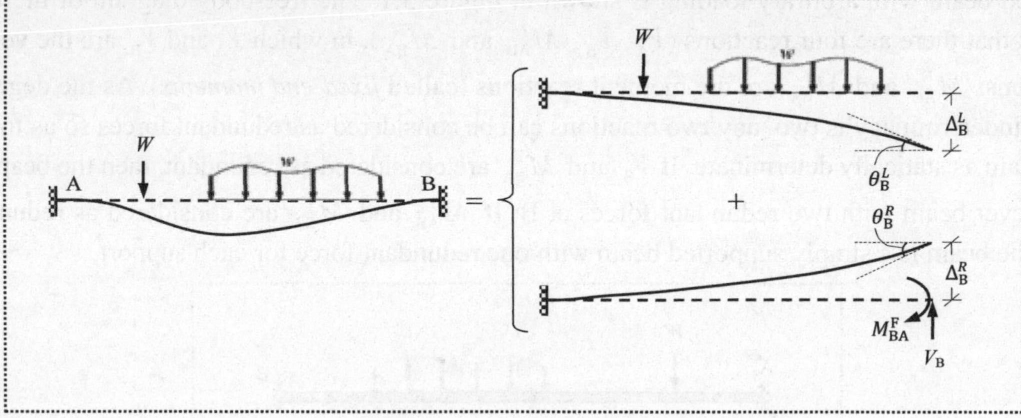

Figure 3.2 Superposition of cantilever beam effects

In Eq. (3.1) and Eq. (3.2), θ_B^L and Δ_B^L can be readily obtained using the formulas (for standard loading cases). In the similar way, θ_B^R and Δ_B^R can be written using the formulas as functions of R_1 and R_2. Therefore, by solving Eq. (3.1) and Eq. (3.2), the values of R_1 and R_2 are obtained.

Consider a fixed beam with mid-span point load as shown in Figure 3.3.

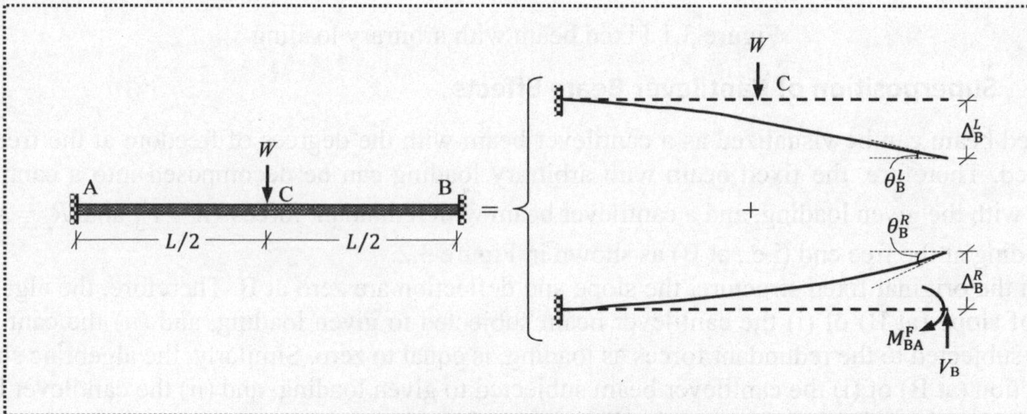

Figure 3.3 Fixed beam with mid-span point load

Since the supports at A and B are fixed, the values of slope and deflection are zero at both the support locations. When the beam is considered as a cantilever beam (fixed at A, and free), the redundant forces at B as $R_1 = V_B$ (vertical force) and $R_2 = M_{BA}^{F}$ (moment force) should be evaluated by applying the compatibility of displacements at B.

$$\theta_B = \theta_B^L + \theta_B^R = 0 \tag{3.3}$$

$$\Delta_B = \Delta_B^L + \Delta_B^R = 0 \tag{3.4}$$

where

$$\theta_B^L = \theta_C^L = \frac{W(L/2)^2}{2EI} = \frac{WL^2}{8EI}$$

$$\Delta_B^L = \Delta_C^L + \theta_C^L \times (L/2)$$

$$= \frac{W(L/2)^3}{3EI} + \frac{W(L/2)^2}{2EI} \times (L/2) = \frac{5WL^3}{48EI}$$

$$\theta_B^R = \theta_B^{R_1} + \theta_B^{R_2} = \frac{-R_1L^2}{2EI} + \frac{R_2L}{EI}$$

$$\Delta_B^R = \Delta_B^{R_1} + \Delta_B^{R_2} = \frac{-R_1L^3}{3EI} + \frac{R_2L^2}{2EI}$$

Therefore, Eq. (3.3) and Eq. (3.4) become;

$$\frac{WL^2}{8EI} + \left(\frac{-R_1L^2}{2EI} + \frac{R_2L}{EI}\right) = 0 \tag{3.5}$$

$$\frac{5WL^3}{48EI} + \left(\frac{-R_1L^3}{3EI} + \frac{R_2L^2}{2EI}\right) = 0 \tag{3.6}$$

By solving Eq. (3.5) and Eq. (3.6);

$$R_1 = \frac{W}{2}$$

$$R_2 = \frac{WL}{8}$$

After getting the values of R_1 and R_2, the force responses (i.e., shear force and bending moment diagrams) of the given fixed beam can be obtained by considering the beam as a cantilever beam with three loads: (i) given load (i.e., W acting at the mid-span in downward direction), (ii) R_1 (i.e., $W/2$ acting at B in upward direction), and (iii) R_2 (i.e., $WL/8$ acting at B in clockwise direction) as shown in Figure 3.4 (ii).

Now, free-body diagram of the cantilever is drawn with support reactions at A as V_A and M_A as shown in Figure 3.4 (iii). By applying the equilibrium conditions;

$$\sum F_y = 0 \Rightarrow V_A - W + \frac{W}{2} = 0$$

$$\Rightarrow V_A = \frac{W}{2}$$

$$\sum M_A = 0 \Rightarrow \frac{W}{2} \times L - \frac{WL}{8} - W \times \frac{L}{2} + M_A = 0$$

$$\Rightarrow M_A = \frac{WL}{8}$$

The obtained values of V_A and M_A are positive, which means the assumed directions of V_A (i.e., upward) and M_A (i.e., anti-clockwise) are correct, and M_A is the fixed end moment at A (i.e., $M_A = M_{AB}^F$).

Shear force diagram:

$$S_A = \frac{W}{2} \text{ kN}$$

$$S_C^{\text{left}} = \frac{W}{2} \text{ kN}$$

$$S_C^{\text{right}} = \frac{W}{2} - W = \frac{-W}{2} \text{ kN}$$

$$S_B = \frac{-W}{2} \text{ kN}$$

Bending moment diagram:

$$M_A = \frac{-WL}{8} \text{ kNm}$$

$$M_C = \frac{-WL}{8} + V_A \times \frac{L}{2}$$

$$= \frac{-WL}{8} + \frac{W}{2} \times \frac{L}{2} = \frac{WL}{8} \text{ kNm}$$

$$M_B = \frac{-WL}{8} \text{ kNm}$$

The values of M_A and M_B are considered negative as these moments cause *hogging* nature. The shear force and bending moment diagrams are shown in Figures 3.4 (iv) and 3.4 (v) respectively.

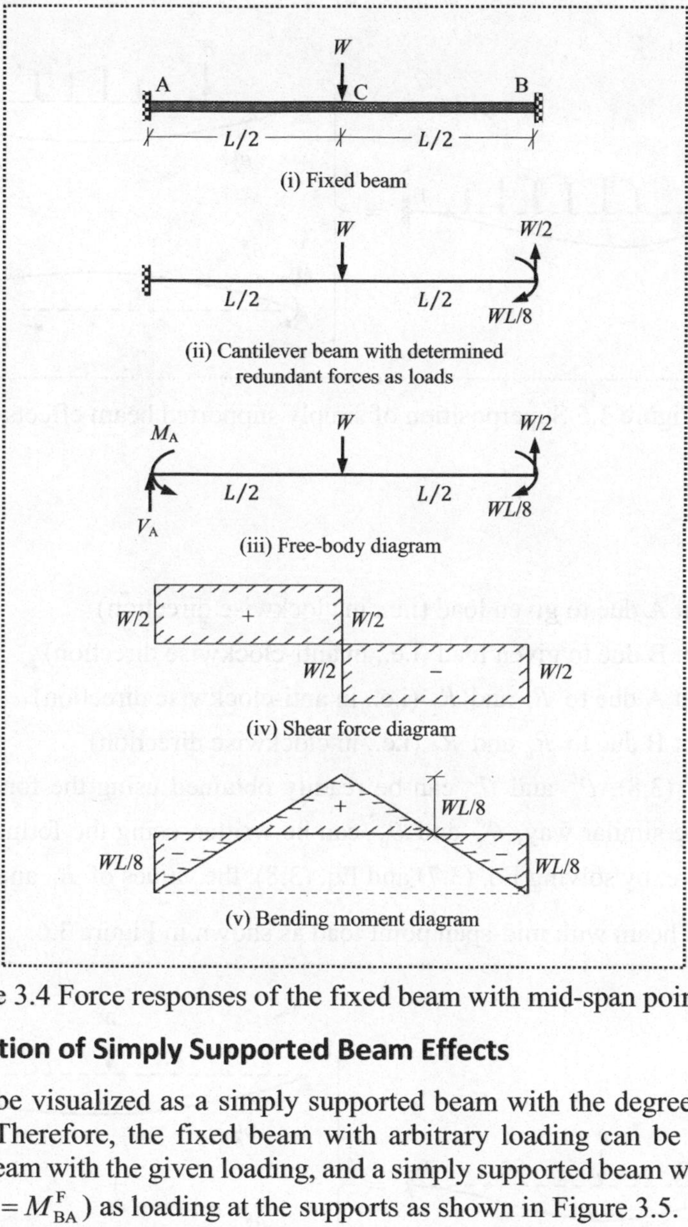

Figure 3.4 Force responses of the fixed beam with mid-span point load

3.3.5 Superposition of Simply Supported Beam Effects

A fixed beam can be visualized as a simply supported beam with the degrees of freedom at the supports arrested. Therefore, the fixed beam with arbitrary loading can be decomposed into a simply supported beam with the given loading, and a simply supported beam with redundant forces ($R_1 = M_{AB}^F$ and $R_2 = M_{BA}^F$) as loading at the supports as shown in Figure 3.5.

In the original fixed structure, the values of slope at A and B are zero. Therefore, the algebraic sum of slope (at A) of (i) the simply supported beam subjected to given loading, and (ii) the simply supported beam subjected to the redundant forces as loading, is equal to zero. Similarly, the algebraic sum of slope (at B) of (i) the simply supported beam subjected to given loading, and (ii) the simply supported beam subjected to the redundant forces as loading, is equal to zero.

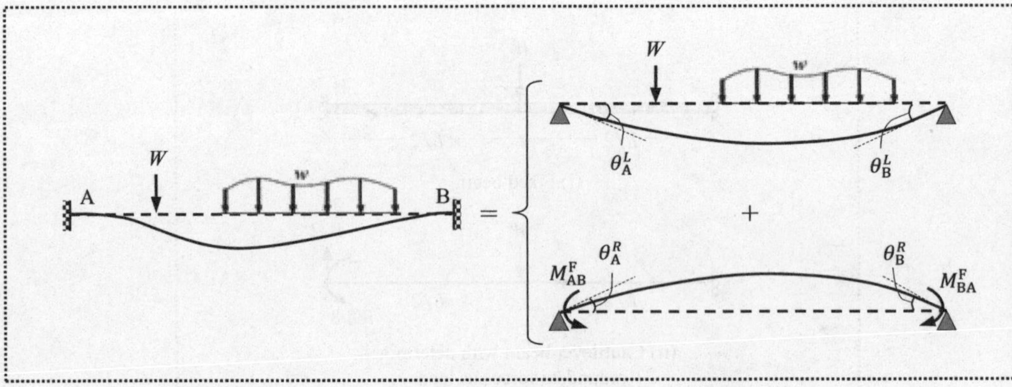

Figure 3.5 Superposition of simply supported beam effects

$$\theta_A^L + \theta_A^R = 0 \tag{3.7}$$

$$\theta_B^L + \theta_B^R = 0 \tag{3.8}$$

where

θ_A^L is the slope at A due to given load (i.e., in clockwise direction)

θ_B^L is the slope at B due to given load (i.e., in anti-clockwise direction)

θ_A^R is the slope at A due to R_1 and R_2 (i.e., in anti-clockwise direction)

θ_B^R is the slope at B due to R_1 and R_2 (i.e., in clockwise direction)

In Eq. (3.7) and Eq. (3.8), θ_A^L and θ_B^L can be readily obtained using the formulas (for standard loading cases). In the similar way, θ_A^R and θ_B^R can be written using the formulas as functions of R_1 and R_2. Therefore, by solving Eq. (3.7) and Eq. (3.8), the values of R_1 and R_2 are obtained.

Consider a fixed beam with mid-span point load as shown in Figure 3.6.

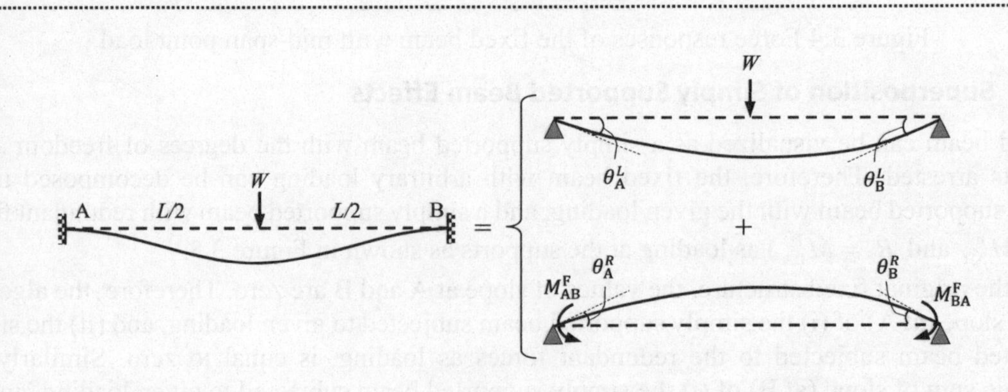

Figure 3.6 Fixed beam with mid-span point load

When the beam is considered as a simply supported beam, the redundant forces at A as $R_1 = M_{AB}^{F}$ (moment force), and at B as $R_2 = M_{BA}^{F}$ (moment force) should be evaluated by applying the compatibility of displacements (i.e., the values of slope at A and B are zero).

$$\theta_A = \theta_A^L + \theta_A^R = 0 \tag{3.9}$$

$$\theta_B = \theta_B^L + \theta_B^R = 0 \tag{3.10}$$

where

$$\theta_A^L = \frac{-WL^2}{16EI}$$

$$\theta_B^L = \frac{WL^2}{16EI}$$

$$\theta_A^R = \theta_A^{R_1} + \theta_A^{R_2} = \frac{R_1 L}{3EI} + \frac{R_2 L}{6EI}$$

$$\theta_B^R = \theta_B^{R_1} + \theta_B^{R_2} = \frac{-R_1 L}{6EI} - \frac{R_2 L}{3EI}$$

Therefore, Eq. (3.3) and Eq. (3.4) become;

$$\frac{-WL^2}{16EI} + \left(\frac{R_1 L}{3EI} + \frac{R_2 L}{6EI}\right) = 0 \tag{3.11}$$

$$\frac{WL^2}{16EI} + \left(\frac{-R_1 L}{6EI} - \frac{R_2 L}{3EI}\right) = 0 \tag{3.12}$$

By solving Eq. (3.11) and Eq. (3.12);

$$R_1 = \frac{WL}{8} \text{ and } R_2 = \frac{WL}{8}$$

After getting the values of R_1 and R_2, the force responses (i.e., shear force and bending moment diagrams) of the given fixed beam can be obtained by considering the beam as a simply supported beam with three loads: (i) given load (i.e., W acting at the mid-span in downward direction), (ii) R_1 (i.e., $WL/8$ acting at A in anti-clockwise direction), and (iii) R_2 (i.e., $WL/8$ acting at B in clockwise direction) as shown in Figure 3.7 (ii).

Now, free-body diagram of the simply supported beam is drawn with support reactions at A as V_A and at B as V_B as shown in Figure 3.7 (iii). By applying the equilibrium conditions;

$$\sum F_y = 0 \Rightarrow V_A - W + V_B = 0$$

$$\sum M_A = 0 \Rightarrow V_B \times L - \frac{WL}{8} - W \times \frac{L}{2} + \frac{WL}{8} = 0$$

$$\Rightarrow V_B = W/2, \text{ and } V_A = W/2.$$

The obtained values of V_A and V_B are positive, which means the assumed directions (i.e., upward) are correct.

Shear force diagram:

$$S_A = \frac{W}{2} \text{ kN}$$

$$S_C^{left} = \frac{W}{2} \text{ kN}$$

$$S_C^{right} = \frac{W}{2} - W = \frac{-W}{2} \text{ kN}$$

$$S_B = \frac{-W}{2} \text{ kN}$$

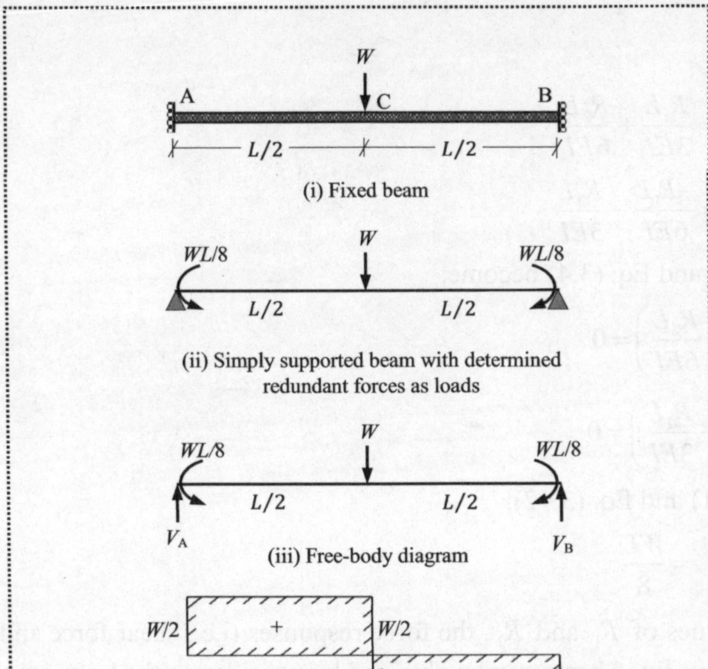

Figure 3.7 Force responses of the fixed beam with mid-span point load

Bending moment diagram:

$$M_{\mathrm{A}} = \frac{-WL}{8} \text{ kNm}$$

$$M_{\mathrm{C}} = \frac{-WL}{8} + V_A \times \frac{L}{2}$$

$$= \frac{-WL}{8} + \frac{W}{2} \times \frac{L}{2} = \frac{WL}{8} \text{ kNm}$$

$$M_{\mathrm{B}} = \frac{-WL}{8} \text{ kNm}$$

The values of M_{A} and M_{B} are considered negative as these moments cause *hogging* nature. The shear force and bending moment diagrams are same as shown in Figures 3.7 (iv) and 3.7 (v) respectively.

Even though the same results are obtained in Figures 3.4 and 3.7, considering the simply supported beam is more convenient for drawing the bending moment diagram. Because, the final bending moment diagram is directly obtained by the superimposition as shown in Figure 3.8. Therefore, if the *fixed end moments* are known for standard load cases, then the fixed beams can be easily analysed for the force responses.

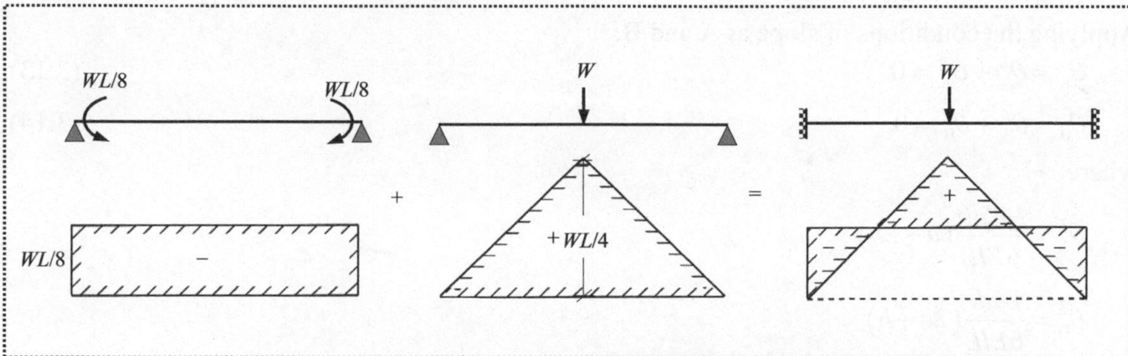

Figure 3.8 Bending moment diagram by superposition

3.3.6 Fixed End Moments

When a fixed beam is treated as a simply supported beam with moment reactions at the supports as two redundant forces, the primary objective is to obtain the values of these redundant forces. These moment reactions are called *fixed end moments*.

Case-1: *A fixed beam with mid-span point load*

From Section 3.6.2,

$$M^{\mathrm{F}}_{\mathrm{AB}} = \frac{WL}{8} \text{ (anti-clockwise)}$$

$$M^{\mathrm{F}}_{\mathrm{BA}} = \frac{WL}{8} \text{ (clockwise)}$$

Case-2: *A fixed beam with a point load at a distance "a" from the left support*

Let a fixed beam be subjected to a point load at a distance of "a" from A, and "b" from B, so that $L = a + b$. The beam is considered as a simply supported beam with the support moments as the redundant forces $R_1 = M_{AB}^F$, and $R_2 = M_{BA}^F$ respectively at A and B as shown in Figure 3.9.

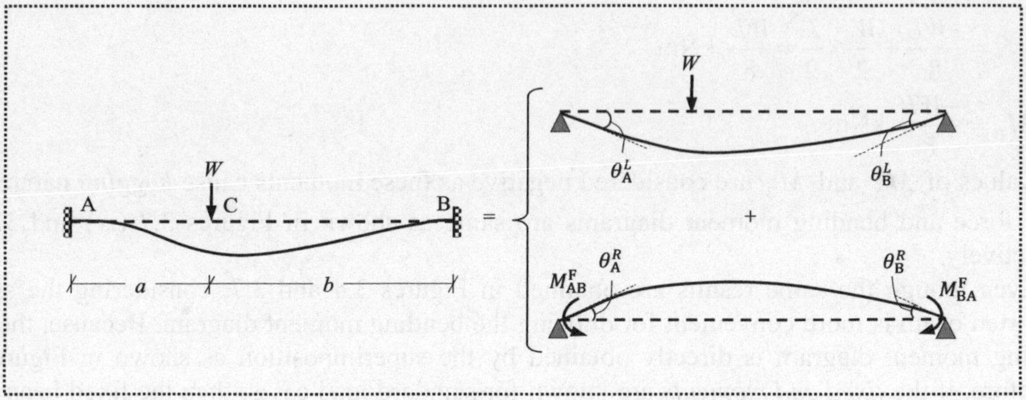

Figure 3.9 Fixed beam with a point load

Applying the conditions of slope at A and B,

$$\theta_A = \theta_A^L + \theta_A^R = 0 \tag{3.13}$$

$$\theta_B = \theta_B^L + \theta_B^R = 0 \tag{3.14}$$

where

$$\theta_A^L = \frac{-Wab}{6EIL}(a + 2b)$$

$$\theta_B^L = \frac{Wab}{6EIL}(2a + b)$$

$$\theta_A^R = \theta_A^{R_1} + \theta_A^{R_2} = \frac{R_1 L}{3EI} + \frac{R_2 L}{6EI}$$

$$\theta_B^R = \theta_B^{R_1} + \theta_B^{R_2} = \frac{-R_1 L}{6EI} - \frac{R_2 L}{3EI}$$

Therefore, Eq. (3.13) and Eq. (3.14) become;

$$\frac{-Wab}{6EIL}(a + 2b) + \left(\frac{R_1 L}{3EI} + \frac{R_2 L}{6EI}\right) = 0 \tag{3.15}$$

$$\frac{Wab}{6EIL}(2a + b) + \left(\frac{-R_1 L}{6EI} - \frac{R_2 L}{3EI}\right) = 0 \tag{3.16}$$

By solving Eq. (3.15) and Eq. (3.16);

$$R_1 = \frac{Wab^2}{L^2}$$

$$R_2 = \frac{Wa^2b}{L^2}$$

Therefore,

$$M_{\mathrm{AB}}^{\mathrm{F}} = \frac{Wab^2}{L^2} \text{ (anti-clockwise)}$$

$$M_{\mathrm{BA}}^{\mathrm{F}} = \frac{Wa^2b}{L^2} \text{ (clockwise)}$$

When more than one load is applied, the fixed end moments can be obtained by superposition of the individual fixed end moments. For example, a fixed beam AB of span "L" is subjected to two point loads: W_1 is acting at a distance of a_1 from A (which means b_1 from B); and W_2 is acting at a distance of a_2 from A (which means b_2 from B), so that $L = a_1 + b_1 = a_2 + b_2$. The fixed end moments are

$$M_{\mathrm{AB}}^{\mathrm{F}} = \frac{W_1a_1b_1^2}{L^2} + \frac{W_2a_2b_2^2}{L^2} \text{ (anti-clockwise)}$$

$$M_{\mathrm{BA}}^{\mathrm{F}} = \frac{W_1a_1^2b_1}{L^2} + \frac{W_2a_2^2b_2}{L^2} \text{ (clockwise)}$$

Case-3: *A fixed beam with uniformly distributed load over the entire length*

Let a fixed beam be subjected to a uniformly distributed load over the entire length. Similar to the previous case, the beam is considered as a simply supported beam with the support moments as the redundant forces ($R_1 = M_{\mathrm{AB}}^{\mathrm{F}}$ at A, and $R_2 = M_{\mathrm{BA}}^{\mathrm{F}}$ at B).

Applying the conditions of slope at A and B,

$$\theta_{\mathrm{A}} = \theta_{\mathrm{A}}^{L} + \theta_{\mathrm{A}}^{R} = 0 \tag{3.17}$$

$$\theta_{\mathrm{B}} = \theta_{\mathrm{B}}^{L} + \theta_{\mathrm{B}}^{R} = 0 \tag{3.18}$$

where

$$\theta_{\mathrm{A}}^{L} = \frac{-wL^3}{24EI}$$

$$\theta_{\mathrm{B}}^{L} = \frac{wL^3}{24EI}$$

$$\theta_{\mathrm{A}}^{R} = \theta_{\mathrm{A}}^{R_1} + \theta_{\mathrm{A}}^{R_2} = \frac{R_1L}{3EI} + \frac{R_2L}{6EI}$$

$$\theta_{\mathrm{B}}^{R} = \theta_{\mathrm{B}}^{R_1} + \theta_{\mathrm{B}}^{R_2} = \frac{-R_1L}{6EI} - \frac{R_2L}{3EI}$$

Therefore, Eq. (3.17) and Eq. (3.18) become;

$$\frac{-wL^3}{24EI}+\left(\frac{R_1L}{3EI}+\frac{R_2L}{6EI}\right)=0 \tag{3.19}$$

$$\frac{wL^3}{24EI}+\left(\frac{-R_1L}{6EI}-\frac{R_2L}{3EI}\right)=0 \tag{3.20}$$

By solving Eq. (3.19) and Eq. (3.20);

$$R_1=\frac{wL^2}{12}$$

$$R_2=\frac{wL^2}{12}$$

Therefore,

$$M^{F}_{AB}=\frac{wL^2}{12} \text{ (anti-clockwise)}$$

$$M^{F}_{BA}=\frac{wL^2}{12} \text{ (clockwise)}$$

The formulas for finding the fixed end moments for standard load cases are given in Table 3.1. When the beam is subjected to multiple loads, the fixed end moments due to individual loads can be superposed to obtain the resultant end moments. The fixed end moments at the left support are considered negative because the direction is anti-clockwise, while the end moment at the right support is positive (clockwise). Therefore, for general gravity loading cases, when the end moments (mostly hogging) are superposed with the moments of simply supported beam (mostly sagging), the sign convention should be strictly followed.

A simple sign convention procedure is presented in Figure 3.10(i). Whether the end moments are drawn below or above the baseline is decided based on the sign (positive or negative) of the end moments. All four possibilities of end moment combinations and their respective bending moments are shown in Figures 3.10(ii)–3.10(v). For example, when M_{AB} (i.e., M^{F}_{AB}) is negative (i.e., anti-clockwise) and M_{BA} (i.e., M^{F}_{BA}) is positive (i.e., clockwise), the bending moment diagram is drawn above the base line. Because, throughout the length, AB is in hogging nature. On the other hand, when both ends are positive (or negative), the bending moment diagrams will be on both sides of the baseline, because both sagging and hogging nature will be there in the beam.

Table 3.1 Formulas for fixed end moments

Beam	FEM at A	FEM at B
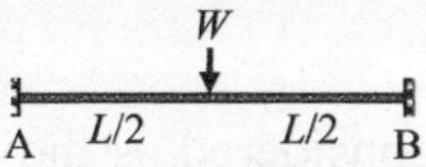	$M^{F}_{AB} = \dfrac{-WL}{8}$	$M^{F}_{BA} = \dfrac{WL}{8}$
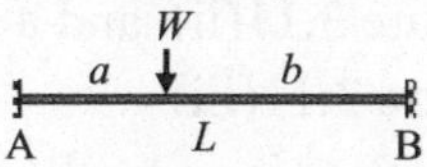	$M^{F}_{AB} = \dfrac{-Wab^2}{L^2}$	$M^{F}_{BA} = \dfrac{Wa^2b}{L^2}$
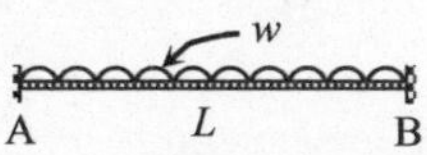	$M^{F}_{AB} = \dfrac{-wL^2}{12}$	$M^{F}_{BA} = \dfrac{wL^2}{12}$
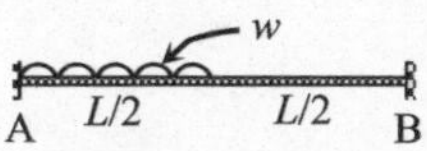	$M^{F}_{AB} = \dfrac{-11}{192}wL^2$	$M^{F}_{BA} = \dfrac{5}{192}wL^2$
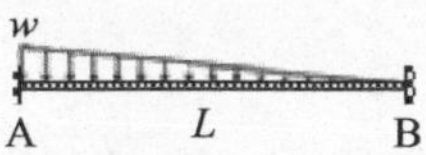	$M^{F}_{AB} = \dfrac{-wL^2}{20}$	$M^{F}_{BA} = \dfrac{wL^2}{30}$
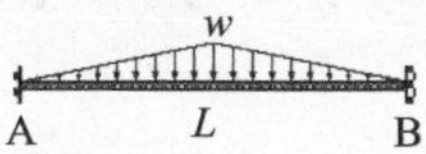	$M^{F}_{AB} = \dfrac{-5}{96}wL^2$	$M^{F}_{BA} = \dfrac{5}{96}wL^2$

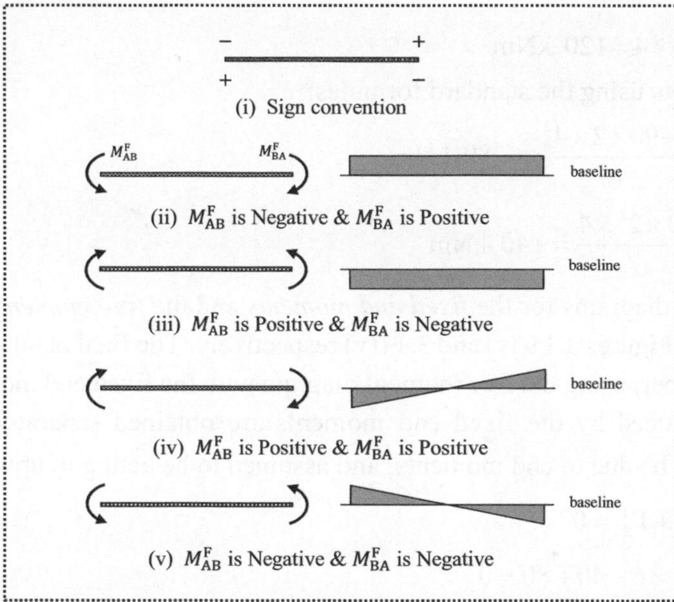

Figure 3.10 Nature of end moments and bending moment diagrams

3.3.7 Numerical Examples

Example 3.1: A fixed beam of span 6 m is subjected to a point load of 90 kN at 2 m from the left end. Draw the shear force and bending moment diagrams.

Solution:

The fixed beam AB is shown in Figure 3.11(i). The beam is considered as the combination of a simply supported beam with the given loading as shown in Figure 3.11(ii), and a simply supported beam with fixed end moments at the supports as shown in Figure 3.11(iii)

The vertical reactions for the simply supported beam with the given loading are obtained by applying the equilibrium equations.

$$\sum F_y = 0 \Rightarrow V_A^L - 90 + V_B^L = 0$$

$$\sum M_A = 0 \Rightarrow V_B^L \times 6 - 90 \times 2 = 0$$

$$V_B^L = 30 \text{ kN}$$

$$V_A^L = 60 \text{ kN}$$

where V_A^L and V_B^L are the vertical reactions at A and B respectively due to the given loading.

Therefore, the moments due to the given loading:

$$M_A^L = 0 \text{ kNm}$$

$$M_B^L = 0 \text{ kNm}$$

$$M_C^L = V_B^L \times 4 = 30 \times 4 = 120 \text{ kNm}$$

The fixed end moments using the standard formulas:

$$M_{AB}^F = \frac{-Wab^2}{L^2} = \frac{-90 \times 2 \times 4^2}{6^2} = -80 \text{ kNm}$$

$$M_{BA}^F = \frac{Wa^2b}{L^2} = \frac{90 \times 2^2 \times 4}{6^2} = +40 \text{ kNm}$$

The bending moment diagrams for the *fixed end moments* and the *free moments* (i.e., due to given loading) are shown in Figures 3.11(iv) and 3.11(v) respectively. The final bending moment diagram can be obtained by superposing the free moment diagram with the fixed end moment diagram. The support, reactions induced by the fixed end moments are obtained separately. Let the vertical reactions V_A^F and V_B^F be due to end moments, and assumed to be acting in upward direction.

$$\sum F_y = 0 \Rightarrow V_A^F + V_B^F = 0$$

$$\sum M_A = 0 \Rightarrow V_B^F \times 6 - 40 + 80 = 0$$

$$V_B^F = -6.67 \text{ kN}$$

$$V_A^F = 6.67 \text{ kN}$$

Since the value of V_B^F is negative, the assumed direction (i.e., upwards) is not correct, but the direction of V_A^F is correct . Therefore, V_A^F is upwards and V_B^F is downwards as corrected in the free-body diagram shown in Figure 3.11(vi).

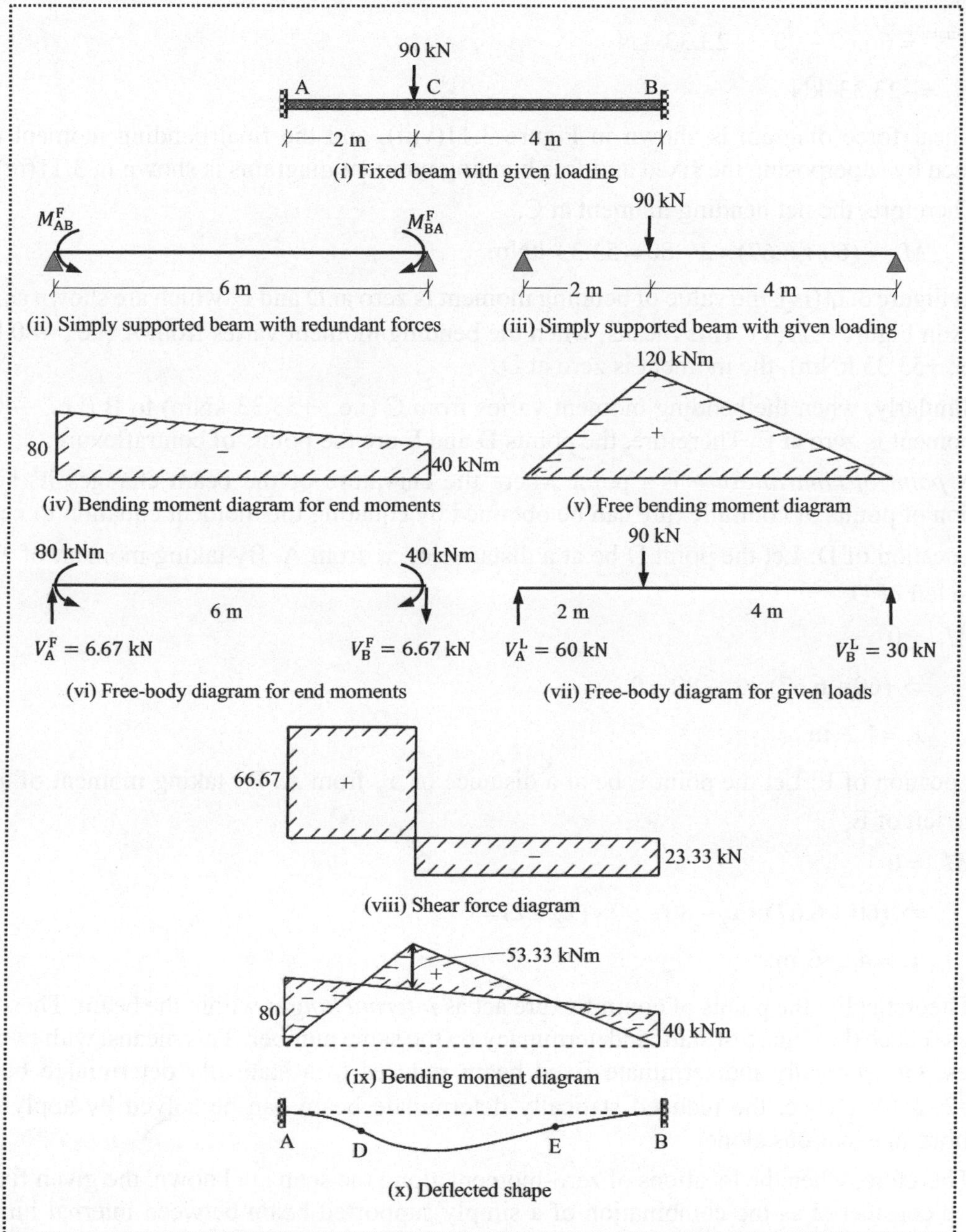

Figure 3.11 Solution for Example 3.1

From Figures 3.11(vi) and 3.11(vii), the values of shear force at various locations are obtained.

$$S_A = V_A = 60 + 6.67 = 66.67 \text{ kN}$$

$$S_C^{\text{left}} = 66.67 \text{ kN}$$

$$S_C^{\text{right}} = 66.67 - 90 = -23.33 \text{ kN}$$

$$S_B = -23.33 \text{ kN}$$

The shear force diagram is shown in Figure 3.11(viii), and the final bending moment diagram obtained by superposing the fixed and free bending moment diagrams is shown in 3.11(ix).

Therefore, the net bending moment at C,

$$M_C = (60 + 6.67) \times 2 - 80 = 53.33 \text{ kNm.}$$

In Figure 3.11(ix), the value of bending moment is zero at D and E, which are shown as *internal hinges* in Figure 3.11(x). This means, when the bending moment varies from A (i.e., –80 kNm) to C (i.e., +53.33 kNm), the moment is zero at D.

Similarly, when the bending moment varies from C (i.e., +53.33 kNm) to B (i.e., –40 kNm), the moment is zero at E. Therefore, the points D and E are the points of contraflexure.

A *point of contraflexure* is a point where the curvature of the beam changes its sign. The location of points of contraflexure can be obtained by equating the moment equation to zero.

Location of D: Let the point D be at a distance of x_1 from A. By taking moment of all forces on the left of D,

$$M_D = 0$$

$$\Rightarrow (60 + 6.67) \times x_1 - 80 = 0$$

$$x_1 = 1.2 \text{ m}$$

Location of E: Let the point E be at a distance of x_2 from A. By taking moment of all forces on the left of E,

$$M_E = 0$$

$$\Rightarrow (60 + 6.67) \times x_2 - 80 - 90 \times (x_2 - 2) = 0$$

$$x_2 = 4.286 \text{ m}$$

Theoretically, the points of contraflexure act as *internal hinges* within the beam. These internal hinges reduce the degree of static indeterminacy by the same number. This means, with two internal hinges, this statically indeterminate fixed beam reduces to a statically determinate beam (i.e., DSI=2–2=0). Hence, the reduced statically determinate beam can be solved by applying static equilibrium equations alone.

Therefore, when the locations of zero-moment along the span are known, the given fixed beam can be considered as the combination of a simply supported beam between internal hinges (i.e., zero-moment locations), and two cantilever beams at the ends. The force responses (e.g., bending moment diagram) can be obtained as shown in Figure 3.12.

First, the mid-portion (i.e., simply supported beam) is analysed using the static equilibrium equations as shown in Figure 3.12(iii). The upward reactions at D and E obtained from the mid-portion, act as the loads at the ends of the cantilevers in the downward direction. Again, the cantilevers are analysed for the force responses as shown in Figure 3.12(iv). The final bending moment diagram is obtained by combining the diagrams of mid-portion and end-portions as shown in Figure 3.12(v).

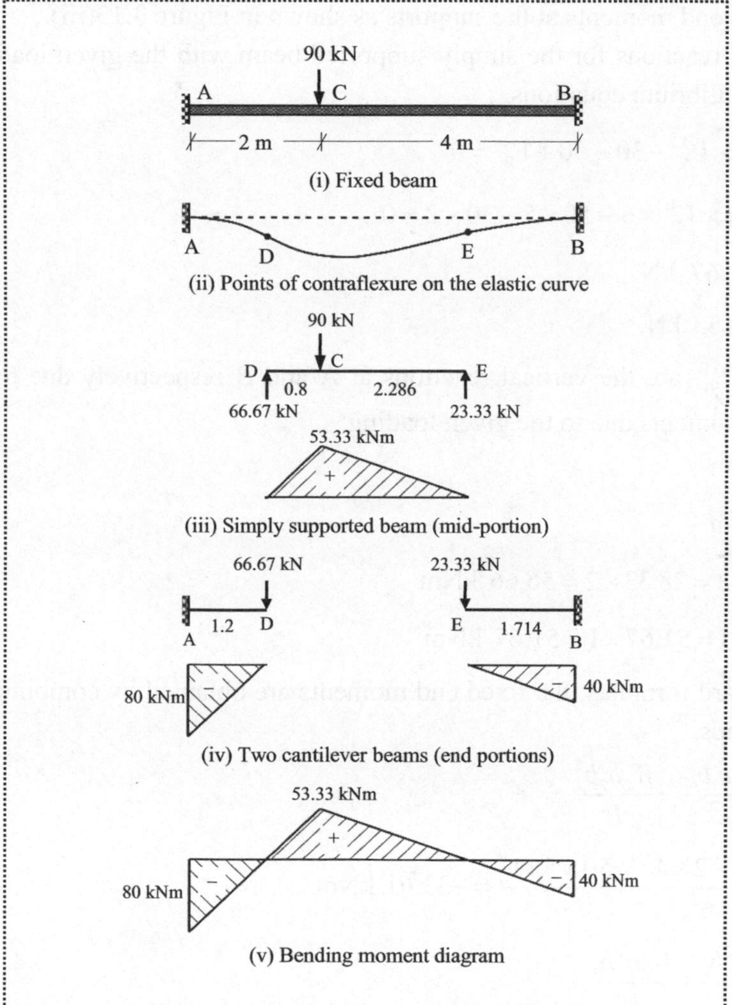

Figure 3.12 Solution for Example 3.1

Example 3.2: A fixed beam of span 6 m is subjected to two point loads of 30 kN and 50 kN at 2 m and 5 m respectively from the left end. Draw the shear force and bending moment diagrams.

Solution:

The fixed beam AB is shown in Figure 3.13(i). The beam is considered as the combination of a simply supported beam with the given loading as shown in Figure 3.13(ii), and a simply supported beam with fixed end moments at the supports as shown in Figure 3.13(iii).

The vertical reactions for the simply supported beam with the given loading are obtained by applying the equilibrium equations.

$$\sum F_y = 0 \Rightarrow V_A^L - 30 - 50 + V_B^L = 0$$

$$\sum M_A = 0 \Rightarrow V_B^L \times 6 - 50 \times 5 - 30 \times 2 = 0$$

$$V_B^L = 51.67 \text{ kN}$$

$$V_A^L = 28.33 \text{ kN}$$

where V_A^L and V_B^L are the vertical reactions at A and B respectively due to the given loading.

Therefore, the moments due to the given loading:

$$M_A^L = 0 \text{ kNm}$$

$$M_B^L = 0 \text{ kNm}$$

$$M_C^L = V_A^L \times 2 = 28.33 \times 2 = 56.66 \text{ kNm}$$

$$M_D^L = V_B^L \times 1 = 51.67 \times 1 = 51.67 \text{ kNm}$$

Using the standard formulas, the fixed end moments are obtained by combining the moments due to individual loads.

$$M_{AB}^F = -\frac{W_1 a_1 b_1^2}{L^2} - \frac{W_2 a_2 b_2^2}{L^2}$$

$$= -\frac{30 \times 2 \times 4^2}{6^2} - \frac{50 \times 5 \times 1^2}{6^2} = -33.61 \text{ kNm}$$

$$M_{BA}^F = \frac{W_1 a_1^2 b_1}{L^2} + \frac{W_2 a_2^2 b_2}{L^2}$$

$$= \frac{30 \times 2^2 \times 4}{6^2} + \frac{50 \times 5^2 \times 1}{6^2} = +48.05 \text{ kNm}$$

The bending moment diagrams for the *free moments* (i.e., due to given loading) and the *fixed end moments* are shown in Figures 3.13(iv) and 3.13(v) respectively. The final bending moment diagram can be obtained by superposing the free moment diagram with the fixed end moment diagram.

The support reactions induced by the fixed end moments are obtained separately. Let the vertical reactions V_A^F and V_B^F be due to end moments, and assumed to be acting in upward direction.

$$\sum F_y = 0 \Rightarrow V_A^F + V_B^F = 0$$

$$\sum M_A = 0 \Rightarrow V_B^F \times 6 - 48.05 + 33.61 = 0$$

$$V_B^F = 2.41 \text{ kN}$$

$$V_A^F = -2.41 \text{ kN}$$

Since the value of V_A^F is negative, the assumed direction (i.e., upwards) is not correct, but the direction of V_B^F is correct. Therefore, V_A^F is downwards and V_B^F is upwards as corrected in the free-body diagram shown in Figure 3.13(vi).

Therefore, from Figures 3.13(vi) and 3.13(vii), the values of shear force at various locations are obtained as

$$S_A = V_A = 28.33 - 2.41 = 25.92 \text{ kN}$$

$$S_C^{left} = 25.92 \text{ kN}$$

$$S_C^{right} = 25.92 - 30 = -4.08 \text{ kN}$$

$$S_D^{left} = -4.08$$

$$S_D^{right} = -4.08 - 50 = -54.08$$

$$S_B = -54.08 \text{ kN}$$

The shear force diagram is shown in Figure 3.13(viii) and the final bending moment diagram is obtained by superposing the fixed and free bending moment diagrams as shown in Figure 3.13(ix).

The net bending moments at C and D are positive (i.e., sagging) which are obtained as follows.

Net moment at C, $M_C = 25.92 \times 2 - 33.61 = 18.23$ kNm

Net moment at D, $M_D = 25.92 \times 5 - 33.61 - 30 \times 3 = 6.0$ kNm

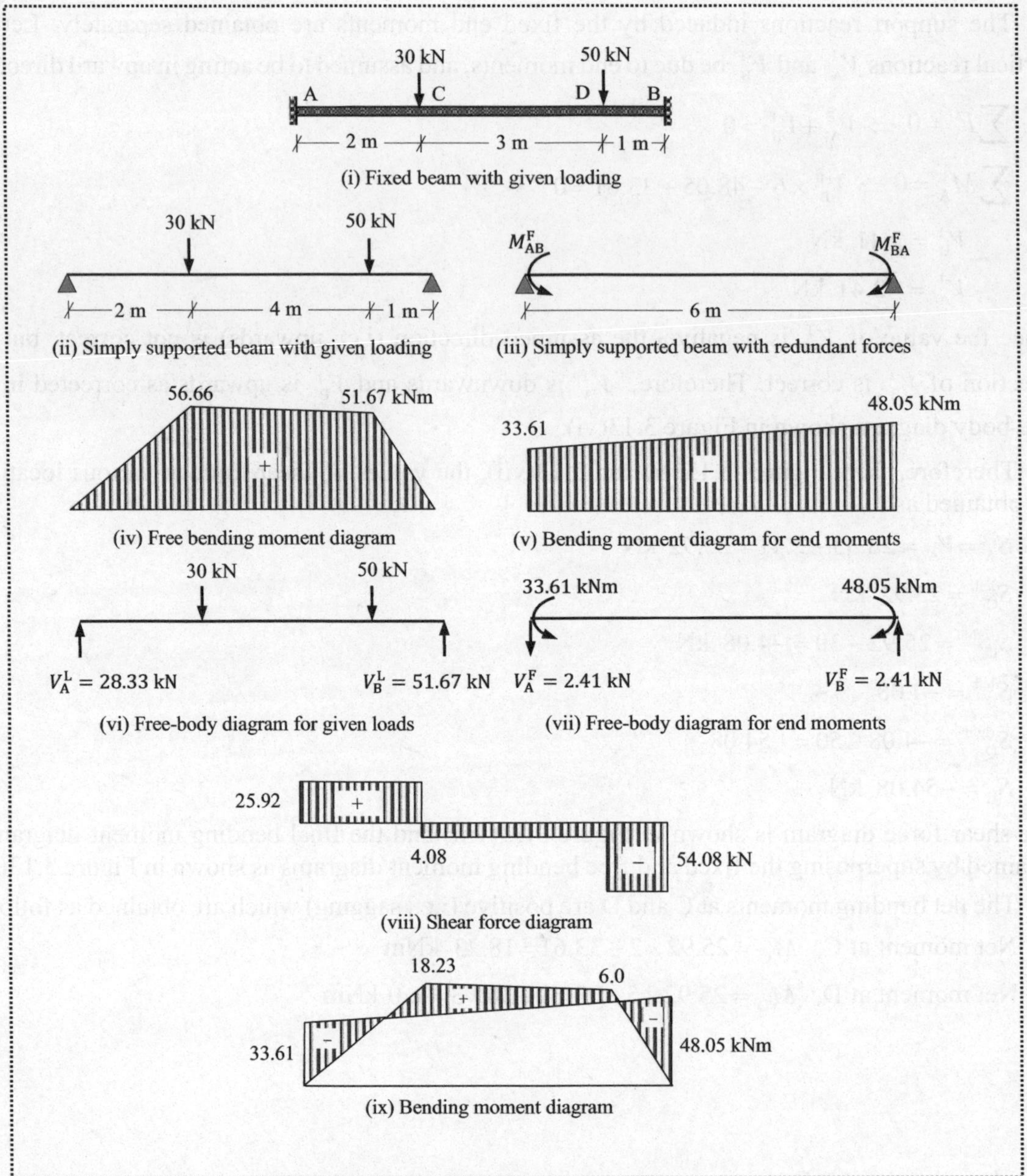

Figure 3.13 Solution for Example 3.2

Example 3.3: A fixed beam of span 6 m is subjected to three point loads of 40 kN, 50 kN and 30 kN at 2 m, 3 m and 5 m respectively from the left end. Draw the shear force and bending moment diagrams.

Solution:

The fixed beam AB is shown in Figure 3.14(i). The beam is considered as the combination of a simply supported beam with the given loading, and a simply supported beam with fixed end moments at the supports.

The vertical reactions for the simply supported beam with the given loading are obtained by applying the equilibrium equations.

$$\sum F_y = 0 \Rightarrow V_A^L - 40 - 50 - 30 + V_B^L = 0$$

$$\sum M_A = 0 \Rightarrow V_B^L \times 6 - 30 \times 5 - 50 \times 3 - 40 \times 2 = 0$$

$$V_B^L = 63.33 \text{ kN}$$

$$V_A^L = 56.67 \text{ kN}$$

where V_A^L and V_B^L are the vertical reactions at A and B respectively due to the given loading.

The moments due to the given loading for simply supported beam:

$$M_A^L = 0 \text{ kNm}$$

$$M_B^L = 0 \text{ kNm}$$

$$M_C^L = V_A^L \times 2 = 56.67 \times 2 = 113.34 \text{ kNm}$$

$$M_D^L = V_A^L \times 2 = 56.67 \times 3 - 40 \times 1 = 130.0 \text{ kNm}$$

$$M_E^L = V_B^L \times 1 = 63.33 \times 1 = 63.33 \text{ kNm}$$

The fixed end moments using the standard formulas:

$$M_{AB}^F = -\frac{40 \times 2 \times 4^2}{6^2} - \frac{50 \times 3 \times 3^2}{6^2} - \frac{30 \times 5 \times 1^2}{6^2} = -77.22 \text{ kNm}$$

$$M_{BA}^F = \frac{40 \times 2^2 \times 4}{6^2} + \frac{50 \times 3^2 \times 3}{6^2} + \frac{30 \times 5^2 \times 1}{6^2} = +76.11 \text{ kNm}$$

The bending moment diagrams for the *free moments* (i.e., due to given loading) and the *fixed end moments* are shown in Figures 3.14(ii) and 3.14(iii) respectively. The final bending moment diagram can be obtained by superposing the free moment diagram with the fixed end moment diagram.

The support reactions induced by the fixed end moments are obtained separately. Let the vertical reactions V_A^F and V_B^F be due to end moments, and assumed to be acting in upward direction.

$$\sum F_y = 0 \Rightarrow V_A^F + V_B^F = 0$$

$$\sum M_A = 0 \Rightarrow V_B^F \times 6 + 77.22 - 76.11 = 0$$

$$\Rightarrow V_B^F = -0.19 \text{ kN and } V_A^F = 0.19 \text{ kN.}$$

Since the value of V_B^F is negative, the assumed direction (i.e., upwards) is not correct, but the direction of V_A^F is correct. Therefore, V_A^F is upwards and V_B^F is downwards. Therefore, the values of shear force at various locations are obtained as

$$S_A = V_A = 56.67 + 0.19 = 56.86 \text{ kN}$$
$$S_C^{\text{left}} = 56.86 \text{ kN}$$
$$S_C^{\text{right}} = 56.86 - 40 = 16.86 \text{ kN}$$
$$S_D^{\text{left}} = 16.86 \text{ kN}$$
$$S_D^{\text{right}} = 16.86 - 50 = -33.14 \text{ kN}$$
$$S_E^{\text{left}} = -33.14 \text{ kN}$$
$$S_E^{\text{right}} = -33.14 - 30 = -63.14 \text{ kN}$$
$$S_B = -63.14 \text{ kN}$$

The shear force and bending moment diagram are shown in Figures 3.14(iv) and 3.14(v) respectively.

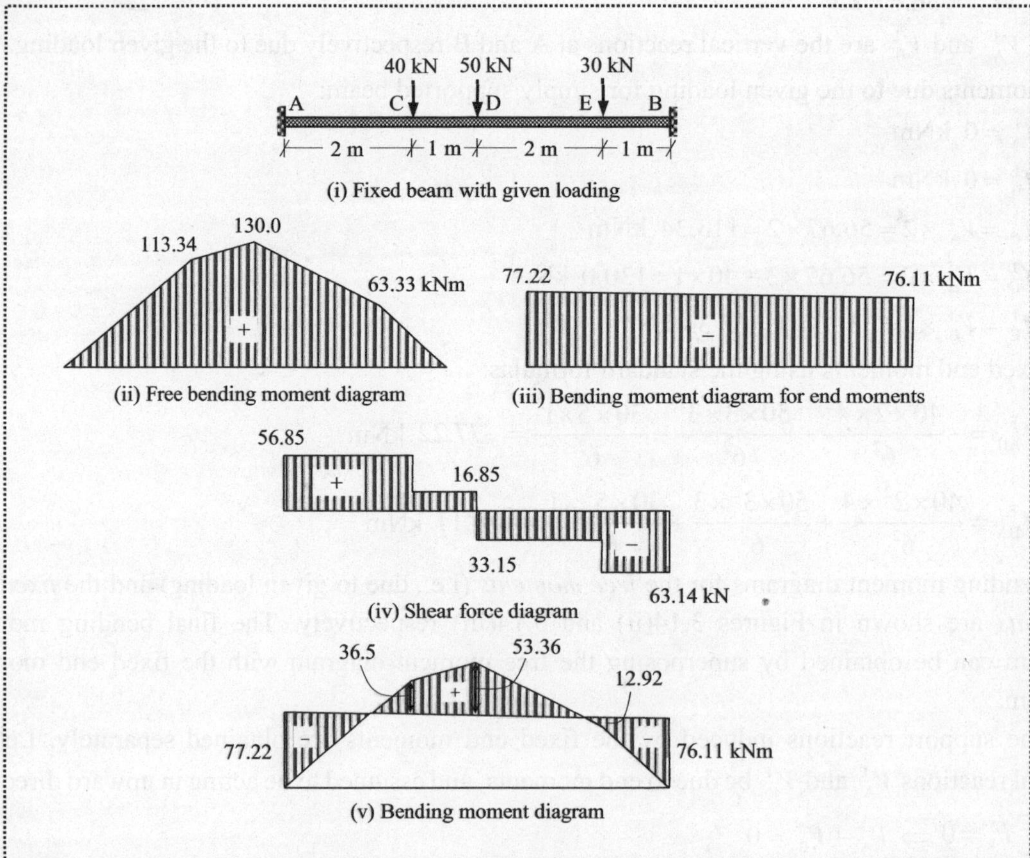

Figure 3.14 Solution for Example 3.3

Net moment at C, $M_C = 56.86\times2-77.22=36.5$ kNm
Net moment at D, $M_D = 56.86\times3-77.22-40\times1=53.36$ kNm
Net moment at D, $M_D = 56.86\times5-77.22-40\times3-50\times2=-12.92$ kNm

Example 3.4: A fixed beam of span 6 m is subjected to a uniformly distributed load of 10 kN/m throughout the length, and a point load of 25 kN at 4 m from the left end. Draw the shear force and bending moment diagrams.

Solution:

The fixed beam AB is shown in Figure 3.15(i). The beam is considered as the combination of a simply supported beam with the given loading, and a simply supported beam with fixed end moments at the supports.

The vertical reactions for the simply supported beam with the given loading are obtained by applying the equilibrium equations.

$$\sum F_y = 0 \Rightarrow V_A^L - 10\times6 - 25 + V_B^L = 0$$

$$\sum M_A = 0 \Rightarrow V_B^L\times6 - 25\times4 - 10\times6\times6/2 = 0$$

$$\Rightarrow V_B^L = 46.67 \text{ kN, and } V_A^L = 38.33 \text{ kN.}$$

where V_A^L and V_B^L are the vertical reactions at A and B respectively due to the given loading.

Therefore, the moments due to the given loading:

$$M_A^L = 0 \text{ kNm}$$

$$M_B^L = 0 \text{ kNm}$$

$$M_C^L = V_A^L\times4 - 10\times4\times4/2 = 38.33\times4 - 10\times4\times2 = 73.32 \text{ kNm}$$

The fixed end moments using the standard formulas:

$$M_{AB}^F = -\frac{wL^2}{12} - \frac{Wab^2}{L^2} = -\frac{10\times6^2}{12} - \frac{25\times4\times2^2 \; -30\times5\times1^2}{6^2 \qquad\qquad 6^2} = -41.11 \text{ kNm}$$

$$M_{BA}^F = +\frac{wL^2}{12} + \frac{Wa^2b}{L^2} = \frac{10\times6^2}{12} + \frac{25\times4^2\times2}{6^2} = +52.22 \text{ kNm}$$

The bending moment diagrams for the *free moments* (i.e., due to given loading) and the *fixed end moments* are shown in Figures 3.15(ii) and 3.15(iii) respectively. The final bending moment diagram can be obtained by superposing the free moment diagram with the fixed end moment diagram.

The support reactions induced by the fixed end moments are obtained separately. Let the vertical reactions V_A^F and V_B^F be due to end moments, and assumed to be acting in upward direction.

$$\sum F_y = 0 \Rightarrow V_A^F + V_B^F = 0$$

$$\sum M_A = 0 \Rightarrow V_B^F\times6 - 52.22 + 41.11 = 0$$

$\Rightarrow V_B^F = 1.85$ kN and $V_A^F = -1.85$ kN.

Since the value of V_A^F is negative, the assumed direction (i.e., upwards) is not correct, but the direction of V_B^F is correct. Therefore, V_A^F is downwards and V_B^F is upwards. Therefore, the values of shear force at various locations are obtained as

$S_A = V_A = 38.33 - 1.85 = 36.48$ kN

$S_C^{left} = 36.48 - 10 \times 4 = -3.52$ kN

$S_C^{right} = -3.52 - 25 = -28.52$ Kn

$S_B = -28.52 - 10 \times 2 = -48.52$ kN

The shear force and bending moment diagrams are shown in Figures 3.15(iv) and 3.15(v) respectively.

Net moment at C, $M_C = 36.48 \times 4 - 41.11 - 10 \times 4 \times 4/2 = 24.81$ kNm.

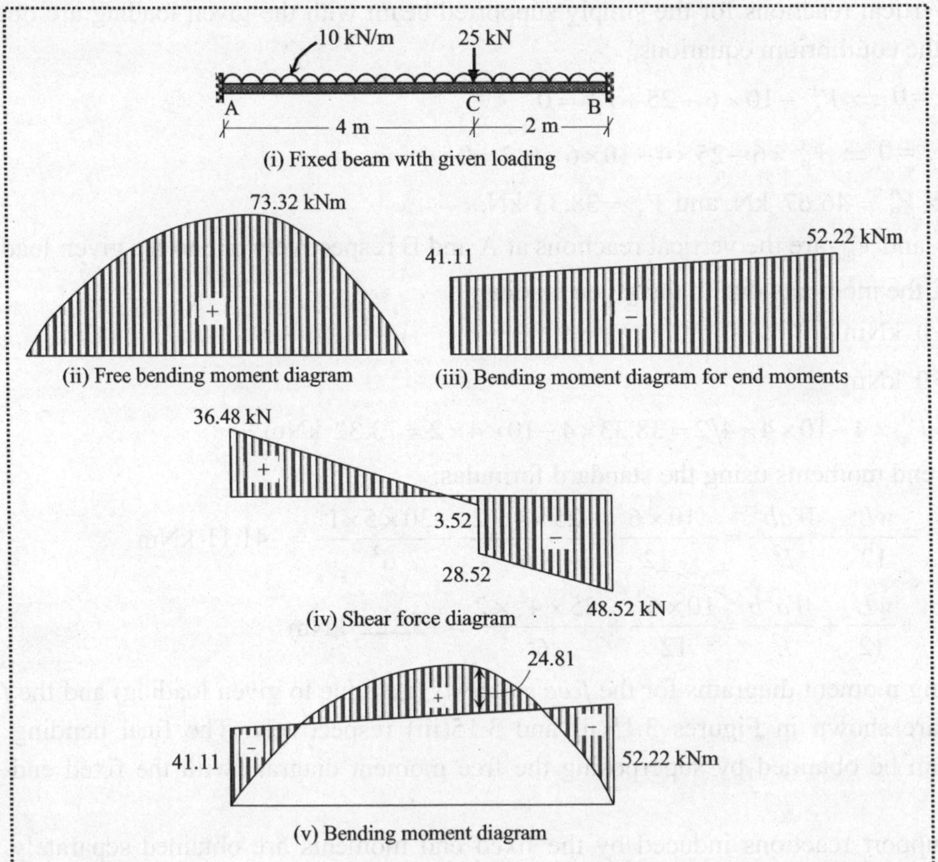

Figure 3.15 Solution for Example 3.4

Example 3.5: A fixed beam of span 6 m is subjected to two-point loads of 20 kN and 30 kN respectively at 1 m and 3 m from the left end, and a uniformly distributed load of 10 kN/m over the entire span. Draw the shear force and bending moment diagrams.

Solution:

The fixed beam AB is shown in Figure 3.16(i). The beam is considered as the combination of a simply supported beam with the given loading, and a simply supported beam with fixed end moments at the supports. The vertical reactions for the simply supported beam with the given loading are obtained by applying the equilibrium equations.

$$\sum F_y = 0 \Rightarrow V_A^L - 20 - 30 - 10\times 6 + V_B^L = 0$$

$$\sum M_A = 0 \Rightarrow V_B^L \times 6 - 10\times 6\times 6/2 - 30\times 3 - 20\times 1 = 0$$

$$\Rightarrow V_B^L = 48.33 \text{ kN, and } V_A^L = 61.67 \text{ kN.}$$

where V_A^L and V_B^L are the vertical reactions at A and B respectively due to the given loading. Therefore, the moments due to the given loading:

$$M_A^L = 0 \text{ kNm}$$

$$M_B^L = 0 \text{ kNm}$$

$$M_C^L = V_A^L \times 1 - 10\times 1\times 1/2 = 61.67\times 1 - 10\times 1\times 1/2 = 56.67 \text{ kNm}$$

$$M_D^L = V_A^L \times 3 - 10\times 3\times 3/2 - 20\times 2 = 61.67\times 1 - 10\times 3\times 3/2 - 20\times 2 = 100.0 \text{ kNm}$$

The fixed end moments using the standard formulas:

$$M_{AB}^F = -\frac{10\times 6^2}{12} - \frac{20\times 1\times 5^2}{6^2} - \frac{30\times 3\times 3^2}{6^2} = -66.39 \text{ kNm}$$

$$M_{BA}^F = \frac{10\times 6^2}{12} + \frac{20\times 1^2\times 5}{6^2} + \frac{30\times 3^2\times 3}{6^2} = +55.28 \text{ kNm}$$

The bending moment diagrams for the *free moments* (i.e., due to given loading) and the *fixed end moments* are shown in Figures 3.16(ii) and 3.16(iii) respectively. The final bending moment diagram can be obtained by superposing the free moment diagram with the fixed end moment diagram.

The support reactions induced by the fixed end moments are obtained separately. Let the vertical reactions V_A^F and V_B^F be due to end moments, and assumed to be acting in upward direction.

$$\sum F_y = 0 \Rightarrow V_A^F + V_B^F = 0$$

$$\sum M_A = 0 \Rightarrow V_B^F \times 6 + 66.39 - 55.28 = 0$$

$$\Rightarrow V_B^F = -1.85 \text{ kN and } V_A^F = 1.85 \text{ kN.}$$

Since the value of V_B^F is negative, the assumed direction (i.e., upwards) is not correct, but the direction of V_A^F is correct. Therefore, V_A^F is upwards and V_B^F is downwards.

The values of shear force at various locations are obtained as

$$S_A = V_A = 61.67 + 1.85 = 63.52 \text{ kN}$$

$$S_C^{left} = 63.52 - 10\times 1 = 53.52 \text{ kN}$$

$$S_C^{right} = 53.52 - 20 = 33.52 \text{ kN}$$

$$S_D^{left} = 33.52 - 10\times 2 = 13.52 \text{ kN}$$

$$S_D^{right} = 13.52 - 30 = -16.48 \text{ kN}$$

$$S_B = -16.48 - 10\times 3 = -46.48 \text{ kN}$$

The shear force and bending moment diagrams are shown in Figures 3.16(iv) and 3.16(v) respectively.

Net moment at C, $M_C = 63.52\times 1 - 66.39 - 10\times 1\times 1/2 = -7.87$ kNm

Net moment at D, $M_D = 63.52\times 3 - 66.39 - 20\times 2 - 10\times 3\times 3/2 = 39.17$ kNm

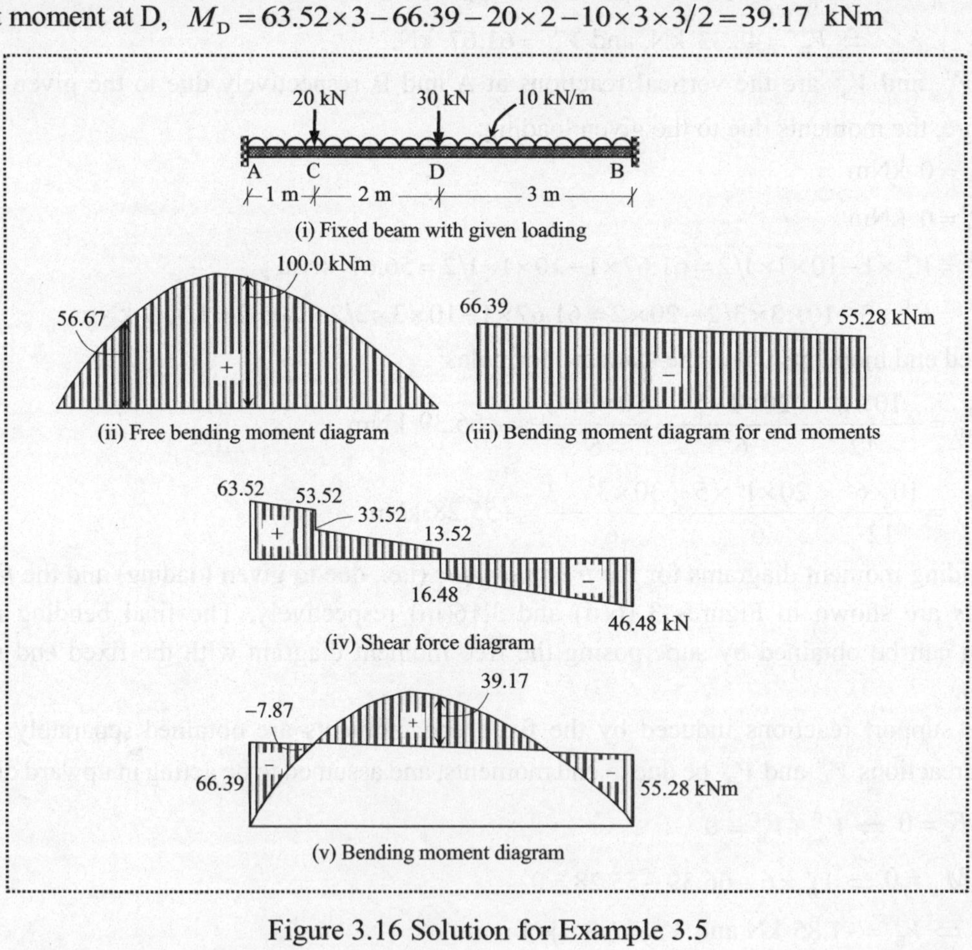

Figure 3.16 Solution for Example 3.5

Example 3.6: A fixed beam of span 6 m is subjected to the concentrated loads of 15 kN, 25 kN and 5 kN respectively at 1 m, 2 m and 3 m from the left end. The beam is also subjected to a uniformly distributed load of 10 kN/m over a span of 3 m from right end. Draw the shear force and bending moment diagrams.

Solution:

The fixed beam AB is shown in Figure 3.17(i). The beam is considered as the combination of a simply supported beam with the given loading, and a simply supported beam with fixed end moments at the supports.

The vertical reactions for the simply supported beam with the given loading are obtained by applying the equilibrium equations.

$$\sum F_y = 0 \Rightarrow V_A^L - 15 - 25 - 5 - 10\times 3 + V_B^L = 0$$

$$\sum M_A = 0 \Rightarrow V_B^L \times 6 - 10\times 3\times(3+1.5) - 5\times 3 - 25\times 2 - 15\times 1 = 0$$

$$\Rightarrow V_B^L = 35.83 \text{ kN, and } V_A^L = 39.17 \text{ kN.}$$

where V_A^L and V_B^L are the vertical reactions at A and B respectively due to the given loading.

Therefore, the moments due to the given loading:

$$M_A^L = 0 \text{ kNm}$$

$$M_B^L = 0 \text{ kNm}$$

$$M_C^L = V_A^L \times 1 = 39.17\times 1 = 39.17 \text{ kNm}$$

$$M_D^L = V_A^L \times 2 - 15 = 39.17\times 2 - 15\times 1 = 63.33 \text{ kNm}$$

$$M_E^L = V_A^L \times 3 - 15\times 2 - 25\times 1 = 39.17\times 3 - 15\times 2 - 25\times 1 = 62.51 \text{ kNm}$$

The fixed end moments using the standard formulas:

$$M_{AB}^F = -\frac{15\times 1\times 5^2}{6^2} - \frac{25\times 2\times 4^2}{6^2} - \frac{5\times 3\times 3^2}{6^2} - \frac{5\times 10\times 6^2}{192} = -45.76 \text{ kNm}$$

$$M_{BA}^F = \frac{15\times 1^2\times 5}{6^2} + \frac{25\times 2^2\times 4}{6^2} + \frac{5\times 3^2\times 3}{6^2} + \frac{11\times 10\times 6^2}{192} = 37.57 \text{ kNm}$$

The bending moment diagrams for the *free moments* (i.e., due to given loading) and the *fixed end moments* are shown in Figures 3.17(ii) and 3.17(iii) respectively. The final bending moment diagram can be obtained by superposing the free moment diagram with the fixed end moment diagram.

The support reactions induced by the fixed end moments are obtained separately. Let the vertical reactions V_A^F and V_B^F be due to end moments, and assumed to be acting in upward direction.

$$\sum F_y = 0 \Rightarrow V_A^F + V_B^F = 0$$

$$\sum M_A = 0 \Rightarrow V_B^F \times 6 + 45.76 - 37.57 = 0$$

$$\Rightarrow V_B^F = -1.37 \text{ kN and } V_A^F = 1.37 \text{ kN.}$$

Since the value of V_B^F is negative, the assumed direction (i.e., upwards) is not correct, but the direction of V_A^F is correct. Therefore, V_A^F is upwards and V_B^F is downwards. Therefore, considering the reactions due to given loads and end moments, the values of shear force at various locations are obtained as

$$S_A = V_A = 39.17 + 1.37 = 40.54 \text{ kN}$$
$$S_C^{\text{left}} = 40.54 \text{ kN}$$
$$S_C^{\text{right}} = 40.54 - 15 = 25.54 \text{ kN}$$
$$S_D^{\text{left}} = 25.54 \text{ kN}$$
$$S_D^{\text{right}} = 25.54 - 25 = 0.54 \text{ kN}$$
$$S_E^{\text{left}} = 0.54 \text{ kN}$$
$$S_E^{\text{right}} = 0.54 - 5 = -4.46 \text{ kN}$$
$$S_B = -4.46 - 10 \times 3 = -34.46 \text{ kN}$$

The shear force and bending moment diagrams are shown in Figures 3.17(iv) and 3.17(v) respectively.

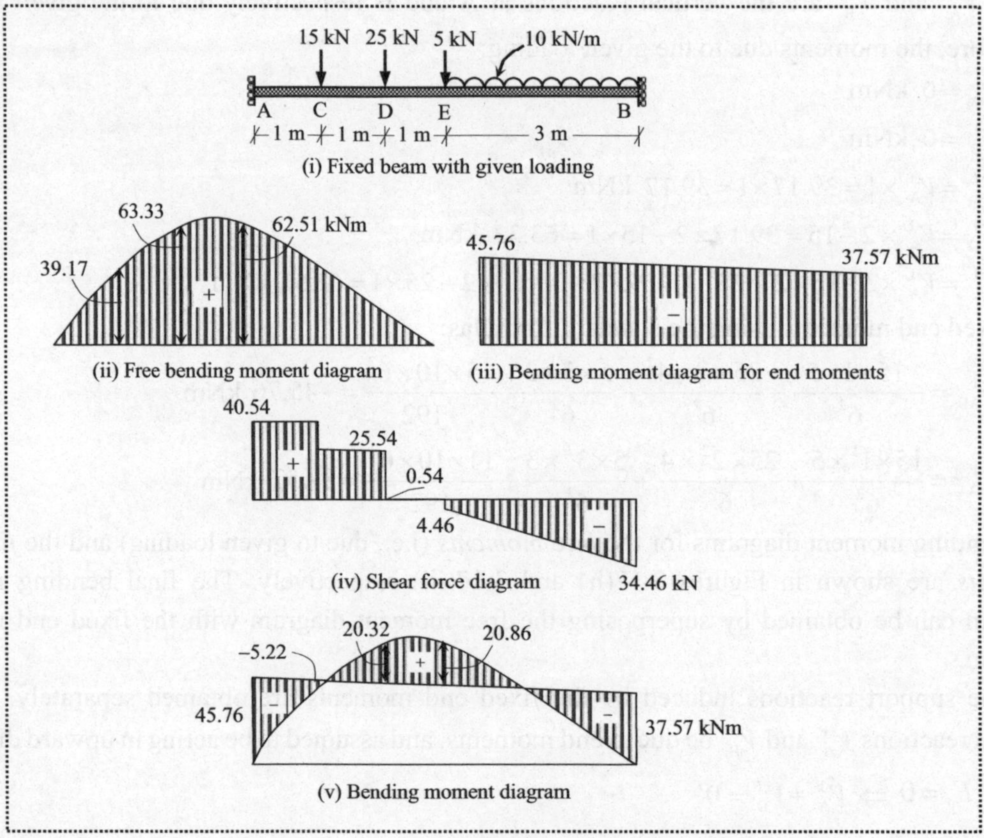

Figure 3.17 Solution for Example 3.6

Net moment at C, $M_C = 40.54 \times 1 - 45.76 = -5.22$ kNm

Net moment at D, $M_D = 40.54 \times 2 - 45.76 - 15 \times 1 = 20.32$ kNm

Net moment at E, $M_E = 40.54 \times 3 - 45.76 - 15 \times 2 - 25 \times 1 = 20.86$ kNm

Example 3.7: A fixed beam of span 6 m is subjected to a uniformly varying load with the intensities of zero at the left end and 30 kN/m at the right end. Draw the shear force and bending moment diagrams.

Solution:

The fixed beam AB is shown in Figure 3.18(i). The beam is considered as the combination of a simply supported beam with the given loading, and a simply supported beam with fixed end moments at the supports.

The vertical reactions for the simply supported beam with the given loading are obtained by applying the equilibrium equations.

$$\sum F_y = 0 \Rightarrow V_A^L - \frac{1}{2} \times 6 \times 30 + V_B^L = 0$$

$$\sum M_A = 0 \Rightarrow V_B^L \times 6 - \left(\frac{1}{2} \times 6 \times 30\right)\left(\frac{2}{3} \times 6\right) = 0$$

$$\Rightarrow V_B^L = 60 \text{ kN, and } V_A^L = 30 \text{ kN.}$$

where V_A^L and V_B^L are the vertical reactions at A and B respectively due to the given loading. Therefore, the moments due to the given loading:

$$M_A^L = 0 \text{ kNm}$$

$$M_B^L = 0 \text{ kNm}$$

$$M_C^L = V_A^L \times 3 - \frac{1}{2} \times 3 \times 15 \times \left(\frac{1}{3} \times 3\right)$$

$$= 30 \times 3 - \frac{1}{2} \times 3 \times 15 \times \left(\frac{1}{3} \times 3\right) = 67.5 \text{ kNm}$$

where, M_C^L is the moment at the mid-span.

The fixed end moments using the standard formulas:

$$M_{AB}^F = -\frac{wL^2}{30} = -\frac{30 \times 6^2}{30} = -36.0 \text{ kNm}$$

$$M_{BA}^F = +\frac{wL^2}{20} = \frac{30 \times 6^2}{20} = 54.0 \text{ kNm}$$

The support reactions induced by the fixed end moments are obtained separately. Let the vertical reactions V_A^F and V_B^F be due to end moments, and assumed to be acting in upward direction.

$$\sum F_y = 0 \Rightarrow V_A^F + V_B^F = 0$$
$$\sum M_A = 0 \Rightarrow V_B^F \times 6 + 36 - 54 = 0$$
$$\Rightarrow V_B^F = 3 \text{ kN and } V_A^F = -3 \text{ kN.}$$

Since the value of V_A^F is negative, the assumed direction (i.e., upwards) is not correct, but the direction of V_B^F is correct. Therefore, V_A^F is downwards and V_B^F is upwards. Therefore, considering the reactions due to given loads and end moments, the values of shear force at various locations are obtained as

$$S_A = V_A = 30 - 3 = 27 \text{ kN}$$
$$S_C^{\text{left}} = 27 - \frac{1}{2} \times 3 \times 15 = 4.5 \text{ kN}$$
$$S_C^{\text{right}} = 4.5 \text{ kN}$$
$$S_B = 27 - \frac{1}{2} \times 6 \times 30 = -63.0 \text{ kN}$$

The shear force and bending moment diagrams are shown in Figures 3.18(ii) and 3.18(iii) respectively.

Net moment at C:

$$M_C = 27.0 \times 3 - 36.0 - \frac{1}{2} \times 15 \times 3 \times \left(\frac{1}{3} \times 3\right) = 22.5 \text{ kNm}$$

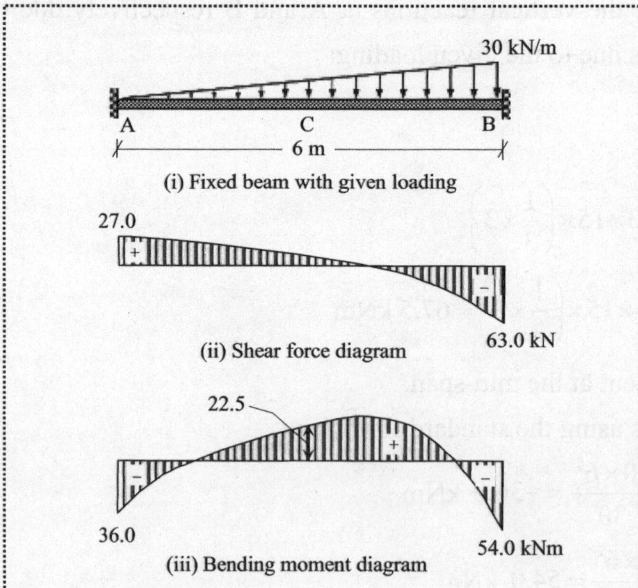

Figure 3.18 Solution for Example 3.7

Example 3.8: A fixed beam of span 6 m is subjected to a triangular load with the intensities of zero at the supports and 30 kN/m at the mid-span. Draw the shear force and bending moment diagrams.

Solution:

The fixed beam AB is shown in Figure 3.19(i). The beam is considered as the combination of a simply supported beam with the given loading, and a simply supported beam with fixed end moments at the supports. The vertical reactions for the simply supported beam with the given loading are obtained by applying the equilibrium equations.

$$\sum F_y = 0 \Rightarrow V_A^L - \frac{1}{2} \times 30 \times 6 + V_B^L = 0$$

$$\sum M_A = 0 \Rightarrow V_B^L \times 6 - \frac{1}{2} \times 6 \times 30 \times \frac{6}{2} = 0$$

$$V_B^L = 45 \text{ kN}$$

$$V_A^L = 45 \text{ kN}$$

where V_A^L and V_B^L are the vertical reactions at A and B respectively due to the given loading. Therefore, the moments due to the given loading:

$$M_A^L = 0 \text{ kNm}$$

$$M_B^L = 0 \text{ kNm}$$

$$M_C^L = V_A^L \times 3 - \frac{1}{2} \times 3 \times 30 \times \left(\frac{1}{3} \times 3\right)$$

$$= 45 \times 3 - \frac{1}{2} \times 3 \times 30 \times \left(\frac{1}{3} \times 3\right) = 90.0 \text{ kNm}$$

where, M_C^L is the moment at the mid-span.

The fixed end moments using the standard formulas:

$$M_{AB}^F = -\frac{5wL^2}{96} = -\frac{5 \times 30 \times 6^2}{96} = -56.25 \text{ kNm}$$

$$M_{BA}^F = \frac{5wL^2}{96} = \frac{5 \times 30 \times 6^2}{96} = 56.25 \text{ kNm}$$

The support reactions induced by the fixed end moments are obtained separately. Let the vertical reactions V_A^F and V_B^F be due to end moments, and assumed to be acting in upward direction.

$$\sum F_y = 0 \Rightarrow V_A^F + V_B^F = 0$$

$$\sum M_A = 0 \Rightarrow V_B^F \times 6 + 56.25 - 56.25 = 0$$

$$V_B^F = 0 \text{ kN}$$

$$V_A^F = 0 \text{ kN}$$

Since the fixed end moments at both supports are equal and opposite, no support reaction is induced.

Therefore, the values of shear force at various locations are obtained as

$S_A = V_A = 45$ kN

$S_C^{left} = 45 - \frac{1}{2} \times 30 \times 3 = 0$ kN

$S_C^{right} = 0$ kN

$S_B = 0 - \frac{1}{2} \times 30 \times 3 = -45$ kN

The shear force and bending moment diagrams are shown in Figures 3.19(ii) and 3.19(iii) respectively.

The net moment at C is, $M_C = 90.0 - 56.25 = 33.75$ kNm

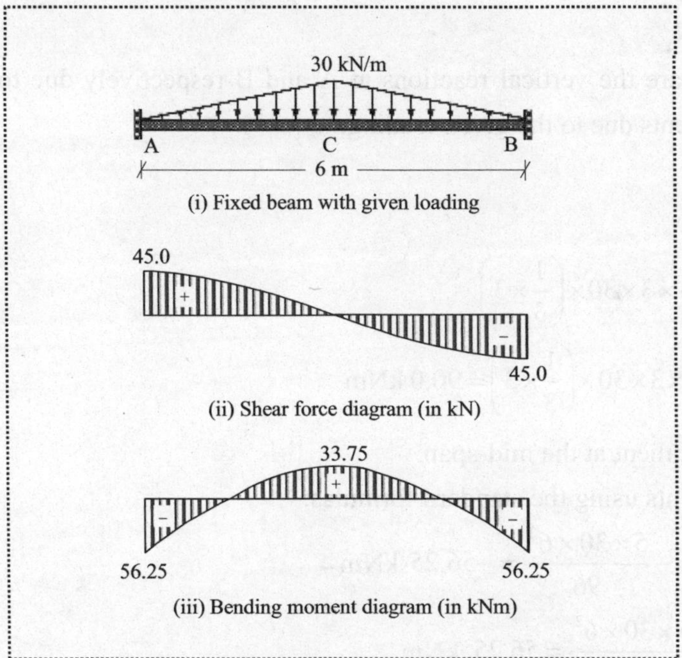

Figure 3.19 Solution for Example 3.8

3.4 Continuous Beam

When a beam has more than two supports, the beam is called a continuous beam. The reactions in the supports of a continuous beam cannot be directly obtained with the equations of static equilibrium only, hence the continuous beams are statically indeterminate.

In order to visualize the effects due to different levels of fixity (i.e., degree of fixity), consider a beam AB subjected a mid-span point load W as shown in Figure 3.20(i), in which, the supports A and B are not restrained against rotation (i.e., free to rotate), hence the moment at B is zero. Therefore, the slope at B is $\theta_B = WL^2/16EI$, which is taken as θ for reference. If the support B is fixed (i.e., restrained completely) as shown in Figure 3.20(ii), the value of θ_B is reduced to zero, hence the moment developed at B is $M_B = 3WL/16$. When the beam is continued over the support B as shown in Figure 3.20(iii), the value of θ_B lies between θ and zero, hence the moment developed at B lies between zero and $3WL/16$. As the elastic curve is continuous over the support B, the tangent drawn to the elastic curve at B forms $\theta_B = \theta_B^{left} = \theta_B^{right}$. Therefore, the intermediate support at B cannot be treated as "*simply supported*" unlike the simple support at the ends, and the adjoining span BC offers restraint to the rotation at B partially. That is why, the value of slope decreases, and the moment increases at B from the original simply supported condition. The amount of reduction/increase depends on the stiffness of the adjoining span. This means, when the stiffness is equal to zero, the behaviour is similar to Figure 3.20(i); and when the stiffness is equal to infinity, the behaviour is similar to Figure 3.20(ii).

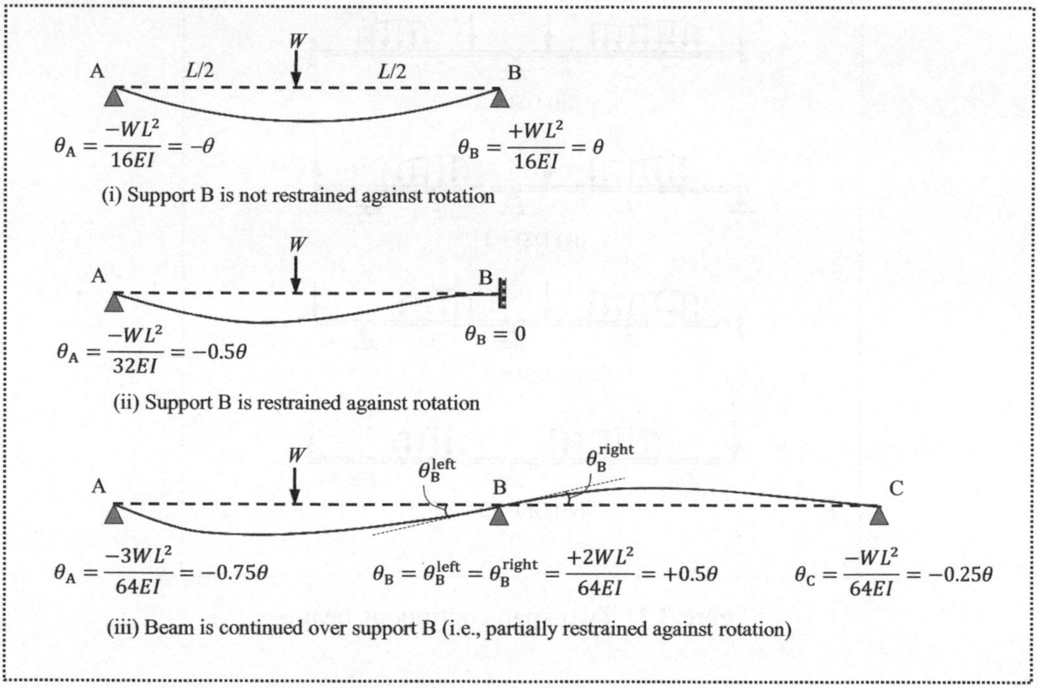

Figure 3.20 Behaviour of a continuous beam

3.4.1 Two-span Continuous Beam

When a beam has three supports, the beam is called a *two-span continuous beam*. Depending on the extreme end support conditions, different types of two-span continuous beam can be obtained as shown in Figure 3.21. The degree of static indeterminacy (DSI) varies from one to three, and the overhanging portions in Figures 3.21(iv)–3.21(vi) are not considered as separate spans of the continuous beam. This means that the value of m remains two for determining the DSI using $DSI = m + r - 2j$. However, the loads on these overhangs contribute to the shear and moment at the support to which the overhang portion is attached. Thus, once the contribution of these loads to the supports are taken into account, the overhanging portions can be suppressed conceptually for the purpose of determining the redundant forces.

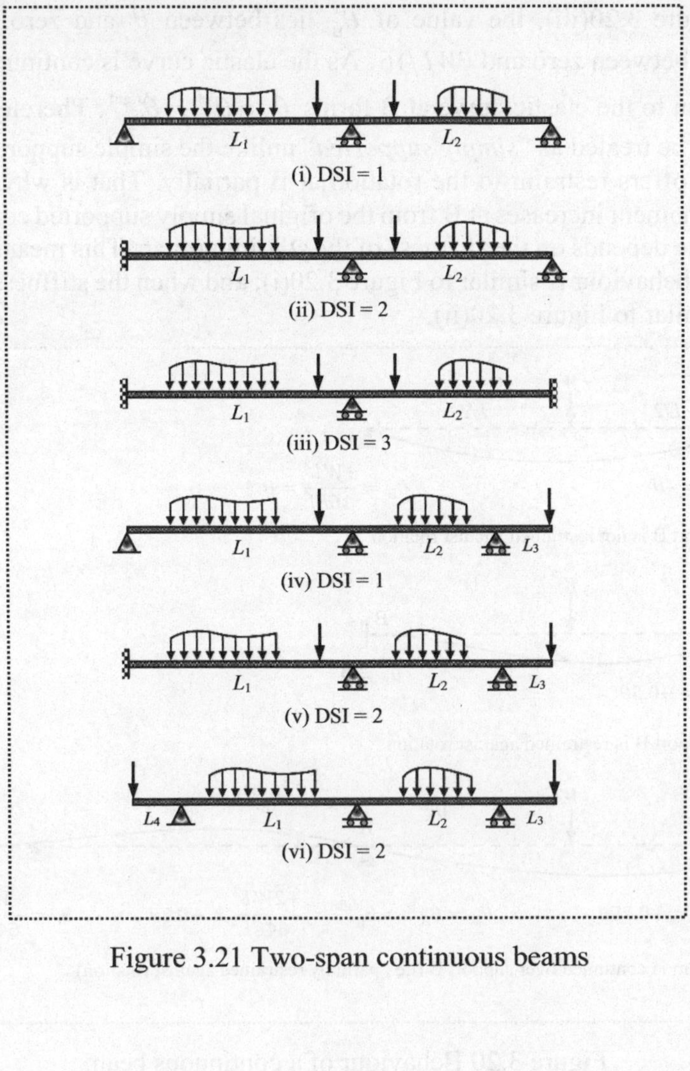

Figure 3.21 Two-span continuous beams

3.4.2 Theorem of Three Moments

Consider a two-span segment ABC of a continuous beam subjected to an arbitrary loading as shown in Figure 3.22. In span AB, the member end moments are M_{AB} and M_{BA}. Similarly, M_{BC} and M_{CB} are the end moments in span BC. These moments are hogging in nature for normal gravity loading. The rotations at A, B and C may be either clockwise or anti-clockwise depending on the relative stiffness and loads. The spans AB and BC can be separated by considering the rotational springs at the ends to accommodate the stiffness of the adjacent spans. The rotation θ_{BA} is the slope at B in the isolated span AB, which can be expressed in terms of the applied loading and end moments. Similarly, the rotation θ_{BC} is the slope at B in the isolated span BC.

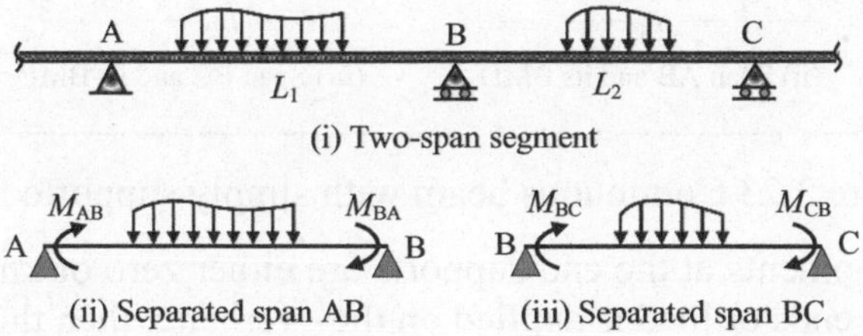

Figure 3.22 Two-span segment of a continuous beam

If each span has a uniform cross-section throughout its length, by applying the compatibility condition (i.e., $\theta_{BA} = \theta_{BC}$), an equation relating the three unknown moments ($M_{AB} = M_A$, $M_{BA} = M_{BC} = M_B$, and $M_{CB} = M_C$) can be established as

$$M_A\left(\frac{L_1}{I_1}\right) + 2M_B\left(\frac{L_1}{I_1} + \frac{L_2}{I_2}\right) + M_C\left(\frac{L_2}{I_2}\right) = -\left(\frac{6A_1\bar{x}_1}{I_1L_1} + \frac{6A_2\bar{x}_2}{I_2L_2}\right) \tag{3.21}$$

where

M_A, M_B, M_C → member end moments

L_1 and L_2 → lengths of span AB and span BC

I_1 and I_2 → moments of inertia of span AB and span BC

A_1 and A_2 → areas of bending moment diagram (i.e., isolated simply supported beams AB and BC)

$\bar{x}_1$ and $\bar{x}_2$ → centroids of bending moment diagram from A and C respectively

Eq. (3.21) is known as the *three-moment equation*, and since it was proposed by Clapeyron in 1857, this method is called *Clapeyron's Theorem of Three Moments*. This can be directly applied to solve two-span continuous beams with a single degree of static indeterminacy. For higher indeterminacy problems, independent three-moment equation should be established for every two adjacent spans. If all the spans have the same cross-section, Eq. (3.21) can be simplified as

$$M_AL_1 + 2M_B\left(L_1 + L_2\right) + M_CL_2 = -\left(\frac{6A_1\bar{x}_1}{L_1} + \frac{6A_2\bar{x}_2}{L_2}\right) \tag{3.22}$$

***Case 1**: Continuous beam with simply supported ends*

Consider a two-span continuous beam with simply supported ends subjected to arbitrary loading as shown in Figure 3.23(i).

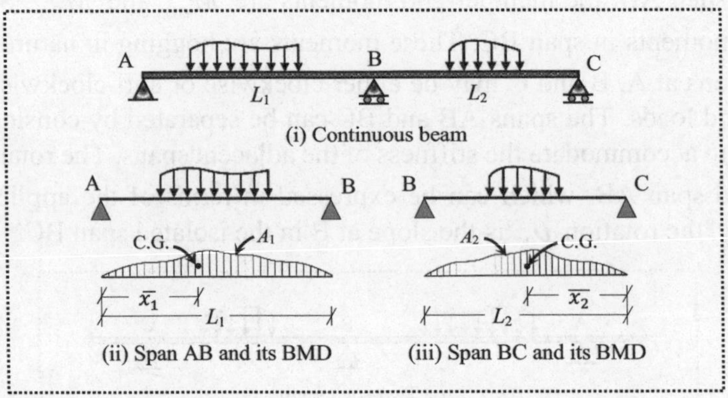

Figure 3.23 Continuous beam with simply supported ends

The values of bending moments at the end supports are either zero or known (i.e., if concentrated moment is applied at the ends or load is applied on the overhang, then the moment can be known). Since the DSI is one, Eq. (3.21) can be directly applied to solve for M_B, which is the only unknown.

$$(0)\times\left(\frac{L_1}{I_1}\right)+2M_B\times\left(\frac{L_1}{I_1}+\frac{L_2}{I_2}\right)+(0)\times\left(\frac{L_2}{I_2}\right)=-\left(\frac{6A_1\bar{x}_1}{I_1L_1}+\frac{6A_2\bar{x}_2}{I_2L_2}\right)$$

$$\Rightarrow 2M_B\left(\frac{L_1}{I_1}+\frac{L_2}{I_2}\right)=-\left(\frac{6A_1\bar{x}_1}{I_1L_1}+\frac{6A_2\bar{x}_2}{I_2L_2}\right)\Rightarrow M_B \text{ can be obtained}$$

The same concepts can be extended to a *three-span continuous beam* ABCD, with simply supported ends at A and D. In this case, the *DSI* is two. The moments $M_A=0$, $M_D=0$, M_B and M_C are the two unknown moments. Eq. (3.21) should be applied twice; by considering adjoining spans AB and BC first, and then BC and CD; thereby getting two equations which can be solved simultaneously to find the redundants M_B and M_C. In a similar manner, if a continuous beam has n spans (with extreme ends simply supported), Eq. (3.21) can be applied $(n-1)$ times for solving the redundant moments (i.e., $DSI=n-1$) associated with the intermediate support locations.

***Case 2**: Continuous beam with fixed ends*

Consider a two-span continuous beam with one extreme end fixed and other extreme end simply supported as shown in Figure 3.24(i). As the *DSI* is two, when Eq. (3.21) is applied for the two spans AB and BC, two unknowns will exist (M_A and M_B); hence they cannot be solved directly. Therefore, as shown in Figure 3.24(ii), assume an imaginary span A′A extending beyond the end A with simple supports both at A′ and A in such a way that the span A′A offers infinite flexural stiffness to restrain the rotation at A. Infinite flexural stiffness (i.e., EI_0/L_0) can be achieved by either having infinite flexural rigidity (i.e., $EI_0=\infty$) or an infinitely small span (i.e., $L_0=0$). It is convenient to choose the latter as it can be easily incorporated in Eq. (3.21). Therefore, the beam becomes a three-span continuous beam, where Eq. (3.21) can be independently applied to two "*two-span continuous beams*" A'AB and ABC. As there is no loading on span A'A, the area of BMD is zero (i.e., $A_0 = 0$).

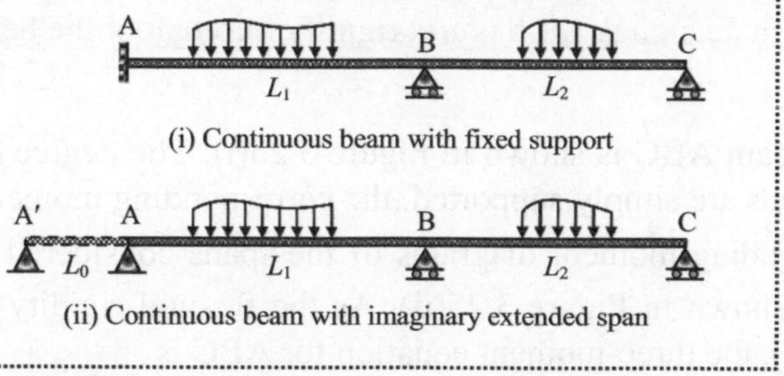

Figure 3.24 Continuous beam with a fixed support at one end

For A'AB:

$$M_{A'}\left(\frac{L_0}{I_0}\right)+2M_A\left(\frac{L_0}{I_0}+\frac{L_1}{I_1}\right)+M_B\left(\frac{L_1}{I_1}\right)=-\left(\frac{6A_0\bar{x}_0}{I_0L_0}+\frac{6A_1\bar{x}_1}{I_1L_1}\right)$$

$$\Rightarrow M_{A'}\left(\frac{0}{I_0}\right)+2M_A\left(\frac{0}{I_0}+\frac{L_1}{I_1}\right)+M_B\left(\frac{L_1}{I_1}\right)=-\left(\frac{6\times(0)\times\bar{x}_0}{I_0L_0}+\frac{6A_1\bar{x}_1}{I_1L_1}\right)$$

$$\Rightarrow 2M_A\left(\frac{L_1}{I_1}\right)+M_B\left(\frac{L_1}{I_1}\right)=-\left(\frac{6A_1\bar{x}_1}{I_1L_1}\right) \tag{3.23}$$

For ABC:

$$M_A\left(\frac{L_1}{I_1}\right)+2M_B\left(\frac{L_1}{I_1}+\frac{L_2}{I_2}\right)+M_C\left(\frac{L_2}{I_2}\right)=-\left(\frac{6A_1\bar{x}_1}{I_1L_1}+\frac{6A_2\bar{x}_2}{I_2L_2}\right)$$

$$\Rightarrow M_A\left(\frac{L_1}{I_1}\right)+2M_B\left(\frac{L_1}{I_1}+\frac{L_2}{I_2}\right)+(0)\left(\frac{L_2}{I_2}\right)=-\left(\frac{6A_1\bar{x}_1}{I_1L_1}+\frac{6A_2\bar{x}_2}{I_2L_2}\right)$$

$$\Rightarrow M_A\left(\frac{L_1}{I_1}\right)+2M_B\left(\frac{L_1}{I_1}+\frac{L_2}{I_2}\right)=-\left(\frac{6A_1\bar{x}_1}{I_1L_1}+\frac{6A_2\bar{x}_2}{I_2L_2}\right) \tag{3.24}$$

By solving Eq. (3.23) and Eq. (3.24), the two unknown moments, M_A and M_B can be obtained.

If the right extreme end is also fixed, then the *DSI* becomes three; hence all three moments M_A, M_B and M_C are the unknowns. Similar to an imaginary span A'A on the left end, an imaginary span CC' on the right end should also be assumed. Therefore, the beam becomes a *four-span continuous beam*, where Eq. (3.21) can be independently applied to three "*two-span continuous beams*" A'AB, ABC and BCC'. As there is no loading on span A'A and CC', the corresponding areas of BMD are zero. The resulting three simultaneous equations can be solved to obtain the unknown moments M_A, M_B and M_C.

3.4.3 Numerical Examples

Example 3.9: A continuous beam ABC is supported at A, B and C. The length of span AB is 6 m and span BC is 4 m. A concentrated load of 50 kN is acting at the mid-span of AB, and a uniformly distributed load of 20 kN/m is acting over the entire span of BC. Draw the shear force and bending moment diagrams. Assume a constant flexural rigidity throughout the beam.

Solution:

The continuous beam ABC is shown in Figure 3.25(i). The degree of static indeterminacy is one, as the extreme ends are simply supported, the corresponding moments are zero (i.e., $M_A = 0$ and $M_C = 0$). The bending moment diagrams of the spans considered independently as simply supported beams are shown in Figure 3.25(ii). As the flexural rigidity is constant for the entire beam (i.e., $I_1 = I_2 = I$), the three-moment equation for ABC is

$$M_A L_1 + 2M_B(L_1 + L_2) + M_C L_2 = -\left(\frac{6A_1\bar{x}_1}{L_1} + \frac{6A_2\bar{x}_2}{L_2}\right)$$

where,

$M_A = 0$; $M_C = 0$; $L_1 = 6$ m; $L_2 = 4$ m

Area of BMD in span AB, $A_1 = \frac{1}{2} \times 6 \times 75 = 225.0$ kNm^2

Area of BMD in span BC, $A_2 = \frac{2}{3} \times 4 \times 40 = 106.667$ kNm^2

Centroid of A_1 from A, $\bar{x}_1 = 6/2 = 3.0$ m (i.e., the shape is symmetrical)

Centroid of A_2 from A, $\bar{x}_2 = 4/2 = 2.0$ m (i.e., the shape is symmetrical)

Substituting the above values in the three-moment equation,

$$(0)(6) + 2 \times M_B \times (6+4) + (0)(4) = -\left(\frac{6 \times 225.0 \times 3}{6} + \frac{6 \times 106.667 \times 2}{4}\right)$$

$$20M_B = -995 \Rightarrow M_B = -49.75 \text{ kNm}$$

The moment M_B is hogging in nature; this typically means that the moment is clockwise at B for the span AB, and anti-clockwise at B for the span BC as represented in the free-body diagram shown in Figure 3.25(iii).

The maximum negative moment occurs at B (i.e., –49.75 kNm). However, the maximum positive moment may occur either in span AB or BC where the shear force changes its sign. Accordingly, in span AB, the shear force changes from positive to negative at D, where the value of moment is

$$M^+_{\max_1} = V_A \times 3 = 16.71 \times 3 = 50.13 \text{ kNm}$$

In span BC, let x be the distance from C, where shear force is zero.

$$20x - 27.56 = 0 \Rightarrow x = 1.378 \text{ m}$$

$$M^+_{\max_2} = V_C \times 1.378 - 20 \times 1.378 \times 1.378/2$$

$$= 27.56 \times 1.378 - 20 \times 1.378 \times 1.378/2 = 18.99 \text{ kNm}$$

Therefore, the maximum positive moment is 50.13 kNm.

The bending moment diagram drawn explicitly with horizontal straight base line is shown in Figure 3.25(vi). Both the bending moment diagrams represented in Figures 3.25(v) and 3.25(vi) are same, however, the only difference lies in the reference line.

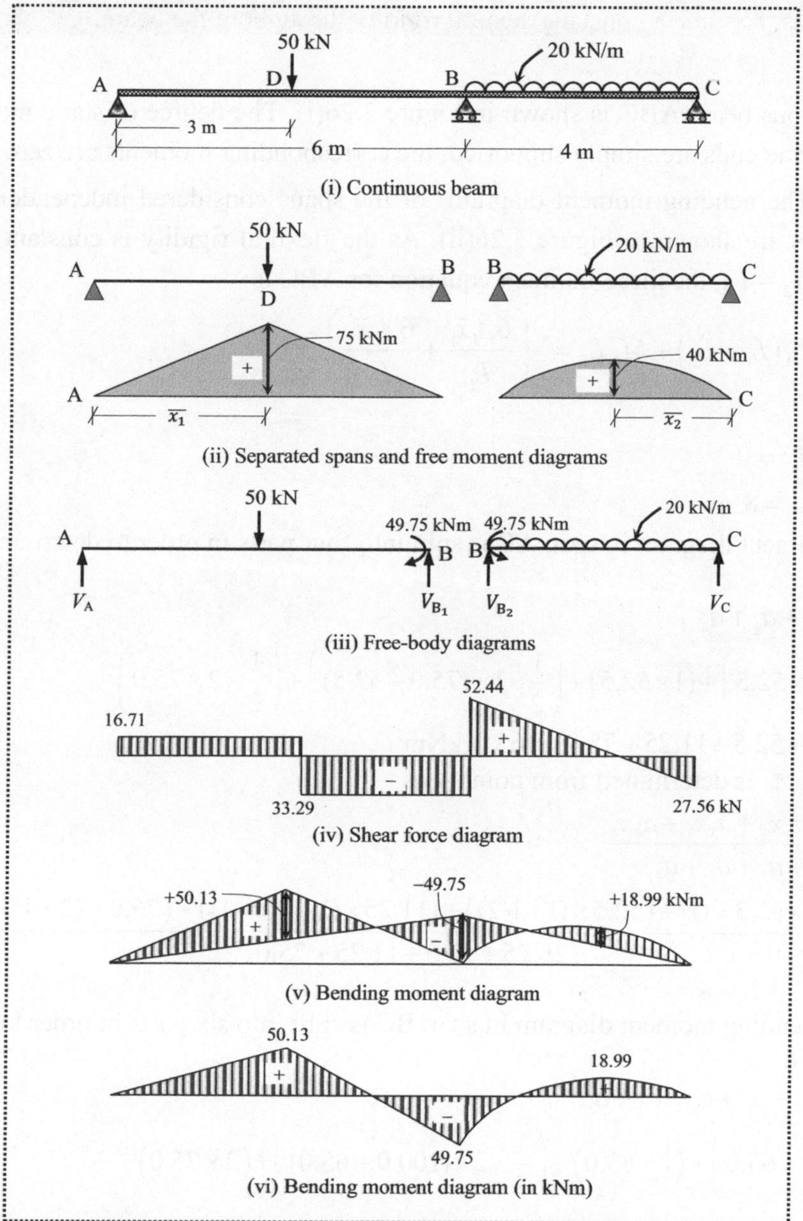

Figure 3.25 Continuous beam with simply supported ends (Example 3.9)

Example 3.10: A two-span continuous beam ABC (span AB is 4 m and span BC is 8 m) has the extreme ends simply supported. The span AB is subjected to two concentrated loads of 30 kN and 60 kN acting at 1 m and 2 m from A. The span BC is subjected to three concentrated loads of 25 kN, 30 kN and 15 kN respectively at 2 m, 4 m and 6 m from B. Draw the shear force and bending moment diagrams. Assume a constant flexural rigidity throughout the beam.

Solution:

The continuous beam ABC is shown in Figure 3.26(i). The degree of static indeterminacy is one, as the extreme ends are simply supported, the corresponding moments are zero (i.e., $M_A = 0$ and $M_C = 0$). The bending moment diagrams of the spans considered independently as simply supported beams are shown in Figure 3.26(ii). As the flexural rigidity is constant for the entire beam (i.e., $I_1 = I_2 = I$), the three-moment equation for ABC is

$$M_A L_1 + 2M_B(L_1 + L_2) + M_C L_2 = -\left(\frac{6A_1\bar{x}_1}{L_1} + \frac{6A_2\bar{x}_2}{L_2}\right)$$

where,

$$M_A = 0;\ M_C = 0$$

$$L_1 = 4\ \text{m};\ L_2 = 8\ \text{m}$$

The bending moment diagram in span AB is split into four parts in order to determine the area and centroid.

$$A_1 = a_1 + a_2 + a_3 + a_4$$

$$= \left(\frac{1}{2}\times 1\times 52.5\right) + (1\times 52.5) + \left(\frac{1}{2}\times 1\times(75.0-52.5)\right) + \left(\frac{1}{2}\times 2\times 75.0\right)$$

$$= 26.25 + 52.5 + 11.25 + 75.0 = 165.0\ \text{kNm}^2$$

The centroid of A_1 is determined from point A as

$$\bar{x}_1 = \frac{a_1x_1 + a_2x_2 + a_3x_3 + a_4x_4}{a_1 + a_2 + a_3 + a_4}$$

$$= \frac{(26.25\times(2/3\times 1)) + (52.5\times(1+1/2)) + (11.25\times(1+2/3\times 1)) + (75.0\times(2+1/3\times 2))}{26.25 + 52.5 + 11.25 + 75.0}$$

$$= 1.91\ \text{m}$$

Similarly, the bending moment diagram in span BC is split into six parts in order to determine the area and centroid.

$$A_2 = a_5 + a_6 + a_7 + a_8 + a_9 + a_{10}$$

$$= \left(\frac{1}{2}\times 2\times 65.0\right) + (2\times 65.0) + \left(\frac{1}{2}\times 2\times(100.0-65.0)\right) + (2\times 75.0)$$

$$+ \left(\frac{1}{2}\times 2\times(100.0-75.0)\right) + \left(\frac{1}{2}\times 2\times 75.0\right)$$

$$= 65.0 + 130.0 + 35.0 + 150.0 + 25.0 + 75.0 = 480.0\ \text{kNm}^2$$

The centroid of A_2 is determined from point C as

$$\bar{x}_2 = \frac{a_5x_5 + a_6x_6 + a_7x_7 + a_8x_8 + a_9x_9 + a_{10}x_{10}}{a_5 + a_6 + a_7 + a_8 + a_9 + a_{10}}$$

$$= \frac{\begin{pmatrix}(65.0\times(2/3\times2))+(130.0\times(2+2/2))+(35.0\times(2+2/3\times2))\\ +(150.0\times(4+2/2))+(25.0\times(4+1/3\times2))+(75.0\times(6+1/3\times2))\end{pmatrix}}{65.0+130.0+35.0+150.0+25.0+75.0}$$

$$= 4.08 \text{ m}$$

Substituting the values of A_1, A_2, x_1 and x_2 in the three-moment equation,

$$(0\times4)+(2\times M_B\times(4+8))+(0\times8) = -\left(\frac{6\times165.0\times1.91}{4}+\frac{6\times480.0\times4.08}{8}\right)$$

$$24M_B = -1941.53$$

$$\Rightarrow M_B = -80.9 \text{ kNm}$$

The moment M_B is hogging in nature; this typically means that the moment is clockwise at B for the span AB, and anti-clockwise at B for the span BC. Therefore, the vertical reactions are obtained by applying equilibrium conditions.

Span AB:

$$\sum F_y = 0 \Rightarrow V_A + V_{B_1} - 30 - 60 = 0$$

$$\sum M_A = 0 \Rightarrow V_{B_1}\times4 - 80.9 - 60\times2 - 30\times1 = 0$$

$$\Rightarrow V_{B_1} = 57.7 \text{ kN and } V_A = 32.3 \text{ kN.}$$

Span BC:

$$\sum F_y = 0 \Rightarrow V_{B_2} + V_C - 25 - 30 - 15 = 0$$

$$\sum M_C = 0 \Rightarrow V_{B_2}\times8 - 80.9 - 25\times6 - 30\times4 - 15\times2 = 0$$

$$\Rightarrow V_{B_2} = 47.6 \text{ kN and } V_C = 22.4 \text{ kN.}$$

The shear force and bending moment diagrams are shown in Figures 3.26(iii) and 3.26(iv) respectively.

Maximum negative moment $M_B = -80.9$ kNm

Maximum positive moment $M_G = 59.5$ kNm

The bending moment diagram drawn explicitly with horizontal straight base line is shown in Figure 3.26(v). Both the diagrams represented in Figures 3.26(iv) and 3.26(v) are same, however, the only difference lies in the reference line.

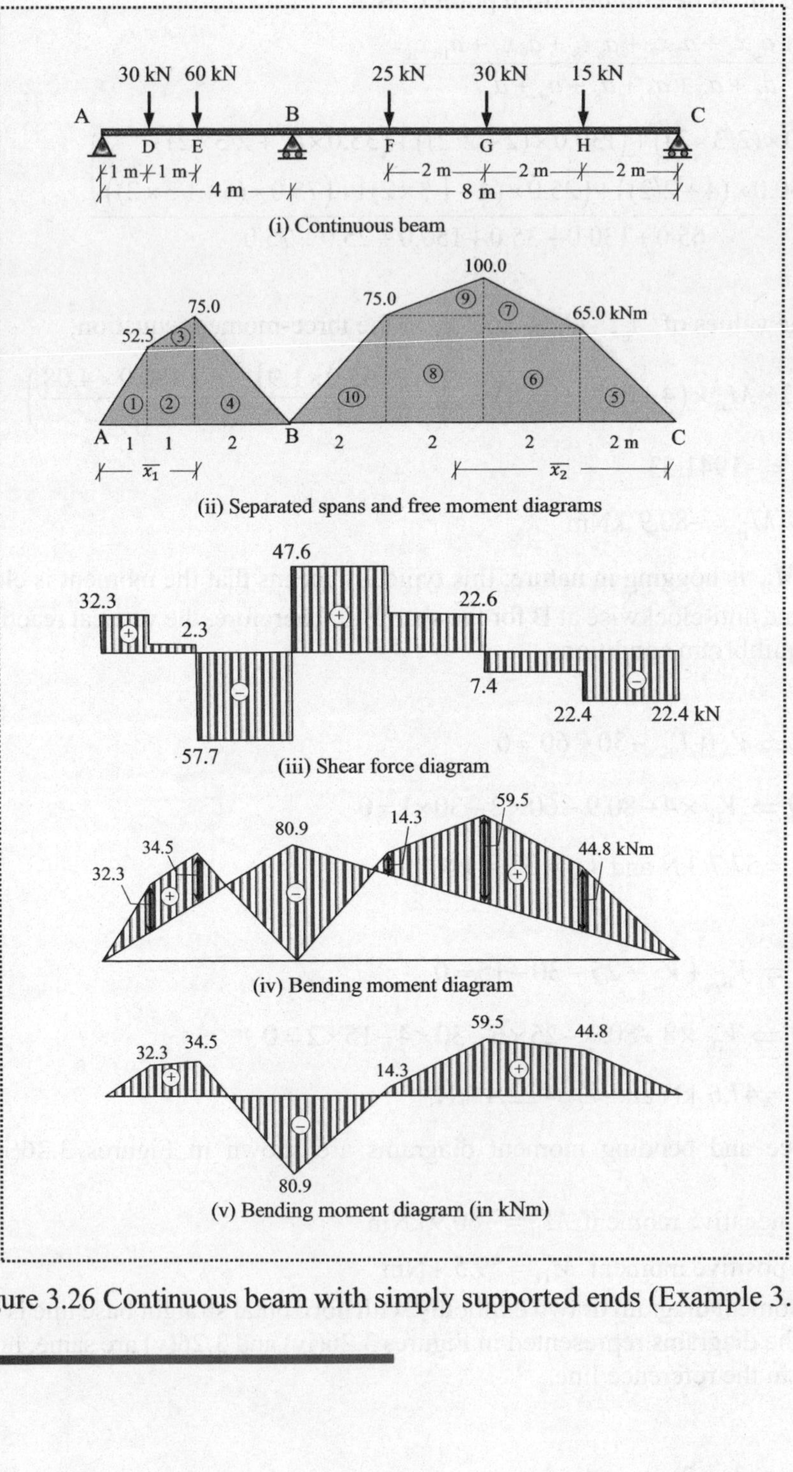

Figure 3.26 Continuous beam with simply supported ends (Example 3.10)

Example 3.11: A two-span continuous beam ABC (span AB is 6 m and span BC is 4 m) has the extreme end A fixed while the end C is hinged. The span AB is subjected to a uniformly distributed load of 10 kN/m over the entire span. The span BC is subjected to a concentrated load of 30 kN acting at 3 m from C. Draw the shear force and bending moment diagrams. Assume a constant flexural rigidity throughout the beam.

Solution:

The continuous beam ABC is shown in Figure 3.27(i). The degree of static indeterminacy is two. Since the extreme end A is fixed, assume an imaginary span A′A extending beyond the end A with simple supports both at A′ and A with a span $L_0 = 0$ as shown in Figure 3.27(ii). The bending moment diagrams of the spans considered independently as simply supported beams are shown in Figure 3.27(iii). As the flexural rigidity is constant for the entire beam (i.e., $I_1 = I_2 = I$), the three-moment equations for A′AB and ABC are written separately.

For A′AB:

$$M_{A'}L_0 + 2M_A\left(L_0 + L_1\right) + M_B L_1 = -\left(\frac{6A_0\bar{x}_0}{L_0} + \frac{6A_1\bar{x}_1}{L_1}\right)$$

where,

$M_{A'} = 0;\ L_0 = 0\ \text{m};\ L_1 = 6$

Area of BMD in span A′A, $A_0 = 0\ \text{kNm}^2$

Centroid of A_0 from A′, $\bar{x}_0 = 0\ \text{m}$

Area of BMD in span AB, $A_1 = \frac{2}{3} \times 6 \times 45 = 180\ \text{kNm}^2$

Centroid of A_1 from B, $\bar{x}_1 = 6/2 = 3.0\ \text{m}$ (i.e., the shape is symmetrical)

Substituting the above values in the three moment-equation for A′AB,

$$(0)(0) + 2M_A \times (0+6) + M_B \times (6) = -\left(0 + \frac{6 \times 180 \times 3}{6}\right)$$

$$12M_A + 6M_B = -540 \qquad (3.25)$$

For ABC:

$$M_A L_1 + 2M_B\left(L_1 + L_2\right) + M_C L_2 = -\left(\frac{6A_1\bar{x}_1}{L_1} + \frac{6A_2\bar{x}_2}{L_2}\right)$$

where,

$M_C = 0;\ L_1 = 6\ \text{m};\ L_2 = 4\ \text{m}$

Area of BMD in span AB, $A_1 = \frac{2}{3} \times 6 \times 45 = 180\ \text{kNm}^2$

Centroid of A_1 from A, $\bar{x}_1 = 6/2 = 3.0\ \text{m}$ (i.e., the shape is symmetrical)

Area of BMD in span BC, $A_2 = \frac{1}{2} \times 4 \times 22.5 = 45.0\ \text{kNm}^2$

Centroid of A_2 from C, $\bar{x}_2 = \dfrac{1+(2\times3)}{3} = 2.33$ m

Substituting the above values in the three moment-equation for ABC,

$$(M_A)(6) + 2M_B \times (6+4) + (0)(4) = -\left(\frac{6\times180.0\times3}{6} + \frac{6\times45.0\times2.33}{4}\right)$$

$$6M_A + 20M_B = -697.28 \tag{3.26}$$

Solving Eqs. (3.25) and (3.26),

$M_A = -32.43$ kNm and $M_B = -25.13$ kNm

The moments M_A and M_B are hogging in nature; this typically means that M_A is anti-clockwise at A, and M_B is clockwise at B for the span AB; and M_B is anti-clockwise at B for the span BC. Therefore, the vertical reactions are obtained by applying equilibrium conditions.

Span AB:

$$\sum F_y = 0 \Rightarrow V_A + V_{B_1} - 10\times6 = 0$$

$$\sum M_A = 0 \Rightarrow V_{B_1}\times6 - 25.13 - 10\times6\times6/2 + 32.43 = 0$$

$$\Rightarrow V_{B_1} = 28.78 \text{ kN and } V_A = 31.22 \text{ kN.}$$

Span BC:

$$\sum F_y = 0 \Rightarrow V_{B_2} + V_C - 30 = 0$$

$$\sum M_C = 0 \Rightarrow V_{B_2}\times4 - 25.13 - 30\times3 = 0$$

$$\Rightarrow V_{B_2} = 28.78 \text{ kN and } V_C = 1.22 \text{ kN.}$$

The shear force and bending moment diagrams are shown in Figures 3.27(iv) and 3.27(v) respectively. The maximum negative moment occurs at A (i.e., −32.43 kNm). However, the maximum positive moment occurs either in span AB or BC, where the shear force changes its sign. Accordingly, in span AB, let x be the distance from A, where shear force is zero.

$$10x - 32.43 = 0 \Rightarrow x = 3.24 \text{ m}$$

$$M^+_{\max_1} = V_A\times3.24 - 32.43 - 10\times3.24\times3.24/2$$

$$= 31.22\times3.24 - 32.43 - 10\times3.24\times3.24/2 = 16.23 \text{kNm}$$

In span BC, the shear force changes from positive to negative at D.

$$M^+_{\max_2} = V_C\times3 = 1.22\times3 = 3.66 \text{ kNm}$$

Therefore, the maximum positive moment is 16.23 kNm.

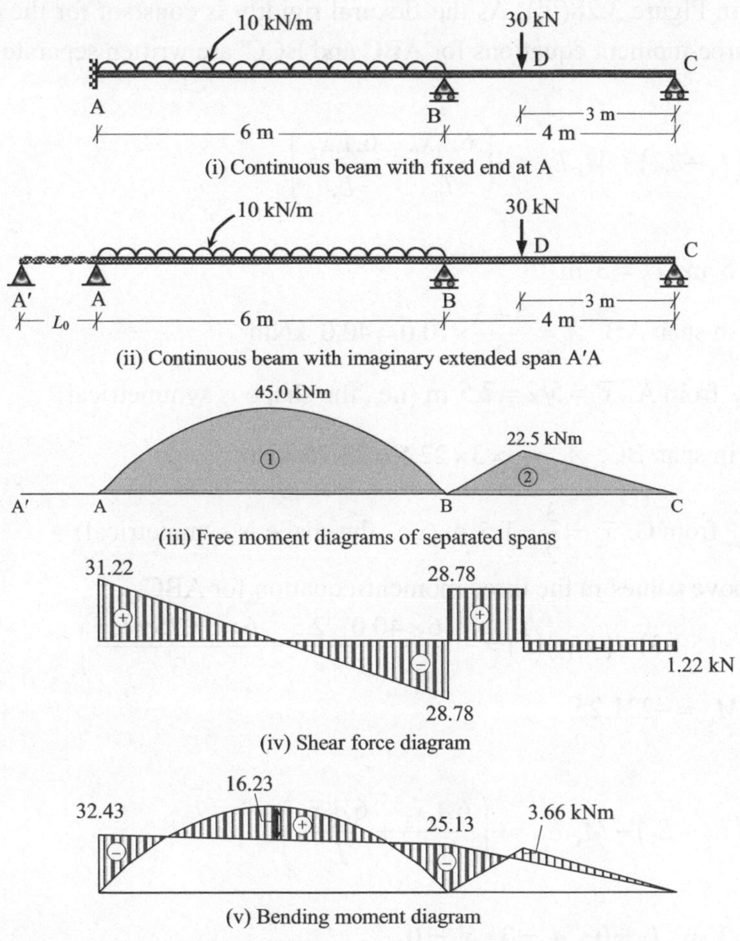

Figure 3.27 Continuous beam with a fixed end (Example 3.11)

Example 3.12: A two-span continuous beam ABC (span AB is 5 m and span BC is 3 m) has the extreme end A hinged while the end C is fixed. The span AB is subjected to two concentrated loads of 10 kN each acting at 1m, and 4 m from A. The span BC is subjected to a mid-span point load of 30 kN. Draw the shear force and bending moment diagrams. Assume a constant flexural rigidity throughout the beam.

Solution:

The continuous beam ABC is shown in Figure 3.28(i). The degree of static indeterminacy is two. Since the extreme end C is fixed, assume an imaginary span CC′ extending beyond the end C with simple supports both at C and C′ with a span $L_3 = 0$ as shown in Figure 3.28(ii).

The bending moment diagrams of the spans considered independently as simply supported beams are shown in Figure 3.28(iii). As the flexural rigidity is constant for the entire beam (i.e., $I_1 = I_2 = I$), the three-moment equations for ABC and BCC′ are written separately.

For ABC:

$$M_A L_1 + 2M_B(L_1 + L_2) + M_C L_2 = -\left(\frac{6A_1\bar{x}_1}{L_1} + \frac{6A_2\bar{x}_2}{L_2}\right)$$

where,

$M_A = 0$; $L_1 = 5$ m; $L_2 = 3$ m

Area of BMD in span AB, $A_1 = \frac{5+3}{2} \times 10.0 = 40.0$ kNm²

Centroid of A_1 from A, $\bar{x}_1 = 5/2 = 2.5$ m (i.e., the shape is symmetrical)

Area of BMD in span BC, $A_2 = \frac{1}{2} \times 3 \times 22.5 = 33.75$ kNm²

Centroid of A_2 from C, $\bar{x}_2 = \frac{3}{2} = 1.5$ m (i.e., the shape is symmetrical)

Substituting the above values in the three moment-equation for ABC,

$$(0)(5) + 2M_B \times (5+3) + (M_C)(3) = -\left(\frac{6 \times 40.0 \times 2.5}{5} + \frac{6 \times 33.75 \times 1.5}{3}\right)$$

$$16M_B + 3M_C = -221.25 \tag{3.27}$$

For BCC′:

$$M_B L_2 + 2M_C(L_2 + L_3) + M_{C'} L_3 = -\left(\frac{6A_2\bar{x}_2}{L_2} + \frac{6A_3\bar{x}_3}{L_3}\right)$$

where,

$M_{C'} = 0$; $L_2 = 3$ m; $L_3 = 0$; $A_3 = 0$; $\bar{x}_3 = 0$

Area of BMD in span BC, $A_2 = 33.75$ kNm²

Centroid of A_2 from B, $\bar{x}_2 = \frac{3}{2} = 1.5$ m (i.e., the shape is symmetrical)

Substituting the above values in the three moment-equation for BCC′,

$$(M_B)(3) + 2M_C \times (3+0) + (0)(0) = -\left(\frac{6 \times 33.75 \times 1.5}{3} + 0\right)$$

$$3M_B + 6M_C = -101.25 \tag{3.28}$$

Solving Eqs. (3.25) and (3.26),

$M_B = -11.77$ kNm and $M_C = -10.99$ kNm

The moments M_B and M_C are hogging in nature; this typically means that M_B is clockwise at B for the span AB; and M_B is anti-clockwise at B and M_C is clockwise at C for the span BC.

Therefore, the vertical reactions are obtained by applying equilibrium conditions.

Span AB:

$$\sum F_y = 0 \Rightarrow V_A + V_{B_1} - 10 - 10 = 0$$

$$\sum M_A = 0 \Rightarrow V_{B_1} \times 5 - 11.77 - 10 \times 4 - 10 \times 1 = 0$$

$$\Rightarrow V_{B_1} = 12.35 \text{ kN and } V_A = 7.65 \text{ kN.}$$

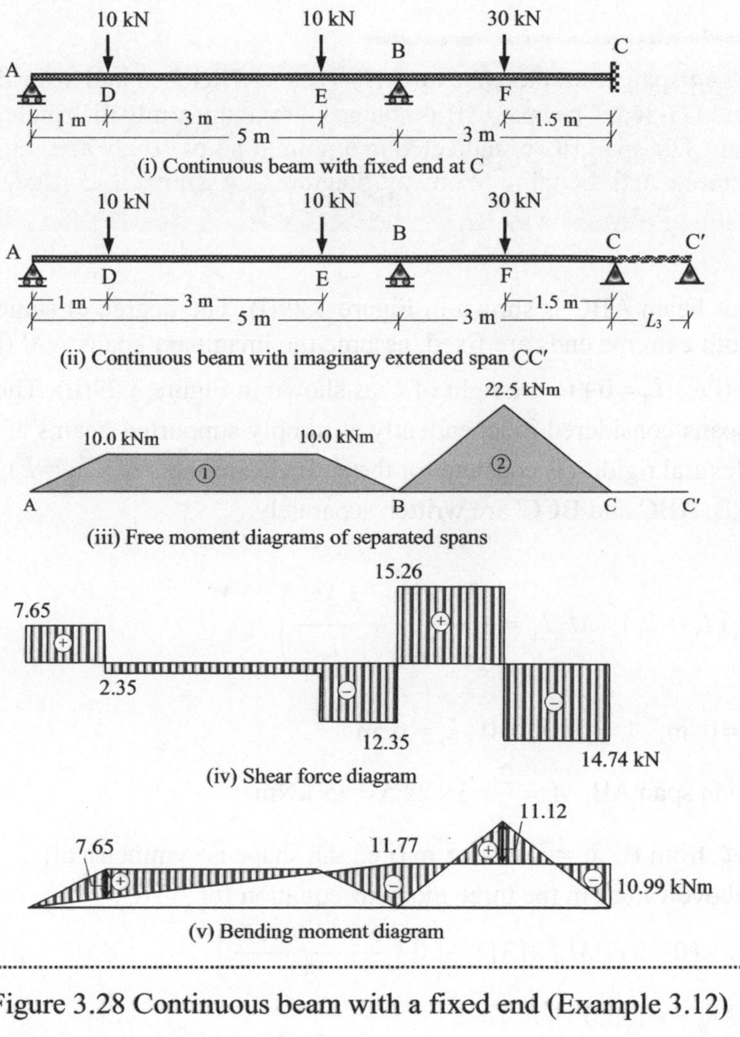

Figure 3.28 Continuous beam with a fixed end (Example 3.12)

Span BC:

$$\sum F_y = 0 \Rightarrow V_{B_2} + V_C - 30 = 0$$

$$\sum M_C = 0 \Rightarrow V_{B_2} \times 3 - 11.77 - 30 \times 1.5 + 10.99 = 0$$

$$\Rightarrow V_{B_2} = 15.26 \text{ kN and } V_C = 14.74 \text{ kN.}$$

The shear force and bending moment diagrams are shown in Figures 3.28(iv) and 3.28(v) respectively.

Net positive moment at D, $M_D = 7.65 \times 1.0 = 7.65$ kNm

Net positive moment at F, $M_F = 14.74 \times 1.5 - 10.99 = 11.12$ kNm

Example 3.13: A two-span continuous beam ABC (span AB is 3 m and span BC is 5 m) has the extreme ends A and C fixed. The span AB is subjected to a uniformly distributed load of 20 kN/m over the entire span. The span BC is subjected to a point load of 30 kN at 3 m from the right end. Draw the shear force and bending moment diagrams. Assume a constant flexural rigidity throughout the beam.

Solution:

The continuous beam ABC is shown in Figure 3.29(i). The degree of static indeterminacy is three. Since the both extreme ends are fixed, assume the imaginary spans AA′ (i.e., $L_0 = 0$) to the left of A and CC′ (i.e., $L_3 = 0$) to the right of C as shown in Figure 3.29(ii). The bending moment diagrams of the spans considered independently as simply supported beams are shown in Figure 3.29(iii). As the flexural rigidity is constant for the entire beam (i.e., $I_1 = I_2 = I$), the three-moment equations for A′AB, ABC and BCC′ are written separately.

For A′AB:

$$M_{A'}L_0 + 2M_A(L_0 + L_1) + M_B L_1 = -\left(\frac{6A_0\bar{x}_0}{L_0} + \frac{6A_1\bar{x}_1}{L_1}\right)$$

where,

$M_{A'} = 0$; $L_0 = 0$ m; $A_0 = 0$; $\bar{x}_0 = 0$; $L_1 = 6$ m

Area of BMD in span AB, $A_1 = \frac{2}{3} \times 3 \times 22.5 = 45$ kNm^2

Centroid of A_1 from B, $\bar{x}_1 = 3/2 = 1.5$ m (i.e., the shape is symmetrical)

Substituting the above values in the three moment-equation for A′AB,

$$(0)(0) + 2M_A \times (0+3) + M_B \times (3) = -\left(0 + \frac{6 \times 45.0 \times 1.5}{3}\right)$$

$$6M_A + 3M_B = -135.0 \qquad (3.29)$$

For ABC:

$$M_A L_1 + 2M_B(L_1 + L_2) + M_C L_2 = -\left(\frac{6A_1\bar{x}_1}{L_1} + \frac{6A_2\bar{x}_2}{L_2}\right)$$

where,

$L_1 = 3$ m; $L_2 = 5$ m

Area of BMD in span AB, $A_1 = 45.0$ kNm^2

Centroid of A_1 from A, $\bar{x}_1 = 3/2 = 1.5$ m (i.e., the shape is symmetrical)

Area of BMD in span BC, $A_2 = \frac{1}{2} \times 5 \times 36.0 = 90.0$ kNm^2

Centroid of A_2 from C, $\bar{x}_2 = \frac{3+5}{3} = 2.67$ m

Substituting the above values in the three moment-equation for ABC,

$$(M_A)(3) + 2M_B \times (3+5) + (M_C)(5) = -\left(\frac{6 \times 45.0 \times 1.5}{3} + \frac{6 \times 90.0 \times 2.67}{5}\right)$$

$$3M_A + 16M_B + 5M_C = -423.36 \tag{3.30}$$

For BCC′:

$$M_B L_2 + 2M_C(L_2 + L_3) + M_{C'} L_3 = -\left(\frac{6A_2\bar{x}_2}{L_2} + \frac{6A_3\bar{x}_3}{L_3}\right)$$

where,

$L_2 = 5$ m; $L_3 = 0$; $M_{C'} = 0$; $A_3 = 0$; $\bar{x}_3 = 0$

Area of BMD in span BC, $A_2 = 90.0$ kNm^2

Centroid of A_2 from B, $\bar{x}_2 = \frac{2+5}{3} = 2.33$ m

Even though the free moment diagram in BC is used the two-span segments ABC and BCC′, the appropriate values of centroid should be used. The centroid $\bar{x}_2 = 2.33$ m is calculated from B for the two-span segment BCC′, while the centroid $\bar{x}_2 = 2.67$ m already calculated was from C for the two-span segment ABC.

Substituting the above values in the three moment-equation for BCC′,

$$(M_B)(5) + 2M_C \times (5+0) + (0)(0) = -\left(\frac{6 \times 90 \times 2.33}{5} + 0\right)$$

$$5M_B + 10M_C = -251.64 \tag{3.31}$$

Solving Eqs. (3.29)–(3.31)

$M_A = -12.92$ kNm

$M_B = -19.17$ kNm

$M_C = -15.58$ kNm

The moments M_A, M_B and M_C are hogging in nature; this typically means that the moment M_A is anti-clockwise at A, and the moment M_B is clockwise at B for the span AB; and the moment M_B is anti-clockwise at B, and the moment M_C is clockwise at C for the span BC. Therefore, the vertical reactions are obtained by applying equilibrium conditions.

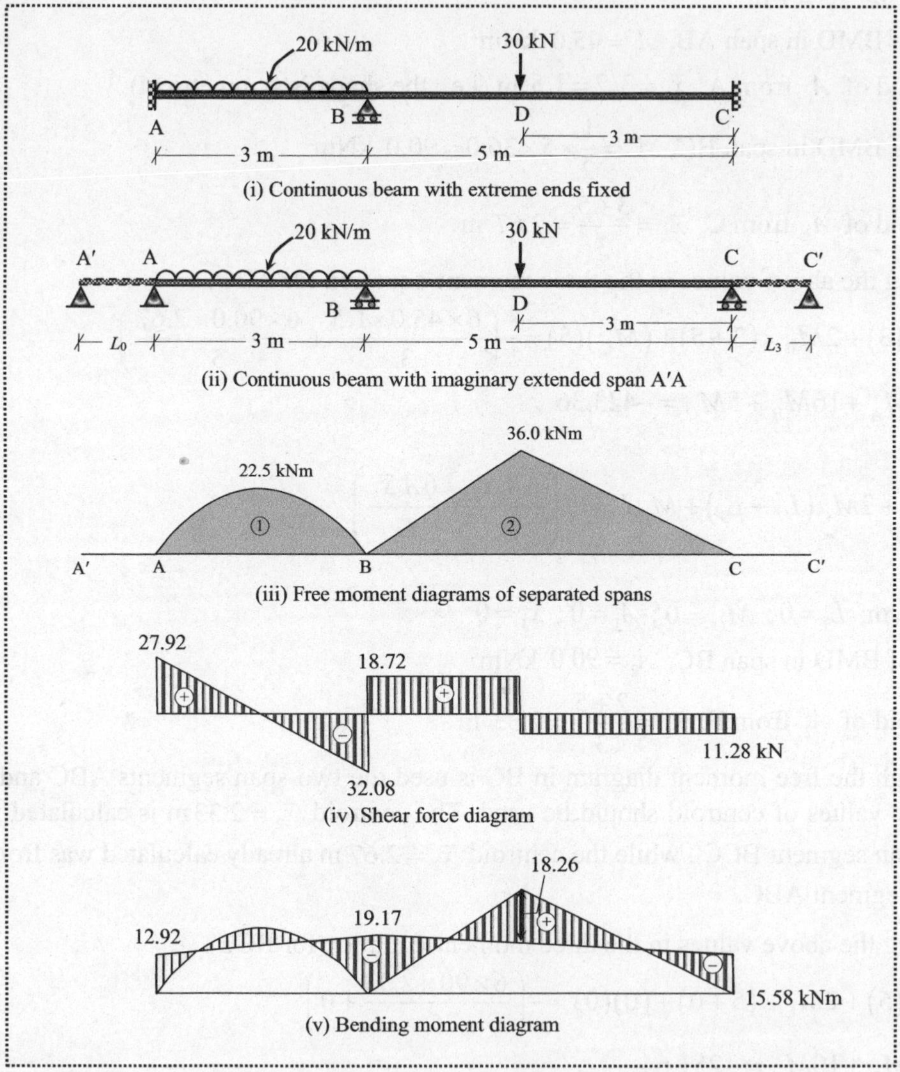

Figure 3.29 Continuous beam with fixed ends (Example 3.13)

Span AB:

$$\sum F_y = 0 \Rightarrow V_A + V_{B_1} - 20\times 3 = 0$$

$$\sum M_A = 0 \Rightarrow V_{B_1}\times 3 - 19.17 - 20\times 3\times 3/2 + 12.92 = 0$$

$\Rightarrow V_{B_1} = 32.08$ kN and $V_A = 27.92$ kN.

Span BC:

$$\sum F_y = 0 \Rightarrow V_{B_2} + V_C - 30 = 0$$

$$\sum M_C = 0 \Rightarrow V_{B_2} \times 5 - 19.17 - 30 \times 3 + 15.58 = 0$$

$$\Rightarrow V_{B_2} = 18.72 \text{ kN and } V_C = 11.28 \text{ kN.}$$

The shear force and bending moment diagrams are shown in Figures 3.29(iv) and 3.29(v) respectively. The maximum negative moment occurs at B (i.e., 19.17 kNm). However, the maximum positive moment occurs either in span AB or BC, where the shear force changes its sign. Accordingly, in span AB, let x be the distance from A, where shear force is zero.

$$27.92 - 20x = 0 \Rightarrow x = 1.40 \text{ m}$$

$$M^+_{max_1} = V_A \times 1.4 - 12.92 - 20 \times 1.4 \times 1.4/2$$

$$= 27.92 \times 1.4 - 12.92 - 20 \times 1.4 \times 1.4/2 = 6.57 \text{ kNm}$$

In span BC, the shear force changes from positive to negative at D.

$$M^+_{max_2} = V_C \times 3 = 11.28 \times 3 - 15.58 = 18.26 \text{ kNm}$$

Therefore, the maximum positive moment is 18.26 kNm.

Example 3.14: A continuous beam ABCD (span AB is 5 m; span BC is 4 m; span CD is 1 m) has the extreme end A fixed and extreme end D is free (i.e., CD is overhanging). The span AB is subjected to a point load of 30 kN at 2 m from A, the span BC is subjected to a mid-span point load of 20 kN, and the span CD is subjected to a point load of 10 kN at the tip. Draw the shear force and bending moment diagrams. Assume a constant flexural rigidity throughout the beam.

Solution:

The continuous beam ABCD is shown in Figure 3.30(i). The degree of static indeterminacy is two. Since the extreme end A is fixed, assume an imaginary span A′A extending beyond the end A with simple supports both at A′ and A with a span $L_0 = 0$ as shown in Figure 3.30(ii).

The bending moment diagrams of the spans considered independently as simply supported beams are shown in Figure 3.30(iii). The value of moment at C is directly obtained from the overhanging portion CD. As the flexural rigidity is constant for the entire beam (i.e., $I_1 = I_2 = I$), the three-moment equations for A′AB and ABC are written separately.

For A′AB:

$$M_{A'}L_0 + 2M_A(L_0 + L_1) + M_B L_1 = -\left(\frac{6A_0\bar{x}_0}{L_0} + \frac{6A_1\bar{x}_1}{L_1}\right)$$

where,

$$M_{A'} = 0$$

$$L_0 = 0 \text{ m; } A_0 = 0;\ \bar{x}_0 = 0;\ L_1 = 5 \text{ m}$$

Area of BMD in span AB, $A_1 = \frac{1}{2} \times 5 \times 36 = 90.0\ \text{kNm}^2$

Centroid of A_1 from B, $\bar{x}_1 = \frac{3+5}{3} = 2.67\ \text{m}$

Substituting the above values in the three moment-equation for A'AB,

$$(0)(0) + 2M_A \times (0+5) + M_B \times (5) = -\left(0 + \frac{6 \times 90.0 \times 2.67}{5}\right)$$

$$10M_A + 5M_B = -288.36 \qquad (3.32)$$

<u>For ABC:</u>

$$M_A L_1 + 2M_B (L_1 + L_2) + M_C L_2 = -\left(\frac{6A_1\bar{x}_1}{L_1} + \frac{6A_2\bar{x}_2}{L_2}\right)$$

where,

$L_1 = 5$ m; $L_2 = 4$ m

$M_C = -10 \times 1 = -10.0$ kNm (due to the load on overhanging portion)

Area of BMD in span AB, $A_1 = 90.0\ \text{kNm}^2$

Centroid of A_1 from A, $\bar{x}_1 = \frac{2+5}{3} = 2.33\ \text{m}$

Area of BMD in span BC, $A_2 = \frac{1}{2} \times 4 \times 20.0 = 40.0\ \text{kNm}^2$

Centroid of A_2 from C, $\bar{x}_2 = \frac{4.0}{2} = 2.0$ m (i.e., the shape is symmetrical)

Substituting the above values in the three moment-equation for ABC,

$$M_A \times (5) + 2M_B \times (5+4) + (-10)(4) = -\left(\frac{6 \times 90.0 \times 2.33}{5} + \frac{6 \times 40.0 \times 2.0}{4}\right)$$

$$5M_A + 18M_B = -331.64 \qquad (3.33)$$

Solving Eqs. (3.32) and (3.33),

$M_A = -22.79$ kNm

$M_B = -12.09$ kNm

The moments M_A, M_B and M_C are hogging in nature; this typically means that the moment M_A is anti-clockwise at A, and the moment M_B is clockwise at B for the span AB; the moment M_B is anti-clockwise at B, and the moment M_C is clockwise at C for the span BC; and the moment M_C is anti-clockwise at C for the span CD. Therefore, the vertical reactions are obtained by applying equilibrium conditions.

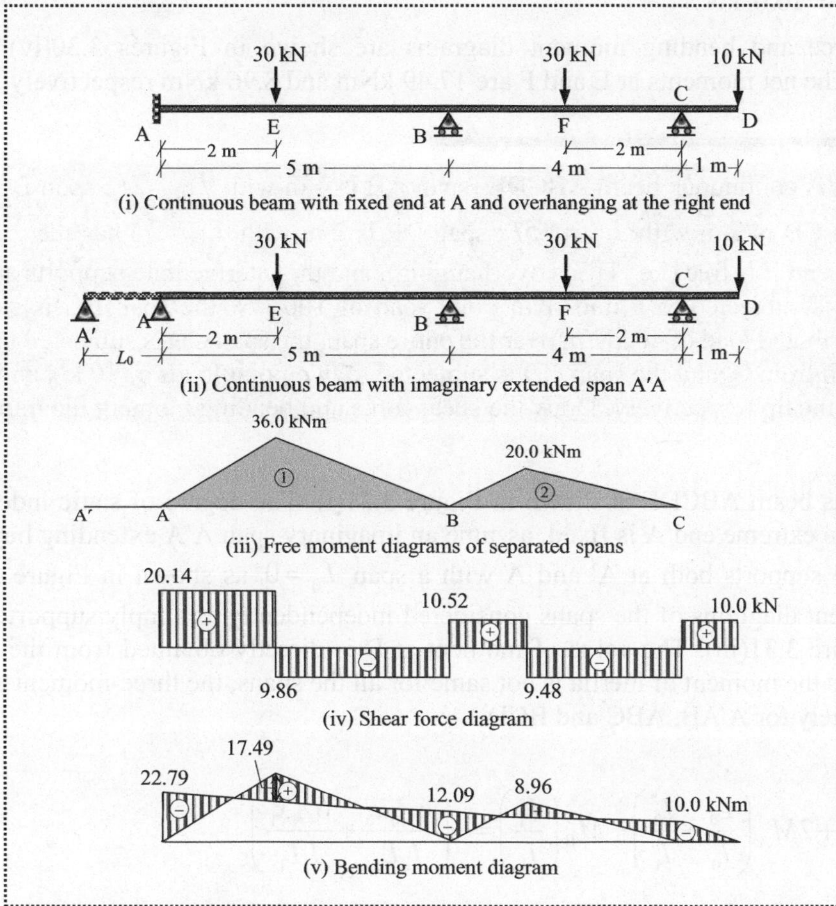

Figure 3.30 Continuous beam with an overhang (Example 3.14)

Span AB:

$$\sum F_y = 0 \Rightarrow V_A + V_{B_1} - 30 = 0$$

$$\sum M_A = 0 \Rightarrow V_{B_1} \times 5 - 12.09 - 30 \times 2 + 22.79 = 0$$

$$\Rightarrow V_{B_1} = 9.86 \text{ kN and } V_A = 20.14 \text{ kN.}$$

Span BC:

$$\sum F_y = 0 \Rightarrow V_{B_2} + V_{C_1} - 20 = 0$$

$$\sum M_C = 0 \Rightarrow V_{B_2} \times 4 - 12.09 - 20 \times 2 + 10.0 = 0$$

$$\Rightarrow V_{B_2} = 10.52 \text{ kN and } V_{C_1} = 9.48 \text{ kN.}$$

Span CD:

$$\sum F_y = 0 \Rightarrow V_{C_2} - 10 = 0$$

$\Rightarrow V_{C_2} = 10.0$ kN

The shear force and bending moment diagrams are shown in Figures 3.30(iv) and 3.30(v) respectively. The net moments at E and F are 17.49 kNm and 8.96 kNm respectively.

Example 3.15: A continuous beam ABCDE (span AB is 4 m with $I_{AB} = 2I$; span BC is 3 m with $I_{BC} = 3I$; span CD is 3 m with $I_{CD} = 1.5I$; span DE is 2 m with $I_{DE} = I$) has the extreme end A fixed, extreme end E is free (i.e., DE is overhanging), and the intermediate supports at B, C and D. The span AB is subjected to a mid-span point load of 100 kN, the span BC is subjected to a uniformly distributed load of 40 kN/m over the entire span, the span CD is subjected to a point load of 90 kN at 1 m from C, and the span CD is subjected to two point loads of 10 kN and 5 kN at 1 m from D and at the tip respectively. Draw the shear force and bending moment diagrams.

Solution:

The continuous beam ABCDE is shown in Figure 3.31(i). The degree of static indeterminacy is three. Since the extreme end A is fixed, assume an imaginary span A′A extending beyond the end A with simple supports both at A′ and A with a span $L_0 = 0$ as shown in Figure 3.31(ii). The bending moment diagrams of the spans considered independently as simply supported beams are shown in Figure 3.31(iii). The value of moment at D is directly obtained from the overhanging portion DE. As the moment of inertia is not same for all the spans, the three-moment equations are written separately for A′AB, ABC and BCD.

For A′AB:

$$M_{A'}\left(\frac{L_0}{I_0}\right) + 2M_A\left(\frac{L_0}{I_0} + \frac{L_1}{I_1}\right) + M_B\left(\frac{L_1}{I_1}\right) = -\left(\frac{6A_0\bar{x}_0}{I_0L_0} + \frac{6A_1\bar{x}_1}{I_1L_1}\right)$$

where,

$M_{A'} = 0$

$L_0 = 0$ m; $A_0 = 0$; $\bar{x}_0 = 0$

$L_1 = 4$ m; $I_1 = 2I$

Area of BMD in span AB, $A_1 = \frac{1}{2} \times 4 \times 100 = 200.0$ kNm^2

Centroid of A_1 from B, $\bar{x}_1 = \frac{4}{2} = 2.0$ m (i.e., the shape is symmetrical)

Substituting the above values in the three moment-equation for A′AB,

$$0 + 2M_A\left(0 + \frac{4}{2I}\right) + M_B\left(\frac{4}{2I}\right) = -\left(0 + \frac{6 \times 200.0 \times 2.0}{2I \times 4}\right)$$

$$4M_A + 2M_B = -300.0 \tag{3.34}$$

For ABC:

$$M_A\left(\frac{L_1}{I_1}\right)+2M_B\left(\frac{L_1}{I_1}+\frac{L_2}{I_2}\right)+M_C\left(\frac{L_2}{I_2}\right)=-\left(\frac{6A_1\bar{x}_1}{I_1L_1}+\frac{6A_2\bar{x}_2}{I_2L_2}\right)$$

where,

$L_1=4$ m; $I_1=2I$; $L_2=3$ m; $I_2=3I$

Area of BMD in span AB, $A_1=200.0\ \text{kNm}^2$

Centroid of A_1 from A, $\bar{x}_1=\frac{4}{2}=2.0$ m (i.e., the shape is symmetrical)

Area of BMD in span BC, $A_2=\frac{2}{3}\times3\times45.0=90.0\ \text{kNm}^2$

Centroid of A_2 from C, $\bar{x}_2=\frac{3}{2}=1.5$ m (i.e., the shape is symmetrical)

Substituting the above values in the three moment-equation for ABC,

$$M_A\left(\frac{4}{2I}\right)+2M_B\left(\frac{4}{2I}+\frac{3}{3I}\right)+M_C\left(\frac{3}{3I}\right)=-\left(\frac{6\times200.0\times2.0}{2I\times4}+\frac{6\times90.0\times1.5}{3I\times3}\right)$$

$$2M_A+6M_B+M_C=-390.0 \qquad (3.35)$$

For BCD:

$$M_B\left(\frac{L_2}{I_2}\right)+2M_C\left(\frac{L_2}{I_2}+\frac{L_3}{I_3}\right)+M_D\left(\frac{L_3}{I_3}\right)=-\left(\frac{6A_2\bar{x}_2}{I_2L_2}+\frac{6A_3\bar{x}_3}{I_3L_3}\right)$$

where,

$L_2=3$ m; $I_2=3I$; $L_3=3$ m; $I_3=1.5I$

$M_D=-5\times2-10\times1=-20.0$ kNm (due to the loads on overhanging portion)

Area of BMD in span BC, $A_2=90.0\ \text{kNm}^2$

Centroid of A_2 from B, $\bar{x}_2=\frac{3}{2}=1.5$ m (i.e., the shape is symmetrical)

Area of BMD in span CD, $A_3=\frac{1}{2}\times3\times60.0=90.0\ \text{kNm}^2$

Centroid of A_3 from D, $\bar{x}_3=\frac{2+3}{3}=1.667$ m

Substituting the above values in the three moment-equation for BCD,

$$M_B\left(\frac{3}{3I}\right)+2M_C\left(\frac{3}{3I}+\frac{3}{1.5I}\right)+(-20.0)\left(\frac{3}{1.5I}\right)=-\left(\frac{6\times90.0\times1.5}{3I\times3}+\frac{6\times90.0\times1.667}{1.5I\times3}\right)$$

$$M_B+6M_C=-250.0 \qquad (3.36)$$

Solving Eqs. (3.34)–(3.36),

$$M_A = -54.48 \text{ kNm}$$

$$M_B = -41.03 \text{ kNm}$$

$$M_C = -34.83 \text{ kNm}$$

The moments M_A, M_B and M_C are hogging in nature; this typically means that the moment M_A is anti-clockwise at A, and the moment M_B is clockwise at B for the span AB; the moment M_B is anti-clockwise at B, and the moment M_C is clockwise at C for the span BC; and the moment M_C is anti-clockwise at C, and the moment M_D is clockwise at D for the span CD; and the moment M_D is anti-clockwise at D for the span DE. Therefore, the vertical reactions are obtained by applying equilibrium conditions.

Span AB:

$$\sum F_y = 0 \Rightarrow V_A + V_{B_1} - 100 = 0$$

$$\sum M_A = 0 \Rightarrow V_{B_1} \times 4 - 54.48 - 100 \times 2 + 41.03 = 0$$

$$V_{B_1} = 53.36 \text{ kN}$$

$$V_A = 46.64 \text{ kN}$$

Span BC:

$$\sum F_y = 0 \Rightarrow V_{B_2} + V_{C_1} - 40 \times 3 = 0$$

$$\sum M_C = 0 \Rightarrow V_{B_2} \times 3 - 41.03 - 40 \times 3 \times 3/2 + 34.83 = 0$$

$$V_{B_2} = 62.07 \text{ kN}$$

$$V_{C_1} = 57.93 \text{ kN}$$

Span CD:

$$\sum F_y = 0 \Rightarrow V_{C_2} + V_{D_1} - 90 = 0$$

$$\sum M_D = 0 \Rightarrow V_{C_2} \times 3 - 34.83 - 90 \times 2 + 20.0 = 0$$

$$V_{C_2} = 64.94 \text{ kN}$$

$$V_{D_1} = 25.06 \text{ kN}$$

Span DE:

$$\sum F_y = 0 \Rightarrow V_{D_2} - 10 - 5 = 0$$

$$V_{D_2} = 15.0 \text{ kN}$$

The shear force and bending moment diagrams are shown in Figures 3.31(iv) and 3.31(v) respectively.

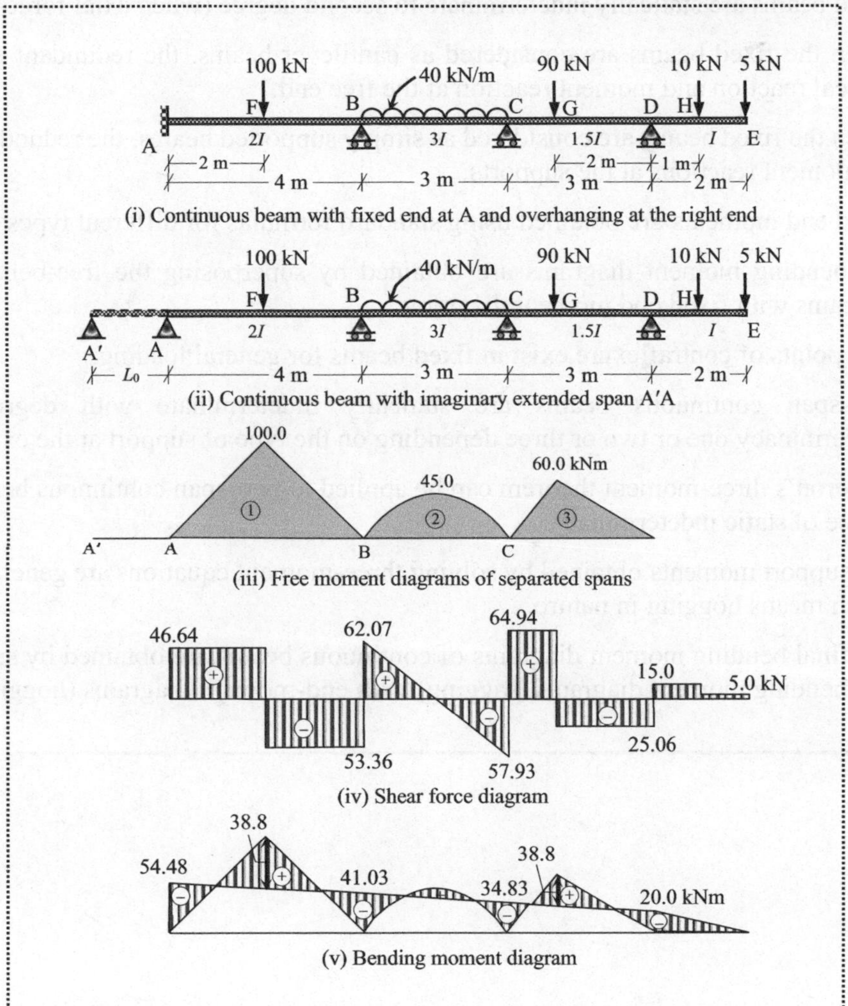

Figure 3.31 Three-span continuous beam (Example 3.15)

UNIT SUMMARY

- ✓ Fixed beams are statically indeterminate to second degree (when axial force is neglected).
- ✓ When the fixed beams are considered as cantilever beams, the redundant forces are the vertical reaction and moment reaction at the free end.
- ✓ When the fixed beams are considered as simply supported beams, the redundant forces are the moment reactions at the supports.
- ✓ Fixed end moments are obtained using standard formulas for different types of loads.
- ✓ Net bending moment diagrams are obtained by superposing the free-bending moment diagrams with fixed end moment diagrams.
- ✓ Two points of contraflexure exist in fixed beams for general loading.
- ✓ Two-span continuous beams are statically indeterminate with degree of static indeterminacy one or two or three depending on the type of support at the extreme ends.
- ✓ Claperon's three-moment theorem can be applied to two-span continuous beams with one degree of static indeterminacy.
- ✓ The support moments obtained by solving three-moment equations are generally negative, which means hogging in nature.
- ✓ The final bending moment diagrams of continuous beams are obtained by superimposing free-bending moment diagrams (sagging) with end-moment diagrams (hogging).

EXERCISES

3.1. A fixed beam of span 6 m is subjected to a point load of 50 kN at 2 m from the left support. Draw the shear force and bending moment diagrams.

3.2. A fixed beam of span 6 m is subjected to two point loads of 50 kN and 75 kN at 2 m and 4 m from the left support. Draw the shear force and bending moment diagrams.

3.3. A fixed beam of span 12 m is subjected to three concentrated loads of 100 kN each at every 3 m interval. Draw the shear force and bending moment diagrams.

3.4. A fixed beam of span 6 m is subjected to a uniformly distributed load of 20 kN/m over the entire span, and a concentrated load of 40 kN at the mid-spam. Draw the shear force and bending moment diagrams.

3.5. A fixed beam of span 6 m is subjected to a uniformly varying load with 30 kN/m at the left support and 20 kN/m at the right support. Draw the shear force and bending moment diagrams.

3.6. A two span continuous beam ABC (AB=6 m; BC=3 m) with extreme ends simply supported is subjected to 30 kN each at the mid-span locations. Analyse the beam for the force responses, and draw the shear force and bending moment diagrams.

3.7. A two-span continuous beam ABC (AB=6 m; BC=3 m) with extreme ends simply supported is subjected a uniformly distributed load of 10 kN/m over the span AB, and two point loads of 20 kN each at every 1 m in the span BC. Draw the shear force and bending moment diagrams.

3.8. A two-span continuous beam ABC (AB=6 m; BC=3 m) with fixed at A and simply supported at C is subjected a uniformly distributed load of 10 kN/m over the span AB, and two point loads of 20 kN each at every 1 m in the span BC. Draw the shear force and bending moment diagrams.

3.9. A two-span continuous beam ABC (AB=6 m; BC=3 m) with extreme ends fixed is subjected a mid-span point load of 30 kN in the span AB, and two point loads of 20 kN each at every 1 m in the span BC. Draw the shear force and bending moment diagrams.

3.10. A continuous beam ABCD (span of AB is 4 m with $I_{AB} = 3I$; span of BC is 3 m with $I_{BC} = 2I$; span of CD is 1 m with $I_{CD} = 1.5I$) with fixed support at A, intermediate supports at B and C, and free at D (i.e., overhanging CD) is subjected a mid-span point load of 30 kN in the span AB, a uniformly distributed load of 15 kN/m in the span BC, and a point load of 5 kN at the tip of span CD. Draw the shear force and bending moment diagrams.

QR Code for *Fixed and Continuous Beams*

NPTEL Lecture: https://www.youtube.com/watch?v=-rB-UB7r55Q

4 Moment Distribution Method

UNIT SPECIFICS

This unit discusses the following aspects.

- Concept of moment distribution method
- Force responses of statically indeterminate beams
- Force responses of statically indeterminate frames

RATIONALE

Force responses of statically indeterminate structures can be obtained by adopting either compatibility or equilibrium based approaches. Irrespective of the method adopted, the resulting equations are solved simultaneously. However, the solution process becomes tedious when the number of equation is more. Therefore, this chapter presents an iterative procedure for analyzing statically indeterminate beams and frames.

UNIT OUTCOMES

List of outcomes of this unit is as follows.

U4-O1: Describe the methods of structural analysis
U4-O2: Application of iterative methods
U4-O3: Development of moment distribution method
U4-O4: Analysis of statically indeterminate beams
U4-O5: Analysis of statically indeterminate frames

Mapping of Unit-4 Outcomes with Course Outcomes *

	CO-1	CO-2	CO-3	CO-4	CO-5
U4-O1	1	1	3	3	1
U4-O2	1	1	3	3	1
U4-O3	1	1	3	3	1
U4-O4	1	1	3	3	1
U4-O5	1	1	3	3	1

* (1- Weak correlation; 2- Medium correlation; 3- Strong correlation)

4.1 Introduction

The analysis of statically determinate structures and statically indeterminate structures necessarily requires the application of static equilibrium conditions. As already seen, the equilibrium equations alone are not sufficient to get a complete set of responses in case of statically indeterminate structures. Therefore, many methods have been developed to analyse the indeterminate structures under two broad approaches namely *compatibility methods* and *equilibrium methods*. In compatibility methods (e.g., consistent deformation method, theorem of three moments etc.), the identified redundants are determined after applying the compatibility conditions. However, in equilibrium methods (e.g., slope-deflection method), displacements are determined after applying the equilibrium conditions, and subsequently the force responses are obtained. Therefore, equilibrium methods are more comprehensive as the complete set of displacements and forces are readily obtained. Nonetheless, the solution process becomes laborious when the number of equations (i.e., equal to number of degrees of kinematic indeterminacy) is large. Hence, an iterative method based on a step-by-step procedure is developed, in which the initial step gives an approximation to the solution, and each subsequent step acts to refine the solution. The iteration can be terminated when the desired degree of accuracy is achieved.

4.2 Slope-Deflection Equations

The slope-deflection method was developed by George A. Maney in 1915 for analyzing statically indeterminate structures. This method is an equilibrium method that accounts for flexural deformations but ignores axial and shear deformations. The general form of force-deformation equation is written as

$$M_{nf} = M_{nf}^{\mathrm{F}} + 2EK_{nf}\left(2\theta_n + \theta_f - 3\psi_{nf}\right) \tag{4.1}$$

where

M_{nf} - member end moment

M_{nf}^{F} - fixed end moment

E - modulus of elasticity

K_{nf} - stiffness factor (equal to I/L)

θ_n and θ_f - member end rotations

ψ_{nf} - chord rotation (equal to Δ_{nf}/L)

Δ_{nf} - transverse displacement between the member ends

and, the subscripts "*n*" and "*f*" refer to the "*near-end*" and "*far-end*" of member nf.

Consider a beam segment AB subjected to arbitrary lateral loading as shown in Figure 4.1(i). In the absence of transverse displacement between the member ends, Eq. (4.1) is written for the end moments as

$$M_{\mathrm{AB}} = M_{\mathrm{AB}}^{\mathrm{F}} + \frac{2EI}{L}\left(2\theta_{\mathrm{A}} + \theta_{\mathrm{B}}\right) \tag{4.2}$$

$$M_{\mathrm{BA}} = M_{\mathrm{BA}}^{\mathrm{F}} + \frac{2EI}{L}\left(2\theta_{\mathrm{B}} + \theta_{\mathrm{A}}\right) \tag{4.3}$$

Eq. (4.2) and Eq. (4.3) can be understood as follows.

(i) The applied loads induce bending of the beam, and the elastic curve rotates by θ_A and θ_B over the supports at A and B respectively. This eventually balances the member end moments at the joints as $M_{AA'} = M_{AB}$ and $M_{BA} = M_{BB'}$.

(ii) Assume the supports A and B are fixed such that the rotations at A and B are arrested. This introduces the fixed end moments M^F_{AB} and M^F_{BA} as shown in Figure 4.1(ii).

(iii) Now support A is allowed to rotate by θ_A (i.e., fixed condition is released) by keeping the support B still fixed. This process develops the end moments in terms of θ_A as $M_{AB} = \dfrac{4EI}{L}\theta_A$ and $M_{BA} = \dfrac{2EI}{L}\theta_A$ as shown in Figure 4.1(iii).

(iv) Similarly, now support B is allowed to rotate by θ_B (i.e., fixed condition is released) by keeping the support A fixed. This process develops the end moments in terms of θ_B as $M_{AB} = \dfrac{2EI}{L}\theta_B$ and $M_{BA} = \dfrac{4EI}{L}\theta_B$ as shown in Figure 4.1(iv).

(v) Therefore, the total moment on the member end is thus seen to be the superposition of the above individual effects.

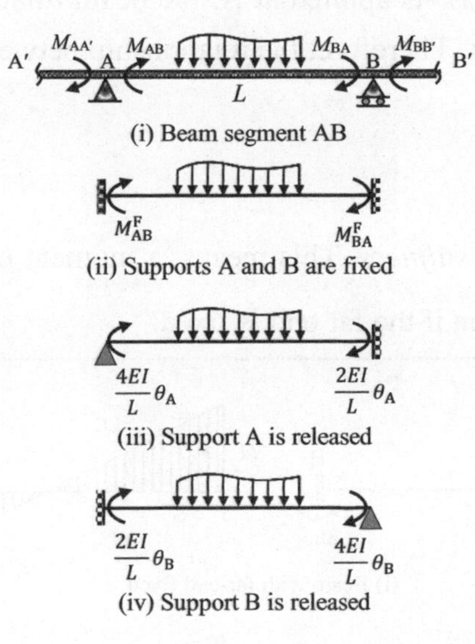

Figure 4.1 Segment of a continuous beam

The end-moment equations are functions of unknown displacements. Therefore, the moment equilibrium conditions are applied at each joint, and the resulting simultaneous equations are solved for the displacements (i.e., number of unknown displacements is equal to number of degrees of kinematic indeterminacy). Finally, the member end moments are obtained by substituting the displacement quantities into the end-moment equations.

4.3 Moment Distribution Method for Beams

Even though the slope-deflection method produces the complete set of displacements and forces, the direct solutions to the simultaneous equations are infeasible for large number of unknown displacements. Moreover, displacements need to be necessarily determined in order to obtain the force responses. Alternatively, an iterative method called the *moment distribution method* was developed by Hardy Cross in 1930, in which the explicit determination of the unknown displacement is avoided, and the various end moments are directly obtained.

The physical significance of the steps in iterative procedure involves fixing the unknown displacements and releasing them one at a time. The process of fixity results in moments accumulating at various joints, which need to be balanced. These moments are distributed to the various connecting elements depending on their relative stiffness, and also the distributed moments are getting carried over to the far-ends. Some of these carried over moments create imbalance, which necessitates further balancing in the subsequent step. This alternating procedure of fixing and releasing (i.e., balancing) is iteratively carried out until the residual unbalanced moments at all joints become negligible.

4.3.1 Bending Stiffness

Consider a prismatic beam AB with a hinged support at A, and fixed support at B as shown in Figure 4.2(i). When a moment M is applied at A, the beam rotates by an angle θ_A at A, and a moment M_{BA} is developed at B. Therefore, the relationship between the applied moment and the rotation is expressed as,

$$M = \left(\frac{4EI}{L}\right)\theta_A = \bar{K}\theta_A \tag{4.4}$$

where $\bar{K} = \frac{4EI}{L}$ is the *bending stiffness*. This means, a moment equal to $\frac{4EI}{L}$ is required to be applied at A to cause unit rotation if the far end is fixed.

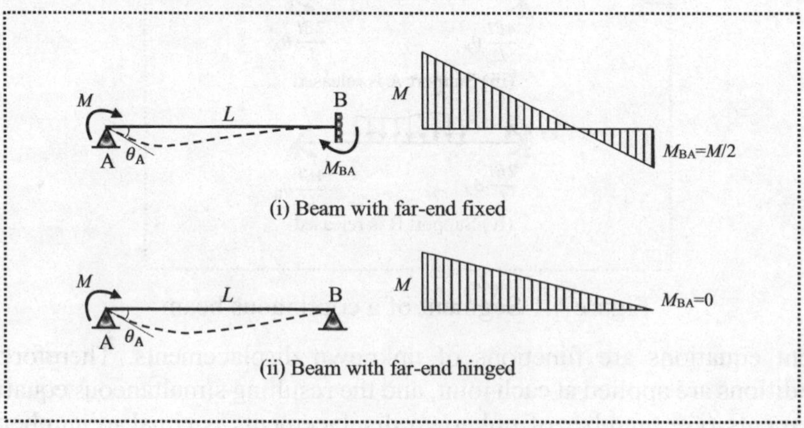

Figure 4.2 A prismatic beam

Similarly, when the far end B is hinged as shown in Figure 4.2(ii), the relationship between the applied moment and the rotation is

$$M = \left(\frac{3EI}{L}\right)\theta_A = \bar{K}\theta_A \tag{4.5}$$

where $\bar{K} = \frac{3EI}{L}$ is the *bending stiffness*. This means, a moment equal to $\frac{3EI}{L}$ is required to be applied at A to cause unit rotation if the far end is hinged.

4.3.2 Carry-Over Moment

When a moment M is applied at A for a beam with the far end fixed as shown in Figure 4.2(i), a moment M_{BA} develops at B which is termed as the *carry-over moment*. Therefore, M_{BA} is expressed in terms of the applied moment.

$$M_{BA} = \left(\frac{2EI}{L}\right)\theta_A = \frac{M}{2} \tag{4.6}$$

Eq. (4.6) indicates, when a moment M is applied at A, one-half of the applied moment is carried over to the far end B if it is fixed. Therefore, the *carry-over factor* (COF) is $1/2$.

Similarly, when the far end is hinged as shown in Figure 4.2(ii), no moment develops at B. Hence, the *carry-over factor* (COF) is zero. The respective bending moment diagrams are also shown in Figure 4.2.

4.3.3 Distribution Factor

Consider a structure with three members connected at B as shown in Figure 4.3. When a moment M is applied at joint B to cause a rotation θ_B, each of the three members connected to the joint B resists the applied moment by a fraction depending on its relative stiffness. From the moment equilibrium at B,

$$\sum M_B = 0 \Rightarrow M + M_{BA} + M_{BC} + M_{BD} = 0$$

$$M = -(M_{BA} + M_{BC} + M_{BD}) \tag{4.7}$$

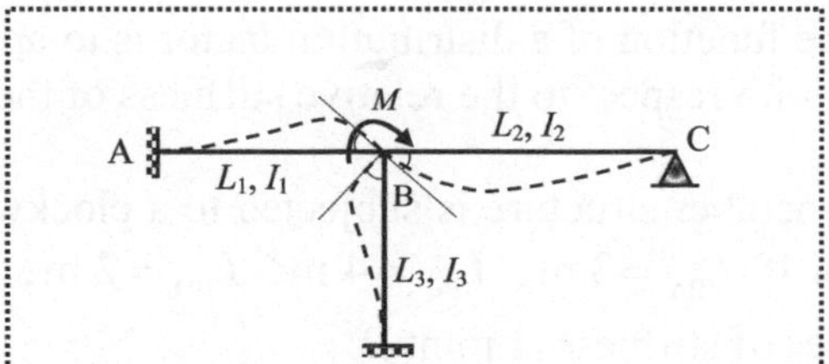

Figure 4.3 Three-member frame structure

When θ_B occurs at joint B, the ends of all members connected to the joint also rotates to the same amount as the members are rigidly connected to joint B. Therefore, the moment resisted by each member can be expressed in terms of joint rotation θ_B.

$$M_{BA} = \bar{K}_{BA}\theta_B \tag{4.8}$$

$$M_{BC} = \bar{K}_{BC}\theta_B \tag{4.9}$$

$$M_{BD} = \bar{K}_{BD}\theta_B \tag{4.10}$$

where $\bar{K}_{BA}$, $\bar{K}_{BC}$, and $\bar{K}_{BD}$ are the bending stiffness of the members. Substitution of Eqs. (4.8)–(4.10) into Eq. (4.7) yields

$$M = -\left(\bar{K}_{BA} + \bar{K}_{BC} + \bar{K}_{BD}\right)\theta_B = -\left(\sum \bar{K}_B\right)\theta_B \tag{4.11}$$

$$\theta_B = \frac{-M}{\left(\sum \bar{K}_B\right)} \tag{4.12}$$

where $\sum \bar{K}_B$ represents sum of the bending stiffness of all the members connected to joint B. Therefore, Eqs. (4.8)–(4.10) become:

$$M_{BA} = \bar{K}_{BA} \times \frac{-M}{\left(\sum \bar{K}_B\right)} = -\left(\frac{\bar{K}_{BA}}{\sum \bar{K}_B}\right) M = -\gamma_{BA} M \tag{4.13}$$

$$M_{BC} = \bar{K}_{BC} \times \frac{-M}{\left(\sum \bar{K}_B\right)} = -\left(\frac{\bar{K}_{BC}}{\sum \bar{K}_B}\right) M = -\gamma_{BC} M \tag{4.14}$$

$$M_{BD} = \bar{K}_{BD} \times \frac{-M}{\left(\sum \bar{K}_B\right)} = -\left(\frac{\bar{K}_{BD}}{\sum \bar{K}_B}\right) M = -\gamma_{BD} M \tag{4.15}$$

where $\gamma_{BA} = \dfrac{\bar{K}_{BA}}{\sum \bar{K}_B}$, $\gamma_{BC} = \dfrac{\bar{K}_{BC}}{\sum \bar{K}_B}$, and $\gamma_{BD} = \dfrac{\bar{K}_{BD}}{\sum \bar{K}_B}$ are the distribution factors of members AB, BC and BD for end B. The function of a distribution factor is to apportion the moment applied at a joint to the member end with respect to the relative stiffness of the member among the members connected to that joint.

For example, a three-member structure is subjected to a clockwise moment of 100 kNm at B as shown in Figure 4.4(i). If $L_{BA} = 3$ m, $L_{BC} = 4$ m, $L_{BD} = 2$ m, $EI_{BA} = 2EI$, $EI_{BC} = 2EI$ and $EI_{BD} = 3EI$, then the values of stiffness at joint B:

$$\bar{K}_{BA} = \frac{3EI_{BA}}{L_{BA}} \quad \text{(i.e., the far end A is hinged)}$$

$$\bar{K}_{BA} = \frac{3 \times (2EI)}{3} = 2EI$$

$$\bar{K}_{BC} = \frac{3EI_{BC}}{L_{BC}} \text{ (i.e., the far end C is hinged)}$$

$$\bar{K}_{BC} = \frac{3\times(2EI)}{4} = 1.5EI$$

$$\bar{K}_{BD} = \frac{4EI_{BD}}{L_{BD}} \text{ (i.e., the far end D is fixed)}$$

$$\bar{K}_{BD} = \frac{4\times(3EI)}{2} = 6EI$$

Therefore, the distribution factors are

$$\gamma_{BA} = \frac{\bar{K}_{BA}}{\sum \bar{K}_B} = \frac{\bar{K}_{BA}}{\bar{K}_{BA}+\bar{K}_{BC}+\bar{K}_{BD}} = \frac{2EI}{2EI+1.5EI+6EI} = 0.21$$

$$\gamma_{BC} = \frac{\bar{K}_{BC}}{\sum \bar{K}_B} = \frac{\bar{K}_{BC}}{\bar{K}_{BA}+\bar{K}_{BC}+\bar{K}_{BD}} = \frac{1.5EI}{2EI+1.5EI+6EI} = 0.16$$

$$\gamma_{BD} = \frac{\bar{K}_{BD}}{\sum \bar{K}_B} = \frac{\bar{K}_{BD}}{\bar{K}_{BA}+\bar{K}_{BC}+\bar{K}_{BD}} = \frac{6EI}{2EI+1.5EI+6EI} = 0.63$$

From the distribution factors, the end moments can be obtained as

$$M_{BA} = -\gamma_{BA}M = -0.21\times100 = -21.0 \text{ kNm}$$

$$M_{BC} = -\gamma_{BC}M = -0.16\times100 = -16.0 \text{ kNm}$$

$$M_{BD} = -\gamma_{BD}M = -0.63\times100 = -63.0 \text{ kNm}$$

Since the far end D is fixed, the moment carried over to DB is $\frac{1}{2}\times(-63.0) = -31.5$ kNm.

No moment is carried over to the far end if hinged/roller. Therefore, the ends AB and CB do not get any carry over moments. The bending moment diagram is as shown in Figure 4.4(ii). It is to be noted that the summation of all moments at the joint is equal to zero.

$$\sum M_B = 0 \Rightarrow 100+(-21.0)+(-16.0)+(-63.0) = 0$$

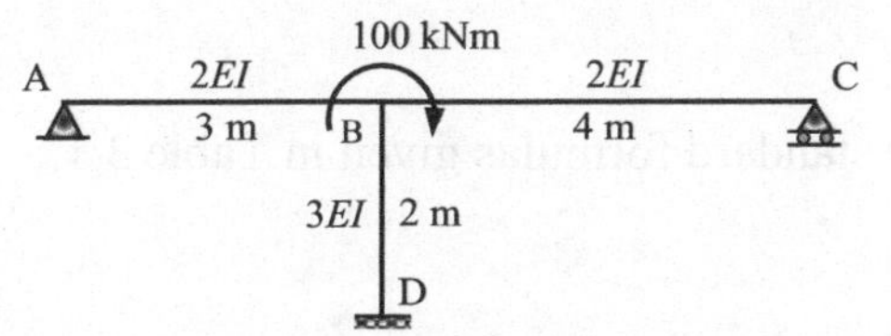

(i) Structure with applied moment

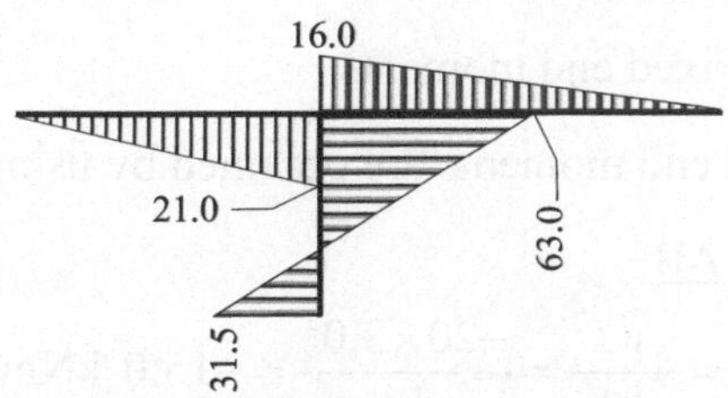

(ii) Bending moment diagram (in kNm)

Figure 4.4 Three-member frame structure

4.3.4 Steps Involved in Moment Distribution Method

The moment distribution method can be adopted to analyze statically indeterminate structures, and it is performed in tabular format. The beam problems can be solved by one moment distribution table. Symmetrical frames subjected to symmetrical loading can also be solved in a same manner. However, the frame problems with unknown sway degree of freedom require more than one distribution table. The steps involved in solving the continuous beam problems are as follows.

(i) Using the standard formulas, the fixed end moments are determined by assuming all the supports as fixed.

(ii) At the joints, the stiffness ($\bar{K}$) of the members connected to the joint, and subsequently the distribution factors (γ) are obtained.

(iii) In the moment distribution table, in case of hinged extreme end (or with an overhang), the unbalanced moment is released at the beginning, and half of the moment is carried over to the far-end (i.e., joint). No further operation is allowed in this support till the end.

(iv) In the first iteration, the unbalanced moments at each joint are distributed (i.e., balanced) using the distribution factors, and the distributed moments are carried over to the respective far-ends using carry over factor.

(v) The step (iv) is repeated until the unbalanced moments at all joints become insignificant.

(vi) The end moments are obtained by algebraic summation of the moments in all iteration cycles.

(vii) The final bending moment diagrams are obtained by superimposing free moment diagram with the end moment diagram.

4.3.5 Numerical Examples

Example 4.1: A two-span continuous beam ABC (span AB is 3 m and span BC is 5 m) has the extreme ends A and C fixed. The span AB is subjected to a uniformly distributed load of 20 kN/m over the entire span. The span BC is subjected to a point load of 30 kN at 3 m from the right end. Draw the shear force and bending moment diagrams. Assume a constant flexural rigidity throughout the beam. [Same as Example 3.13]

Solution:

Step (i): Fixed end moments

The fixed end moments are obtained by using the standard formulas given in Table 3.1.

<u>Span AB:</u>

$$M^{F}_{AB} = \frac{-wL^2}{12} = \frac{-20\times 3.0^2}{12} = -15.0 \text{ kNm}$$

$$M^{F}_{BA} = \frac{+wL^2}{12} = \frac{+20\times 3.0^2}{12} = +15.0 \text{ kNm}$$

Span BC:

$$M_{BC}^{F} = \frac{-Wab^2}{L^2} = \frac{-30 \times 2 \times 3^2}{5^2} = -21.6 \text{ kNm}$$

$$M_{CB}^{F} = \frac{-Wa^2b}{L^2} = \frac{-30 \times 2^2 \times 3}{5^2} = +14.4 \text{ kNm}$$

Step (ii): Stiffness and distribution factors

Joint B:

Stiffness, $\bar{K}_{BA} = \frac{4EI_{BA}}{L_{BA}} = \frac{4EI}{3} = 1.333EI$ (i.e., the far end A is fixed)

Stiffness, $\bar{K}_{BC} = \frac{4EI_{BC}}{L_{BC}} = \frac{4EI}{5} = 0.8EI$ (i.e., the far end C is fixed)

Distribution factor, $\gamma_{BA} = \frac{\bar{K}_{BA}}{\sum \bar{K}_B} = \frac{\bar{K}_{BA}}{\bar{K}_{BA} + \bar{K}_{BC}} = \frac{1.333EI}{1.333EI + 0.8EI} = 0.625$

Distribution factor, $\gamma_{BC} = \frac{\bar{K}_{BC}}{\sum \bar{K}_B} = \frac{\bar{K}_{BC}}{\bar{K}_{BA} + \bar{K}_{BC}} = \frac{0.8EI}{1.333EI + 0.8EI} = 0.375$

Step (iii): Moment distribution table

(a) The table is created with one column for each end moment. The respective distribution factors are entered for every joint ($\gamma_{BA} = 0.625$ and $\gamma_{BC} = 0.375$).

(b) Fixed end moments are entered ($M_{AB}^{F} = -15.0$, $M_{BA}^{F} = +15.0$, $M_{BC}^{F} = -21.6$, $M_{BC}^{F} = +14.4$)

(c) Since the extreme ends are fixed, no moment is released at the extreme end locations.

(d) At joint B, the unbalanced moment is $+15.0 - 21.60 = -6.6$. Therefore, $+6.6$ is required to be applied at B to balance the joint moments. Out of $+6.6$, based on the distribution factors, $0.625 \times (+6.6) = +4.13$ is distributed for the end BA and $0.375 \times (+6.6) = +2.48$ is distributed for the end BC.

(e) Half of the distributed moments (i.e., balancing) are carried over to the respective far ends. This means, $\frac{1}{2} \times (+4.13) = +2.06$ is carried over to AB, and $\frac{1}{2} \times (+2.48) = +1.24$ is carried over to CB.

(f) The steps involved in (d) and (e) constitute one cycle of iteration (i.e., balancing and carrying over to the far end).

(g) At this stage, no unbalanced moment exists in joint B. Therefore, no further cycle of iteration is possible.

(h) Now, the end moments are obtained by algebraic summation of all the moments in every column.

$$M_{AB} = -15.0 + 2.06 = -12.94 \text{ kNm}$$

$$M_{BA} = +15.0 + 4.13 = +19.13 \text{ kNm}$$

$$M_{BC} = -21.6 + 2.48 = -19.13 \text{ kNm}$$

$$M_{CB} = +14.4 + 1.24 = +15.64 \text{ kNm}$$

As a check, the summation of joint moments should be equal to zero.

$$M_{BA} + M_{BC} = +19.13 + (-19.13) = 0$$

	Joint	A	B		C
	End	AB	BA	BC	CB
	DF		**0.625**	**0.375**	
	FEM	−15.00	+15.00	−21.60	+14.40
Cycle 1	Balance		+4.13	+2.48	
Cycle 1	COM	+2.06			+1.24
	End moments	−12.94	+19.13	−19.13	+15.64

Step (iii): Final moments

The final bending moment diagram is obtained by superimposing the free bending moment diagram (Figure 4.5(ii)) with the end moment diagram (Figure 4.5(iii)). The same sign convention is followed as given in Figure 3.10 for the end moment diagram. This means, the anti-clockwise moment at the end AB (–12.94 kNm) and the clockwise moment at the end BA for the member AB cause hogging curvature, hence the diagram is drawn on one side of the reference axis. Similarly, the member BC is also in hogging nature. When the free moment and end moment diagrams are superposed, the net moment diagram is resulted.

The shear force and bending moment diagrams are shown in Figures 4.5(iv) and 4.5(v) respectively.

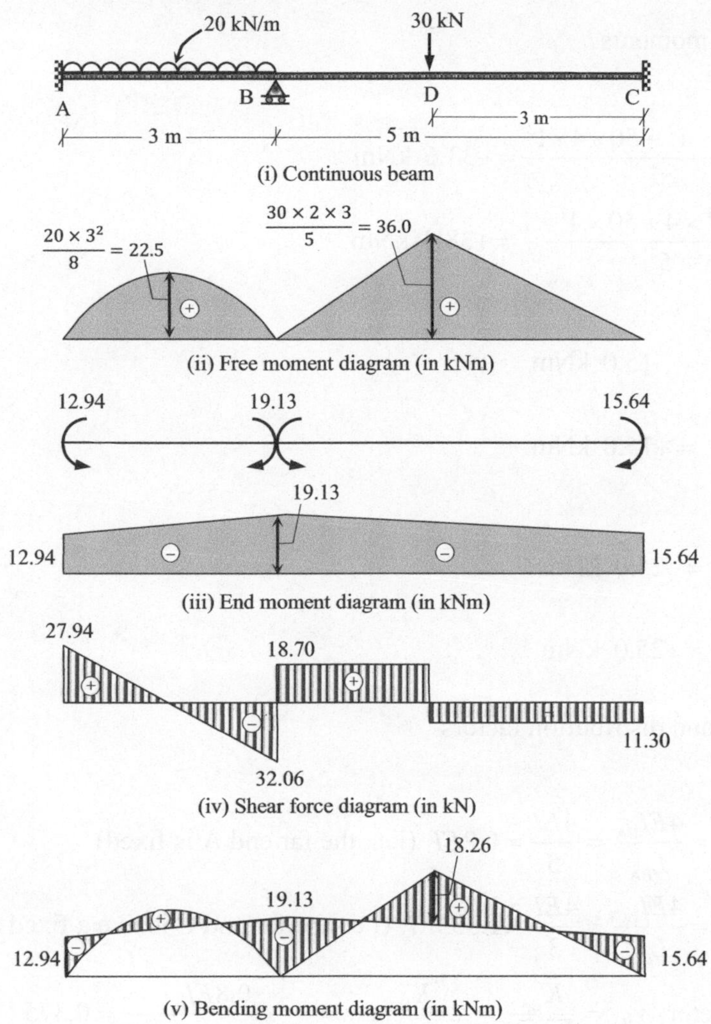

Figure 4.5 Two-span continuous beam (Example 4.1)

Example 4.2: A three-span continuous beam ABCD ($L_{AB} = 5\,\text{m}$; $L_{BC} = 3\,\text{m}$; $L_{CD} = 4\,\text{m}$) has the extreme ends A and D fixed, and intermediate supports at B and C. The span AB is subjected to two point loads of 40 kN and 50 kN at 1 m and 4 m respectively from A. The span BC is subjected to a uniformly distributed load of 20 kN/m over the entire span. The span BC is subjected to a mid-span point load of 50 kN. Draw the shear force and bending moment diagrams. Assume a constant flexural rigidity throughout the beam.

Solution:

Step (i): Fixed end moments

Span AB:

$$M^{F}_{AB} = \frac{-40\times1\times4^2 - 50\times4\times1^2}{5^2} = -33.6 \text{ kNm}$$

$$M^{F}_{BA} = \frac{+40\times1^2\times4 + 50\times4^2\times1}{5^2} = +38.4 \text{ kNm}$$

Span BC:

$$M^{F}_{BC} = \frac{-20\times3^2}{12} = -15.0 \text{ kNm}$$

$$M^{F}_{CB} = \frac{+20\times3^2}{12} = +15.0 \text{ kNm}$$

Span CD:

$$M^{F}_{CD} = \frac{-50\times4}{8} = -25.0 \text{ kNm}$$

$$M^{F}_{DC} = \frac{+50\times4}{8} = +25.0 \text{ kNm}$$

Step (ii): Stiffness and distribution factors

Joint B:

Stiffness, $\bar{K}_{BA} = \frac{4EI_{BA}}{L_{BA}} = \frac{4EI}{5} = 0.8EI$ (i.e., the far end A is fixed)

Stiffness, $\bar{K}_{BC} = \frac{4EI_{BC}}{L_{BC}} = \frac{4EI}{3} = 1.333EI$ (i.e., the far end C is like a fixed support)

Distribution factor, $\gamma_{BA} = \frac{\bar{K}_{BA}}{\sum \bar{K}_{B}} = \frac{\bar{K}_{BA}}{\bar{K}_{BA} + \bar{K}_{BC}} = \frac{0.8EI}{0.8EI + 1.333EI} = 0.375$

Distribution factor, $\gamma_{BC} = \frac{\bar{K}_{BC}}{\sum \bar{K}_{B}} = \frac{\bar{K}_{BC}}{\bar{K}_{BA} + \bar{K}_{BC}} = \frac{1.333EI}{0.8EI + 1.333EI} = 0.625$

Joint C:

Stiffness, $\bar{K}_{CB} = \frac{4EI_{CB}}{L_{CB}} = \frac{4EI}{3} = 1.333EI$ (i.e., the far end B is like a fixed support)

Stiffness, $\bar{K}_{CD} = \frac{4EI_{CD}}{L_{CD}} = \frac{4EI}{4} = EI$ (i.e., the far end D is fixed)

Distribution factor, $\gamma_{CB} = \frac{\bar{K}_{CB}}{\sum \bar{K}_{C}} = \frac{\bar{K}_{CB}}{\bar{K}_{CB} + \bar{K}_{CD}} = \frac{1.333EI}{1.333EI + EI} = 0.571$

Distribution factor, $\gamma_{CD} = \frac{\bar{K}_{CD}}{\sum \bar{K}_C} = \frac{\bar{K}_{CD}}{\bar{K}_{CB} + \bar{K}_{CD}} = \frac{EI}{1.333EI + EI} = 0.429$

Step (iii): Moment distribution table

(a) The table is created with one column for each end moment. The respective distribution factors are entered for every joint.

(b) Fixed end moments are entered.

(c) Since the extreme ends are fixed, no moment is released at the extreme end locations.

(d) At joint B, the unbalanced moment is $+38.4 - 15.0 = +23.4$. Therefore, -23.4 is required to be applied at B to balance the joint moments. Out of -23.4, based on the distribution factors, $0.375 \times (-23.4) = -8.78$ is distributed to the end BA and $0.625 \times (-23.4) = -14.62$ is distributed to the end BC. The moment $\frac{-8.78}{2} = -4.39$ is carried over to the far end AB, and $\frac{-14.62}{2} = -7.31$ is carried over to the far end CB.

(e) At joint C, the unbalanced moment is $+15.0 - 25.0 = -10.0$. Therefore, $+10.0$ is required to be applied at C to balance the joint moments. Out of $+10.0$, based on the distribution factors, $0.571 \times (+10.0) = +5.71$ is distributed to the end CB and $0.429 \times (+10.0) = +4.29$ is distributed to the end CD. The moment $\frac{+5.71}{2} = +2.86$ is carried over to the far end BC, and $\frac{+4.29}{2} = +2.15$ is carried over to CD.

(f) At the end of cycle 1, the unbalanced moment at joint B is $+2.86$, which is balanced again (i.e., distributed to BA and BC) based on the distribution factors, and then carried over to the respective far ends (i.e., AB and CB). Similarly, the unbalanced moment at joint C is -7.31, which is balanced again (i.e., distributed to CB and CD) based on the distribution factors, and then carried over to the respective far ends (i.e., BC and DC).

(g) The above step (f) is repeated until the unbalanced moment at all the joints become insignificant (i.e., close to zero).

(h) Now, the end moments are obtained by algebraic summation of all the moments in every column.

$$M_{AB} = -33.6 - 4.39 - 0.54 - 0.39 - 0.05 - 0.03 = -39.0 \text{ kNm}$$

$$M_{BA} = +38.4 - 8.78 - 1.07 - 0.78 - 0.10 - 0.07 - 0.01 - 0.01 = +27.58 \text{ kNm}$$

$$M_{BC} = -15.0 - 14.62 + 2.86 - 1.78 + 2.09 - 1.31 + 0.25 - 0.15 + 0.19 - 0.12 + 0.02 - 0.01 + 0.02 - 0.01 = -27.58 \text{ kNm}$$

$$M_{CB} = +15.0 + 5.71 - 7.31 + 4.17 - 0.89 + 0.51 - 0.65 + 0.37 - 0.08 + 0.05 - 0.06 + 0.03 - 0.01 = 16.84 \text{ kNm}$$

$$M_{CD} = -25.0 + 4.29 + 3.14 + 0.38 + 0.28 + 0.03 + 0.03 = -16.84 \text{ kNm}$$

$$M_{DC} = +25.0 + 2.15 + 1.57 + 0.19 + 0.14 + 0.02 = +29.08 \text{ kNm}$$

As a check, the summation of joint moments should be equal to zero.

$$M_{BA} + M_{BC} = +27.58 + (-27.58) = 0$$

$$M_{CB} + M_{CD} = +16.84 + (-16.84) = 0$$

	Joint	A	B		C		D
	End	AB	BA	BC	CB	CD	DE
	DF		**0.375**	**0.625**	**0.571**	**0.429**	
	FEM	−33.60	38.40	−15.00	15.00	−25.00	25.00
Cycle 1	Balance		−8.78	−14.62	5.71	4.29	
	COM	−4.39		2.86	−7.31		2.15
Cycle 2	Balance		−1.07	−1.78	4.17	3.14	
	COM	−0.54		2.09	−0.89		1.57
Cycle 3	Balance		−0.78	−1.31	0.51	0.38	
	COM	−0.39		0.25	−0.65		0.19
Cycle 4	Balance		−0.10	−0.15	0.37	0.28	
	COM	−0.05		0.19	−0.08		0.14
Cycle 5	Balance		−0.07	−0.12	0.05	0.03	
	COM	−0.03		0.02	−0.06		0.02
Cycle 6	Balance		−0.01	−0.01	0.03	0.03	
	COM	0.00		0.02	−0.01		0.02
Cycle 7	Balance		−0.01	−0.01	0.00	0.00	
	COM	0.00		0.00	0.00		0.00
	End moments	−39.00	27.58	−27.58	16.84	−16. 84	29.08

Step (iii): Final moments

The final bending moment diagram is obtained by superimposing the free bending moment diagram (Figure 4.6(ii)) with the end moment diagram (Figure 4.6(iii)). The shear force and bending moment diagrams are shown in Figures 4.6(iv) and 4.6(v) respectively.

Note: In Example 4.1, the ends BA and BC in joint B did not get any carry-over moment. Therefore, the next cycle of iteration was not possible. However, in Example 4.2, the end BC in joint B got a carry-over moment from the end CB. Similarly, the end CB in joint C got a carry-over moment from the end BC. These carry-over moments remain as the unbalanced moments in the respective joints, and prompted for the next cycle of iteration. This process continues till the carryover moments become insignificant (i.e., close to zero).

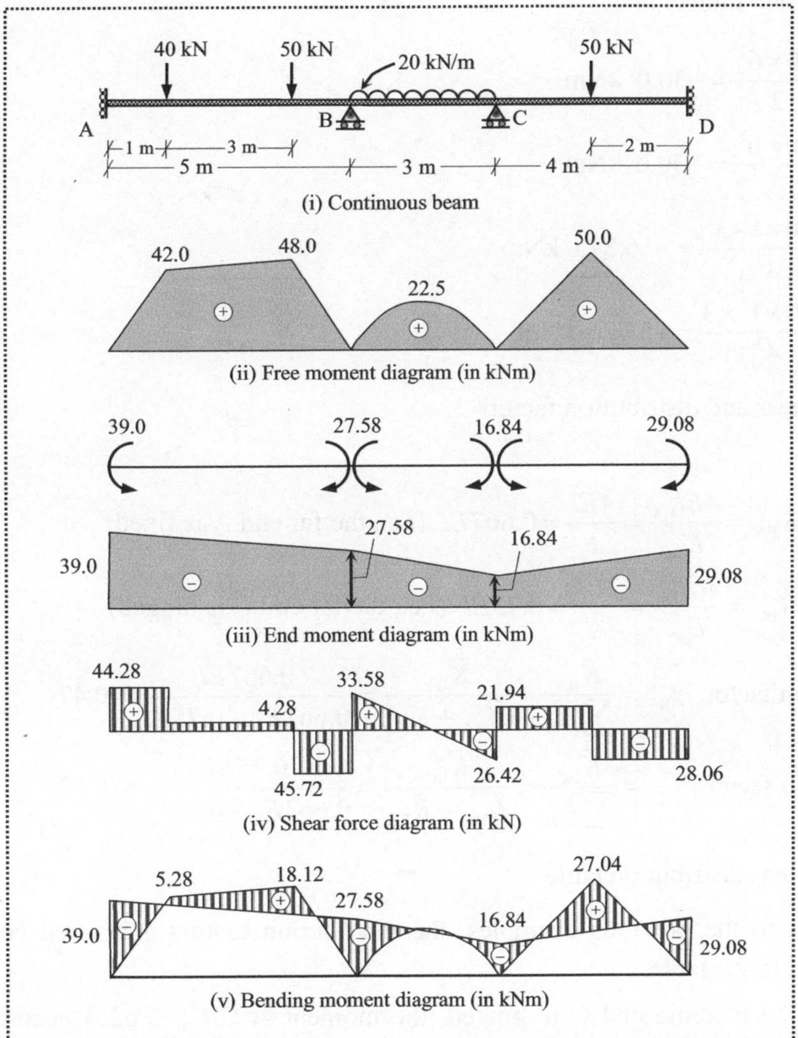

Figure 4.6 Three-span continuous beam (Example 4.2)

Example 4.3: A two-span continuous beam ABC (span AB is 6 m and span BC is 4 m) has the extreme end A fixed while the end C is hinged. The span AB is subjected to a uniformly distributed load of 10 kN/m over the entire span. The span BC is subjected to a concentrated load of 30 kN acting at 3 m from C. Draw the shear force and bending moment diagrams. Assume a constant flexural rigidity throughout the beam. [same as Example 3.11]

Solution:

Step (i): Fixed end moments

$$M_{AB}^{F} = \frac{-10 \times 6^2}{12} = -30.0 \text{ kNm}$$

$$M_{BA}^{F} = \frac{+10 \times 6^2}{12} = +30.0 \text{ kNm}$$

$$M_{BC}^{F} = \frac{-30 \times 1 \times 3^2}{4^2} = -16.875 \text{ kNm}$$

$$M_{CB}^{F} = \frac{+30 \times 1^2 \times 3}{4^2} = +5.625 \text{ kNm}$$

Step (ii): Stiffness and distribution factors

Joint B:

Stiffness, $\bar{K}_{BA} = \frac{4EI_{BA}}{L_{BA}} = \frac{4EI}{6} = 0.667EI$ (i.e., the far end A is fixed)

Stiffness, $\bar{K}_{BC} = \frac{3EI_{BC}}{L_{BC}} = \frac{3EI}{4} = 0.75EI$ (i.e., the far end C is hinged)

Distribution factor, $\gamma_{BA} = \frac{\bar{K}_{BA}}{\sum \bar{K}_B} = \frac{\bar{K}_{BA}}{\bar{K}_{BA} + \bar{K}_{BC}} = \frac{0.667EI}{0.667EI + 0.75EI} = 0.47$

Distribution factor, $\gamma_{BC} = \frac{\bar{K}_{BC}}{\sum \bar{K}_B} = \frac{\bar{K}_{BC}}{\bar{K}_{BA} + \bar{K}_{BC}} = \frac{0.75EI}{0.667EI + 0.75EI} = 0.53$

Step (iii): Moment distribution table

(a) Similar to the previous examples, the distribution factors and fixed end moments are entered in the table.

(b) Since the extreme end C is hinged, the moment at CB (+5.625) needs to be released. Therefore, −5.625 is added at CB, and then $-5.625/2 = -2.81$ is carried over to the far end BC. By releasing the moment at CB, the moment at CB has become zero, which is the final moment. Therefore, no further operations are carried out at the end CB.

(c) Now the initial moment is revised by including the moment received at BC as carryover moment.

(d) At joint B, the unbalanced moment is $+30.0-19.69=+11.31$. Therefore, -11.31 is distributed to the ends BA (-4.85) and BC (-5.47), and then $-4.85/2=-2.42$ is carried over to the far end AB. Since the extreme end CB is hinged, no moment is carried over to CB from BC.

(e) At this stage, no unbalanced moment exists in joint B. Therefore, no further cycle of iteration is possible.

(f) Now, the end moments are obtained by algebraic summation of all the moments in every column.

$$M_{AB}=-30.0-2.42=-32.42 \text{ kNm}$$

$$M_{BA}=+30.0-4.85=+25.15 \text{ kNm}$$

$$M_{BC}=-19.69-5.47=-25.16 \text{ kNm}$$

$$M_{CB}=0 \text{ kNm}$$

As a check, the summation of joint moments should be equal to zero.

$$M_{BA}+M_{BC}=+25.15+(-25.16)=-0.01\simeq 0$$

Note: The reason for not getting the summation of joint moments exactly equal to zero is the round-off error resulting from the distribution factor, balancing and carry-over moments.

	Joint	A	B		C
	End	AB	BA	BC	CB
	DF		**0.47**	**0.53**	
	FEM	−30.00	+30.00	−16.88	+5.63
	Release				−5.63
	COM			−2.81 ↙	
	Initial moment	−30.00	+30.00	−19.69	0
Cycle 1	Balance		−4.85	−5.47	
Cycle 1	COM	−2.42 ↙			
	End moments	−32.42	+25.15	−25.16	0

Step (iii): Final moments

The final bending moment diagram is obtained by superimposing the free bending moment diagram with the end moment diagram. The shear force and bending moment diagrams are shown in Figures 4.7(ii) and 4.7(iii) respectively.

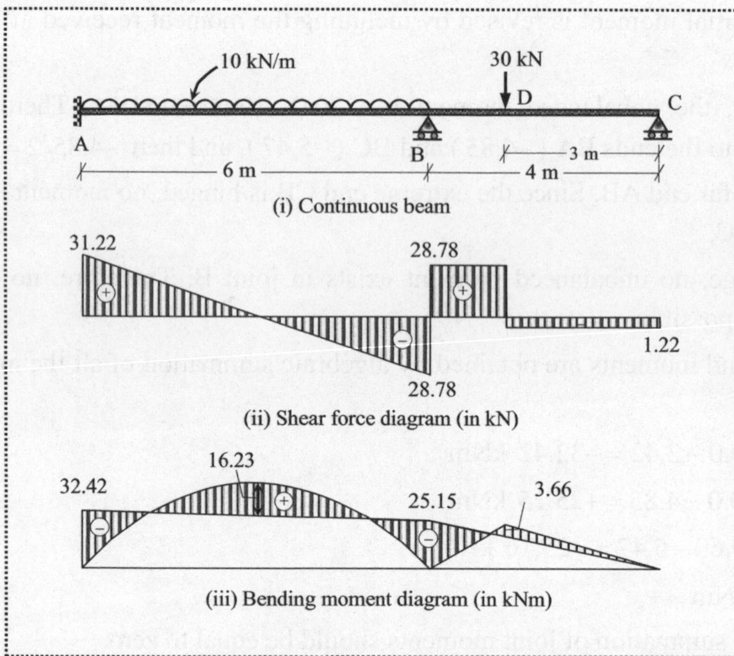

Figure 4.7 Two-span continuous beam (Example 4.3)

Example 4.4: A two-span continuous beam ABC (span AB is 5 m and span BC is 3 m) has the extreme end A hinged while the end C is fixed. The span AB is subjected to two concentrated loads of 10 kN each acting at 1m, and 4 m from A. The span BC is subjected to a mid-span point load of 30 kN. Draw the shear force and bending moment diagrams. Assume a constant flexural rigidity throughout the beam. [same as Example 3.12]

Solution:

Step (i): Fixed end moments

$$M_{AB}^{F} = \frac{-10\times1\times4^2 - 10\times4\times1^2}{5^2} = -8.0 \text{ kNm}$$

$$M_{BA}^{F} = \frac{+10\times1^2\times4 + 10\times4^2\times1}{5^2} = +8.0 \text{ kNm}$$

$$M_{BC}^{F} = \frac{-30\times3}{8} = -11.25 \text{ kNm}$$

$$M_{CB}^{F} = \frac{+30\times3}{8} = +11.25 \text{ kNm}$$

Step (ii): Stiffness and distribution factors

<u>Joint B</u>:

$$\text{Stiffness, } \bar{K}_{BA} = \frac{3EI_{BA}}{L_{BA}} = \frac{3EI}{5} = 0.6EI \text{ (i.e., the far end A is hinged)}$$

$$\text{Stiffness, } \bar{K}_{BC} = \frac{4EI_{BC}}{L_{BC}} = \frac{4EI}{3} = 1.333EI \text{ (i.e., the far end C is fixed)}$$

$$\text{Distribution factor, } \gamma_{BA} = \frac{\bar{K}_{BA}}{\sum \bar{K}_B} = \frac{\bar{K}_{BA}}{\bar{K}_{BA} + \bar{K}_{BC}} = \frac{0.6EI}{0.6EI + 1.333EI} = 0.31$$

$$\text{Distribution factor, } \gamma_{BC} = \frac{\bar{K}_{BC}}{\sum \bar{K}_B} = \frac{\bar{K}_{BC}}{\bar{K}_{BA} + \bar{K}_{BC}} = \frac{1.333EI}{0.6EI + 1.333EI} = 0.69$$

Step (iii): Moment distribution table

(a) Similar to the previous examples, the distribution factors and fixed end moments are entered in the table.

(b) Since the extreme end A is hinged, the moment at AB (–8.0) needs to be released. Therefore, +8.0 is added at AB, and then $+8.0/2 = +4.0$ is carried over to the far end BA. By releasing the moment at AB, the moment at AB has become zero, which is the final moment. Therefore, no further operations are carried out at the end AB.

(c) Now the initial moment is revised by including the moment received at BA as carryover moment.

(d) At joint B, the unbalanced moment is balanced and distributed to BA and BC, then the moment is carried over to the far end CB. Since the extreme end AB is hinged, no moment is carried over to AB from BA.

(e) At this stage, no unbalanced moment exists in joint B. Therefore, no further cycle of iteration is possible.

(f) Now, the end moments are obtained by algebraic summation of all the moments in every column.

	Joint	A	B		C
	End	AB	BA	BC	CB
	DF		**0.31**	**0.69**	
	FEM	−8.00	+8.00	−11.25	+11.25
	Release	+8.00			
	COM		+4.00		
	Initial moment	0	+12.00	−11.25	+11.25
Cycle 1	Balance		−0.23	−0.52	
	COM	-			−0.26
	End moments	0	+11.77	−11.77	+10.99

Step (iii): Final moments

The final bending moment diagram is obtained by superimposing the free bending moment diagram with the end moment diagram. The shear force and bending moment diagrams are shown in Figures 4.8(ii) and 4.8(iii) respectively.

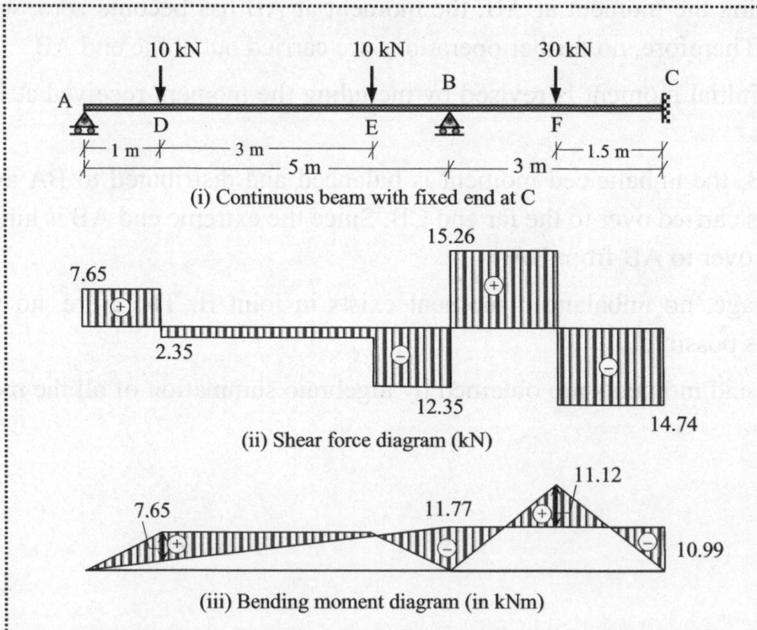

Figure 4.8 Two-span continuous beam (Example 4.4)

Example 4.5: A two-span continuous beam ABC (span AB is 4 m and span BC is 8 m) has the extreme ends simply supported. The span AB is subjected to two concentrated loads of 30 kN and 60 kN acting at 1 m and 2 m from A. The span BC is subjected to three concentrated loads of 25 kN, 30 kN and 15 kN respectively at 2 m, 4 m and 6 m from B. Draw the shear force and bending moment diagrams. Assume a constant flexural rigidity throughout the beam. [same as Example 3.10]

Solution:

Step (i): Fixed end moments

$$M_{AB}^{F} = \frac{-30\times1\times3^2-60\times2\times2^2}{4^2} = -46.875 \text{ kNm}$$

$$M_{BA}^{F} = \frac{+30\times1^2\times3+60\times2^2\times2}{4^2} = +35.625 \text{ kNm}$$

$$M_{BC}^{F} = \frac{-25\times2\times6^2-30\times4\times4^2-15\times6\times2^2}{8^2} = -63.75 \text{ kNm}$$

$$M_{CB}^{F} = \frac{+25\times2^2\times6+30\times4^2\times4+15\times6^2\times2}{8^2} = +56.25 \text{ kNm}$$

Step (ii): Stiffness and distribution factors

Joint B:

Stiffness, $\bar{K}_{BA} = \frac{3EI_{BA}}{L_{BA}} = \frac{3EI}{4} = 0.75EI$ (i.e., the far end A is hinged)

Stiffness, $\bar{K}_{BC} = \frac{3EI_{BC}}{L_{BC}} = \frac{3EI}{8} = 0.375EI$ (i.e., the far end C is hinged)

Distribution factor, $\gamma_{BA} = \frac{\bar{K}_{BA}}{\sum \bar{K}_B} = \frac{\bar{K}_{BA}}{\bar{K}_{BA}+\bar{K}_{BC}}$

$$= \frac{0.75EI}{0.75EI+0.375EI} = 0.667$$

Distribution factor, $\gamma_{BC} = \frac{\bar{K}_{BC}}{\sum \bar{K}_B} = \frac{\bar{K}_{BC}}{\bar{K}_{BA}+\bar{K}_{BC}}$

$$= \frac{0.375EI}{0.75EI+0.375EI} = 0.333$$

Step (iii): Moment distribution table

(a) Similar to the previous examples, the distribution factors and fixed end moments are entered in the table.

(b) Since the extreme end A is hinged, the moment at AB (–46.875) needs to be released. Therefore, +46.875 is added at AB, and then $+46.875/2 = +23.438$ is carried over to the far end BA. By releasing the moment at AB, the moment at AB has become zero, which is the final moment. Therefore, no further operations are carried out at the end AB. Similarly, as the extreme end C is also hinged, the moment at CB (+56.25) needs to be released. Therefore, –56.25 is added at CB, and then $-56.25/2 = +28.125$ is carried over to the far end BC. By releasing the moment at CB, the moment at CB has become zero, which is the final moment. Therefore, no further operations are carried out at the end CB.

(c) Now the initial moment is revised by including the moments received at BA and BC as carryover moments.

(d) At joint B, the unbalanced moment is balanced and distributed to BA and BC. No moment is carried over to the far ends AB and CB as these ends are hinged.

(e) At this stage, no unbalanced moment exists in joint B. Therefore, no further cycle of iteration is possible.

(f) Now, the end moments are obtained by algebraic summation of all the moments in every column.

	Joint	A	B		C
	End	AB	BA	BC	CB
	DF		**0.667**	**0.333**	
	FEM	–46.875	+35.625	–63.750	+56.250
	Release	+46.875			–56.250
	COM		+23.438	–28.125	
	Initial moment	0	+59.063	–91.875	0
Cycle 1	Balance		+21.886	+10.926	
	COM	-			-
	End moments	0	+80.949	+80.949	0

Step (iii): Final moments

The final bending moment diagram is obtained by superimposing the free bending moment diagram with the end moment diagram. The shear force and bending moment diagrams are shown in Figures 4.9(ii) and 4.9(iii) respectively.

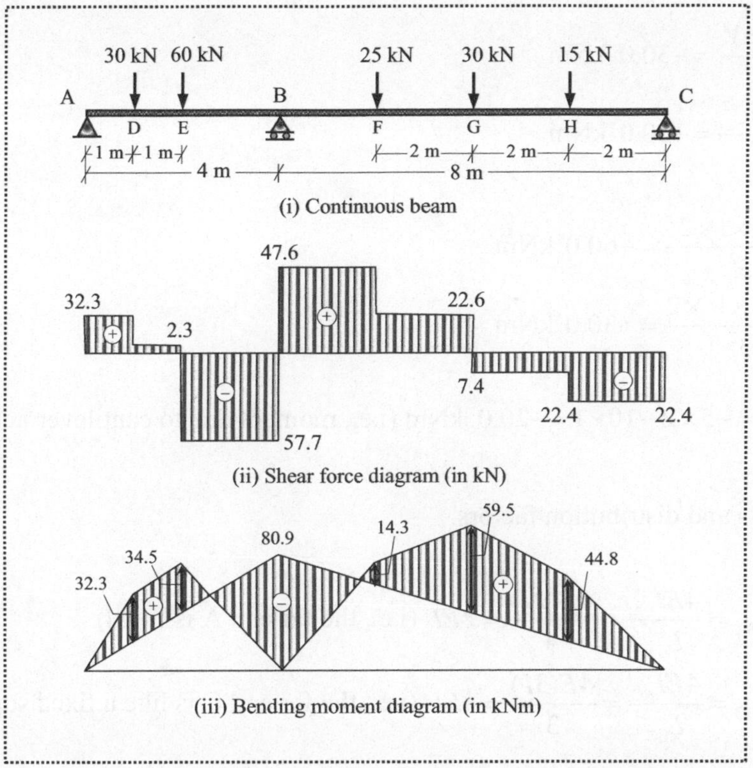

Figure 4.9 Continuous beam with simply supported ends (Example 4.5)

Example 4.6: A continuous beam ABCDE (span AB is 4 m with $I_{AB} = 2I$; span BC is 3 m with $I_{BC} = 3I$; span CD is 3 m with $I_{CD} = 1.5I$; span DE is 2 m with $I_{DE} = I$) has the extreme end A fixed, extreme end E is free (i.e., DE is overhanging), and the intermediate supports at B, C and D. The span AB is subjected to a mid-span point load of 100 kN, the span BC is subjected to a uniformly distributed load of 40 kN/m over the entire span, the span CD is subjected to a point load of 135 kN at 1 m from C, and the span DE is subjected to two point loads of 10 kN and 5 kN at 1 m from D and at the tip respectively. Draw the shear force and bending moment diagrams.

Solution:

Step (i): Fixed end moments

Span AB:

$$M_{AB}^{F} = \frac{-100 \times 4}{8} = -50.0 \text{ kNm}$$

$$M_{BA}^{F} = \frac{+100 \times 4}{8} = +50.0 \text{ kNm}$$

Span BC:

$$M^{F}_{BC} = \frac{-40\times 3^2}{12} = -30.0 \text{ kNm}$$

$$M^{F}_{CB} = \frac{+40\times 3^2}{12} = +30.0 \text{ kNm}$$

Span CD:

$$M^{F}_{CD} = \frac{-135\times 1\times 2^2}{3^2} = -60.0 \text{ kNm}$$

$$M^{F}_{DC} = \frac{+135\times 1^2\times 2}{3^2} = +30.0 \text{ kNm}$$

Span DE:

$M^{F}_{DE} = M_{DE} = -5\times 2 - 10\times 1 = -20.0$ kNm (i.e., moment due to cantilever action)

$M_{ED} = 0$

Step (ii): Stiffness and distribution factors

Joint B:

Stiffness, $\bar{K}_{BA} = \frac{4EI_{BA}}{L_{BA}} = \frac{4E(2I)}{4} = 2EI$ (i.e., the far end A is fixed)

Stiffness, $\bar{K}_{BC} = \frac{4EI_{BC}}{L_{BC}} = \frac{4E(3I)}{3} = 4EI$ (i.e., the far end C is like a fixed support)

Distribution factor, $\gamma_{BA} = \frac{\bar{K}_{BA}}{\sum \bar{K}_{B}} = \frac{\bar{K}_{BA}}{\bar{K}_{BA} + \bar{K}_{BC}} = \frac{2EI}{2EI + 4EI} = 0.333$

Distribution factor, $\gamma_{BC} = \frac{\bar{K}_{BC}}{\sum \bar{K}_{B}} = \frac{\bar{K}_{BC}}{\bar{K}_{BA} + \bar{K}_{BC}} = \frac{4EI}{2EI + 4EI} = 0.667$

Joint C:

Stiffness, $\bar{K}_{CB} = \frac{4EI_{BA}}{L_{BA}} = \frac{4E(3I)}{3} = 4EI$ (i.e., the far end B is like a fixed support)

Stiffness, $\bar{K}_{CD} = \frac{3EI_{BC}}{L_{BC}} = \frac{3E(1.5I)}{3} = 1.5EI$ (i.e., the far end D is hinged)

With reference to joint C, the perspective of the far ends (i.e., supports at B and D) is different, even though they appear to be simply supported. The support B has an adjoining span BA that resists the free rotation of joint B, while the adjoining span DE (i.e., overhanging portion) does not resist the free rotation of joint D. That is why the support D is considered as hinged.

Distribution factor, $\gamma_{CB} = \frac{\bar{K}_{CB}}{\sum \bar{K}_{C}} = \frac{\bar{K}_{CB}}{\bar{K}_{CB} + \bar{K}_{CD}} = \frac{4EI}{4EI + 1.5EI} = 0.727$

Distribution factor, $\gamma_{CD} = \frac{\bar{K}_{CD}}{\sum \bar{K}_{C}} = \frac{\bar{K}_{CD}}{\bar{K}_{CB} + \bar{K}_{CD}} = \frac{1.5EI}{4EI + 1.5EI} = 0.273$

Step (iii): Moment distribution table

(a) The distribution factors and fixed end moments are entered in the table.
(b) Since the extreme end E is free, the moment at ED is zero.
(c) The final moment at the end DE is −20.0 kNm due to the loads acting on the overhanging portion. Therefore, for the joint equilibrium, the final moment at the end DC should be equal to +20.0 kNm.
(d) Since the support at D is considered as hinged, the unbalanced moment ($-20.0+30.0=+10.0$) should be released at the initial stage itself. Therefore, −10.0 is added at DC, and $-10.0/2=-5.0$ is carried over to CD. No further operations are carried out at the ends DC, DE and ED.
(e) The initial moments are revised by including the carryover moment.
(f) In the first cycle of iteration, the unbalanced moments at the joints are balanced, and carried over to the respective far ends.
(g) The iteration is continued till the unbalanced moments at joints B and C become negligibly small.
(h) Now, the end moments are obtained by algebraic summation of all the moments.

	Joint	A	B		C		D		E
	End	AB	BA	BC	CB	CD	DC	DE	ED
	DF		**0.333**	**0.667**	**0.727**	**0.273**			
	FEM	−50.00	+50.00	−30.00	+30.00	−60.00	+30.00	−20.00	0
	Release						−10.00		
	COM					−5.00			
	Initial moments	−50.00	+50.00	−30.00	+30.00	−65.00	+20.00	−20.00	0
Cycle 1	Balance		−6.66	−13.34	25.45	9.56			
	COM	−3.33		12.72	−6.67				
Cycle 2	Balance		−4.24	−8.49	4.85	1.82			
	COM	−2.12		2.42	−4.24				
Cycle 3	Balance		−0.81	−1.62	3.08	1.16			
	COM	−0.40		1.54	−0.81				
Cycle 4	Balance		−0.51	−1.03	0.59	0.22			
	COM	−0.26		0.29	−0.51				
Cycle 5	Balance		−0.10	−0.20	0.37	0.14			
	COM	−0.05		0.19	−0.10				
Cycle 6	Balance		−0.06	−0.12	0.07	0.03			
	COM	−0.03		0.04	−0.06				
Cycle 7	Balance		−0.01	−0.02	0.05	0.02			
	COM	−0.01		0.02	−0.01				
	End moments	−56.19	37.61	−37.59	52.05	−52.06	20.00	−20.00	0

Step (iii): Final moments

The final bending moment diagram is obtained by superimposing the free bending moment diagram with the end moment diagram. The shear force and bending moment diagrams are shown in Figures 4.10(ii) and 4.10(iii) respectively.

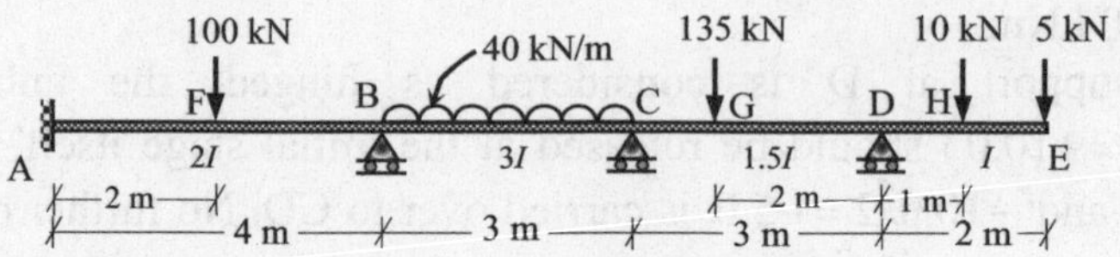

(i) Continuous beam an overhanging at the right end

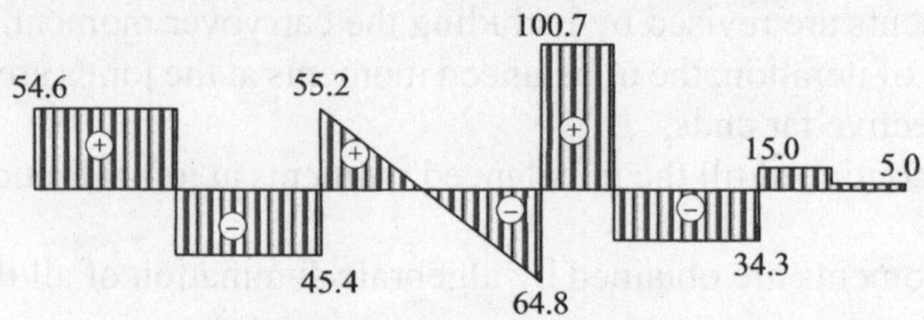

(ii) Shear force diagram (in kN)

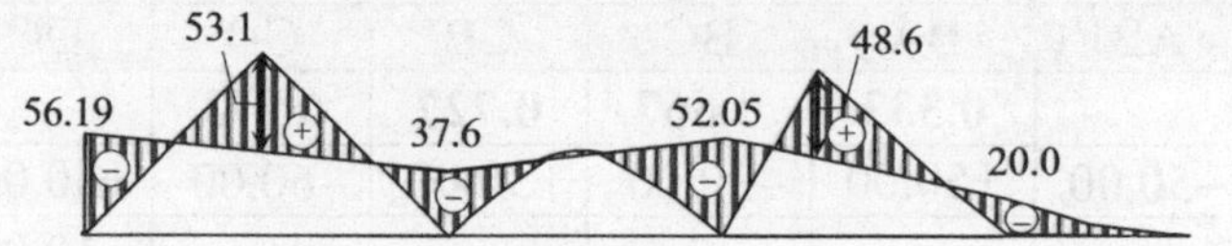

(iii) Bending moment diagram (in kNm)

Figure 4.10 Three-span continuous beam with an overhang (Example 4.6)

Example 4.7: Analyse the frame shown in Figure 4.11(i) using the moment distribution method.

Solution:

The given frame does not have any unknown sway degree of freedom. This means, the horizontal translation of the column elements (members BD and CE) is prevented owing to the beam element AB fixed at A. In case, if the extreme end at A was a roller support, then the frame would translate in the horizontal direction resulting in an unknown sway degree of freedom.

Therefore, the frame problems with no unknown sway degree of freedoms are solved using the same procedure adopted for analyzing the beams.

Step (i): Fixed end moments

Span AB:

$$M^{F}_{AB} = \frac{-50 \times 4}{8} = -25.0 \text{ kNm}$$

$$M_{BA}^{F} = \frac{+50\times 4}{8} = +25.0 \text{ kNm}$$

<u>Span BC:</u>

$$M_{BC}^{F} = \frac{-20\times 6^2}{12} = -60.0 \text{ kNm}$$

$$M_{CB}^{F} = \frac{+20\times 6^2}{12} = +60.0 \text{ kNm}$$

<u>Span CE:</u>

$$M_{CE}^{F} = \frac{-30\times 4}{8} = -15.0 \text{ kNm}$$

$$M_{EC}^{F} = \frac{+30\times 4}{8} = +15.0 \text{ kNm}$$

<u>Span DB:</u>

$$M_{DB}^{F} = \frac{-45\times 1\times 2^2}{3^2} = -20.0 \text{ kNm}$$

$$M_{BD}^{F} = \frac{+45\times 1^2\times 2}{3^2} = +10.0 \text{ kNm}$$

Step (ii): Stiffness and distribution factors

Joint	Stiffness ($\bar{K}$)	Distribution factor (γ)
B	$\bar{K}_{BA} = \frac{4E(I)}{4} = EI$	$\gamma_{BA} = \frac{\bar{K}_{BA}}{\sum \bar{K}_B} = \frac{EI}{EI+EI+2EI} = 0.25$
	$\bar{K}_{BC} = \frac{4E(1.5I)}{6} = EI$	$\gamma_{BC} = \frac{\bar{K}_{BC}}{\sum \bar{K}_B} = \frac{EI}{EI+EI+2EI} = 0.25$
	$\bar{K}_{BD} = \frac{4E(1.5I)}{3} = 2EI$	$\gamma_{BD} = \frac{\bar{K}_{BD}}{\sum \bar{K}_B} = \frac{2EI}{EI+EI+2EI} = 0.5$
C	$\bar{K}_{CB} = \frac{4E(1.5I)}{6} = EI$	$\gamma_{CB} = \frac{\bar{K}_{CB}}{\sum \bar{K}_C} = \frac{EI}{EI+1.5EI} = 0.4$
	$\bar{K}_{CE} = \frac{3E(2I)}{4} = 1.5EI$	$\gamma_{CE} = \frac{\bar{K}_{CE}}{\sum \bar{K}_C} = \frac{1.5EI}{EI+1.5EI} = 0.6$

Step (iii): Moment distribution table

(a) Similar to the previous examples, the distribution factors and fixed end moments are entered in the table.

(b) Since the extreme end E is hinged, the moment at EC (+15.00) needs to be released. Therefore, –15.00 is added at EC, and then –7.50 is carried over to the far end CE. By releasing the moment at EC, the moment at EC has become zero, which is the final moment.

Therefore, no further operations are carried out at the end EC. The initial moments are revised by including the carryover moment.

(c) At joint B, the unbalanced moment is $+25.0-60.0+10.0=-25.0$. Therefore, +25.00 is required to be applied at B to balance the joint moments. Based on the distribution factors, +6.25, +6.25 and +12.5 are entered at the ends BA, BC and BD respectively. Consequently, +3.13, +3.13 and +6.25 are carried over to AB, CB and DB respectively.

(d) Similarly, the unbalanced moment at joint C is $+60.0-22.5=+37.5$. Therefore, –37.5 is distributed between CB and CE as –15.0 and –22.5 respectively. Consequently, –7.5 is carried over to the far end BC. No moment is carried over to the far end DB.

(e) After the first cycle of iteration, the unbalanced moment at the joint B is –7.5. Therefore +7.5 is distributed to BA, BC and BD respectively as +1.88, +1.88 and +3.75, and then carried over to AB, CB and DB respectively as +0.94, +0.94 and +1.88. Similarly, the unbalanced moment at C is +3.13. Therefore, –3.13 is distributed to CB and CE respectively as –1.25 and –1.88, and –0.63 is carried over to BC.

(f) The iteration is continued till the unbalanced moments at the joints B and C become negligibly small.

(g) Now, the end moments are obtained by algebraic summation of all the moments in every column.

	Joint	A	B			C		D	E
	End	AB	BA	BC	BD	CB	CE	DB	EC
	DF		**0.25**	**0.25**	**0.50**	**0.40**	**0.60**		
	FEM	–25.00	+25.00	–60.00	+10.00	+60.00	–15.00	–20.00	+15.00
	Release								–15.00
	COM						–7.50		
	Initial moments	–25.00	+25.00	–60.00	+10.00	+60.00	–22.50	–20.00	0
Cycle 1	Balance		+6.25	+6.25	+12.50	–15.00	–22.5		
	COM	+3.13		–7.50		+3.13		+6.25	
Cycle 2	Balance		+1.88	+1.88	+3.75	–1.25	–1.88		
	COM	+0.94		–0.63		+0.94		+1.88	
Cycle 3	Balance		+0.16	+0.16	+0.31	–0.38	–0.56		
	COM	+0.08		–0.19		+0.08		+0.16	
Cycle 4	Balance		+0.05	+0.05	+0.09	–0.03	–0.05		
	COM	+0.02		–0.02		+0.02		+0.05	
Cycle 5	Balance		+0.00	+0.00	+0.01	–0.01	–0.01		
	COM	+0.00		–0.00		+0.00		+0.00	
	End moments	–20.83	+33.33	–60.00	+26.66	+47.50	–47.50	–11.67	0

Step (iii): Final moments

The final bending moment diagram is obtained by superimposing the free bending moment diagram with the end moment diagram. The shear force and bending moment diagrams are shown in Figures 4.11(ii) and 4.11(iii) respectively.

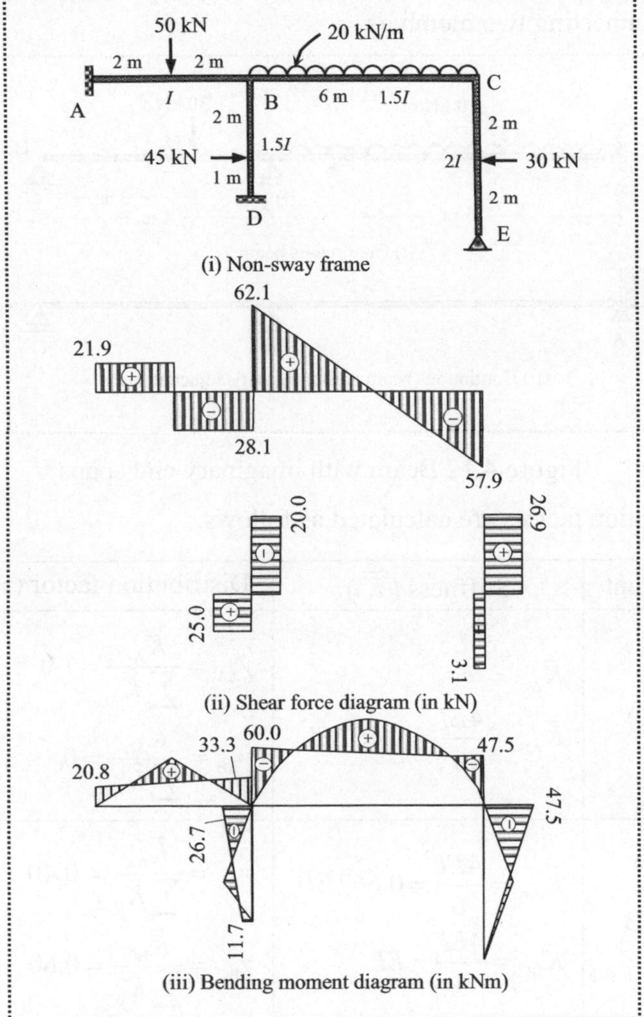

Figure 4.11 Non-sway frame (Example 4.7)

Note: In the numerical examples, the distribution factors are considered only at the joints wherein at least two members are connected, and the extreme ends are not considered as joints. Theoretically, the extreme ends can also be considered, but it will result in more cycles of iteration for convergence.

Consider a two-span continuous beam already solved in Example 4.3 as shown in Figure 4.12(i). The beam has a fixed support at A, an intermediate support at B and a hinged support at C. Assume an imaginary span A′A with infinitely rigid (i.e., $\bar{K}_{AA'} = \infty$) so that the rotation at A is prevented. Similarly, assume an imaginary span CC′ with infinitely flexible (i.e., $\bar{K}_{CC'} = 0$) so that the rotation at C is freely permitted. Thus, with two imaginary end spans, the supports A and C have become joints connecting two members.

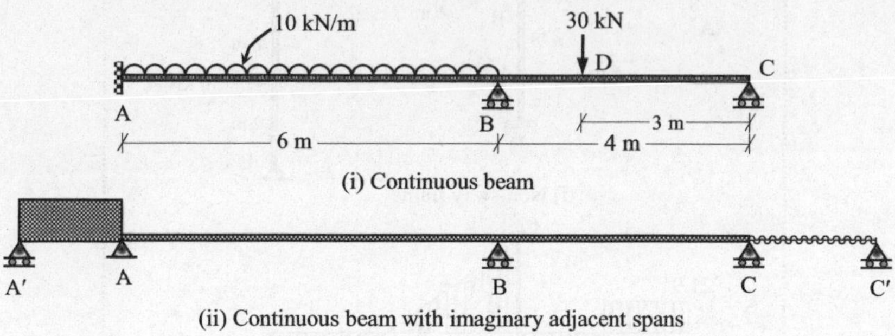

Figure 4.12 Beam with imaginary end spans

Therefore, the distribution factors are calculated as follows.

Joint	Stiffness ($\bar{K}$)	Distribution factor (γ)
A	$\bar{K}_{AA'} = \infty$ $\bar{K}_{AB} = \frac{4EI}{6} = 0.667EI$	$\gamma_{AA'} = \frac{\bar{K}_{AA'}}{\sum \bar{K}_A} = 1.0$ $\gamma_{AB} = \frac{\bar{K}_{AB}}{\sum \bar{K}_A} = 0$
B	$\bar{K}_{BA} = \frac{4EI}{6} = 0.667EI$ $\bar{K}_{BC} = \frac{4EI}{4} = EI$	$\gamma_{BA} = \frac{\bar{K}_{BA}}{\sum \bar{K}_B} = 0.40$ $\gamma_{BC} = \frac{\bar{K}_{BC}}{\sum \bar{K}_B} = 0.60$
C	$\bar{K}_{CB} = \frac{4EI}{4} = EI$ $\bar{K}_{CC'} = 0$	$\gamma_{CB} = \frac{\bar{K}_{CB}}{\sum \bar{K}_C} = 1.0$ $\gamma_{CC'} = \frac{\bar{K}_{CE}}{\sum \bar{K}_C} = 0$

In the moment distribution table, the distribution factors and fixed end moments are entered. The unbalanced moments at the joints A, B and C are balanced according to the respective distribution factors, and then carried over to the far ends. The iteration is continued until the unbalanced moments become negligibly small.

The end moments exactly match with the solutions obtained in Example 4.3. However, the effort required (i.e., number of cycles) to obtain the solution is more when compared with the procedure adopted in Example 4.3.

	Joint	A′	A		B		C		C′
	End	A′A	AA′	AB	BA	BC	CB	CC′	C′C
	DF		**1.0**	**0**	**0.4**	**0.6**	**1.0**	**0**	
	FEM			−30.00	+30.00	−16.88	+5.63		
Cycle 1	Balance		+30.00	+0.00	−5.25	−7.88	−5.63	−0.00	
	COM			−2.63	+0.00	−2.81	−3.94		
Cycle 2	Balance		+2.63	+0.00	+1.13	+1.69	+3.94	+0.00	
	COM			+0.56	+0.00	+1.97	+0.84		
Cycle 3	Balance		−0.56	−0.00	−0.79	−1.18	−0.84	−0.00	
	COM			−0.39	−0.00	−0.42	−0.59		
Cycle 4	Balance		+0.39	+0.00	+0.17	+0.25	+0.59	+0.00	
	COM			0.08	+0.00	+0.30	+0.13		
Cycle 5	Balance		−0.08	−0.00	−0.12	−0.18	−0.13	−0.00	
	COM			−0.06	−0.00	−0.06	−0.09		
Cycle 6	Balance		+0.06	+0.00	+0.03	+0.04	+0.09	+0.00	
	COM			0.01	+0.00	+0.04	+0.02		
Cycle 7	Balance		−0.01	−0.00	−0.02	−0.03	−0.02	−0.00	
	COM			−0.01	−0.00	−0.01	−0.01		
Cycle 8	Balance		+0.01	+0.00	+0.00	+0.01	+0.01	+0.00	
	COM			+0.00	0.00	+0.01	+0.00		
	End moments		**32.43**	**−32.43**	**25.15**	**−25.14**	**0.00**	**0.00**	

UNIT SUMMARY

- ✓ Moment distribution method is a displacement method in which the end moments are obtained iteratively.
- ✓ Stiffness of an element at a joint is $4EI/L$ for the far-end fixed, whereas the stiffness is $3EI/L$ if the far end is hinged.
- ✓ Distribution factor is the ratio between stiffness of a member and total stiffness of members connected at the joint.
- ✓ The summation of distribution factors at a joint is one.
- ✓ Carry over factor is $1/2$ for the fixed end, and zero for the hinged end.
- ✓ From the fixed end moments stage, the unbalanced moments at each joint is balanced and subsequently carried over to the respective far ends depending on the end conditions.
- ✓ The iteration should be repeated until the unbalanced moment becomes insignificant at every joint.
- ✓ Final end moments are obtained by algebraic summation of all the moments (distributed and carried over moments) at each joint.
- ✓ Final bending moment diagram is obtained by superposing the free moment diagram with the end moment diagram.
- ✓ Beams and frames without any unknown sway degree of freedom can be solved using a single the moment distribution table.

EXERCISES

4.1. A two-span continuous beam ABC (AB=6 m; BC=3 m) with extreme ends fixed is subjected a mid-span point load of 30 kN in the span AB, and two point loads of 20 kN each at every 1 m in the span BC. Draw the shear force and bending moment diagrams.

4.2. A two-span continuous beam ABC (AB=6 m; BC=3 m) with fixed at A and simply supported at C is subjected a uniformly distributed load of 10 kN/m over the span AB, and two point loads of 20 kN each at every 1 m in the span BC. Draw the shear force and bending moment diagrams.

4.3. A two span continuous beam ABC (AB=6 m; BC=3 m) with extreme ends simply supported is subjected to 30 kN each at the mid-span locations. Analyse the beam for the force responses, and draw the shear force and bending moment diagrams.

4.4. A two-span continuous beam ABC (AB=6 m; BC=3 m) with extreme ends simply supported is subjected a uniformly distributed load of 10 kN/m over the span AB, and two point loads of 20 kN each at every 1 m in the span BC. Draw the shear force and bending moment diagrams.

4.5. A continuous beam ABCD (span of AB is 4 m with $I_{AB} = 3I$; span of BC is 3 m with $I_{BC} = 2I$; span of CD is 1 m with $I_{CD} = 1.5I$) with fixed support at A, intermediate supports at B and C, and free at D (i.e., overhanging CD) is subjected a mid-span point load of 30 kN in the span AB, a uniformly distributed load of 15 kN/m in the span BC, and a point load of 5 kN at the tip of span CD. Draw the shear force and bending moment diagrams.

QR Code for *Moment Distribution Method*

NPTEL Lecture: https://www.youtube.com/watch?v=LORmHAC_vPo

5 Simple Trusses

UNIT SPECIFICS

This unit discusses the following aspects.

- Different types of truss structures
- Analysis of simples trusses by the method of joints
- Analysis of simples trusses by the method of sections

RATIONALE

In structures with large spans, providing beams as major transverse load carrying elements becomes uneconomical. In such situations, trusses are preferred. The truss is composed of short and straight discrete elements arranged into triangulated patterns connected at their ends to form a stable configuration. This chapter presents various methods for analyzing simple trusses for the force response.

UNIT OUTCOMES

List of outcomes of this unit is as follows.

U5-O1: Importance of truss structures
U5-O2: Different types of trusses
U5-O3: Assumptions for analyzing the trusses
U5-O4: Analysis of simple trusses using the method of joints
U5-O5: Analysis of simple trusses using the method of sections

Mapping of Unit-5 Outcomes with Course Outcomes *

	CO-1	CO-2	CO-3	CO-4	CO-5
U5-O1	1	1	1	3	1
U5-O2	1	1	1	1	1
U5-O3	1	1	2	1	2
U5-O4	1	1	2	2	3
U5-O5	1	1	2	2	3

*** (1- Weak correlation; 2- Medium correlation; 3- Strong correlation)**

5.1 Introduction

A truss is an assemblage of straight members arranged in a triangle or a combination of triangles, and connected by means of pins for transmitting the externally applied loads by developing axial forces in the members. Mostly, trusses are constructed using structural steel or aluminum shapes or wood struts with bolted or welded connections. Timber trusses were built for function (rather than the architectural fancy) in the past, but nowadays they are replaced by metal trusses owing to the structural efficiency. Trusses are widely used in many applications such as industrial structures, bridges, roofs of buildings, towers and space stations. The top and bottom truss members are called *chords* and the members between the chords are called *web* members. The compressive web members are called *struts* and tensile web members are called *ties*.

5.2 Types of Trusses

The basic shape of a truss is a triangle formed by three members connected at the common joints. Hence, the triangle arrangement with three members and three joints is a rigid structure. When another two members are connected to two of the joints forming another triangle, the structure becomes a five-member rigid structure. Therefore, the whole structure is suitably built-up from the basic triangle by adding two members (sometimes one member is sufficient, by keeping two existing members as common). This kind of arrangement makes the structure rigid and internally stable. Moreover, when the structures are supported in such a way that all the reactions are neither parallel nor concurrent, the external stability is also achieved.

If all the members of a truss lie in one plane, the structure is called a *plane truss*. Similarly, if the configuration of the structure encloses three-dimensional space, the structure is called a *space truss*. In reality, planar trusses are not two-dimensional; this means that the existence of a dimension normal to the plane should be realized. Because, the member cross sections carry the third dimension, and also the physical joining of the members involves a layered nonplanar assemblage of members. However, the minor eccentricities of the member axes with respect to the plane of the structure are unimportant in the analysis of the truss structure as a whole. On the other hand, when the truss structures enclose a three-dimensional space, it is appropriate to consider the full spatial interconnection of the members when analyzing structures such as towers, complicated roof systems and aerospace structures. However, in many cases such as bridges structures and simple roof systems, the framework can be subdivided into planar components for simplifying the analysis procedure without compromising the accuracy of the results.

Depending on the overall configuration, two categories of trusses namely the *flat* trusses (i.e., with parallel chord or girders) and *pitched/common* trusses (i.e., for sloped roof) can be seen in practice. Different types of truss structures are shown in Figure 5.1. The choice of the truss is mainly governed by many factors such as the span of the structure, main purpose of the structure, topographical conditions, economy etc.

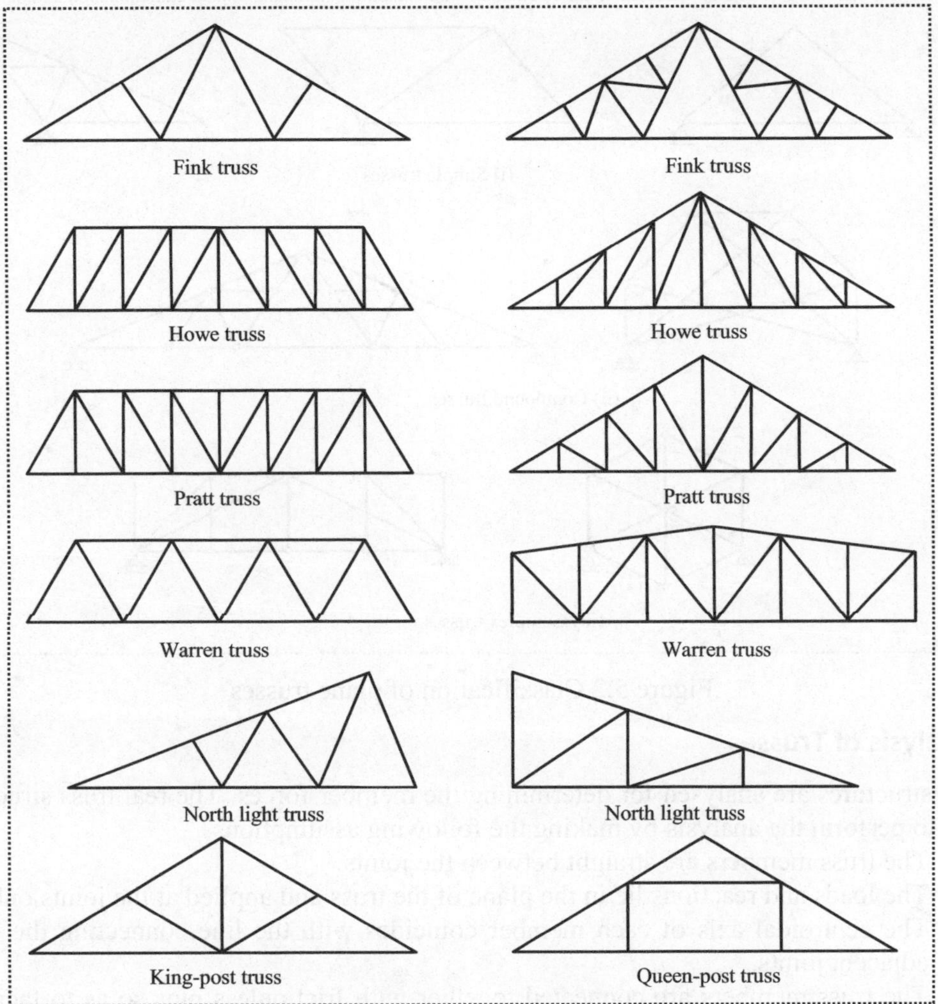

Figure 5.1 Common types of trusses

5.2.1 Classification of Plane Trusses

Planar truss structures are classified as *simple*, *compound* and *complex* trusses. A *simple truss* is a plane truss which begins with a basic triangular shape and can be expanded by adding two members and a joint. The simple trusses do not need to be made entirely of triangles, nevertheless, the non-triangular cells do not ensure the stability conditions in some cases. A *compound truss* is formed by either modifying the simple truss by readjusting the members or by combining simple trusses. The compound trusses are commonly adopted in long-span bridges. A *complex truss* adopts a general layout of members which is different from the simple and compound trusses. It often contains overlapping members (i.e., no joints at many apparent intersections of members). Analysis of such structures is complicated as the equilibrium equations are generally coupled. Examples of *simple*, *compound* and *complex* truss structures are shown in Figure 5.2.

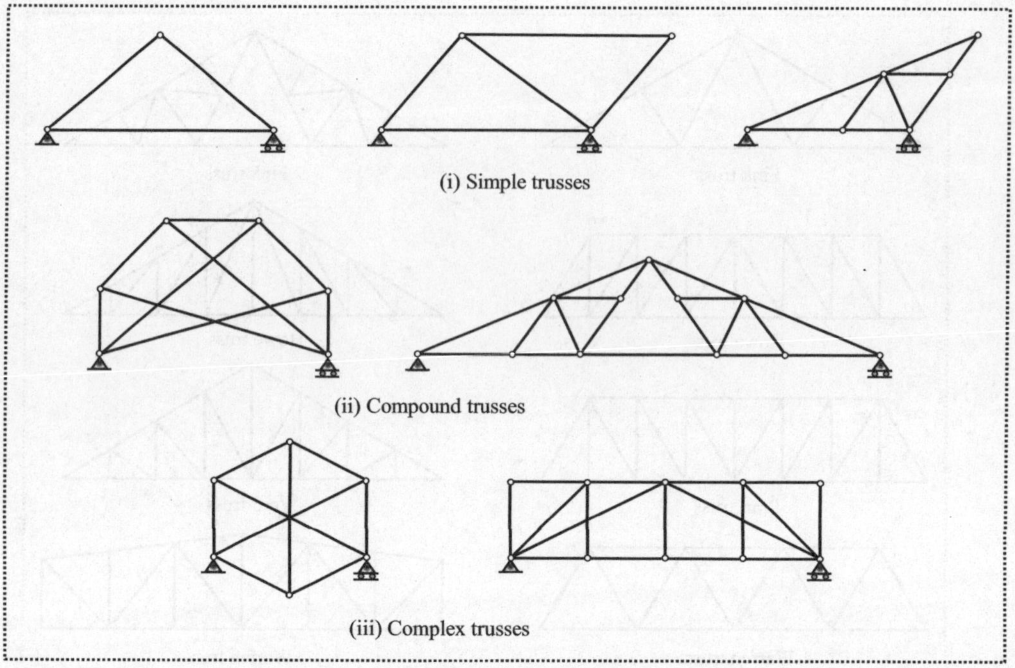

Figure 5.2 Classification of plane trusses

5.3 Analysis of Trusses

The truss structures are analysed for determining the member forces. The real truss structures are idealized to perform the analysis by making the following assumptions.

(i) The truss members are straight between the joints.

(ii) The loads and reactions lie in the plane of the truss and applied at the joints only.

(iii) The centroidal axis of each member coincides with the line connecting the centre of adjacent joints.

(iv) The truss members are connected together with frictionless pins so as to facilitate the members to rotate freely at the joints.

(v) The deformation of a truss under applied loads caused by change in length of the individual members is small enough to cause appreciable change in the overall shape and dimensions of the truss.

Since the members transmit the applied loads through axial action, the two end forces must be collinear and opposite to each other for equilibrium, making the nature of forces in each member either tension or compression. The representation of member forces (also called bar forces) is illustrated in Figure 5.3. The simple truss shown in Figure 5.3(i) is decomposed into joints and members to realize the action of joints on the member and the subsequent reaction of the member on the joints as illustrated in Figure 5.3(ii). On an isolated member, the *tension* in member is represented by inward arrows from the joints, and the *compression* in member is represented by outward arrows to the joints as shown in Figure 5.2(iii). Thus, the direction of forces away from the joint indicates *tensile force*, while the direction towards the joint indicates *compressive force* in the members as indicated in Figure 5.3(iv).

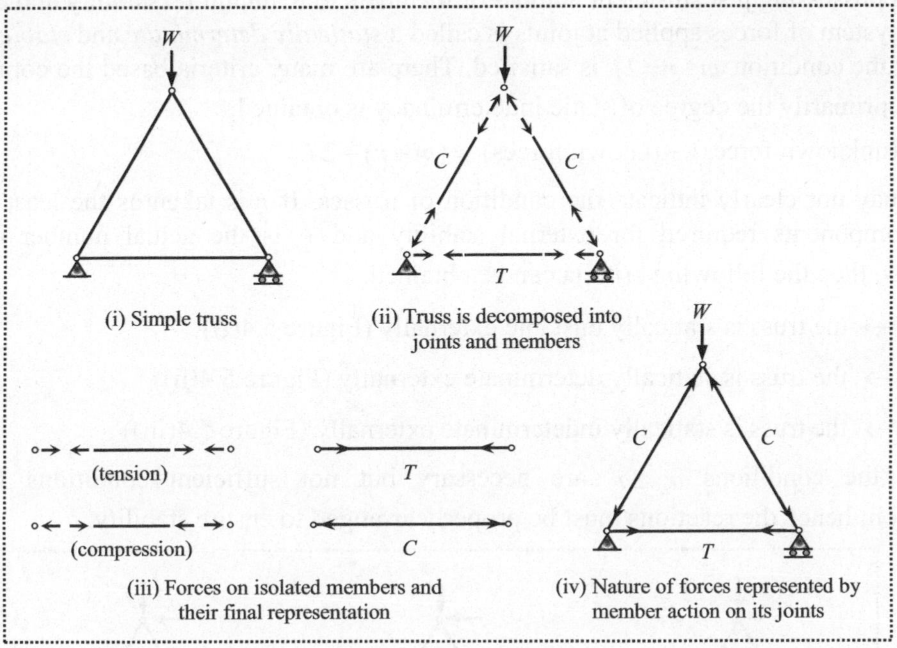

Figure 5.3 Representation of member forces in truss analysis

In truss analysis, a *tension* (T) is designated as a positive bar force while a *compression* (C) is a negative bar force. First, the free-body diagram is isolated in which the desired bar forces are exposed as unknowns. The directions of unknown forces are assumed to be positive (i.e., tension) on the cut face, and the static equilibrium equation equations are applied to solve for the unknown bar forces. If the solution produces a positive force, the assumed direction is correct (i.e., tension). On the other hand, a negative force indicates that the assumed direction is incorrect, hence the member is in compression. This means that the numerical value is correct regardless of the sign.

5.3.1 Stability and Determinacy of Trusses

The fundamental configuration (i.e., triangle) of a planar truss with pin joints at the connections is internally stable. This means, the configuration does not get modified abruptly before or after application of external loads. When this configuration is supported externally by providing a hinged support at any one joint and a roller support at another joint, the structure becomes externally just-rigid. This essentially means, with one hinged and one roller supports, minimum three reaction components are introduced to satisfy the requirement of equilibrium conditions. As the only internal force in each member is the axial force, the total number of unknown forces is equal to six (i.e., three member forces and three reactions). However, each joint offers two equilibrium equations $\left(\sum F_x = 0 \text{ and } \sum F_y = 0\right)$. If m denotes the number of members and r denotes the number of reaction components (at the supports), and j denotes the number of joints, then $m + r = 2j$ for the basic configuration.

A truss possessing just sufficient number of members to maintain its stability and equilibrium under any system of forces applied at joints is called a *statically determinate* and *stable* truss. This means that the condition $m+r=2j$ is satisfied. There are many criteria based the composition of m, r, and j; primarily the degree of static indeterminacy is obtained.

$$DSI = \text{(unknown forces)} - \text{(known forces)} = (m+r)-2j \quad (5.1)$$

Eq. (5.1) may not clearly indicate the condition of trusses. If r is taken as the least number of reaction components required for external stability and r_a is the actual number of reaction components, then the following criteria can be obtained.

$r_a < r \rightarrow$ the truss is statically unstable externally (Figure 5.4(i))

$r_a = r \rightarrow$ the truss is statically determinate externally (Figure 5.4(ii))

$r_a > r \rightarrow$ the truss is statically indeterminate externally (Figure 5.4(iii))

Therefore, the conditions $r_a \geq r$ are necessary but not sufficient conditions for statical classification; hence the reactions must be properly arranged to ensure stability.

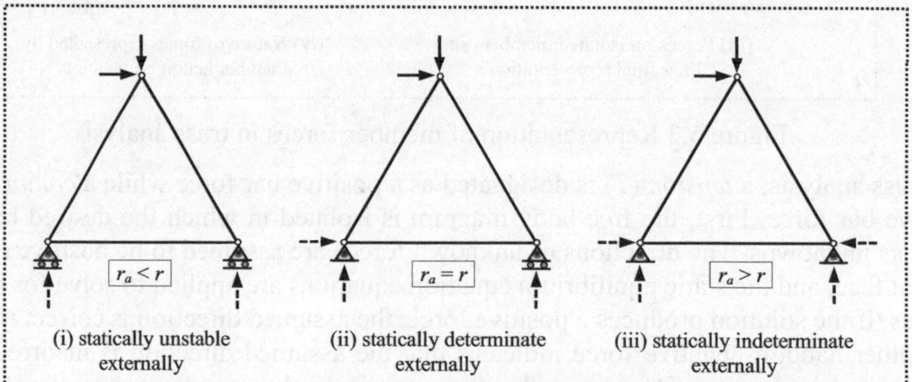

Figure 5.4 External classification of truss

For internal classification, let the condition $m+r=2j$ be rewritten as $m=2j-r$. In this form, m is the number of members required to form an internally statically determinate truss. If m_a is the actual number of members in the truss, then the following criteria can be obtained.

$m_a < m \rightarrow$ the truss is statically unstable internally (Figure 5.5(i))

$m_a = m \rightarrow$ the truss is statically determinate internally (Figure 5.5(ii))

$m_a > m \rightarrow$ the truss is statically indeterminate internally (Figure 5.5(iii))

Therefore, if $m_a < m$, the truss is definitely unstable, but if $m_a \geq m$, it does not necessarily mean that the truss is stable. This may be due to improper arrangement of members to ensure internal stability. Such trusses are said to have *critical form*.

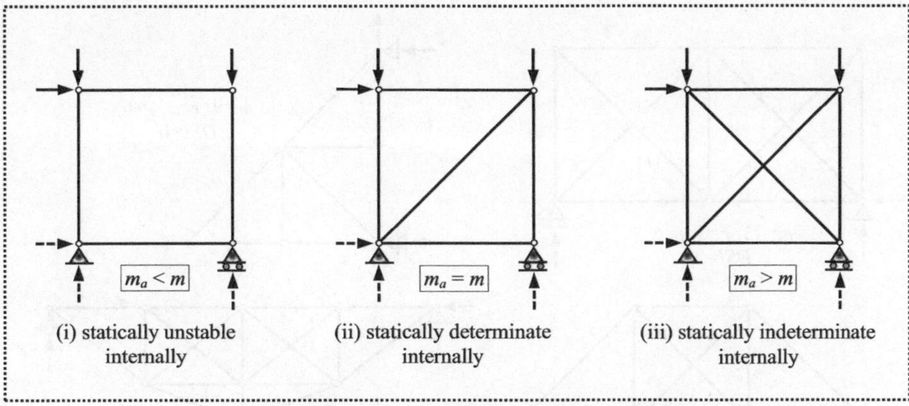

Figure 5.5 Internal classification of truss

Based on the degree of static indeterminacy, if $DSI = 0$ the truss is termed as *just-rigid*; if $DSI < 0$ the truss is *under-rigid*; and $DSI > 0$ the truss is *over-rigid*. Figure 5.6 shows a few examples of trusses which are statically determinate (i.e., $DSI = 0$), but unstable. The unstable structures cannot function as load transfer system, and hence cannot be solved for the force or displacement responses.

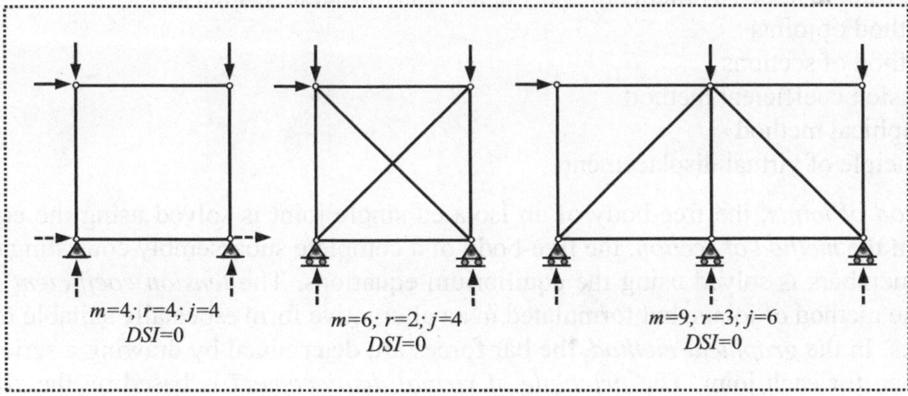

Figure 5.6 Examples of unstable trusses with *DSI*=0

Figure 5.7 shows various stable trusses with the details of static indeterminacy. When $DSI > 0$, the trusses are statically indeterminate, hence the equilibrium equations alone are inadequate to determine the member forces.

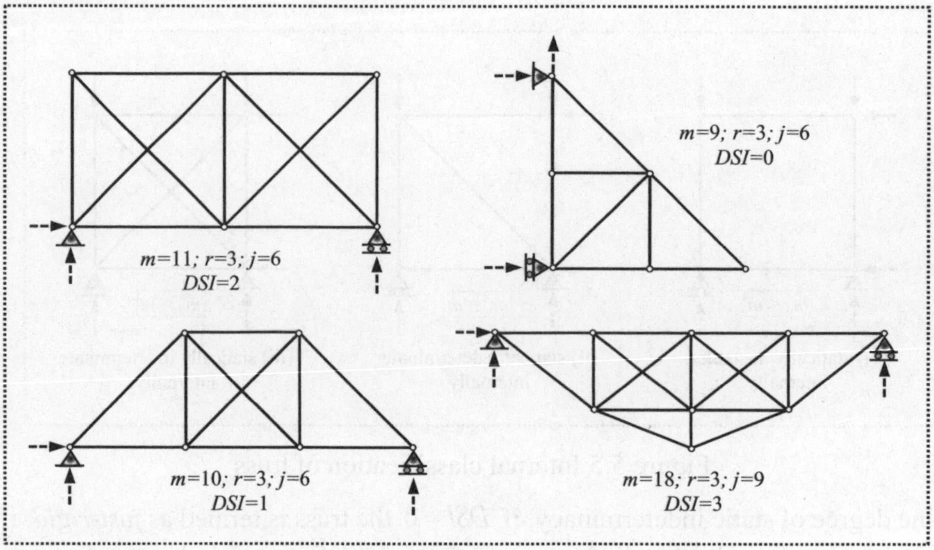

Figure 5.7 Examples of stable trusses

5.3.2 Methods of Analysis

There are several methods available to analyse the truss structures, such as

(i) Method of joints
(ii) Method of sections
(iii) Tension coefficient method
(iv) Graphical method
(v) Principle of virtual displacement

In the *method of joints*, the free-body of an isolated single joint is solved using the equilibrium equations. In the *method of section*, the free-body of a complete subassembly consisting of several joints and members is solved using the equilibrium equations. The *tension coefficient method* is similar to the method of joints, but formulated in an alternative form especially suitable for solving space trusses. In the *graphical method*, the bar forces are determined by drawing a series of force polygons, one for each joint. The *principle of virtual displacement* is based on the concepts of virtual work when the body is subjected to a small imaginary displacement.

5.4 Method of Joints

Truss is assumed to be composed of a series of members and joints. Any portion of a structure must be in a state of equilibrium is the basis for all analysis techniques directed at determining forces in truss members. First, the support reactions are obtained by considering the rigid-body equilibrium conditions (i.e., $\sum F_x = 0$, $\sum F_y = 0$ and $\sum M = 0$) of the whole structure. Each joint is isolated, and the system of forces acting at the joint is defined by the unknown forces (i.e., member forces at the joint) and by the known forces (i.e., external loads and support reactions), if available. The actual direction of the known forces is used, and the nature of the unknown forces is arbitrarily considered to be the tension. Since all the forces in the joint act through the same point (called concurrent system), only two equilibrium equations (i.e., $\sum F_x = 0$ and $\sum F_y = 0$) are valid, and the moment equilibrium (i.e., $\sum M = 0$) is not a concern. The unknown forces are determined by applying the equilibrium equations (i.e., $\sum F_x = 0$ and $\sum F_y = 0$). In a joint, since only two conditions are available, no more than two unknowns can be solved. In general, the truss analysis is started at a support where two members meet, because the support reactions are already known, and only two member forces are unknown. Once all the forces acting at the initial point have been found, the adjacent joint is considered for the analysis.

5.4.1 Numerical Examples

Example 5.1: Analyse the truss shown in Figure 5.8 for the bar forces.

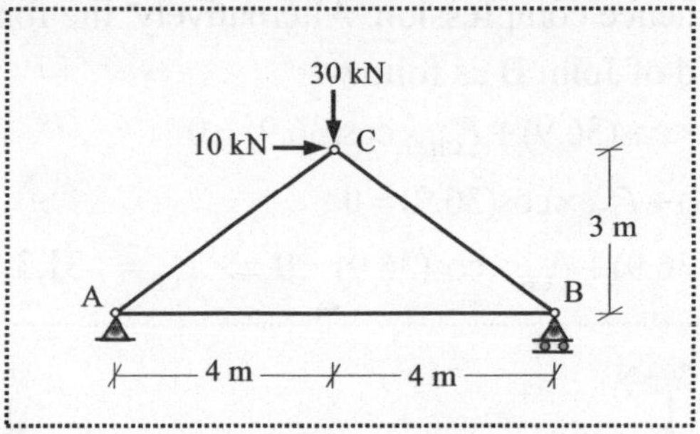

Figure 5.8 Three-member truss (Example 5.1)

Solution:

The free-body diagram of the whole structure is shown in Figure 5.9(i). First, the truss needs to be checked for the determinacy. There are three members (AB, BC and CA), three joints (A, B and C), and three reactions (V_A, V_B and H_A). Therefore, the degree of static indeterminacy is $DSI = m + r - 2j = 3 + 3 - 2(3) = 0$, hence the structure is statically determinate. The support reactions are determined by applying the equilibrium conditions.

$$\sum F_x = 0 \Rightarrow -H_A + 10 = 0$$

$$\Rightarrow H_A = 10.0 \text{ kN}$$

$$\sum F_y = 0 \Rightarrow V_A + V_B - 30 = 0$$

$$\sum M_A = 0 \Rightarrow V_B \times 8 - 30 \times 4 - 10 \times 3 = 0$$

$$\Rightarrow V_B = 18.75 \text{ kN} \ \& \ V_A = 11.25 \text{ kN}$$

The internal forces are marked as $F_{AB} = F_{BA}$, $F_{AC} = F_{CA}$, $F_{BC} = F_{CB}$ in the free-body diagram with the nature of internal forces assumed as tension (i.e., the arrows are placed for the members at the ends pointing away from the joints) as shown in Figure 5.9(ii).

Joint A is isolated as shown in Figure 5.9(iii), and the equilibrium equations are applied. The inclined forces (i.e., forces in the inclined members) are resolved into horizontal and vertical directions while applying the equilibrium conditions.

$$\sum F_x = 0 \Rightarrow -10.0 + F_{AB} + F_{AC} \times \cos(36.9) = 0$$

$$\sum F_y = 0 \Rightarrow +11.25 + F_{AC} \times \sin(36.9) = 0 \Rightarrow F_{AC} = -18.7 \text{ kN}$$

Therefore, $-10.0 + F_{AB} + (-18.7) \times \cos(36.9) = 0 \Rightarrow F_{AB} = +25.0 \text{ kN}$

The sign of F_{AC} is negative; hence compression. However, the sign should not be changed until the analysis is completed for all the joints.

Joint C is isolated as shown in Figure 5.9(iv), and the equilibrium equations are applied.

$$\sum F_x = 0 \Rightarrow -F_{BA} - F_{BC} \times \cos(36.9) = 0$$

$$-F_{AB} - F_{BC} \times \cos(36.9) = 0 \Rightarrow -25.0 - F_{BC} \times \cos(36.9) = 0 \Rightarrow F_{BC} = -31.3 \text{ kN}$$

The sign of F_{BC} is negative; hence compression. Alternatively, the force F_{BC} can be obtained by considering the joint C instead of Joint B as follows.

$$\sum F_x = 0 \Rightarrow +10.0 - F_{CA} \times \cos(36.9) + F_{CB} \times \cos(36.9) = 0$$

$$+10.0 - F_{AC} \times \cos(36.9) + F_{CB} \times \cos(36.9) = 0$$

$$+10.0 - (-18.7) \times \cos(36.9) + F_{CB} \times \cos(36.9) = 0 \Rightarrow F_{CB} = -31.3 = F_{BC}$$

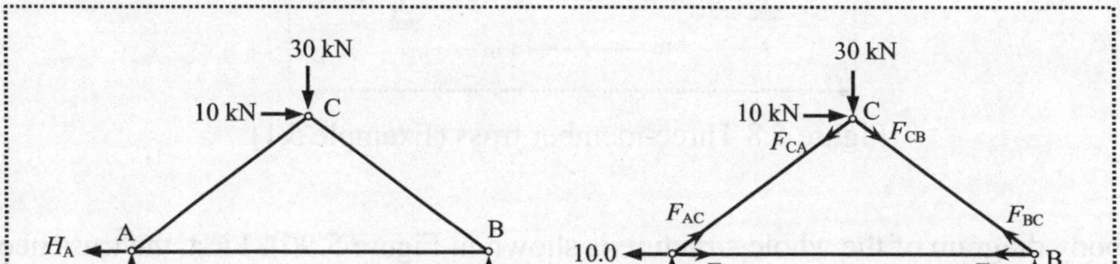

Figure 5.9 Truss analysis (Example 5.1)

Final member forces:

$F_{AB} = F_{BA} = +25.0$ kN (Tension)

$F_{AC} = F_{CA} = -18.7$ kN (Compression)

$F_{BC} = F_{CB} = -31.3$ kN (Compression)

The member forces are represented as shown in Figure 5.9(v).

Example 5.2: Analyse the truss shown in Figure 5.10 for the bar forces.

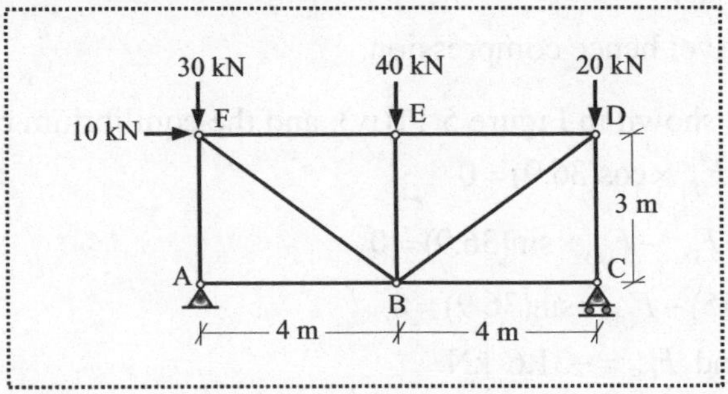

Figure 5.10 Nine-member truss (Example 5.2)

Solution:

The free-body diagram of the whole structure is shown in Figure 5.11(i). First, the truss needs to be checked for the determinacy.

$DSI = m + r - 2j = 9 + 3 - 2(6) = 0$, hence the structure is statically determinate. The support reactions are determined by applying the equilibrium conditions.

$$\sum F_x = 0 \Rightarrow -H_A + 10 = 0$$

$$\Rightarrow H_A = 10.0 \text{ kN}$$

$$\sum F_y = 0 \Rightarrow V_A + V_C - 30 - 40 - 20 = 0$$

$$\sum M_A = 0 \Rightarrow V_C \times 8 - 20 \times 8 - 40 \times 4 - 30 \times 0 - 10 \times 3 = 0$$

$$\Rightarrow V_C = 43.75 \text{ kN} \ \& \ V_A = 46.25 \text{ kN}$$

The nature of the internal forces is assumed as tension (i.e., the arrows are placed for the members at the ends pointing away from the joints) as shown in the free-body diagram.

Joint A is isolated as shown in Figure 5.11(ii), and the equilibrium equations are applied.

$$\sum F_x = 0 \Rightarrow -10.0 + F_{AB} = 0$$

$$\Rightarrow F_{AB} = +10.0 \text{ kN}$$

$$\sum F_y = 0 \Rightarrow +46.25 + F_{AF} = 0$$

$$\Rightarrow F_{AF} = -46.25 \text{ kN}$$

The sign of F_{AF} is negative; hence compression. However, the sign should not be changed until the analysis is completed for all the joints.

Now, Joint B cannot be considered as an isolated joint for determining the next set of internal forces, because there are member forces in which four forces are unknown.

Therefore, the joint C is isolated as shown in Figure 5.11(iii), and the equilibrium equations are applied.

$$\sum F_x = 0 \Rightarrow F_{CB} = 0$$

$$\sum F_y = 0 \Rightarrow +43.75 + F_{CD} = 0$$

$$\Rightarrow F_{CD} = -43.75 \text{ kN}$$

The sign of F_{CD} is negative; hence compression.

The joint D is isolated as shown in Figure 5.11(iv), and the equilibrium equations are applied.

$$\sum F_x = 0 \Rightarrow -F_{DE} - F_{DB} \times \cos(36.9) = 0$$

$$\sum F_y = 0 \Rightarrow -20.0 - F_{DC} - F_{DB} \times \sin(36.9) = 0$$

Therefore, $-20.0 - (-43.75) - F_{DB} \times \sin(36.9) = 0$

$$\Rightarrow F_{DB} = +40.0 \text{ kN and } F_{DE} = -31.6 \text{ kN}$$

The sign of F_{DE} is negative; hence compression.

The joint E is isolated as shown in Figure 5.11(v), and the equilibrium equations are applied.

$$\sum F_x = 0 \Rightarrow F_{ED} - F_{EF} = 0 \Rightarrow (-31.6) - F_{EF} = 0$$

$$\Rightarrow F_{EF} = -31.6 \text{ kN}$$

$$\sum F_y = 0 \Rightarrow -40.0 - F_{EB} = 0$$

$$\Rightarrow F_{EB} = -40.0 \text{ kN}$$

The sign of F_{EF} and F_{EB} is negative; hence compression.

The joint F is isolated as shown in Figure 5.11(vi), and the equilibrium equations are applied.

$$\sum F_x = 0 \Rightarrow +10.0 + F_{FE} + F_{FB} \times \cos(36.9) = 0$$

$$+10.0 - 31.6 + F_{FB} \times \cos(36.9) = 0$$

$$\Rightarrow F_{FB} = +27.0 \text{ kN}$$

$$\sum F_y = 0 \Rightarrow -30.0 - F_{FA} - F_{FB} \times \sin(36.9) = 0$$

$$-30.0 - F_{FA} - 27.0 \times \sin(36.9) = 0$$

$$\Rightarrow F_{FA} = -46.2 \text{ kN}$$

The force F_{FA} was already obtained by considering Joint A; same result is obtained while considering Joint F.

Table 5.1 presents the forces along with the nature of all the members. The member forces are represented as shown in Figure 5.11(vii).

Table 5.1 Member forces (Example 5.2)

Member	Force (kN)	Nature
AB	10.0	Tension
BC	0	-
CD	43.8	Compression
DE	31.6	Compression
EF	31.6	Compression
AF	46.3	Compression
BD	40.0	Tension
BE	40.0	Compression
BF	27.0	Tension

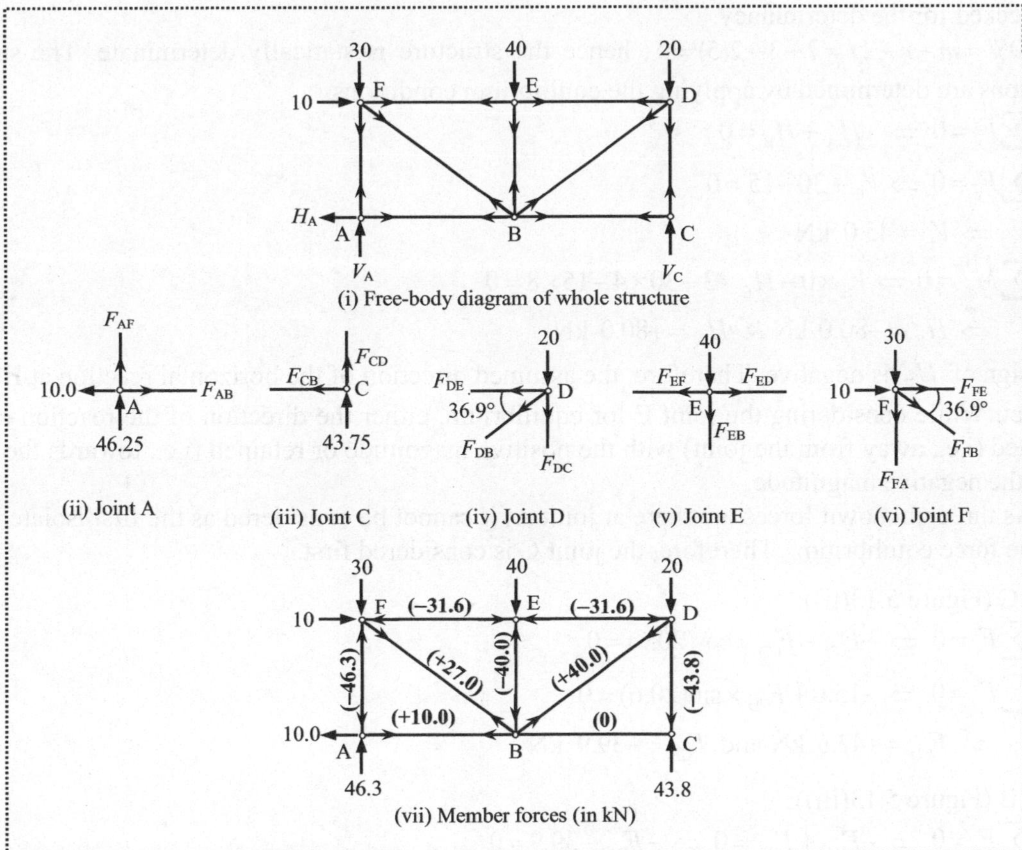

Figure 5.11 Truss analysis (Example 5.2)

Example 5.3: Analyse the truss shown in Figure 5.12 for the bar forces.

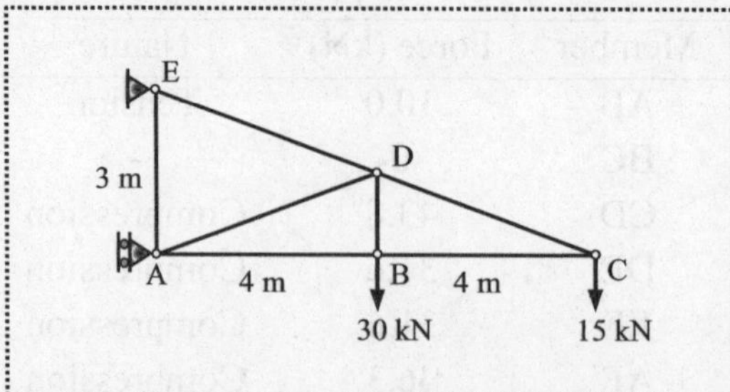

Figure 5.12 Seven-bar truss (Example 5.3)

Solution:

The free-body diagram of the whole structure is shown in Figure 5.13(i). First, the truss needs to be checked for the determinacy.

$DSI = m + r - 2j = 7 + 3 - 2(5) = 0$; hence the structure is statically determinate. The support reactions are determined by applying the equilibrium conditions.

$$\sum F_x = 0 \Rightarrow +H_A + H_E = 0$$

$$\sum F_y = 0 \Rightarrow V_E - 30 - 15 = 0$$

$$\Rightarrow V_E = 45.0 \text{ kN}$$

$$\sum M_A = 0 \Rightarrow V_E \times 0 - H_E \times 3 - 30 \times 4 - 15 \times 8 = 0$$

$$\Rightarrow H_E = -80.0 \text{ kN } \& \ H_A = +80.0 \text{ kN}$$

The sign of H_E is negative. Therefore, the assumed direction of the horizontal reaction at E is not correct. While considering the joint E for equilibrium, either the direction of the reaction can be updated (i.e., away from the joint) with the positive magnitude or retained (i.e., towards the joint) with the negative magnitude.

As three unknown forces are there at joint A, it cannot be considered as the first isolated joint for the force equilibrium. Therefore, the joint C is considered first.

Joint C (Figure 5.13(ii)):

$$\sum F_x = 0 \Rightarrow -F_{CB} - F_{CD} \times \cos(20.6) = 0$$

$$\sum F_y = 0 \Rightarrow -15.0 + F_{CD} \times \sin(20.6) = 0$$

$$\Rightarrow F_{CD} = +42.6 \text{ kN and } F_{CB} = -39.9 \text{ kN}$$

Joint B (Figure 5.13(iii)):

$$\sum F_x = 0 \Rightarrow -F_{BA} + F_{BC} = 0 \Rightarrow -F_{BA} - 39.9 = 0$$

$$\Rightarrow F_{BA} = -39.9 \text{ kN}$$

$$\sum F_y = 0 \Rightarrow +F_{BD} - 30.0 = 0$$

$$\Rightarrow F_{BD} = +30.0 \text{ kN}$$

Joint A (Figure 5.13(iv)):

$$\sum F_x = 0 \Rightarrow +80.0 + F_{AB} + F_{AD} \times \cos(20.6) = 0$$
$$\Rightarrow +80.0 - 39.9 + F_{AD} \times \cos(20.6) = 0$$
$$\Rightarrow F_{AD} = -42.8 \text{ kN}$$
$$\sum F_y = 0 \Rightarrow +F_{AE} + F_{AD} \times \sin(20.6) = 0$$
$$\Rightarrow +F_{AE} - 42.8 \times \sin(20.6) = 0$$
$$\Rightarrow F_{AE} = +15.0 \text{ kN}$$

Joint E (Figure 5.13(v)):

$$\sum F_x = 0 \Rightarrow -80.0 + F_{ED} \times \sin(69.4) = 0$$
$$\Rightarrow F_{ED} = +85.5 \text{ kN}$$
$$\sum F_y = 0 \Rightarrow +45 - F_{EA} - F_{ED} \times \cos(69.4) = 0$$
$$\Rightarrow +45 - F_{EA} - 85.5 \times \cos(69.4) = 0$$
$$\Rightarrow F_{EA} = +15.0 \text{ kN}$$

The force F_{EA} was already obtained by considering Joint A; same result is obtained while considering Joint E.

Table 5.2 presents the forces along with the nature of all the members. The member forces are represented as shown in Figure 5.13(vi).

Table 5.2 Member forces (Example 5.3)

Member	Force (kN)	Nature
AB	39.9	Compression
BC	39.9	Compression
CD	42.6	Tension
DE	85.5	Tension
AE	15.0	Tension
AD	42.8	Compression
BD	30.0	Tension

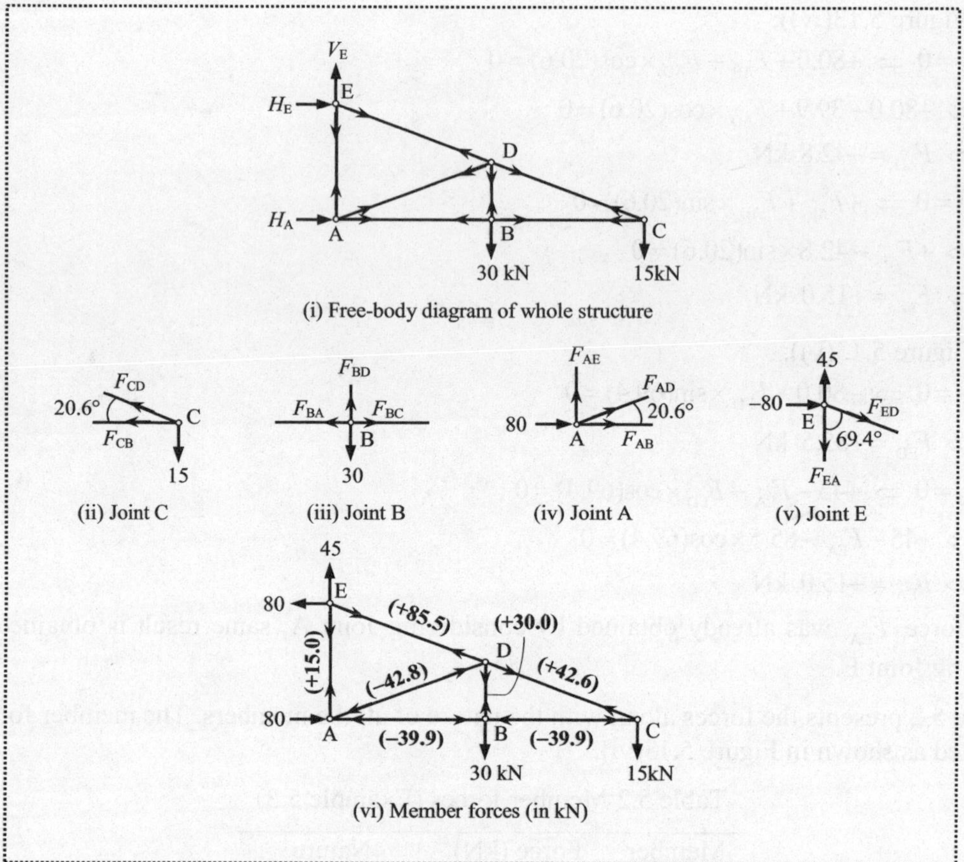

Figure 5.13 Truss analysis (Example 5.3)

Example 5.4: Analyse the truss shown in Figure 5.14 for the bar forces.

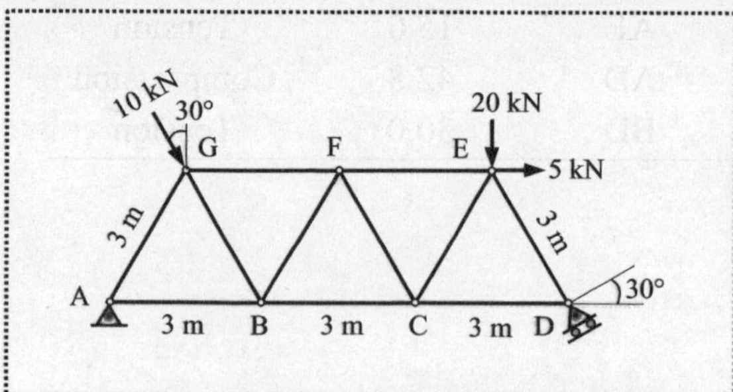

Figure 5.14 Eleven-bar truss (Example 5.4)

Solution:

The free-body diagram of the whole structure is shown in Figure 5.15(i). Both vertical and horizontal reactions exist at A. The roller support at D offers resistance in one direction that is normal to the plane (i.e., 30° to the horizontal plane). Therefore, the reaction at D (i.e., R_D) is acting normal to the inclined plane. The components of the reaction R_D are resolved in horizontal and vertical directions as $H_D = R_D \sin 30$ and $V_D = R_D \cos 30$ respectively. Similarly, the inclined load applied at G is resolved into both horizontal and vertical directions as shown in Figure 5.15(ii).

The degree of static indeterminacy, $DSI = m + r - 2j = 11 + 3 - 2(7) = 0$; hence the structure is statically determinate. The support reactions are determined by applying the equilibrium conditions.

$$\sum F_x = 0 \Rightarrow +H_A - R_D \sin 30 + 10 \sin 30 + 5.0 = 0$$

$$\sum F_y = 0 \Rightarrow +V_A + R_D \cos 30 - 10 \cos 30 - 20 = 0$$

$$\sum M_A = 0 \Rightarrow R_D \cos 30 \times 9 - 5 \times 2.6 - 20 \times 7.5 - 10 \cos 30 \times 1.5 - 10 \sin 30 \times 2.6 = 0$$

$$R_D = 24.247 \text{ kN}$$

$$H_A = +2.124 \text{ kN}$$

$$V_A = +7.662 \text{ kN}$$

Joint A (Figure 5.15(iii)):

$$\sum F_x = 0 \Rightarrow +2.1 + F_{AB} + F_{AG} \times \cos(60) = 0$$

$$\sum F_y = 0 \Rightarrow +7.7 + F_{AG} \times \sin(60) = 0$$

$$F_{AG} = -8.9 \text{ kN}$$

$$F_{AB} = +2.3 \text{ kN}$$

Joint D (Figure 5.15(iv)):

$$\sum F_x = 0 \Rightarrow -F_{DC} - F_{DE} \times \cos(60) - 12.1 = 0$$

$$\sum F_y = 0 \Rightarrow +21.0 + F_{DE} \times \sin(60) = 0$$

$$F_{DE} = -24.2 \text{ kN}$$

$$F_{DC} = 0 \text{ kN}$$

Joint E (Figure 5.15(v)):

$$\sum F_x = 0 \Rightarrow -F_{EF} - F_{EC} \times \cos(60) + F_{ED} \times \cos(60) + 5.0 = 0$$

$$\sum F_y = 0 \Rightarrow -20.0 - F_{EC} \times \sin(60) - F_{ED} \times \sin(60) = 0$$

$$F_{EC} = +1.1 \text{ kN}$$

$$F_{EF} = -7.7 \text{ kN}$$

Joint C (Figure 5.15(vi)):

$$\sum F_x = 0 \Rightarrow -F_{CB} - F_{CF} \times \cos(60) + F_{CE} \times \cos(60) + F_{CD} = 0$$

$$\sum F_y = 0 \Rightarrow +F_{CF} \times \sin(60) + F_{CE} \times \sin(60) = 0$$

$$F_{CF} = -1.1 \text{ kN}$$

$$F_{CB} = +1.1 \text{ kN}$$

Joint B (Figure 5.15(vii)):

$$\sum F_x = 0 \Rightarrow -F_{BA} - F_{BG} \times \cos(60) + F_{BF} \times \cos(60) + F_{BC} = 0$$

$$\Rightarrow F_{BF} - F_{BG} = 2.4$$

$$\sum F_y = 0 \Rightarrow +F_{BG} \times \sin(60) + F_{BF} \times \sin(60) = 0$$

$$\Rightarrow F_{BF} + F_{BG} = 0$$

$$F_{BF} = +1.2 \text{ kN}$$

$$F_{BG} = -1.2 \text{ kN}$$

Joint F (Figure 5.15(viii)):

$$\sum F_x = 0 \Rightarrow -F_{FG} - F_{FB} \times \cos(60) + F_{FC} \times \cos(60) + F_{FE} = 0$$

$$F_{FG} = -8.9 \text{ kN}$$

The member forces determined are presented in Table 5.3, and represented as shown in Figure 5.15(ix).

Table 5.3 Member forces (Example 5.4)

Member	Force (kN)	Nature
AB	2.3	Tension
BC	1.1	Tension
CD	0	Tension
DE	24.2	Compression
EF	7.7	Compression
FG	8.9	Compression
GA	8.9	Compression
BF	1.2	Tension
BG	1.2	Compression
CE	1.1	Tension
CF	1.1	Compression

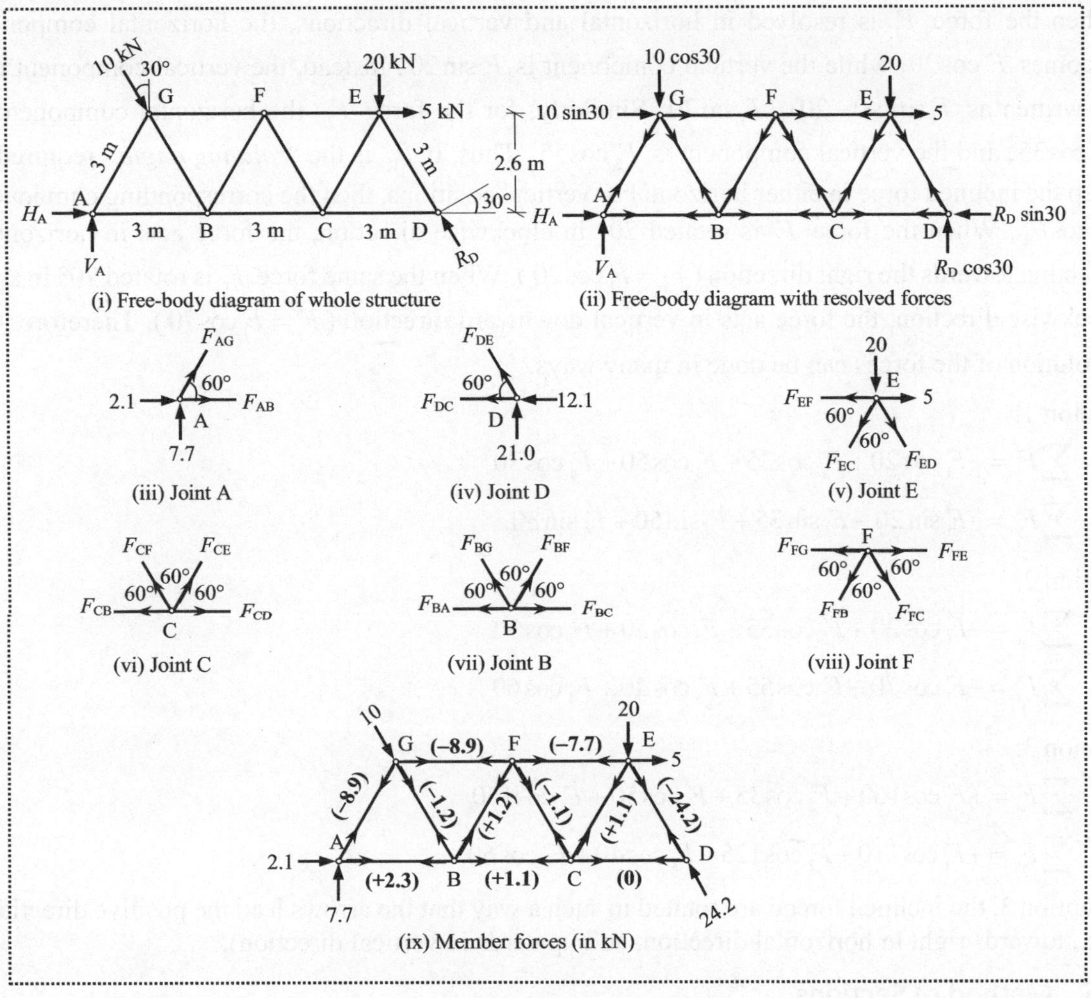

Figure 5.15 Truss analysis (Example 5.4)

Note: While resolving the inclined forces in horizontal and vertical directions, it is convenient to use only "*cosine*". For example, consider a force system shown in Figure 5.16.

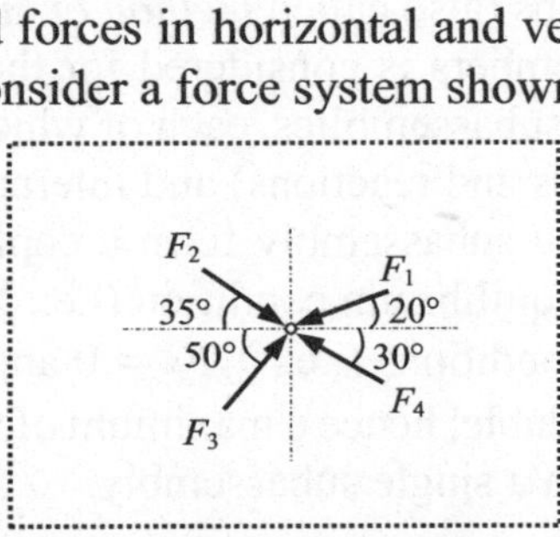

Figure 5.16 System of inclined forces

When the force F_1 is resolved in horizontal and vertical directions, the horizontal component becomes $F_1 \cos 20$, while the vertical component is $F_1 \sin 20$. Instead, the vertical component can be written as $F_1 \sin(90-20) = F_1 \sin 70$. Similarly, for the force F_2, the horizontal component is $F_2 \cos 35$, and the vertical component is $F_2 \cos 55$. Thus, if θ_R is the "*rotating angle*" required to keep the inclined force in either horizontal or vertical positions, then the corresponding component is $\cos\theta_R$. When the force F_1 is rotated 20° in clockwise direction, the force acts in horizontal, directing towards the right direction ($F_x = F_1 \cos 20$). When the same force F_1 is rotated 70° in anti-clockwise direction, the force acts in vertical downward direction ($F_y = F_1 \cos 70$). Therefore, the resolution of the forces can be done in many ways.

Option 1:

$$\sum F_x = -F_1 \cos 20 + F_2 \cos 35 + F_3 \cos 50 + F_4 \cos 30$$

$$\sum F_y = -F_1 \sin 20 - F_2 \sin 35 + F_3 \sin 50 + F_4 \sin 30$$

Option 2:

$$\sum F_x = -F_1 \cos 20 + F_2 \cos 35 + F_3 \cos 50 + F_4 \cos 30$$

$$\sum F_y = -F_1 \cos 70 - F_2 \cos 55 + F_3 \cos 40 + F_4 \cos 60$$

Option 3:

$$\sum F_x = +F_1 \cos 160 + F_2 \cos 35 + F_3 \cos 50 + F_4 \cos 150$$

$$\sum F_y = +F_1 \cos 110 + F_2 \cos 125 + F_3 \cos 40 + F_4 \cos 60$$

In option 3, the inclined forced are rotated in such a way that the arrows lead the positive directions (i.e., towards right in horizontal direction, and upwards in vertical direction).

5.5 Method of Sections

In the method of joints, the elemental portions of the truss considered for equilibrium were the joints. All the joints are considered one by one until all the member forces of the truss are determined. In the method of sections (also called *method of moments*), the complete subassembly consisting of several joints and members is considered for the equilibrium. An imaginary cut is made to partition the truss into two subassemblies, each of which is in equilibrium under the action of external forces (i.e., applied loads and reactions) and internal forces (i.e., member forces in the cut). Since the forces acting on the subassembly form a coplanar, but non-concurrent and non-parallel force system, the moment equilibrium condition (i.e., $\sum M = 0$) should also be used along with the translational equilibrium conditions (i.e., $\sum F_x = 0$ and $\sum F_y = 0$). This means that all the three equilibrium equations are available; hence a maximum of three unknown forces cutting across three members can be determined in a single subassembly.

Thus, conceptually, the method of joints can be considered in terms of a section line around each joint, wherein the moment equilibrium condition (i.e., $\sum M = 0$) becomes null-and-void owing to the concurrent nature. In numerical examples, the method of joints is preferred when all the member forces in a truss are to be determined, whereas the method of sections is particularly useful when only a selected member forces are to be determined.

5.5.1 Numerical Examples

Example 5.5: Analyse the truss shown in Figure 5.17 for the bar forces. [Same as Example 5.1]

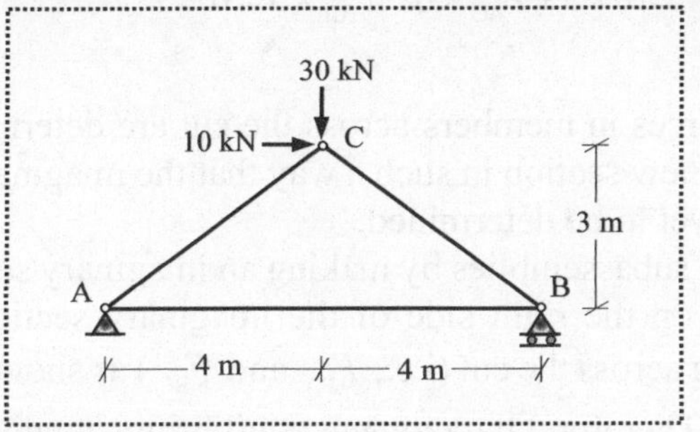

Figure 5.17 Three-member truss (Example 5.5)

Solution:

This example is already solved using the method of joints. The free-body diagram of the whole structure with the assumed nature of member forces is shown in Figure 5.18(i). The support reactions are computed by applying the equilibrium conditions on the whole structure.

$$\sum F_x = 0 \Rightarrow -H_A + 10 = 0$$

$$\Rightarrow H_A = 10.0 \text{ kN}$$

$$\sum F_y = 0 \Rightarrow V_A + V_B - 30 = 0$$

$$\sum M_A = 0 \Rightarrow V_B \times 8 - 30 \times 4 - 10 \times 3 = 0$$

$$V_B = 18.75 \text{ kN}$$

$$V_A = 11.25 \text{ kN}$$

The truss is cut into two subassemblies by making an imaginary section 1-1 as shown in Figure 5.18(ii). The subassembly on the left side of the imaginary section 1-1 is considered for the member forces which are lying across the cut (i.e., F_{AB} and F_{AC}) as shown in Figure 5.18(iii). Since the subassembly is in equilibrium, the moment of all forces in the subassembly about any point on the plane should be equal to zero (i.e, moment equilibrium condition).

First, the moment equilibrium condition is applied at point B, and then applied at point C (it need not be at the locations of joints; it can be even outside the structure configuration, but it is convenient to consider the joint locations). There are four forces in the subassembly (i.e., 10.0 kN, 11.25 kN, F_{AB} and F_{AC}). Therefore, the algebraic summation of the moments of these forces (i.e., force multiplied by the respective normal distance up to B) should be considered.

$$\sum M_B = 0 \Rightarrow +11.25\times 8 + 10\times 0 + F_{AC}\times 4.8 + F_{AB}\times 0 = 0$$

$$\Rightarrow F_{AC} = -18.75 \text{ kN}$$

All clockwise moments are considered as positive and anti-clockwise moments are considered as negative. The forces 10 kN and F_{AB} will pass through the point B; hence the perpendicular distance is zero. The perpendicular distance from the axis of force F_{AC} to the point B is 4.8 m as shown in Figure 5.18(iii).

Now, the moment equilibrium condition is applied at point C.

$$\sum M_C = 0 \Rightarrow +11.25\times 4 + 10\times 3 + F_{AC}\times 0 - F_{AB}\times 3 = 0$$

$$\Rightarrow F_{AB} = +25.0 \text{ kN}$$

With the section 1-1, the forces in members across the cut are determined. Therefore, the truss is now considered for another new section in such a way that the imaginary cut is passing through the members whose forces are yet to be determined.

The truss is cut into two subassemblies by making an imaginary section 2-2 as shown in Figure 5.18(iv). The subassembly on the right side of the imaginary section 2-2 is considered for the member forces that are lying across the cut (i.e., F_{BA} and F_{BC}) as shown in Figure 5.18(v), in which F_{BA} is already determined. Therefore, the moment equilibrium condition is applied at point A.

$$\sum M_A = 0 \Rightarrow -18.75\times 8 + F_{AB}\times 0 - F_{BC}\times 4.8 = 0$$

$$\Rightarrow F_{BC} = -31.25 \text{ kN}$$

Final member forces:

$F_{AB} = F_{BA} = +25.0$ kN (Tension)

$F_{AC} = F_{CA} = -18.75$ kN (Compression)

$F_{BC} = F_{CB} = -31.25$ kN (Compression)

The member forces are represented as shown in Figure 5.18(vi).

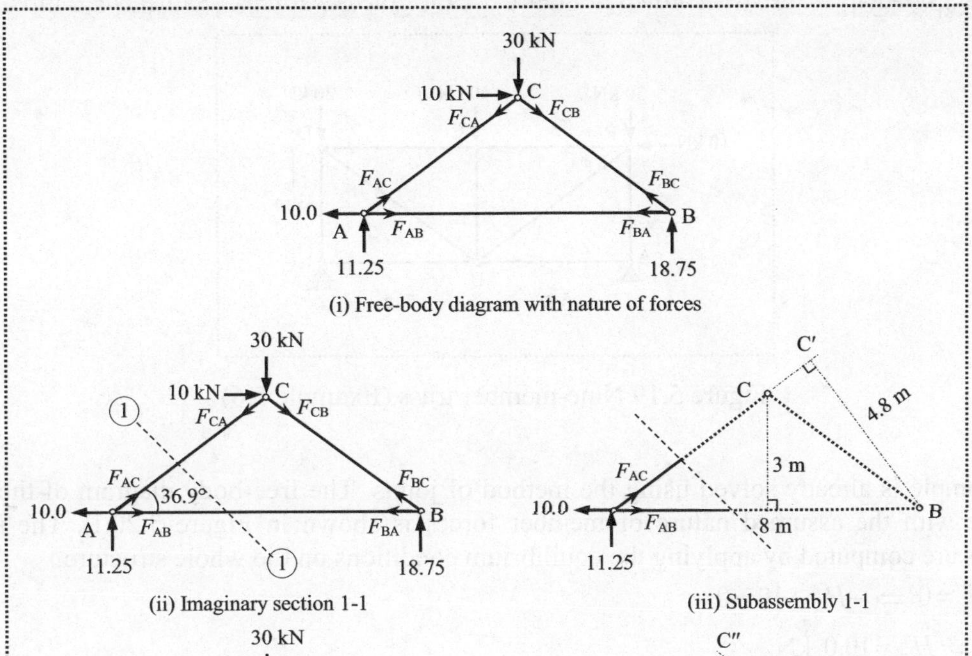

Figure 5.18 Truss analysis (Example 5.5)

Example 5.6: Analyse the truss shown in Figure 5.19 for the bar forces. [Same as Example 5.2]

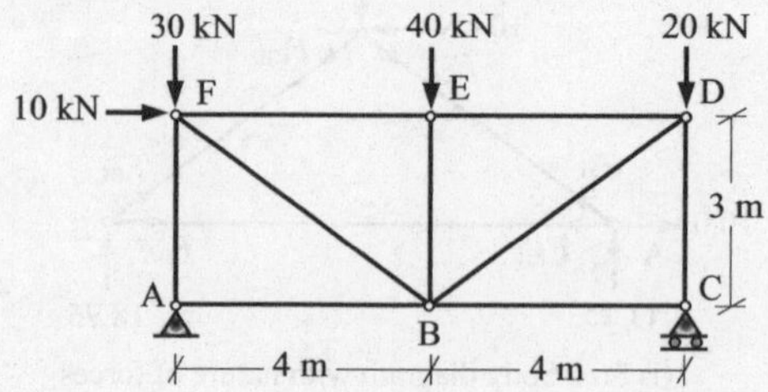

Figure 5.19 Nine-member truss (Example 5.6)

Solution:

This example is already solved using the method of joints. The free-body diagram of the whole structure with the assumed nature of member forces is shown in Figure 5.20(i). The support reactions are computed by applying the equilibrium conditions on the whole structure.

$$\sum F_x = 0 \Rightarrow -H_A + 10 = 0$$

$$\Rightarrow H_A = 10.0 \text{ kN}$$

$$\sum F_y = 0 \Rightarrow V_A + V_C - 30 - 40 - 20 = 0$$

$$\sum M_A = 0 \Rightarrow V_C \times 8 - 20 \times 8 - 40 \times 4 - 30 \times 0 - 10 \times 3 = 0$$

$$\Rightarrow V_C = 43.75 \text{ kN \& } V_A = 46.25 \text{ kN}$$

The truss is cut into two subassemblies by making an imaginary section 1-1 as shown in Figure 5.20(ii). The subassembly on the left side of the imaginary section 1-1 is considered for the member forces F_{AB}, F_{FB} and F_{FE}) as shown in Figure 5.20(iii). Since the subassembly is in equilibrium, all three equilibrium conditions can be applied.

$$\sum F_x = 0 \Rightarrow +10 - 10.0 - F_{AB} - F_{FE} - F_{FB} \times \cos 36.9 = 0$$

$$\sum F_y = 0 \Rightarrow +46.25 - 30 - F_{FB} \times \sin 36.9 = 0$$

$$\Rightarrow F_{FB} = +27.0 \text{ kN}$$

$$\sum M_B = 0 \Rightarrow 46.25 \times 4 + 10 \times 3 - 30 \times 4 + F_{FE} \times 3 = 0$$

$$\Rightarrow F_{FE} = -31.6 \text{ kN}$$

By substituting F_{FB} and F_{FE} in $\sum F_x = 0$;

$$F_{AB} = +10.0$$

It is not necessary to apply all three equilibrium conditions (i.e., $\sum F_x = 0$, $\sum F_y = 0$ and $\sum M = 0$) to solve for three unknown member forces that are exposed in the section 1-1. Alternatively, all the three forces can be determined by applying only moment equilibrium condition at three locations separately.

$$\sum M_B = 0 \Rightarrow 46.25\times4+10\times3-30\times4+F_{FE}\times3=0$$
$$\Rightarrow F_{FE} = -31.6 \text{ kN}$$
$$\sum M_C = 0 \Rightarrow 46.25\times8+10\times3-30\times8+F_{FE}\times3-F_{FB}\times2.4=0$$
$$\Rightarrow F_{FB} = +27.0 \text{ kN}$$
$$\sum M_E = 0 \Rightarrow 46.25\times4+10.0\times3-F_{AB}\times3-30\times4-F_{FB}\times2.4=0$$
$$\Rightarrow F_{AB} = +10.0$$

Now, the truss is cut into two subassemblies by making an imaginary section 2-2 as shown in Figure 5.20(iv). The subassembly on the right side of the imaginary section 2-2 is considered for the member forces F_{CB}, F_{DB} and F_{DE} as shown in Figure 5.20(v). Since the subassembly is in equilibrium, all three equilibrium conditions can be applied.

$$\sum F_x = 0 \Rightarrow -F_{CB}-F_{DE}-F_{DB}\times\cos36.9=0$$
$$\sum F_y = 0 \Rightarrow +43.75-20-F_{DB}\times\sin36.9=0$$
$$\Rightarrow F_{DB} = +40.0 \text{ kN}$$
$$\sum M_B = 0 \Rightarrow -43.75\times4+20\times4-F_{DE}\times3=0$$
$$\Rightarrow F_{DE} = -31.6 \text{ kN}$$

By substituting F_{DB} and F_{DE} in $\sum F_x = 0$;

$$F_{CB} = 0$$

Now, the truss is cut into two subassemblies by making an imaginary section 3-3 as shown in Figure 5.20(vi). The subassembly above the imaginary section 3-3 exposes the member forces F_{BE}, F_{BF}, F_{BD}, and F_{CD} as shown in Figure 5.20(vii).

Since F_{EF} and F_{BD} are already obtained, the subassembly can be considered for the remaining three forces. Moment equilibrium condition is applied at B and C.

$$\sum M_B = 0 \Rightarrow -F_{EF}\times3+20\times4+F_{DC}\times4=0$$
$$\Rightarrow F_{DC} = 43.8 \text{ kN}$$
$$\sum M_C = 0 \Rightarrow -F_{DB}\times2.4-40\times4-F_{EB}\times4-F_{EF}\times3=0$$
$$\Rightarrow F_{EB} = -40.0 \text{ kN}$$

Again, the truss is cut into two subassemblies by making an imaginary section 4-4 as shown in Figure 5.20(viii). The subassembly above the imaginary section 4-4 exposes the member forces F_{AF}, and F_{AB} as shown in Figure 5.20(ix).

Since F_{AB} is already obtained, the subassembly can be considered for the remaining force. Moment equilibrium condition is applied at B.

$$\sum M_B = 0 \Rightarrow +F_{AF}\times4+46.25\times4=0$$
$$\Rightarrow F_{AF} = -46.25 \text{ kN}$$

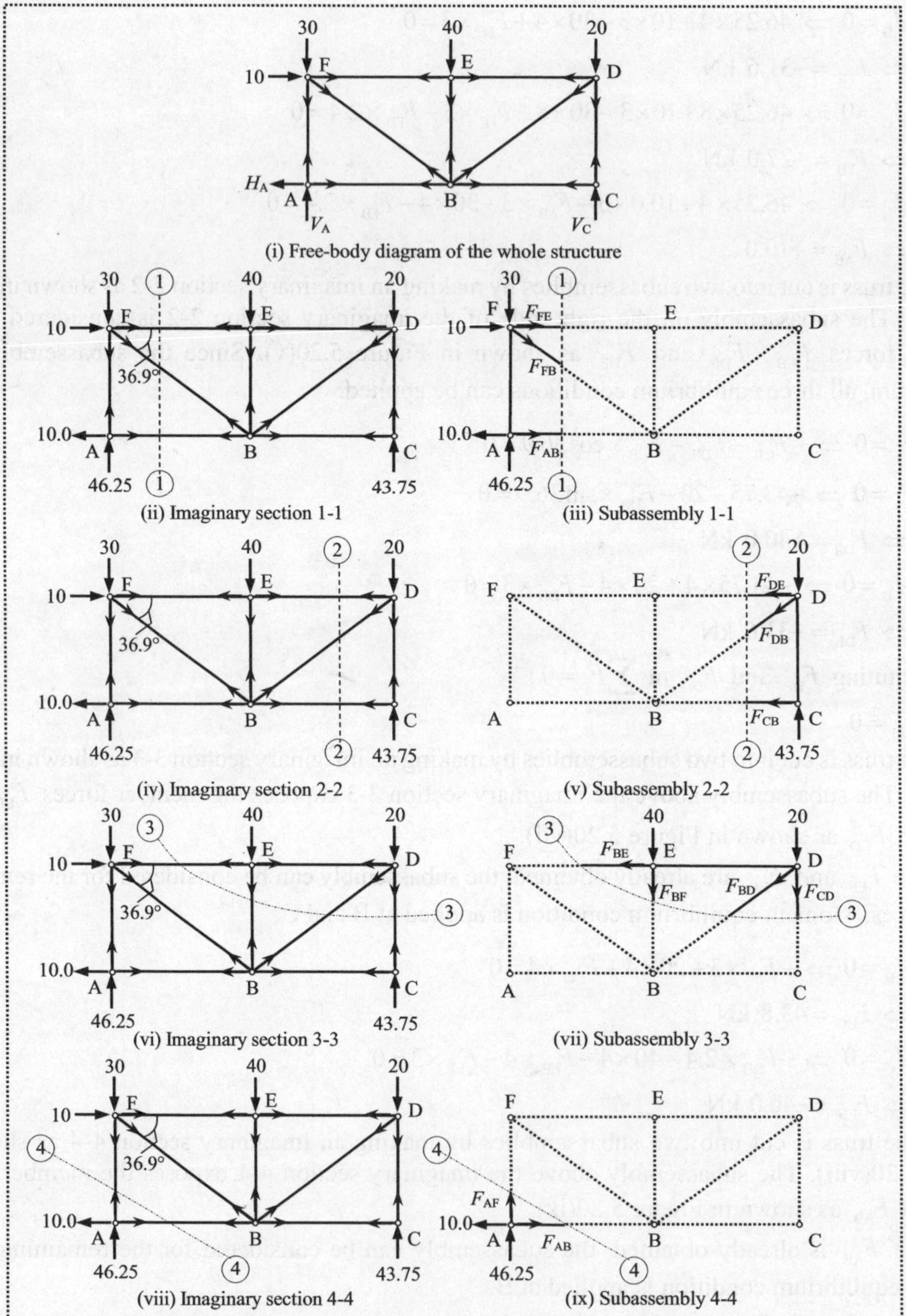

Figure 5.20 Truss analysis (Example 5.6)

Alternatively, the vertical force equilibrium condition can be applied.

$$\sum F_y = 0 \Rightarrow +F_{AF} + 46.25 = 0$$

$$\Rightarrow F_{AF} = -46.25 \text{ kN}$$

The member forces are represented as shown in Figure 5.21.

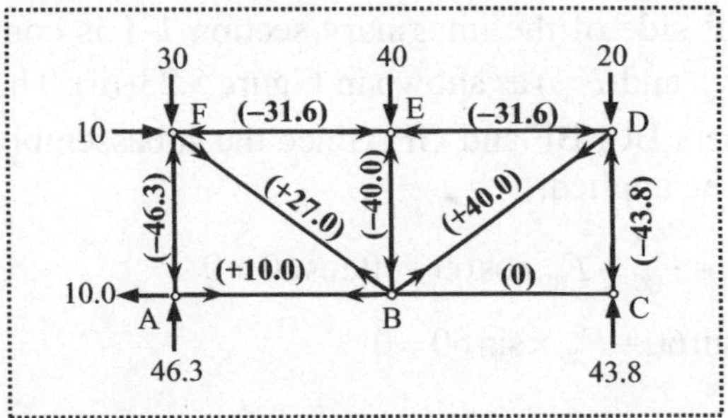

Figure 5.21 Member forces in kN (Example 5.6)

Example 5.7: Determine the member forces of BC, BF and GF in the truss shown in Figure 5.22.

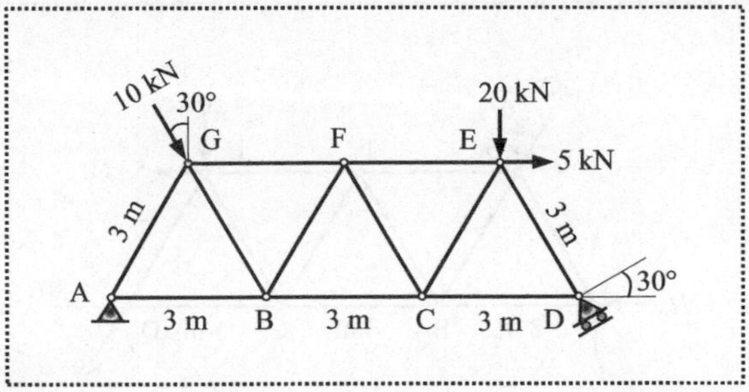

Figure 5.22 Eleven-member truss (Example 5.7)

Solution:

The free-body diagram of the whole structure is shown in Figure 5.23(i). The truss is statically determinate with three support reactions (H_A, V_A and R_D) in which is acting normal to the inclined plane. The components of the reaction R_D are resolved in horizontal and vertical directions as $H_D = R_D \sin 30$ and $V_D = R_D \cos 30$ respectively. Similarly, the inclined load applied at G is resolved into both horizontal and vertical directions as shown in Figure 5.23(i).

The support reactions are determined by applying the equilibrium conditions.

$$\sum F_x = 0 \Rightarrow +H_A - R_D \sin 30 + 10 \sin 30 + 5.0 = 0$$

$$\sum F_y = 0 \Rightarrow +V_A + R_D \cos 30 - 10 \cos 30 - 20 = 0$$

$$\sum M_A = 0 \Rightarrow R_D \cos 30 \times 9 - 5 \times 2.6 - 20 \times 7.5 - 10 \cos 30 \times 1.5 - 10 \sin 30 \times 2.6 = 0$$

$$\Rightarrow R_D = 24.247 \text{ kN},\ H_A = +2.124 \text{ kN} \ \& \ V_A = +7.662 \text{ kN}$$

Since the forces in the selected members need to be obtained, the imaginary section should pass through those members. In one imaginary section, a maximum of three members can be cut, as three equilibrium conditions can be applied. Accordingly, the truss is cut into two subassemblies by making an imaginary section 1-1 such that the section exposes the members whose forces are to be determined as shown in Figure 5.23(ii).

The segment on the left side of the imaginary section 1-1 is considered for determining the member forces (i.e., F_{BC}, F_{BF} and F_{GF}) as shown in Figure 5.23(iii). The nature of forces is assumed to be tension for the members BC, BF and GF. Since the subassembly is in equilibrium, all three equilibrium conditions can be applied.

$$\sum F_x = 0 \Rightarrow +2.1 + F_{GF} + F_{BC} + F_{BF}\cos 60 + 10\cos 60 = 0$$

$$\sum F_y = 0 \Rightarrow +7.7 - 10\sin 60 + F_{BF} \times \sin 60 = 0$$

$$\Rightarrow F_{BF} = +1.1 \text{ kN}$$

$$\sum M_F = 0 \Rightarrow +7.7 \times 4.5 - 2.1 \times 2.6 - 10\cos 30 \times 3 - F_{BC} \times 2.6 = 0$$

$$\Rightarrow F_{BC} = +1.2 \text{ kN}$$

By substituting F_{BF} and F_{BC} in $\sum F_x = 0$, $F_{GF} = -8.9$ kN

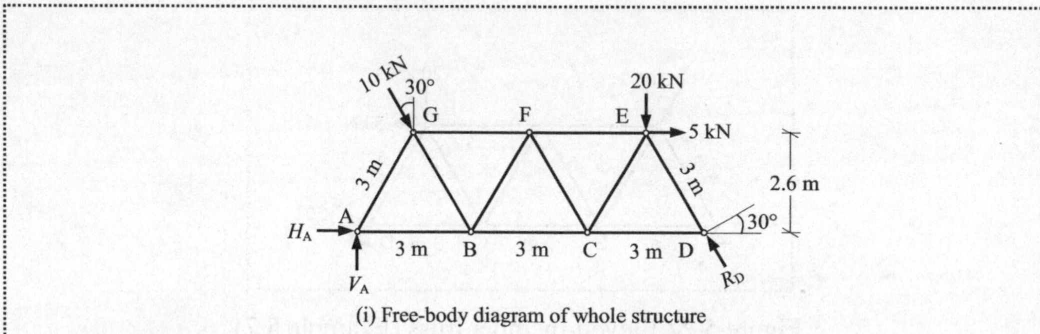

Figure 5.23 Truss analysis (Example 5.7)

Note: If this example is to be solved using the method of joints for determining the specific member forces (i.e., F_{BC}, F_{BF} and F_{GF}), the separated joints A, B and G should be sequentially solved.

5.6 Simplifying Conditions

Sometimes a qualitative inspection of the joints enables the analyst for quick determination of member forces, especially for identifying the *zero-force* members. If a joint has only two non-collinear members and there is no external load or support reaction at that joint, then those two members are *zero-force* members. Similarly, if a joint has only three members (with no external load or reaction), in which two members are collinear, then the third non-collinear member is a *zero-force* member. In truss structures, the *zero-force* members are used to increase stability and rigidity of the truss, and to provide support for various different loading conditions. Consider a truss as shown in Figure 5.24.

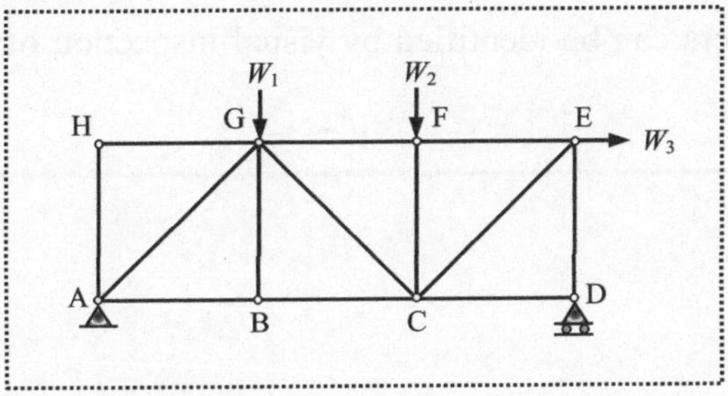

Figure 5.24 Qualitative inspection of a truss

A simple inspection of the truss structure shown in Figure 5.24 reveals the following.

(i) Joint B: $F_{BD} = 0$ (i.e., the vertical force equilibrium condition will consist of only F_{BD}; the third non-collinear member in a joint that has only three members)

(ii) Joint B: $F_{BA} = F_{BC}$ (i.e., by the horizontal force equilibrium condition)

(iii) Joint D: $F_{DC} = 0$ (i.e., the horizontal force equilibrium condition will consist of only F_{DC})

(iv) Joint D: $F_{DE} = V_D$ (i.e., by the vertical force equilibrium condition; if V_D is upwards then F_{DE} is compression)

(v) Joint F: $F_{FC} = -W_2$ (i.e., by the vertical force equilibrium condition)

(vi) Joint F: $F_{FE} = F_{FG}$ (i.e., by the horizontal force equilibrium condition)

(vii) Joint H: $F_{HA} = 0$ and $F_{HG} = 0$ (i.e., by the horizontal and vertical force equilibrium conditions; non-collinear members in a joint that has only two members)

UNIT SUMMARY

- ✓ A truss is an assembly of members connected together by rivets/welds, and all joints are assumed to be pinned/hinged.
- ✓ The only internal force is the axial member force; tension or compression.
- ✓ Statically determinate stable structures are considered for analysis using the method of joints and method of section.
- ✓ The method of joints is useful when all the member forces are to be determined, and the method of section is preferred when a selected member forces are required.
- ✓ *Zero-force* members can be identified by visual inspection of the trusses to simplify the solution process.

EXERCISES

5.1 Analyse the trusses shown in Figure 5.25 for the member forces using the method of joints.

5.2 Analyse the trusses shown in Figure 5.25 for the member forces using the method of sections.

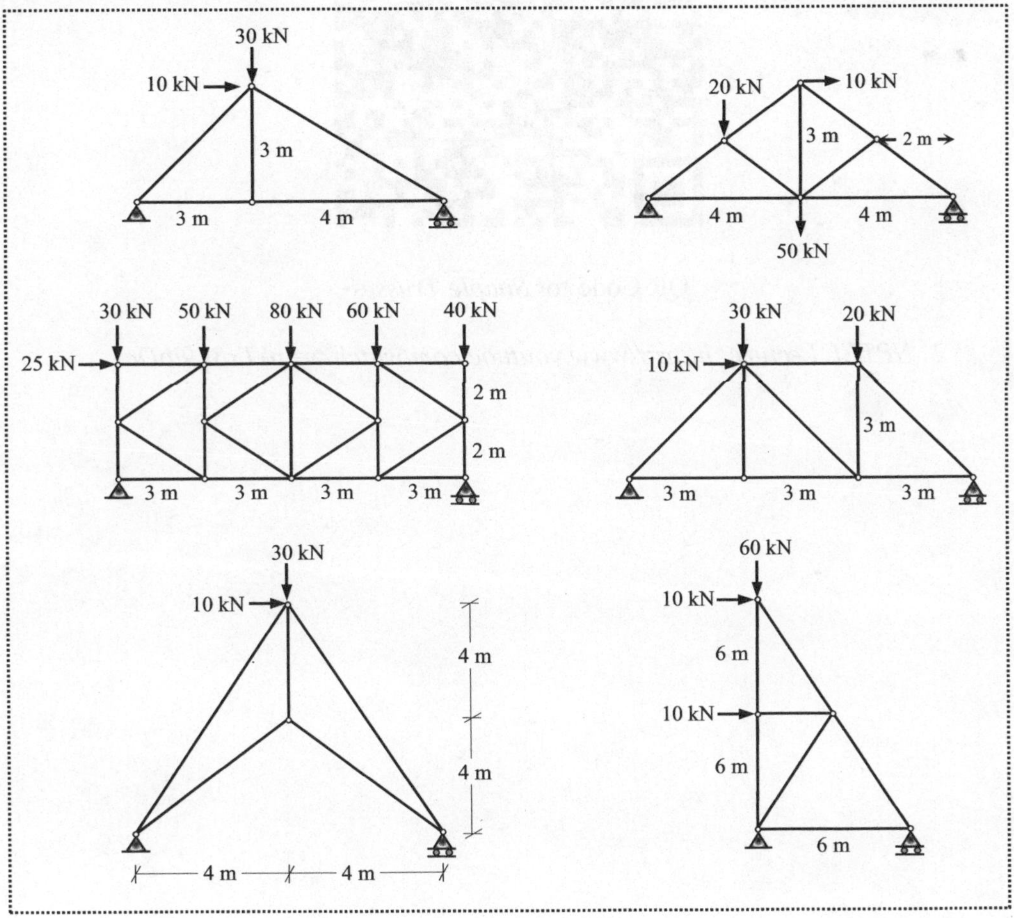

Figure 5.25 Truss examples for exercise

QR Code for *Simple Trusses*

NPTEL Lecture: https://www.youtube.com/watch?v=pkTx8L9ibDc

APPENDICES

APPENDIX-A: Area and Centroid

Shape		$\bar{x}$	$\bar{y}$	Area, A
Square	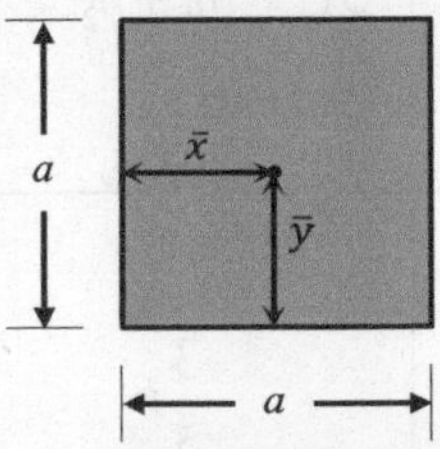	$\frac{a}{2}$	$\frac{a}{2}$	a^2
Rectangle	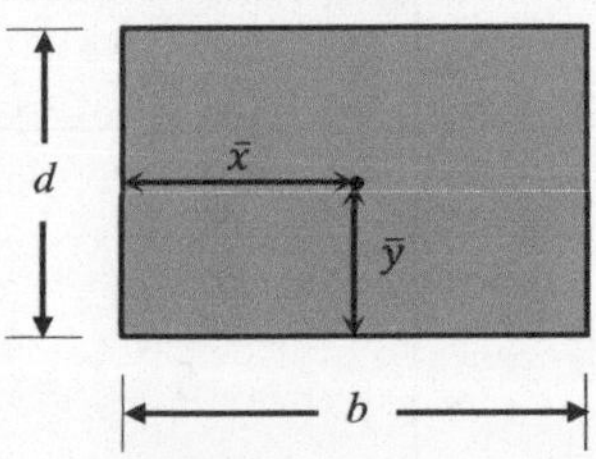	$\frac{b}{2}$	$\frac{d}{2}$	bd
Triangle	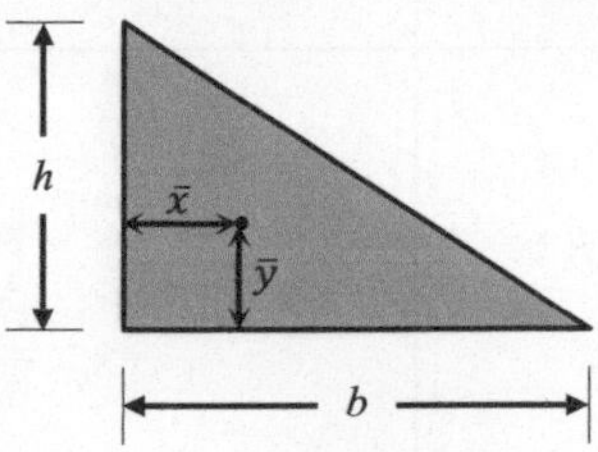	$\frac{b}{3}$	$\frac{h}{3}$	$\frac{1}{2}bh$
Triangle	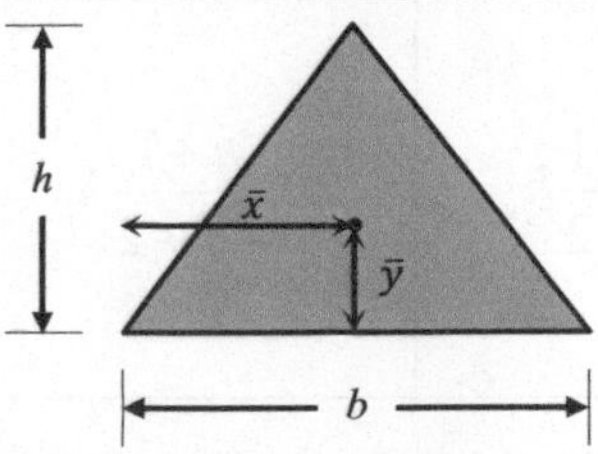	$\frac{b}{2}$	$\frac{h}{3}$	$\frac{1}{2}bh$
Triangle	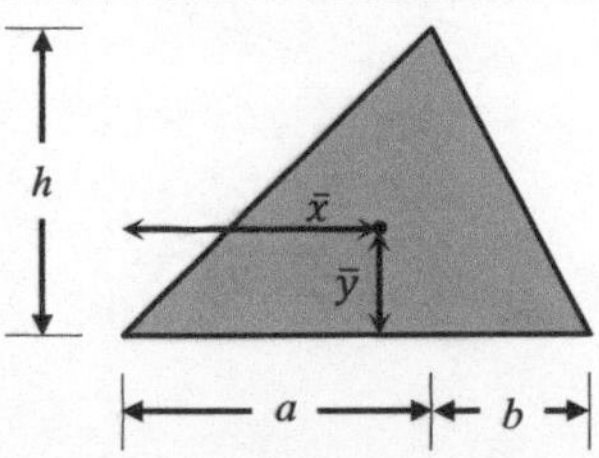	$\frac{2a+b}{3}$	$\frac{h}{3}$	$\frac{1}{2}bh$

APPENDIX-A: Area and Centroid (contd.)

Shape		$\bar{x}$	$\bar{y}$	Area, A
Trapezoid	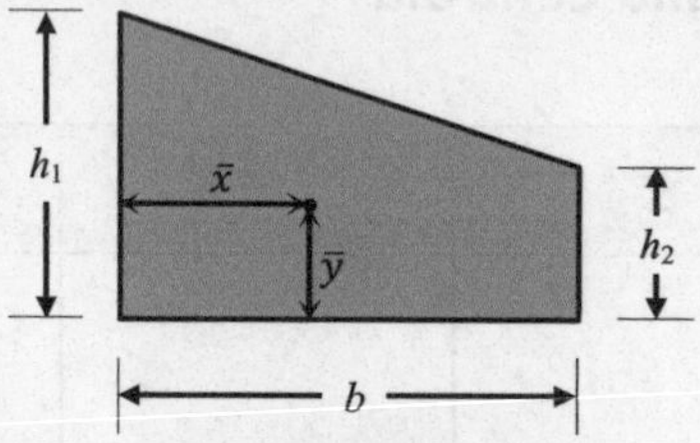	$\frac{b}{3}\left(\frac{h_1+2h_2}{h_1+h_2}\right)$	$\frac{1}{3}\left(\frac{h_1^2+h_1h_2+h_2^2}{h_1+h_2}\right)$	$b\left(\frac{h_1+h_2}{2}\right)$
Parabolic area	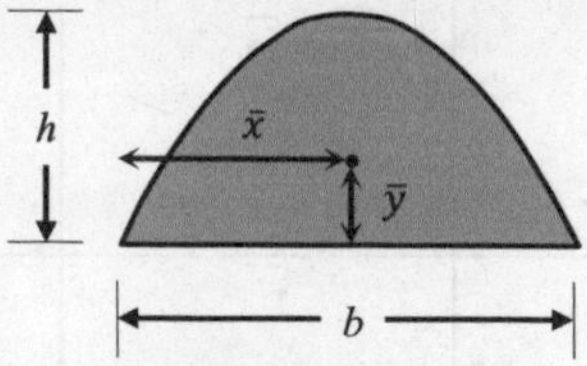	$\frac{b}{2}$	$\frac{3}{5}h$	$\frac{2}{3}bh$
Half-parabola	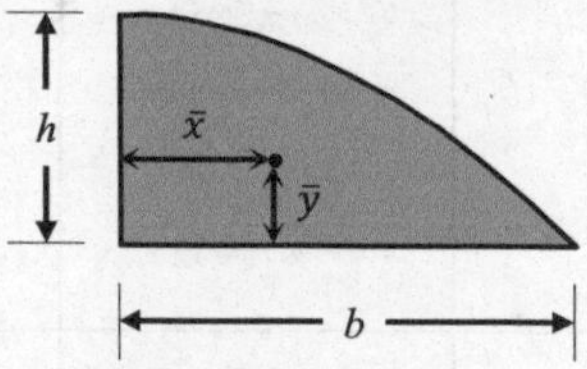	$\frac{3}{8}b$	$\frac{3}{5}h$	$\frac{2}{3}bh$
Parabolic spandrel	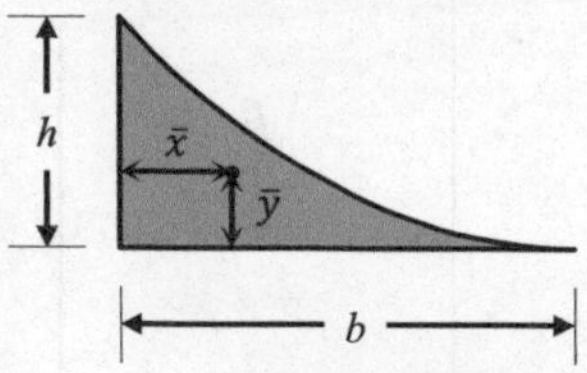	$\frac{1}{4}b$	$\frac{3}{10}h$	$\frac{1}{3}bh$
General spandrel	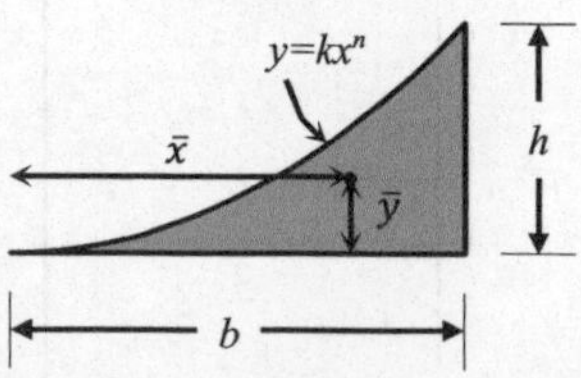	$\frac{n+1}{n+2}b$	$\frac{n+1}{4n+2}h$	$\frac{1}{n+1}bh$

APPENDIX-B: Slope and Deflection

Beam	Slope	Deflection
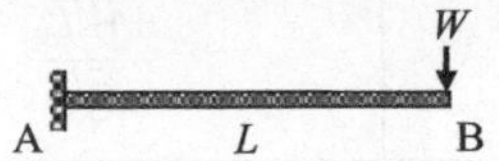	$\theta_A = 0$ $\theta_B = \frac{-WL^2}{2EI}$	$\Delta_A = 0$ $\Delta_B = \frac{WL^3}{3EI}$
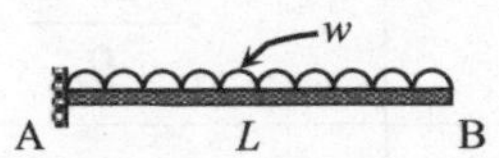	$\theta_A = 0$ $\theta_B = \frac{-wL^3}{6EI}$	$\Delta_A = 0$ $\Delta_B = \frac{wL^4}{8EI}$
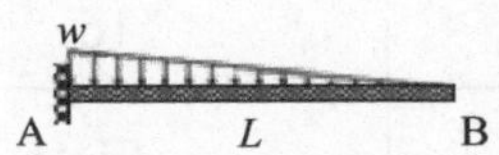	$\theta_A = 0$ $\theta_B = \frac{-wL^3}{24EI}$	$\Delta_A = 0$ $\Delta_B = \frac{wL^4}{30EI}$
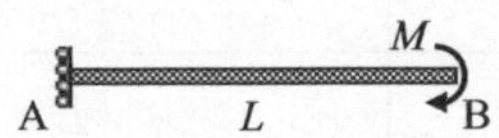	$\theta_A = 0$ $\theta_B = \frac{-ML}{EI}$	$\Delta_A = 0$ $\Delta_B = \frac{ML^2}{2EI}$
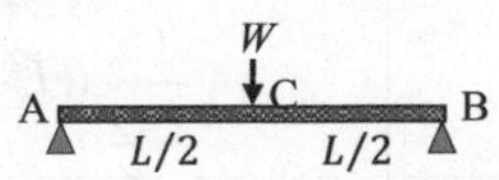	$\theta_A = \frac{-WL^2}{16EI}$ $\theta_B = \frac{WL^2}{16EI}$	$\Delta_A = \Delta_B = 0$ $\Delta_C = \frac{WL^3}{48EI}$
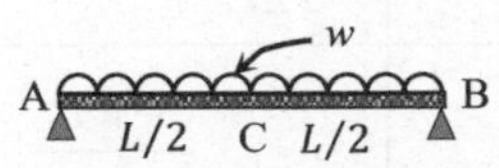	$\theta_A = \frac{-wL^3}{24EI}$ $\theta_B = \frac{wL^3}{24EI}$	$\Delta_A = \Delta_B = 0$ $\Delta_C = \frac{5}{384}\frac{wL^4}{EI}$
	$\theta_A = \frac{-wL^3}{45EI}$ $\theta_B = \frac{7}{360}\frac{wL^3}{EI}$	$\Delta_A = \Delta_B = 0$ $\Delta_C = \frac{5}{768}\frac{wL^4}{EI}$ $\Delta_{max} = 0.006522\frac{wL^4}{EI}$ (at $0.481L$ from A)
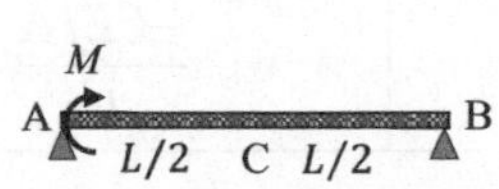	$\theta_A = \frac{-ML}{3EI}$ $\theta_B = \frac{ML}{6EI}$	$\Delta_A = \Delta_B = 0$ $\Delta_C = \frac{ML^2}{16EI}$ $\Delta_{max} = 0.06415\frac{ML^2}{EI}$ (at $0.423L$ from A)

APPENDIX-C: Fixed End Moments

Beam	M^{F}_{AB}	M^{F}_{BA}
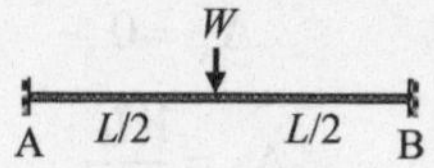	$\dfrac{-WL}{8}$	$\dfrac{+WL}{8}$
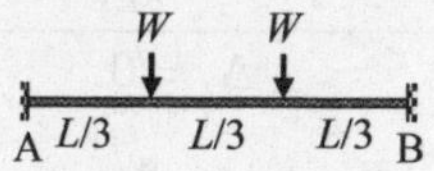	$\dfrac{-2WL}{9}$	$\dfrac{+2WL}{9}$
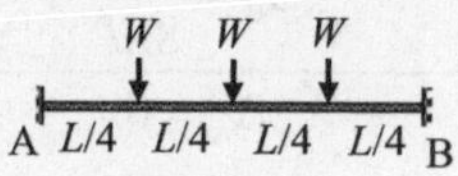	$\dfrac{-5WL}{16}$	$\dfrac{+5WL}{16}$
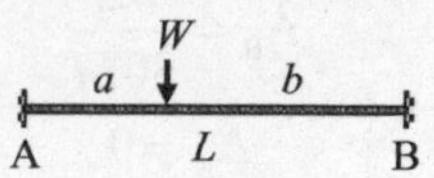	$\dfrac{-Wab^2}{L^2}$	$\dfrac{+Wa^2b}{L^2}$
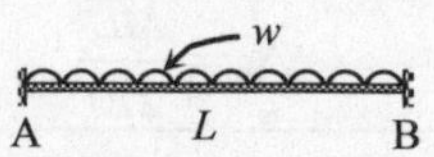	$\dfrac{-wL^2}{12}$	$\dfrac{+wL^2}{12}$
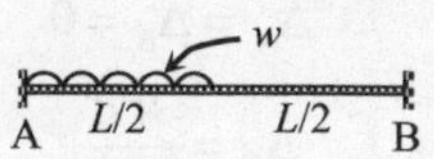	$\dfrac{-11}{192}wL^2$	$\dfrac{+5}{192}wL^2$
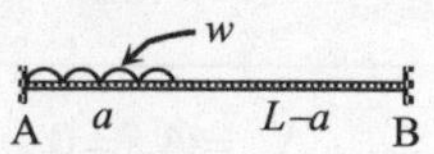	$\dfrac{-Wa^2}{12L^2}\left(3a^2-8aL+6L^2\right)$	$\dfrac{+Wa^2}{12L^2}\left(-3a^2+4aL\right)$
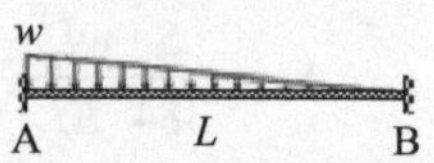	$\dfrac{-wL^2}{20}$	$\dfrac{+wL^2}{30}$
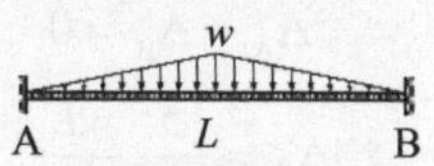	$\dfrac{-5}{96}wL^2$	$\dfrac{+5}{96}wL^2$
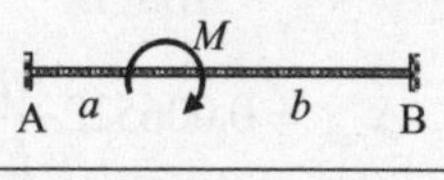	$\dfrac{+M}{L^2}\left(2ab-b^2\right)$	$\dfrac{+M}{L^2}\left(2ab-a^2\right)$
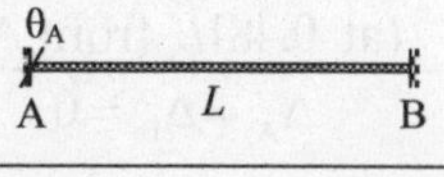	$\dfrac{+4EI\theta_A}{L}$	$\dfrac{+2EI\theta_A}{L}$
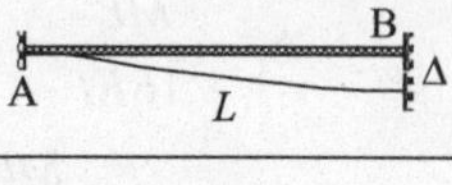	$\dfrac{-6EI\Delta}{L^2}$	$\dfrac{-6EI\Delta}{L^2}$

REFERENCES FOR FURTHER LEARNING

1. Menon D (2008), *Structural Analysis*, Narosa Publishing House, New Delhi.
2. Reddy C S (2011), *Basic Structural Analysis*, McGraw Hill, New Delhi.
3. Gambhir M L (2014), *Fundamentals of Structural Mechanics and Analysis*, PHI Learning, New Delhi.
4. Timoshenko S P & Young D H (1965), *Theory of Structures*, McGraw-Hill, New York.
5. Hibbeler R C (2012), *Structural Analysis*, Pearson Prentice Hall, New Jersey.
6. Kassimali A (2014), *Structural Analysis*, Cengage Learning, Stamford.
7. West H H & Geshwinder L F (2002), *Fundamentals of Structural Analysis*, John Wiley, New York.
8. Megson T H G (2005), *Structural and Stress Analysis*, Elsevier Butterworth-Heinemann, Burlington.
9. Norris C H, Wilbur J B & Utku S (1977), *Elementary Structural Analysis*, McGraw-Hill, Singapore.
10. Conner J J (1976), *Analysis of Structural Member Systems*, The Ronald Press, New York.
11. Schodek D L, & Bechthold M (2011), *Structures*, PHI Learning, New Delhi.
12. Brohn D (1987), *Understanding Structural Analysis*, Granada Publishing, London.
13. Sozen M A & Ichinose T (2009), *Understanding Structures: An Introduction to Structural Analysis*, CRC Press, Florida.
14. Leet K, Uang C & Gilbert A (2013), *Fundamentals of Structural Analysis*, McGraw Hill, New Delhi.
15. Ghali A, Neville A M & Brown T G (2009), *Structural Analysis – A unified Classical and Matrix Approach*, Taylor & Francis, New York.
16. Jennings A (2004), *Structures: From Theory to Practice*, Taylor & Francis, New York.
17. Gutkowski R M (1990), *Structures: Fundamental Theory and Behaviour*, Van Nostrand Reinhold, New York.
18. Kurrer K E (2008), *The History of the Theory of Structures: From Arch Analysis to Computational Mechanics*, Ernst & Sohn, Berlin.
19. Kinney S J (1957), *Indeterminate Structural Analysis*, Addison-Wesley, Massachusetts.
20. Wang C K (1983), *Intermediate Structural Analysis*, McGraw-Hill, Singapore.

CO AND PO ATTAINMENT TABLE

Course outcomes (COs) for this course can be mapped with the programme outcomes (POs) after the completion of the course and a correlation can be made for the attainment of POs to analyze the gap. After proper analysis of the gap in the attainment of POs necessary measures can be taken to overcome the gaps.

Table for CO and PO attainment

	PO-1	PO-2	PO-3	PO-4	PO-5	PO-6	PO-7
CO-1	3	3	3	2	1	1	3
CO-2	3	3	2	2	1	1	3
CO-3	3	3	2	1	1	1	3
CO-4	3	3	3	1	1	1	3
CO-5	3	3	2	1	1	1	3

*** (1- Weak correlation; 2- Medium correlation; 3- Strong correlation)**

The data filled in the above table can be used for gap analysis.

INDEX